Contents

Contributors   vi

Introduction   1

1 The Child in Psychology   15
John Sants

2 Neurological Development and the Growth of Psychological
Functions   46
Colwyn Trevarthen

3 The Relevance of Ethology   96
P. J. B. Slater

4 Some Methodological Issues in Developmental Research   120
Harry McGurk

5 Piagetian Perspectives   142
Hans Furth

6 Two Decades of Research into Early Language   169
Roger Goodwin

7 The Nature of Educational Competence   218
J. G. Wallace

8 The Significance of Sex Differences in Developmental Psychology   253
John Archer and *Barbara Lloyd*

9 Universality and Plasticity, Ontogeny and Phylogeny:
The Resonance Between Culture and Cognitive Development   290
Neil Warren

10 Society's Cradle: An Anthropological Perspective on the
Socialisation of Cognition   327
Billie Jean Isbell and *Lauris McKee*

11 Developmental Psychology and Society   365
John Sants

Index   385

Contributors

JOHN ARCHER
School of Psychology, Preston Polytechnic, Preston, Lancashire, England

HANS FURTH
The Boys Town Center for the Study of Youth Development, The Catholic University of America, Washington, USA

ROGER GOODWIN
School of Cultural and Community Studies, University of Sussex, Falmer, Brighton, Sussex, England

BILLIE JEAN ISBELL
Department of Anthropology, Cornell University, McGraw Hall, Ithaca, New York, USA

BARBARA LLOYD
School of Social Sciences, University of Sussex, Falmer, Brighton, Sussex, England

HARRY McGURK
Department of Psychology, University of Surrey, Guildford, Surrey, England

LAURIS McKEE
Department of Anthropology, Cornell University, McGraw Hall, Ithaca, New York, USA

JOHN SANTS
School of Cultural and Community Studies, University of Sussex, Falmer, Brighton, Sussex, England

P. J. B. SLATER
Ethology and Neurophysiology Group, School of Biological Sciences, University of Sussex, Falmer, Brighton, Sussex, England

COLWYN TREVARTHEN
Department of Psychology, University of Edinburgh, Edinburgh, Scotland

J. G. WALLACE
School of Education, Deakin University, Victoria, Australia

NEIL WARREN
School of African and Asian Studies, University of Sussex, Falmer, Brighton, Sussex, England

Developmental Psychology and Society

DEVELOPMENTAL PSYCHOLOGY AND SOCIETY

Edited by

John Sants

Reader in Developmental Psychology, School of Cultural and Community Studies, University of Sussex

First published 1980 by
THE MACMILLAN PRESS LTD
London and Basingstoke
Associated companies in Delhi Dublin
Hong Kong Johannesburg Lagos Melbourne
New York Singapore and Tokyo

British Library Cataloguing in Publication Data

Developmental psychology and society.
  1. Developmental psychology
  I. Sants, John
  155   BF 713

  ISBN 978-1-349-16333-5   ISBN 978-1-349-16331-1 (eBook)
  DOI 10.1007/978-1-349-16331-1

Introduction

JOHN SANTS

(*School of Cultural and Community Studies, University of Sussex, Falmer, Brighton, Sussex, England*)

Many months ago, when I started thinking about this book, I came across a striking passage by Margaret Mead. Under the heading *A New Understanding of Childhood* I found the following:

'. . . as an anthropologist concerned primarily with our understanding of ourselves as human beings I believe that, looking back, our descendants will regard as one of the great accomplishments of our age the discovery of the nature of childhood and our attempt to put this new knowledge to work in the upbringing of our children' (Mead, 1972).

This book took shape as I thought about Dr Mead's surprising suggestions. A number of questions occurred to me. (1) Have we only recently discovered the nature of childhood? (2) What have we discovered? (3) Are we using the discoveries? (4) If so, what are the consequences? All four questions were in my mind as I began to think about authors for this volume but, as the reader will have already decided, the answers could well have filled four separate books each as long as this one. Consequently, it is perhaps a little absurd to try to set the scene in this introduction by taking the questions in turn but the device does allow me to cover ground which I think will help the reader to place the chapters to follow in a useful context.

The Discovery and Study of Childhood

The systematic study of children has usually been left to psychologists. An important consequence is that our notions about the nature of childhood are derived almost exclusively from children of this century in developed societies. Fortunately, childhood has recently caught the attention of anthropologists, sociobiologists and historians. Indeed, it was an historian who got everyone thinking about the question of the invention of childhood. Phillippe Aries is rightly quoted in most contemporary introductions (as he is here) for drawing our attention to the fact that childhood was not always recognised as it is now. He showed, moreover, that the study of childhood need not be dependent on specialists (like psychologists) who consciously attend to the concepts: what any adults do to children—how they dress, feed and train them, for example—can, if systematically examined in cultural manifestations, reveal the implicit child psychology of those who do not claim to be specialists in children. The history of childhood has burgeoned enormously since Aries wrote his pioneer *Centuries of Childhood* in 1962. I have room in this introduction for a brief look at just three contrasting historical studies: Lloyd de Mause's *The History of Childhood* (1974), Laurence Stone's *The Family, Sex and Marriage in England 1500–1800* (1977) and Philip Greven's *The Protestant Temperament* (1977).

de Mause, with nine fellow historians associated with his Institute for Psychohistory and its *Journal of Psychohistory* in New York, set out to compile a history of childhood. The result, however, turned out to be ' . . . a long and mournful story of the abuse of children from the earliest times even to the present day.' de Mause distinguishes six modes of parent–child relations and it is only in the last two (from the nineteenth century onwards) that the child is afforded any recognition in his own right. His six modes represent

> 'the psychogenically most advanced part of the population in the most advanced countries, and the dates given are the first in which I found examples of that mode in the sources'.

de Mause first identifies the *Infanticidal Mode* (antiquity to fourth century AD). Killing infants was a regular practice in antiquity. There was an explicit culling of the unwanted, the deformed or sickly, infant girls being particularly vulnerable. The killing of legitimate children was only slowly reduced during the Middle Ages and illegitimate children continued regularly to be killed into the nineteenth century. Baby battering is still with us. Next, there was the *Abandonment Mode* (fourth to thirteenth century AD). A striking illustration is quoted in Stone from as late as 1756–60 in London. Fifteen thousand children were dumped in four years in the London Foundling Hospital established by Thomas Coram. Ten thousand died: it became 'a charnel house for the dead'. In the *Ambivalent Mode* (fourteenth to seventeenth centuries) the child is seen as 'soft wax, plaster, or clay to be beaten into shape'. There was an increase in the number of child instruction manuals. With the *Intrusive Mode* (eighteenth century) parents turned their attentions to conquering the mind. The child was nursed by the mother and not swaddled, prayed with but not played with, hit but not regularly whipped. In the *Socialization Mode* (nineteenth to mid-twentieth centuries) the raising of a child became less a process of conquering its will than of training it, guiding it into proper paths, teaching it to conform, socialising. Finally we get the *Helping Mode* (begins mid-twentieth century) in which the parents become the servants of the child. The history of childhood is thus seen as a series of closer approaches between adult and child. The further back one goes in history, the less effective parents are in meeting the child's developing needs.

The successive modes described by de Mause are derived in the first place from psychoanalytical theory, but similar child-rearing modes are identified by Laurence Stone. For him 'the key to the story of the evolution of child-rearing is the principle of stratified diffusion, by which new attitudes first take hold among those classes which are most literate and most open to new ideas'. His class-based modes are (1) *Negligent* (aristocracy); (2) *Child-oriented, Affectionate and Permissive* (upper bourgeoisie and squirearchy); (3) *Child-oriented but Repressive* (upper bourgeoisie and squirearchy); (4) *Egocentric Intrusive* (pious nonconformists); (5) *Brutal but Careful* (cottager and artisan); (6) *Indifferent and Exploitative* (poor). Philip Greven, in his history of the shaping of the Protestant temperament in America, also has a look at patterns of child-rearing. He distinguishes three forms of Protestant temperament: Evangelical, Moderate and Genteel. Within each group, he argues, the temperaments of the early Americans were shaped by the formative experiences of their childhoods. For him, an understanding of childhood experience enables the historian to bridge the gap between the public and private realms of consciousness and thought. The public world of ideas gives only a partial understanding of the three distinctive patterns of temperament. Again we have identification of modes of child-rearing, although Greven warns that these modes continue over long periods of time, rather than being in constant evolution. Nevertheless, an analysis of changes in the modes may help us to understand the evolution of societies.

Psychologists, for the most part, have not tried to identify and describe modes of socialisation in this manner; but the way the historians go about their business has something in common with the clinical psychologists. First, spot the categories, then describe them and then identify further categories so as to include all cases without remainder. The method has the merits of beginning with the richness of human activity rather than by imposing external concepts. The use of plain language—as in *Brutal but Careful*—also has its merits as a preliminary device in that it conveys a picture of physical cruelty as a means of control by poor parents just above the line of absolute destitution together with a view of children as economic assets.

Socialisation, as an interaction of adults and children, is a concept more commonly found in sociology than in psychology. For example, Hans Dreitzel (1973) argues that

'socialisation can only be understood if seen as a complex interaction process governed by the reciprocity of needs, demands, and perspectives. In other words, rather than treating the adult's behaviour as an independent variable, both the behaviour of adults and of children must be seen as mutually dependent variables. Children are not simply a *tabula rasa* which mysteriously responds to the input of stimuli by adults, and adults are not simply stable factors of the child's social environment, but are themselves prone to change under the impact of their offsprings challenge'.

Psychologists have been surprisingly slow to attend to what is taken for granted by historians and sociologists. Laboratory-based behaviourism must take the blame but fortunately its hold is now weakening. Psychologists have been frightened by the prospect of tottering 'over the cliff of phenomenological introspection, where every man's introspective report is the ultimate datum' (Rafky, 1973). But Rafky is surely right in suggesting that socialisation will never be understood until psychologists cast their nets more widely and seek to identify and codify the underlying assumptions in the complexities of adult–child interactions. We need more 'thick descriptions'.

The term is Gilbert Ryle's and is explored by the anthropologist, Clifford Geertz (1975) in his essay 'Thick description: toward an interpretive theory of culture'. Geertz takes Ryle's example of a boy 'rapidly contracting his right eye-lid'. From this 'thin description' one cannot tell whether the boy is winking or twitching, or even parodying a wink. In order to make a correct interpretation of what is happening, one needs a 'thick description' of the act as part of the culture. For example, if it is a wink, then the boy is 'communicating in a quite precise and special way: (1) deliberately, (2) to someone in particular, (3) to impart a particular message, (4) according to a socially established code, (5) without cognizance of the rest of the company.' The thin descriptions of behaviourist psychology will not take us very far if we are looking for meaning in social behaviour. We will not understand men without knowing them. Geertz faces up to the critics of his view of anthropology as a search for meaning in the symbolic forms in human life. He accepts that cultural analysis is intrinsically incomplete and, moreover, characteristically asserts that ' . . . interpretive anthropology is a science whose progress is marked less by a perfection of consensus than by a refinement of debate. What gets better is the precision with which we vex each other'. In the science of behaviourist developmental psychology, debates about the child in his social world have produced some consensus but an unimpressive refinement of our understanding.

Fortunately, however, the search for meaning in social behaviour has recently inspired a number of psychologists in touch with colleagues in the social sciences. The analysis of social behaviour in terms of its social rules is one example. Nevertheless, there are already those who fear that this expanding exercise in ethnomethodology may harden too quickly into formal descriptions of rule structures so that once again the nuances of personal meaning will have escaped.

In cross-cultural cognitive psychology, the emic/etic distinction has been called upon as a way of dealing with the problem of establishing a science of human behaviour in which we the actors are recognisable in our distinctive ways. In the emic approach, the search for meaning makes use of how the actors themselves are construing the world. Etic analyses 'depend upon phenomenal distinctions judged appropriate by the community of scientific observers' (Harris, 1968). The problem, of course, is to get from the richness of emics to the general objectivity of etics and so avoid an apparently endless collection of exotic descriptions from the native's point of view. Berry's research is promising in this respect (see Berry and Dasen, 1974). In looking at other cultures we can begin by asking, 'How well can they do our tricks?' (Wober, 1969), and, as a result, modify our hypotheses so that they can apply to both cultures. Thus universal hypotheses are 'derived etics' which began as 'imposed etics'. I give a more detailed account in chapter 11.

Once again, however, the dangers of consensus at the expense of refinement do not seem to be very far away. The thick descriptions of emics may get short shrift in the psychologist's time-honoured world of etics. The experimental psychologist is not at ease exploring the native's point of view. The clinical psychologist, in contrast, does it all the time and some of the most promising advances in developmental psychology have started with his methods. Piaget's use of the 'clinical method' has paid off, and so has Erikson's. Clinical psychologists working with children have always aimed to understand what it is like to be at the centre of the child's world, surrounded by his significant persons, responding to the demands of home and school. Trying to discover why a child is unhappy in school will usually require more than seeing what he does in the classroom. The clinician patiently prompts the child to reveal his world in his own time and in his own way. Piaget's use of the method in the 1920s opened up the world of childhood for adults who had long forgotten their own. Erikson's approach to childhood and society (Erikson, 1965) is best understood by reading his case-history of the boy Sam where biology, psychology and sociology are not separated. Sam gives meaning to the apparent triteness of the Berger and Luckman (1971) generalisation that 'socialisation always takes place in the context of a specific social structure'.

I have said something about historians, sociologists and anthropologists. We can now turn to the sociobiologists. Their work has allowed developmental psychologists the opportunity to return to the great issues of biology and culture which characterised genetic psychology at the turn of the century, but which disappeared as child psychologists succumbed to the pressures of their experimental colleagues. (Piaget's strengths, it can be noted in passing, are that he retained a preoccupation with the grand questions which preoccupied Darwin (and Freud) at the birth of psychology. He has lived to see child psychology come back to him.)

Sociobiology is founded on the theory of evolution. It seems astonishing that psychologists should have almost lost sight of Darwinism until the ethologists came into view. In the fascinating *Culture and Infancy* (Leiderman *et al.* 1977), Melvin Konner claims that the

'study of behaviour, which is a feature of living organisms, is simply a branch of biology, and behaviour development research above all should be cognizant of this; because, with the exception of behaviourism and

associationism in perception, every major advance in behaviour development research has been biological'.

As illustrations, Konner (somewhat provocatively but correctly, I believe)
cites the work of Freud, Piaget, Gessell, Carmichael, Bower, Bowlby and
Roger Brown. Konner then goes on to list five current trends concerning the
biological basis of behaviour development: (1) individual differences in the
infant's shaping of the mother–infant relation; (2) the genetic basis of
behavioural differences of different populations; (3) the highly resilient
maturation of fundamental features of the nervous system, cushioned against
environmental insult and products of natural selection; (4) studies of infancy
in the human environment of evolutionary adaptedness, i.e. in hunter-
gatherers; (5) natural selection theory, kin selection and the biology of
altruism.

The first three trends make clear that it is now acceptable to explore forms
of genetic control in the development of behaviour but the fourth and fifth
trends listed by Konner illustrate the power of the theory of natural selection:
the environment as a selecting agent acts on the variability in genetic
endowment, due to mutation and recombination in sexual reproduction, so
that there is differential representation of each individual's offspring in
succeeding generations. Evolutionary change comes about through differences in reproductive success or fitness (Barash, 1977). The environment
selects behaviours which give a reproductive advantage. Studies of infants in
the tree-less plains in which man became adapted by natural selection may
therefore explain functions of infancy not easily apparent in the environment
of our own times. Strategies of parenting may be explained in terms of
parental investment, i.e. behaviour toward offspring which 'increases the
chances of the offspring's survival at the cost of the parent's ability to invest in
future offspring' (Trivers, 1972). Parents and offspring both seek to increase
their own contributions to the gene pool so that, for example, conflict can
occur between them over the optimal time of weaning. Fascinating analyses
of mate selection, reproduction and parenting can be seen in Barash's answers
to his questions: 'How much should be invested in each reproductive effort?
Who takes care of the kids? Should parents and off-spring disagree?' No developmental psychologist should ignore his explanations but, in so far as the
examples are drawn from animals other than man, the psychologist must also
be mindful of E. O. Wilson's caution (in his foreword to Barash's book) that to
'devise a naturalistic description of human social behaviour is to note a set of
facts for further investigation, not to pass a value judgement or to deny that a
great deal of behaviour can be deliberately changed if individual societies so
wish'. What, in other words, are the consequences of human culture? To that
question, it is not surprising to find that sociobiologists begin by considering
culture as biological adaptation. Their strategy is sound but an oversimplified biology can lead us astray when we turn to contemporary culture.

Konner looks at some complexities in Bowlby's theory of infant–mother attachment and invokes the concept of selection funnels, i.e. intensive selection at a particular stage in the life-cycle. When mortality is very high, as it is in early human infancy in the environment of natural adaptation, proximity of parent and infant is essential to ensure survival in the presence of predators; but it is a characteristic of selection funnels that the adaptation required at one stage of the life-cycle may be a disadvantage at a later stage. Overdependence of infant on mother may inhibit later independence and in our predator-free culture is not required. A sensible conclusion is that we should be mindful of our biological constraints but not accept that we are their prisoners. The term 'constraints' has recently been introduced to remind psychologists that varieties of adaptation by natural selection in the animal kingdom make the search for general laws of learning a premature objective (Hinde and Stevenson-Hinde, 1973). The term, however, rather begs the question about man's biological inheritance. Whether we are constrained or promoted by our biology is discussed with differing emphases in the chapters by Trevarthen and Slater.

The Achievements of Developmental Psychology

This volume sets out some of the things that psychologists have to say after nearly a century's systematic study of child development. At times, as the reader works his way through the technicalities of the psychologists' experiments and theories, he may think that our understanding of childhood is a long way removed from the child he sees in the home, the school or in other social gatherings. Earlier in this introduction I conceded that psychologists are not strong on social development. Nevertheless, I do believe that a century's activity has brought us to the brink of more than the psychologists themselves fully realise. The discipline, it must be said, has not encouraged the grand theorist: Darwin, Freud and Piaget opened up vistas precisely because they were not bothered by pernickety needs to justify themselves to fellow members of a professional community uncertain of its status. But the way in which child psychology has at last absorbed Piaget gives exciting promise that we are on the threshold of the kind of understanding of the nature of childhood which Mead discerns.

Unfortunately, only the more recent text-books in child psychology give immediate support to Mead's claims. Established texts do not appear to have much to say about the nature of childhood. They do of course tell us a good deal about the capacities of children of different ages. A century of systematic child study has given parents and teachers answers to many of their questions, but we are only just beginning to get glimpses of an understanding of what childhood is all about. What I would like to do in the remainder of this section is grasp at the grander visions of the few general theorists who have, in my view, laid the foundations for an understanding of the nature of childhood, and in particular say something about Freud, who hovers in the wings in this book but is rarely seen on stage.

The popular notion of psychoanalysis is that it has shown that what we do is unconsciously influenced by sexual phantasies. Furthermore, the popular assumption is that these phantasies have their origins in early childhood. Freud discovered that if his patients were asked to talk freely about themselves, uninhibited by normal social constraints, they sooner or later began reviving memories of earliest childhood. The layman accepts the Freudian emphasis on childhood because the revival of childhood memories is a common experience in any soliloquy. He also readily accepts that as a child he was stirred by his own sexuality in its clash with the sexuality of his parents. Thus popular culture has thoroughly absorbed the essence of Freud, i.e. that our adult character is an outcome of the way in which in early infancy we establish our sexual identities in our first relationships with our parents. The layman does not bother much about the scientific status of the belief.

An essential feature of this common Freudian belief is that it is child-centred: development is seen as an ever recurring construction by the child. The part played by adults tends to be generalised and taken for granted. But Freud himself was fully aware of the way in which parents' phantasies of infantile origins within themselves act upon the child. In a letter to Jung, he wrote: 'the transfer of one's hopes to one's children is certainly an excellent way of appeasing one's unresolved complexes . . .' (McGuire, 1977). Erikson, as we have seen, has shown how these hopes are bound up with culture as well as with personal phantasies.

It is a paradox of Freudian theory that it should give a central place to childhood in its explanations of human behaviour but in the hands of its master rarely study childhood in action. What Freud studied was the child acting within the adult. His indirect approach to childhood has been ridiculed by some of his critics, but Freud's rejoinder in the preface to the fourth edition of *Three Essays on the Theory of Sexuality* is fair comment: 'If mankind had been able to learn from a direct observation of children, these three essays could have remained unwritten'. (I discuss possible barriers in the observation of children in my first chapter in this book.)

What can be said in summary about the understanding of childhood now entrenched in our culture from the grander visions of the great pioneers, Darwin, Freud and Piaget? From them we get notions of the functions of childhood. Our knowledge of the capacities of childhood is, as I have said, detailed, comprehensive and valuable. But how we use the knowledge of capacities depends upon our grasp of functions. The Darwinian concept of the functions of childhood has been set out by Bruner in his paper on 'The nature and uses of immaturity' (Bruner, 1972). The human race, Bruner argues, has a biological past. The human infant has been selected to adapt during a prolonged infancy in which he learns to prepare for unforseeable change. His 'tutor proneness'—or readiness to learn from adults, and itself perhaps the outcome of natural selection—enables him to acquire in play the characteristic social and technical skills of mankind. The human infant is distinctively adaptable but rooted in ancient, biological modes. At present we tend to underestimate the scope of the adaptability as well as the strength of the constraints.

Freud also emphasises the adult's role as tutor in the establishment of social skills, although of course putting it that way does not convey Freud's concentration on the sexual nature of relationships and personal identity. Piaget has explored and described the nature of the child's acquisition of cognitive skills. In all of them we can see childhood as the expression of an astonishing verve in the pursuit of participation in the human, social scene. The child is not a *tabula rasa*, neither is he some form of defective adult. He is essentially an active, self-organising constructor of what it means to be human.

Childhood and Society

The terms *ontogeny* and *phylogeny* will be found in many places in this book. How the evolution of the individual from birth to maturity interacts with the evolution of his species has long been a tricky problem for biologists and it is no less troublesome for psychologists and historians. For them, the general question is how are childhood and society connected? If adult character is formed by childhood experiences then the evolution of society is determined by its modes of child-rearing. But that, of course, is only a partial explanation. We must next ask where the modes of child-rearing come from. Are they passed from one generation to the next in the kind of successive socialisation processes that have been invoked to explain 'cycles of disadvantage'? Or are modes of child-rearing externally determined by ecological changes following scientific and technical discoveries? Responses to these questions probably depend on one's predilections about the relative weights to be assigned to family dynamics and socio-economic factors. But in either case we are still left with the question of the source of change. Cycles of disadvantage within families can persist despite radical interventions from outside and socio-economic changes have often been held in check by strong family traditions. All that seems certain is that modes of child-rearing are extraordinarily resilient.

The historian, de Mause, firmly believes that child-rearing modes are the source of all historical change and that historical change depends upon the ability of parents to divest themselves of anxieties retained from their own childhood and on their ability to participate in the new emerging childhood. He rejects the view of social scientists that what parents do is determined by 'society'. de Mause's rejection of social structures as inevitable determinants is, however, more of an outcome of his belief in the power of the individual psyche as revealed in psychoanalysis than of any refutation of Durkheimian analyses. Nevertheless, de Mause does raise the possibility that if child-rearing were to be undertaken by adults who are unhampered by the presence of the child within themselves, then the evolution of society would be very different. Freud's moments of optimism were based on this possibility.

Laurence Stone's orthodox analyses and conclusions are less contentious. In his first chapter he dismisses the hope that the historian can discover any simple linear or cyclical models for changes in family life, if only because of the slowness and apparent irregularity of cultural change and its variations within different social groups. For analytical convenience, Stone tackles changes in the family from six points of view: biological, sociological, political, economic, psychological and sexual. He does, however, work within three distinct types of families: (1) Open Lineage (1450–1630) (2) Restricted, Patriarchal Nuclear (1550–1700) and (3) Closed Domesticated Nuclear (1640–1800) which saw the 'growth of affective individualism'. It might be thought that the contemporary psychologist could confine himself to Stone's analysis of the third kind of family, but Stone ends with hints of the demise of this form of family life. His final conclusions on family change and historical development illustrate an historian's manner of analysing childhood and society.

Stone considers development as an outcome of the ebb and flow of a battle between kin, state, nuclear family and individual. By the late eighteenth century the happiness of the individual was being given priority over its older rivals but in the nineteenth century the interests of family, patriarch, school, religion and state reasserted themselves. In the twentieth century the priority of 'affective individualism' was restored but, Stone argues, we should not conclude that our present family life in the pursuit of affective individualism is necessarily a sign of moral progress. The pursuit of satisfying personal fulfilment, accompanied by the consequent intense sexual and affective bonding, places strains on the family group which in the end may rip it apart. Striving to keep the family together, moreover, reduces the proper con-sideration of external demands which successful societies require. The Closed Domesticated Nuclear Family is 'geographically, chronologically and socially a most restricted and unusual phenomenon, and there is as little reason to have any more confidence in its survival and spread in the future as there is for democracy itself'. Stone's predictions about the break-up of our present nuclear family have a ring of plausibility. Man's affective and sexual bonding, evolved for adaptation in the less complex life of the Savannah, may be incompatible with the prolonged childhood created by contemporary society. Margaret Mead also predicts that we are 'going to move away from the isolated nuclear family which is the worst possible place to bring up a child' (Senn, 1977, p. 146). Whether we do or not may be the crucial event of our time.

The Chapters in this Volume

My notes to authors for this book began with the quotation from Margaret Mead given at the beginning of this introduction. It seemed to me that Mead's claims for the recent surge in developmental psychology deserved a careful scrutiny. The reader will find that our main concern has been the presentation of what is known. What it all means for the upbringing of our children (and for society) is less explicit. Nevertheless, the device of keeping a constant eye on social relevance has, I think, enabled us to some extent to lessen the detachment and pedantry of the text-book style.

Some themes crop up in a number of chapters. Colwyn Trevarthen's fascinating and detailed description of brain growth, which culminates in his appraisal of the functions of infancy, brings out the new awareness of the cultural aspects of infant activity:

> 'Of all the foresightful explorations of experience made by the infant brain, those directed to an emotion-charged social life are by far the most powerful . . . infants possess the germ of cultural co-operation'.

In our other biological chapter, Peter Slater demonstrates the power of evolutionary theory in recent analyses of animal behaviour but parts company somewhat with his fellow sociobiologists as he approaches humans. Evolutionary perspectives have been valuable in the study of infants but, as Slater reminds us, 'the behaviour of the newborn human is more the product of evolution than is that of the adult'. Adults become modified by the institutions and structures of human culture. The power of evolutionary ideas in the analysis of human social behaviour remains exciting but as yet uncertain.

Harry McGurk explains the methods used in developmental research. He thus extends the discussion of what we know about children to how we know it. He concedes that despite the value of experiments in controlled conditions in establishing causal relationships, 'it must be acknowledged that the ultimate goal of developmental research is to provide the basis for a comprehensive and systematic understanding of the nature of developmental processes *in their natural context*'. The move towards 'rich' descriptions in natural social settings is a general trend. Roger Goodwin, for example, shows how developmental psycholinguistics has shifted in its short history from the detailed analyses of separate utterances to broader analyses of children's conversations. Iain Wallace is fully aware of the varieties of sub-cultures from which children come to school but his argument for a precise analysis of cognitive processes in manageable steps is a good illustration of the continuing value of the experimental attack. The method may not give immediate answers to general questions of practical importance but it must always be the bed-rock of a scientific psychology.

John Archer and Barbara Lloyd suggest that the scientific study of sex differences reflects the history of psychology and thus reflects 'the growing concern with process'. The topic in their review covers perhaps one decade of research and theory (rather than the two decades of developmental psycholinguistics) and illustrates *par excellence* the characteristics of contemporary developmental psychology. Biology and anthropology here join forces with psychology:

> 'the developmental processes are best described as an interaction between biological and environmental influences in their wider sense, including not only broad cultural influences but also physical and social inputs'.

When Neil Warren looks at commonalities and differences in cognitive development across cultures he moves almost without comment from psychology to anthropology, except to note in passing that, when drawing on disciplines other than one's own, care must be taken not to fall foul of theoretical differences in the other discipline. His main conclusion is that although cognitive development can be potentially much the same in all cultures 'one must allow that there are probably elaborate forms of "rationality" which are not captured by Piaget's concept of "formal operations" or by his logicism in general. Institutionalised operativity confronts children in many forms. The point is reaffirmed by the anthropologists, Billy Jean Isbell and Lauris McKee. The tragic and remarkable case of the isolated *Genie*, together with analyses of more fortunate infants in a variety of family settings, illustrates an interactive model of cognitive development and demonstrates the value of cross-cultural research in revealing the early structures of cognition, both verbal and non-verbal. Isbell and McKee have no doubt that cultural differences are at work on the infant's cognition:

> 'Each culture has a customary mode of infant caretaking which patterns the relationships between caretaker and infant. We suggest that differences in cognitive orientations—in the development of anticipatory schemata—arise from differences in these patterned relationships, and the consequent differences in salient stimuli which are presented to infants'.

I have chosen to end this introduction with Hans Furth's chapter on Piaget because *genetic epistemology* is 'a science in its own right, straddling philosophy and psychology, without being either . . . '. But if one understands the Piagetian perspective then every aspect of developmental psychology is transformed, social as well as cognitive. Furth doubts whether the popularity of Piaget's theory is matched by an adequate understanding; but his own expositions of Piagetian theory (e.g. Furth, 1969, 1970 and 1972) have done more than any other to show how Piaget's perspective 'turns an unsolvable epistemological quest into a solvable empirical enterprise'. On the way, Piaget has described 'the development of the intelligence that made science possible as observed in and interpreted from children's spontaneous construction of their knowledge structures'. The epistemological quest has transformed our understanding of childhood, not only because we have made discoveries about children but because we can now understand more about the functions of childhood in man's evolution.

References

Aries, P. (1962). *Centuries of Childhood*, Jonathan Cape, London

Barash, D. P. (1977). *Sociobiology and Behavior*, Elsevier, New York

Berger, P. L. and Luckman, T. (1971). *The Social Construction of Reality: a Treatise in the Sociology of Knowledge*, Penguin Books, London

Berry, J. W. and Dasen, P. R. (eds) (1974). *Culture and Cognition: Readings in Cross-Cultural Psychology*, Methuen, London

Bruner, J. S. (1972). Nature and uses of immaturity, *Amer. Psychol.* 27. Reprinted in *Play–Its Role in Development and Evolution* (ed. J. S. Bruner, A. Jolly and K. Sylva), Penguin Books, London

Dreitzel, H. P. (ed.) (1973). *Childhood and Socialization*, Macmillan, New York

Erikson, E. H. (1965). *Childhood and Society*, Penguin Books, London

Furth, H. G. (1969). *Piaget and Knowledge: Theoretical Foundations*, Prentice-Hall, Englewood Cliffs, N.J.

Furth, H. G. (1970). *Piaget for Teachers*, Prentice-Hall, Englewood Cliffs, N.J.

Furth, H. G. and Wachs, H. (1972). *Thinking Goes to School: Piaget's Theory in Practice*, Oxford University Press, London

Geertz, C. (1975). *The Interpretation of Cultures*, Hutchinson, London

Greven, P. (1977). *The Protestant Temperament: Patterns of Child Rearing, Religious Experience, and the Self in Early America*, Alfred A. Knopf, New York

Harris, M. (1968). *The Rise of Anthropological Theory*, Thomas Y. Cromwell Company, New York

Hinde, R. A. and Stevenson-Hinde, J. (eds) (1973). *Constraints on Learning: Limitations and Predispositions*, Academic Press, London

Leiderman, P. H., Tulkin, S. R. and Rosenfeld, A. (eds) (1977). *Culture and Infancy: Variations in the Human Experience*, Academic Press, New York

McGuire, W. (ed.) (1977). *The Freud/Jung Letters: the Correspondence between Sigmund Freud and C. G. Jung*, Hogarth Press and Routledge and Kegan Paul, London

de Mause, L. (ed.) (1974). *The History of Childhood*, Souvenir Press, London

Mead, M. (1972). A new understanding of childhood, *Redbook Magazine*, January 1972. Reprinted in *Annual Editions: Readings in Human Development, '73–'74*, Annual Editions, Dushkin, Connecticut

Rafky, D. M. (1973). Phenomenology and socialization: some comments on the assumptions underlying socialization theory, in *Childhood and Socialization* (ed. H. P. Dreitzel), Macmillan, New York

Senn, J. E. (1977). *Speaking Out for America's Children*, Yale University Press, New Haven and London

Stone, L. (1977). *The Family, Sex and Marriage in England 1500–1800*, Weidenfeld and Nicholson, London

Trivers, R. L. (1972). Parental investment and sexual selection, in *Sexual Selection and the Descent of Man 1871–1971* (ed. B. Campbell), Heinemann, London

Wober, M. (1969). Distinguishing centri-cultural from cross cultural tests and research, *Percept. Mot. Skills*, **28**

1 The Child in Psychology

JOHN SANTS

(School of Cultural and Community Studies, University of Sussex, Falmer, Brighton, Sussex, England)

Generalisations about the Nature of Childhood

The child got off to a good start in psychology. Stanley Hall, who founded the first experimental psychology laboratory in America in 1883, also launched the Child Study Movement at the Exposition at Chicago in 1893. In England, James Sully established the laboratory at University College, London in 1897 and also published *Studies of Childhood* in 1895. Both these pioneers had made tours of Germany in search of the 'New Psychology' and had there encountered its two major influences: Wundtian experimental psychology and Darwinian evolutionary theory. The laboratory experiment and the biology of the developing child were of equal interest for Hall, Sully and other founding fathers, but few psychologists were ever able to pursue the two approaches together.

Darwinian child psychology and Wundtian experimental psychology soon became alternatives. For most psychologists, the scientific respectability of the laboratory proved the more attractive alternative and the child almost disappeared from general psychology texts in the hey-day of Behaviourism between 1930 and 1950. One man, Stanley Hall, played a decisive part in the formation of both of these branches of psychology. Hall's oscillations from one to the other provide a fascinating illustration of the forces which lead psychologists to their choice of topics and methods. Hall finally gave his allegiance to genetic psychology but he did not live to see the child established at the centre of the new psychology. Experimental psychology flourished and child studies became less and less respectable. Some explanations for the decline of the child in the history of psychology can be found in the section of this chapter on the career of Stanley Hall, and his immediate successors, but the chapter begins with an exploratory analysis of what may be general barriers in the study of children.

Few of us have observed children with any great care yet we all generalise about them. My argument will be that we use generalisations because at some time or other we all have to deal with children. We do not relate to them as individuals, because children make us apprehensive. How then do parents and others generalise about children? The Newsons' Nottingham mothers (Newson and Newson, 1963) responded readily with generalisations: 'They

get to know if you give in . . . . At this time now—at this age—they're trying
to see who's master. . . . You find with children . . .'. In an interesting
discussion in a more recent publication from the Nottingham survey, the
Newsons' consider how mothers begin to be bothered when their repertoire of
generalisations about children conflicts with their growing perceptions of the
child as an individual within the family (Newson and Newson, 1976). But even
in the intimacies of the family, generalisations would appear to be a main
determinant of relating. The Nottingham mothers display a mixture of
generalisations about the nature of childhood and generalisations about the
care of children.

When we generalise about the nature of children we draw from our general
concepts of human nature. Most of us conclude that the uncultured child
must behave as he does because it is in his nature to do so. Ausubel and
Sullivan (1970) have classified basic concepts of human development as
preformationist, predeterminist and *tabula rasa*. The preformationist view
assumes that all capacities of intellect and personality exist at birth in the
'little adult' or homunculus. Few people today believe in the instantaneous
creation of each little Adam or each little Eve (as did van Leeuwenhock in
1677 when he looked through his new compound microscope and reported
seeing 'animalcules' in sperm) but some forms of the preformationist view
remain. Astrologers still contend that all has been decided by the state of the
heavens at the moment of birth and there are still midwives and mothers who
look for significant portents. If this view of development is held, then child-
care becomes a matter of helping the preformed child to adjust to the rules of a
particular culture. Most adults, however, hold some form of the predeterminist concepts of human development where it is assumed that heredity is
an important determinant but where there is modification as a result of
experience in the interactions of nature and nurture. In this view, child-care is
very much a consequence of the particular concept of human nature held by
the adult. Some concepts, biological or religious, classify the child as
essentially 'bad', i.e. natural instincts are anti-social, or children are born
ignorant and evil, although salvation is possible through education and
correction. Other concepts classify the child as 'good', i.e. the natural child is
innocent and virtuous, although in danger of corruption by society. It is
doubtful whether any of us believe in the third category as a concept of human
development and view the child as a *tabula rasa*. The concept of innate
neutrality is attractive as a political principle, but not even Watson really
believed that any outcome is possible for any child.

It may well be argued that parents and teachers surely do not behave as if
their generalisations about human nature in children take identifiable forms.
There can be no doubt, however, that educational reformers, poets and others
preoccupied with childhood, write as if they do hold clear, identifiable
concepts. The generalisations of Rousseau, Blake or A. S. Neil have an
unequivocal and passionate ring. These are the generalisations which parents

or teachers will find when they turn to child specialists for guidance. It may be true that Rousseau and other reformers couch their generalisations in strong and simple terms in order to replace a popular generalisation with its converse; but this in itself suggests an assumption by the reformers that children are indeed controlled by the generalisations of their parents and teachers. In the absence of relevant surveys we can reasonably conclude that the generalisations of the Nottingham mothers, or the generalisations given freely to probationary teachers in the school staff-room, support the argument that all adults hold a limited but powerful repertoire of generalisations about children. The second part of my argument is that the generalisations are required because our apprehensions inhibit the close study of children and the pursuit of relaxed relationships with them.

Barriers in the Study of Children

Why do most of us fail to get to know children well enough to understand them? The intimacies of parenthood do bring some weakening of control by generalisations as we saw with the Nottingham mothers. The study of children by psychologists often begins when they first become parents. James Mark Baldwin chose genetic psychology for this reason. Describing his professional life, he wrote:

'It was with the birth of the first child, Helen (the "H" of the books on mental development) that interest on the problems of genesis—origin, development, evolution—became prominent; the interest which was to show itself in all the subsequent years. "H" became (with, later on, her sister "E"), from her extreme infancy, the focus through which all the problems of general biology and psychology presented themselves' (Baldwin, 1961).

'H' and 'E', together with Darwin's infant son 'Doddy', Binet's Armande and Marguerite, Piaget's Jacqueline, Lucienne and Laurent form a distinguished company of child subjects in the history of psychology! Before parenthood, psychologists are inclined to believe that an understanding of human behaviour can be found with adult or animal subjects in the laboratory. Controlled experiments are undoubtedly easier with adults and rats. Children are rarely suitable subjects with whom to test hypotheses from general psychology. But appropriate hypotheses in developmental psychology are surely best generated from observations culled from prolonged sessions in the company of children themselves. There appears however, to be an irrational avoidance of the company of children, sufficiently striking to justify analysis. Unfortunately, I know of no established theory or research with which to conduct this analysis. Consequently, for this section of the chapter I can only offer some questions which may take us to the heart of the matter.

Do we fear children because they are familiar yet different?

Hebb's discussion of the origins of fear may be suggestive. His experiments showed that chimpanzees were terrified by a plaster replica of the head of a chimpanzee. A possible explanation for their terror was given support by Hebb's other finding that chimpanzees reared blindfold, and therefore without experience of the sight of fellow chimpanzees, were not afraid of a plaster head, at most they showed mild curiosity but usually indifference. Hebb concluded that their fear is produced by 'events that combine the familiar and the unfamiliar—not by the totally unfamiliar event'. He describes a further observation to support the notion:

> 'Dr R and Mr T are regular attendants in a chimpanzee nursery; the infants are attached to both, and eagerly welcome being picked up by either. Now, in full sight of the infants, Dr R puts on Mr T's coat. At once he evokes fear reactions identical with those made to a stranger, and just as strong. An unfamiliar combination of familiar things, by itself, can therefore produce a violent emotional reaction' (Hebb, 1958).

For humans too, the violation of expectations can be alarming. If someone appears to be familiar and predictable, and yet behaves unexpectedly, the disturbance is not just surprising but profoundly disturbing. It could be argued that this can hardly explain adult fear of children since all adults surely have experience of social interactions with the very young: we were all children once and played with other children. Yet few of us retain clear memories of the world of childhood. When, as children, we played with other children we had only the partly formed conceptual systems necessary for this kind of understanding. It is not enough to have been a child oneself in order to understand children. For most adults, children are strange and alarming cuckoos in the nest.

Is there a fear of primitive, uncontrolled behaviour?

Allied to the fear of the familiar yet different is the fear of primitive, uncontrolled behaviour, an apprehension readily seen in the student teacher, or indeed in anyone else who may be called upon to supervise a group of children, whether in the village hall or at a birthday party. Roger Brown (1965) recalls Talcott Parsons' description of new generations of children as 'recurrent barbarian invasions'. Barbarians are a frightening image because they are strange, primitive and brutish. Associating children with brutes has a long history. Aristotle held that 'children and brutes pursue pleasure'. In popular belief therefore children are held to have much in common with animals. If we add the doctrine, once fashionable in child psychology, that ontogeny reciptulates phlylogeny, we easily assume that the younger the child the nearer it is to the animals. There is a strongly held popular belief, reinforced in various forms by some Darwinians, that man's animal heritage of instinctive aggression is liable to break out at any moment and is only slowly and precariously brought under control in the course of childhood. For many, the animal nature of the young child is a constant threat.

The fear, however, that a group of children may go wild is not just a fear of people getting hurt. The disintegration of social structure is alarming when a group becomes a mob. Le Bon (1960) suggested that in crowds 'the heterogeneous is swamped by the homogenous, and the unconscious qualities obtain the upper hand'. Adults may be frightened of children running amok, not only because it can so easily happen but because primitive, collective behaviour is a particularly haunting idea, popular in science fiction. When children are responding only to the excitement of the group, the adult loses his means of control through appeals to individuals. Anxiety follows the loss of social structure within a group because this brings a loss of personal identity to its individual members.

The most widely recognized cause of adult avoidance of the company of children is that their very childishness is embarrassing. Some men may not like being seen with young children, especially as part of their work, because, in our society, such work is thought to be a job for women. If a man overcomes this prejudice he may sometimes be thought by others to be spurred on by latent sexual perversions or immaturity. There is also the common taunt about liking children because of a failure to grow up and compete successfully in the adult world. Apart from a fear of what others may think, the child has a capacity to embarrass the adult directly, because he is a child. The 'he' in the last sentence is appropriately ambiguous: it is the child's capacity to arouse the child in the adult which many grown-ups find disturbing.

Are children disturbing because they arouse the child within us?

This time we can turn to psychoanalysis to get the beginnings of an explanation. A further description of Melanie Klein's Object Relations Theory will appear later in this chapter when we discuss the interactions between child psychology and general psychology, but the usefulness of the psychoanalytic viewpoint in describing the child within all of us can be glimpsed in these quotations from Klein and then Erick Erikson. First, Klein:

'If we look at our adult world from the viewpoint of its roots in infancy, we gain an insight into the way our mind, our habits and our views have been built up from the earliest infantile phantasies and emotions to the most complex and sophisticated adult manifestations. There is one more conclusion to be drawn, which is that nothing that ever existed in the unconscious completely loses its influence on the personality.' (Klein, 1960).

Next, Erikson:

'Moralistic man and rationalising man continues to identify himself with abstractions of himself, but refuses to see how he became what he really is and how, as an emotional and political being, he undoes with infantile confusions and impulsions what his thought has invented and what his hands have built' (Erikson, 1965).

The view that Klein and Erikson are expressing, is that the rational attitudes of adults, such as they are, have developed from the irrational, emotional impulses of infancy. These emotional impulses subsequently become dormant but they can be triggered off once again if the original infantile experiences are forced upon us, as they may be when we interact with children. The view is perhaps illustrated by an example from everyday life. If we go back to our example of the adult recruited to look after children at a birthday party and imagine the usual adjudications which are required to settle squabbles over sharing toys and food or disputes about the rules of the game, one plausible explanation of the adult's eventual shouting, clouting and consequent anxiety might be that his adult sophistication has given way to aroused infantile memories. Some adults may do their best to escape mixing with children in situations of this kind because they dislike noise and buffeting; but many may evade these encounters in order to avoid a return to the anxieties of their childhood.

Does a belief in the foundational nature of childhood impede our study of children?

A generalization about childhood which has been held steadfastly from Plato to Bowlby, despite the inadequacy of the supporting evidence (Clarke and Clarke, 1976) is that infancy is of crucial importance for future development: 'Just as the twig is bent, the tree's inclined'. This belief presents the child researcher with a problem. If human development is founded on the experiences of childhood, then the study of children gives us our best chance of understanding human psychology. On the other hand, if childhood experiences are crucial, the experimental intervention itself may be crucial and should not be undertaken unless we can be assured that the intervention will at least not be harmful. Many early experimental child psychologists appear to have come close to child abuse in the interests of science. Little Albert's experiences with Watson and Rayner in 1917 may have added something to psychology but they leave one with misgivings about the child's subsequent development. The Watson and Rayner experiment does in fact quite clearly illuminate the problem. The experimenters reveal their awareness of the danger of their intervention in Albert's life when they claim that their activities would 'do him relatively little harm'. But presenting a nine-month-old infant with a rat, a rabbit, a dog, a monkey, masks with and without hair, cotton wool, burning newspapers—and banging loudly on a steel bar—makes the claim sound unduly optimistic within the context of our understanding 60 years later. We would now doubt whether Albert's life in a home for invalid children could justifiably be described as 'normal'. However, it is the subsequent research in developmental psychology which makes us worry about Albert's fate. The classic experiment illustrates the dilemma: we need to study children in order to discover what may harm them, but in studying them we may ourselves be harmful. The problem is still with us. The more we discover about childhood the more prudent it is to assume that all childhood experiences are formative. We must therefore assume that all empirical interventions become part of a child's learning experiences. Before starting an experiment with children, psychologists must surely attempt to judge its likely effects in the light of what they have already discovered, just as they would if asked to give advice on interventions in a child's life by parents or teachers. Anyone surveying the history of experimental psychology might well wonder whether enough thought has been given to the experiment as a learning experience for the child subject.

Children are good subjects in that they sit down eagerly awaiting what the adult is going to get out of his box and ask them to do next. What they remember, however, may not be the experimental task but their attempts to decide what the experimenter thought of their successes and failures and why they were asked to show what they could do with such funny, repetitive problems. The many hours that hundreds of children have spent discriminating squares of different sizes or trying to remember pairs of words presented together may have helped the psychologist chasing publications, but they have not added a great deal to our understanding of human development. Fortunately there has been a shift in recent years to more child-centred research programmes. Hypotheses are increasingly derived from getting to know children by observations in natural settings rather than from the laboratory experiments with animals and adults. When the experimenter's hypotheses are generated from observations of the spontaneous activities of children then the psychologist may only be asking children to do what they might very well do without him. We may have some years to go before we quite reach this happy position and so resolve the dilemma.

The Conflicting Interests of Stanley Hall

Dorothy Ross's biography of Stanley Hall, *G. Stanley Hall: The Psychologist as Prophet* (Ross, 1972) gives a throughly documented and fascinating account of Hall's professional life. This puzzling, controversial founder of experimental psychology and child psychology oscillated between the attractions of both so that within one man we can see the nature of the tensions which have affected the child's place in psychology ever since. Hall came to psychology from theology and philosophy after reading Wundt's *Granduze der physiologischen Psycholgie* (which reached America in 1873) and Spencer's evolutionary *Principles of Psychology*. Hall's introduction to the new experimental psychology of consciousness and to Darwinian theory was extended by two visits to Germany. On his second, in 1878—as a psychologist with a doctorate supervised by William James—he eventually settled at the laboratory in Leipzig. What he has to say about Wundt is surprising. In a letter to James in December 1878, he wrote: 'Wundt is more and more exasperating. He seems to me a grand importer of English ideas . . . and an exporter of the generalized commonplaces of German physiology . . . inexact . . . and as a man who has done more speculation and less valuable observing than any man I know who has had his career. His experiments, which I attend, I think utterly unreliable and defective in method' (Ross, 1972, p. 85). One is not surprised that the visitor from Harvard was confident enough to criticise the great man. James himself was never unreservedly enthusiastic. A few years after Hall's stay at Leipzig, James wrote in a letter that Wundt 'made a very pleasant and personal impression, on me, with his agreeable voice and ready, tooth-showing smile' (Allen, 1969, p. 251). What is surprising is Hall's outright rejection of Wundt as an experimentalist. Spearman contradicts the view and describes an incident where Wundt solved a technical, experimental problem in the laboratory: 'No sooner did we mention our trouble to him than he with consummate ease forthwith solved it for us' (Spearman, 1961). Admittedly, Hall was writing a letter and not publishing a comment. And also, at that time, he was proud of his ability as an experimentalist. Yet one does perhaps discern that, on reaching the source of the new experimental psychology, Hall had an early premonition that in the end he would fail to find the discipline personally satisfying. When Hall did praise Wundt, many years later in a public lecture in 1912, it was for his 'broad philosophical interests leading out of science'.

On Hall's return to America, his ambition was to find a post in psychology and make a name for himself as an experimental psychologist. But jobs were hard to get: as Jastrow wrote, the 'problem that intimately concerned the graduate student was that of securing a position. There were as yet no teaching positions in psychology alone. Psychology was associated with philosophy, and the smaller colleges were likely to continue in that tradition'.

(Jastrow was talking about his own predicament after the award of his Ph.D. in 1886.) Hall's thoughts then turned to education. With the lack of openings, he feared that 'neither psychology nor philosophy would ever make bread' and decided that 'the most promising line of work would be to study the applications of psychology to education'. We can see here the ways in which the progress of a science is influenced by the needs of its practitioners for prestige and remuneration. Decisions about what to do next are seldom the outcome of an academic logic of inquiry unaffected by personal needs. Hall persuaded Harvard to let him lecture on Pedagogy on Saturday mornings in 1881. The lectures were a great success, attended by local educationists and teachers, and repeated in the following two years.

The lectures were given at just the right time. Hall had been right about finding a 'promising line'. Teachers were beginning to look for a sounder basis for their professionalism and were excited about the scientific child studies of Preyer, Sully and others, reported from Europe. Hall gave indications of what could be done in America. His assertions have a post-Piagetian ring: 'it is the fundamental law of mental development, as well of action and assimilation, that must be made the basis of methods of teaching, topics chosen and their order' (Ross, 1972, p. 126). He published the results of his questionnaires administered by 60 teachers to 'three or more children each' in *The Contents of Children's Minds* (1883). His conclusions were that 'there is next to nothing of pedagogic value the knowledge of which it is safe to assume at the outset of school-life. Hence the need of objects and the danger of books and word-cram.' (From the excerpt in Dennis (1972).) Rousseau would have been pleased with the first findings of the new scientific child study.

But already Hall was uneasy about his growing fame in the world of teachers: 'Just as soon as I fully see my way clearly to a livelihood in (psychology) the educational line of study will be speedily subordinated to it, as it is only one facet of *applied psychology*' (Ross, 1972, p. 133). For Hall, at this stage, pure experimental psychology was still the way in which he could best earn the approval of his peers and also find a satisfying approach to the understanding of man. In 1882, he was offered an appointment as lecturer in psychology and pedagogics at Johns Hopkins, two years later as professor, and in 1888 he went to Clark as its first president. His enthusiasm and hopes for experimental psychology were unlimited. He founded the first psychology laboratory, the first journal (the *American Journal of Psychology* in 1887) and the American Psychological Association, of which he was the first president. Psychology, Hall announced in his first editorial, must be scientific and not speculative. Controversy, and topics like psychical research, should have no place. Hall argued that 'science offered a truly religious world-view, of greater weight than philosophic and religious myths tied to merely personal or historic speculation' (Ross, 1972, pp. 142–143). He thought he had found his profession as well as his faith. For a time, Hall's energy and ability swept him along as a founder of experimental psychology, but in the space of a decade he had quarrelled with his fellow experimentalists and turned finally to child study—and genetic psychology—as the subject in which he could satisfy his needs for a psychology which would encompass the emotional and dynamic aspects of man. He finally expressed outright those early criticisms of Wundtian laboratory work with adult consciousness of perceptual processes observed among the apparatus of the laboratory. The principles on which he was to found genetic psychology were drawn from Darwin and not from Wundt.

In 1894 Hall reached the age of fifty. His wife and daughter had died and he had quarrelled with his colleagues in experimental psychology. He felt that life was rushing away and he had done nothing. Academics, he said, are afflicted by a 'dawdling erudition . . . . They live in an atmosphere of criticism, they collect notes, they wait, they dream, their youth goes by, and the night comes when no man can work' (Ross, 1972, p. 253). As with Wordsworth and Rousseau, Hall sought to replenish his flagging spirits by drawing from the vitality of childhood, his own and others. He drew especially from his adolescence and his best known publication *Adolescence* (Hall, 1904) is also his best outline of genetic psychology.

The theory of recapitulation pervades Hall's child studies. Ontogeny and phylogeny were first distinguished and related in this way by Haeckel in 1866: 'Ontogenesis is a brief and rapid recapitulation of phylogenesis'. Hall saw the ontogenesis of the child's mind (or soul) as a recapitulation drawn from the entire history of the human race.

In child study we are dealing, he claimed, with the 'archeology of mind', with its heredity of 'unconscious, instinctive, prehuman or animal traits'. Not that each individual recapitulates the totality of human experience: in the 'instinct-feelings' in contrast to conscious mind, 'man is a microcosm' and nothing 'human or prehuman is alien'. Much, of course, is alien to the man of Wundtian psychology. 'A true science of character', however, 'goes beyond eye, ear, and motor mindedness'. In seeing the child as recapitulation of man's total past, Hall was able to find a psychology which could encompass those varied aspects of human existence which, for him, gave it any acceptable meaning. He could—and did—turn to ethology, and psychoanalysis to explore the totality of human experience. In his study of *Adolescence* (from which these quotations are taken) Hall describes adolescence as the second stage in individual development—the first being infancy—when the 'floodgates of heredity are thrown open'. One can see how his exotic language convinced his colleagues in the new experimental psychology that Hall had finally left their company. Even James was irritated by his 'religious cant'. Some, however, like Jastrow, while conceding that Hall abandoned the standards of the scientific method, nevertheless considered that Hall's imaginative approach opened up approaches in child study which otherwise would have remained closed (Jastrow, 1961). In full flight, Hall's extravagances are worth quoting:

'As in the prenatal and infant stage man hears from his remoter forbears back perhaps to primitive organisms, now the later and higher ancestry takes up the burden of the song of life, and the voices, of our extinct and perhaps forgotten, and our later and more human ancestry are heard in the soul. Just as in the first birth the gifts of nature are of fundamental psycho-physic qualities, which are later elaborated and differentiated by development, so now her rich donations are generic, and the accessory qualities that are unfolded out of them arise slowly from the feelings, instincts, impulses, dispositions, *Anlangen* and *Triebe*, which are the products of this later heritage . . . In some respects, early adolescence is thus the infancy of man's higher nature, when he receives from the great all-mother his last capital of energy and evolutionary momentum' (Excerpt in Grinder (1967)).

Hall, the experimentalist bold enough to criticise Wundt's techniques is now a different tack in psychology! In Hall's speculations the theory of recapitulation does not result in the mere search for gill slits or tails—or even the reflex grasping of arboreal man—but in a study of the child in whom might be seen the full scope of man's potential. Hall's romantic enthusiasm and energy did in a sense lead to a scientific psychology of child study but as much in reaction to as in the direct following of his example. Hall's principle method of investigation—the questionnaire—was attacked by Munsterberg as the 'seductive but rude and untechnical gathering of cheap and vulgar material' and 'a caricature and not an improvement of psychology' (Ross, 1972, p. 342). The same criticism could be made of many surveys in schools today; but if only one follower goes on to a more rigorous study, an original and legitimate line of inquiry may be started. Hall suggested to Gessell, when he was looking for a thesis topic, that Gessell should study the infants at the Foundling Hospital of New York. Gessell did not in fact do this until many years later but submitted as his doctorate topic 'the manifestations of jealousy, normal and abnormal, in animals and in man at ascending age periods beginning with infancy'. Gessell's view of Hall, rather like Jastrow's, was that Hall's energy and empathy, amounting to genius, 'lifted psychology above the sterilities of excessive analysis and pedantry' (Gessell, 1952). Hall's enthusiasm for genetic psychology lead him to psychoanalysis and to invite Freud to lecture at the Clark anniversary in 1909. Hall's experimentalist colleagues at Clark had suggested Ebbinghaus but Hall wrote to Freud on his own initiative. Of those psychologists who reacted to Hall and founded their own specialised branches of educational psychology, the best known are Terman and Thorndike, founders, respectively, of mental testing and the psychology of learning. Both of these topics had their origins in the child-study movement centred around Hall, despite his dislike of their tedium.

Men like Hall, if they have genius, stimulate followers by example and reaction. Reading him today can be more profitable than reading either

Terman or Thorndike, since the psychologies pioneered by the latter two were given an initial circumscribed precision which has now virtually run its course. Many, if not most, of Hall's insights and preoccupations are still outside conventional psychology and thus unsolved. His work is strewn with problems which sound interesting now, such as the possible effects of the predominance of female teachers in schools for the young. If Hall had been no more than a speculator, psychology would have passed him by. He influenced its course because he acquired its techniques and understood its theories before campaigning about its limitations. Yet like so many critics he failed to devise the techniques and theories of an alternative more satisfying psychology. What he did do was to show how a developmental perspective in psychology can produce a profitable expansion of the subject. Fortunately, as we shall see in the next section, there were others with the patience to develop these expansions within a scientific psychology.

Reactions to Genetic Psychology

The genetic psychology of Stanley Hall has much in common with the developmental psychology of today. The common theme is evolution. Hall was in love with the very word:

'As soon as I first heard it in my youth I think I must have been almost hypnotized by the word "evolution", which was music to my ear and seemed to fit my mouth better than any other' (Hall, 1927, p. 357).

Similar enthusiasm can be seen in Bruner (1976):

'I would only urge that in considering deep issues of educability we keep our perspective broad and remember that the human race has a biological past from which we can read lessons for the culture of the present.'

What happened to the evolutionary perspective in child psychology between Hall and Bruner? It did not disappear entirely, and remained to guide some approaches to normative studies, but evolutionary thinking was soon obliterated by the technicalities of the other major movements in child psychology between 1920 and 1950, intelligence testing and school learning. Darwin is one of three who laid the foundations for developmental psychology. The other two are Freud and Piaget. In the heyday of 'child psychology' all three failed to gain general recognition amongst child psychologists. Even today psychologists tend to be seen as predominantly testers of children's intelligence. But why did child psychologists spend so much time trying to perfect the classification of children from their performances on tests? Terman is a good example. He also had read his

Spencer and Haeckel as well as Darwin (Terman, 1961) when his interests first turned to psychology and he was yet another psychologist to have those interests confirmed with the birth of his first child. His grounding in the experimental psychology of the day was gained at Indiana University before he moved to his fellowship at Clark with Hall. Terman's admiration for Hall was somewhat grudging: he admired Hall's hypnotic energy and imagination but was disillusioned about him as a scientist just as Hall had been about Wundt. This led Terman to reject Hall's questionnaire techniques and turn instead to the precision of testing. Criticisms of the limitations of testing the range of human subtleties as a form of inquiry might well have weakened Terman's resolution and that of the few other testers if the demands of World War I had not enhanced the value and status of the movement. Thereafter, Terman's belief that mental testing would be 'an integral part of experimental psychology' was never shaken. Unlike most of the psychologists in the volumes of *History of Psychology in Autobiography* Terman is well satisfied with his life's work. Perhaps he did share with his father 'an obstinate persistence in completing any task he had undertaken'. It was the public demand for the classification of abilities, of course, which gave Terman a status in his preferred topic. The lasting influence of Hall can perhaps be seen in Terman's rejection of Watson's exclusion of heredity, and in his beliefs in the importance of animal psychology and Freud, but his heroes in psychology were Galton and Binet. Paradoxically, it is not Binet's intelligence test which he admired but his 'originality, insight, open-mindedness and charm'. The pioneer of the assessment of intelligence in England, Spearman, also names Galton as one of his most admired predecessors. The other was Wundt. The impetus for Spearman's work was the search for laws of cognition in the here and now of the laboratory and in his rejection of the 'romantic' spirit in science (Spearman, 1961).

In studies of children's school learning, dominant in the child psychology of the 1920s and 1930s, Thorndike was the pioneer. Did he also find his life's work by reacting against Hall? In reviewing Hall's *Adolescence*, Thorndike conceded as much: 'The great service of President Hall's studies may be to inspire others which will replace their data and refute their conclusions, but which will nonetheless be true offspring' (Ross, 1972, p. 347). Thorndike joined in the attack by the experimental psychologists on the child-study movement at the turn of the century and *Notes on Child Study* (1901) was his first book. Newly appointed in 1901 at the Teachers College of Columbia University, with his puzzle-box animal experiments behind him, Thorndike wanted to reform the movement as a scientist from within. Trained in methodology and statistics by Catell (who asked him to apply his findings from animals to humans), he first sought to refine Hall's questionnaires, but more importantly his theory of recapitulation, before shifting his focus to children's learning. In all this, Thorndike's guiding principle was to stick to the facts from observations and like Spearman he had no place for the 'romantic' spirit in the new science. Consequently Thorndike soon found the theory of recapitulation woefully short of supporting evidence. No one, he suggested, would mistake the human embryo at any stage for an adult fish. He was even more scathing about cultural recapitulation and concluded that the popularity of the theory depended on the rhetoric of its presentation. The disappearance of the evolutionary perspective in Thorndike's later work on school learning and testing must also be due to his respect for the hard psychology of the early experimentalists. His initial reaction to the animal studies of Romanes and other Darwinians was to seek clear evidence in the laboratory, remove reliance on anecdote and anthropomorphic speculation, and urge parsimony in all scientific explanation. Once one embarks on this course there is little place for constant reminders about the wonders of the complexity of children. Reminders of that sort can only diminish the significance of what strict scientific psychology has established.

In America, in the wake of Terman and Thorndike the grand visions of genetic psychology gave way to the toughness of measurement and the parsimony of S-R psychology. Freud, Piaget and Darwin still had their followers, but 'respectable' child psychologists from the late 1930s until the late 1950s were hard at work gathering research findings about children within the framework of the learning theories of general psychology. It was an effort which was both rewarding and disappointing but rarely very exciting. The ethologists have recently blown a fresh wind of Darwinism into the study of children. Piaget is now generally influential and the insights of Freud are productive rather than provocative. These trends have now firmly merged into the developmental psychology which began in the late 1950s. Before describing the developmental psychology of today, however, we can fill the gap between genetic psychology and its contemporary, evolutionary counterpart with a look at the nature–nurture arguments arising from the growth of intelligence testing.

Nature and Nurture in Child Psychology

Taking sides in the nature versus nurture contest is rather like being for or against capital punishment, comprehensive schools or sex equality: we tend to have an instant preference strongly resistant to argument. So much so, that once we know which side has been taken by anyone on the issues just mentioned we can make a fair prediction about whether nature or nurture will be given preference as the more important determinant of development. Not surprisingly, the emotive force which impels us to take sides has caught the attention of psychoanalysts. Flugel (1955) classifies the two camps as those who are parent-regarding (i.e. those who accept parental authority, especially paternal authority, as an inherent part of the social structure) and those who are child-regarding (i.e. those who rebel against acceptance of the inevitability of parental authority and who adopt the child's standpoint). The explanation has a ring of plausibility: the concept of genetic endowment is attractive if you admire your father but a nuisance if you do not. On the other hand, an acceptance of the logic of the genetic argument may lead to an admiration in an effort to avoid cognitive dissonance. Whatever the mechanisms, the link between family life and attitudes to heredity can be seen clearly enough in the 'insubordinate' environmentalist, Watson, and in the nativist, Gessell, who described his family as 'closely united' (Watson, 1961 and Gessell, 1952).

We have seen that child psychology was launched on the tide of Darwinism at the end of the nineteenth century. Psychology in general in its early days followed Darwin in his search for instincts in man (and reasoning in animals) in order to support a theory of continuity in evolutionary development. But in 1919, Dunlap wrote his classic article 'Are there any instincts?' and radical Behaviourists soon established 'A psychology without heredity' (Kuo, 1924). Thereafter, the majority of learning theorists, who dominated general psychology until the 1950s (Beach, 1955), were happy to exclude genetics. This climate was partly responsible for the isolation of the leading child psychologist of the years between the Wars: Arnold Gessell. He tends to be dismissed as unduly preoccupied with norm-gathering and maturation, but Gessell is less old-fashioned now as a theorist. The reader will have a job to find his name in the author index of any of the better known textbooks in general psychology and, even in child psychology, Gessell is used for his data on developmental schedules rather than for his approach as a theorist. Moreover, his adherence to chronological ages tends to be criticised and he is accused of thinking 'that proving the importance of maturation justified his neglect of environmental influences'. He is said to be out of tune with more recent experimental research which is 'aimed at studying the interaction of maturational and environmental influences, recognizing the general importance and interdependence of both' (Zigler and Child, 1973). Yet a truly sympathetic reading of Gessell in the light of our renewed tolerance of heredity does not lead one to describe him as neglecting interaction.

In the heat of debate, psychologists have talked about each other as if there are some who would want to lay claim to either environment or heredity as a sole determinant of development. Interaction is a relatively new term in the academic debates but we are surely all interactionists. Even Watson did not deny the importance of inherited structures: he overstated his environmentalist case in order to shift the emphasis. For him, behaviour is an outcome of 'a certain type of structure plus early training' (Watson, 1926), but he put the emphasis on training. Gessell in reaction may have put the emphasis on heredity but the interactionism of his position is apparent in the following:

'The supreme genetic law appears to be this: All present growth hinges on past growth. Growth is not a simple function neatly determined by x units of inheritance plus y units of environment, but is an historical complex which reflects at every stage the past which it incorporates. In other words we are led astray by an artificial dualism of heredity and environment, if it blinds us to the fact that growth is a continuous, self-conditioning process, rather than a drama controlled, *ex machina*, by two forces . . . it is important to avoid any over simplification of the problem' (Gessell, 1928).

Gessell's description of growth as 'a continuous, self-conditioning process' is similar to Piaget's: 'The child comes by his mind as he comes by his body, through the organizing processes of growth' (Gessell, 1952).

Gessell remained steadfastly faithful to the Darwinian psychology of Hall. Why then does he not occupy a central place in child psychology and almost fail completely to find a place in general psychology? Stolz (1958) believes that Gessell and Thompson's books on infants were 'a major contribution to the understanding of human development which has been lost sight of', but is content to explain the neglect as due to Gessell's later use of chronological age as a measure of development. The explanation does not credit psychologists with much ingenuity in the use of published work. Chronological age is a useful statistic but its value for parents, teachers and researchers should not have led to its being seen by psychologists as a fixed component of Gessell's theory. Other explanations of Gessell's lack of prestige occur if we remind ourselves of the attitudes of children discussed earlier in this chapter. Gessell does not figure prominently in general psychology because he observed and described children and did not conduct experiments with them. He did not formulate theories which provided hypothesis for experimental testing. He preferred to lay some foundations for the science of man by means of a clinical science of child development. Experimentalists, as his mentor Stanley Hall found, do not like looking for their starting points outside the laboratory. For child psychologists striving to retain the respect of experimental colleagues Gessell was seen as a paediatrician responding to requests for developmental norms from doctors, teachers and parents. Child psychologists who became specialists in intelligence testing, in response to demands from parents and teachers, felt rather more respectable and 'scientific' because of the support from their statistical techniques. Their work has supplied the ammunition for the continuing battle in nature–nurture arguments and any survey of the child in psychology must take note of the battle.

Lewis Terman, who enabled psychologists to give IQs to children, joined Stanley Hall at Clark University in 1903 when it was 'still the American Mecca for aspiring young psychologists' (Terman, 1961). In his need for a 'solid footing for research' Terman avoided Hall's questionnaires and turned to tests. Hall disapproved of the 'quasi-exactness of quantitative methods' but characteristically gave his blessing. Acknowledging his own clumsiness with laboratory apparatus, Terman rejected a career in experimental psychology and began, for him, the more congenial work of mental testing. It prospered at Stanford during the first World War when psychologists using tests in selection for the Armed Forces got the 'recognition they deserved'. Terman's chosen specialism in child psychology gave him both scientific respectability and general status. His favourite psychologists, it can be noted, were Galton and Binet.

At the time when Terman went to Clark in 1903, Burt and Spearman had begun their work on tests in England. Spearman explained in the 1904 article which he sent to the *American Journal of Psychology* (reprinted in Wiseman, 1967) that the experimental psychology of Wundt was failing to produce results of any use in applied psychology, especially education. He proposed a 'correlational psychology' as a better bet than laboratory experiments in the general study of the integration of mental phenomena. Experimental psychology, he believed, was far too strongly contaminated by faculty psychology. For psychologists disappointed by Wundtian psychology's failure to provide a human psychology, Sir Francis Galton made a splendid father figure. We have seen that Terman was happy to relate to this scientific Darwinian and Burt also rested happily in the view that Galton was the first to study individual characteristics by strict scientific techniques, i.e. standardised measurement, experimental tests and mathematical analysis of the data (Burt, 1952). Around 1905, therefore, the correlational study of abilities was founded on a sound basis on both sides of the Atlantic and before long became a focus for clashes between hereditarians and environmentalists. The first rows had some of the ferocity of the recent Jensen exchanges (Kamin, 1977). Educational psychologists who have included intelligence tests as part of their stock in trade in the assessment and prediction of scholastic ability are often surprised to come across attempts to settle nature–nurture issues from the results of these tests. The assumption of a constancy in IQ has a professional convenience but does, of course, in certain political climates give rise to heated resentments. Nevertheless, the psychologists who have sparked off the rows have rarely been engaged in the practice of educational psychology. Arguments about the genetic contribution to IQ have not been a particular preoccupation of child psychologists themselves. They have, however, supplied the data for psychologists and others who feel compelled to take sides in this basic and emotive division of attitudes.

Darwin, Freud, Piaget: Founders of Developmental Psychology

We have seen that the founders of both genetic and experimental psychology were enthusiastic Darwinians. By the 1930s, however, Darwin's influence had waned. The experimental psychologists of animal learning had been lured by the data derived from laboratory mazes and other apparatus into the belief that there was a realistic hope of formulating general laws of learning which would apply to all living species, including humans. All that was needed were more laboratory experiments to refine the theories. The foundations of a general psychology of learning could be achieved with the rat. At the same time, in the 1930s and 1940s, child psychologists became less interested in speculations about developmental processes and turned their attentions to the statistical intricacies of the analysis of intellectual abilities, the gathering of normative data *per se*, and correlational studies of educational and social variables. They also pursued a general psychology of learning. Somewhere around 1960, however, Darwinism returned.

In the psychology of animal learning, the paper by Breland and Breland (1961) is a useful landmark with a dramatic setting. The story is now told with some relish in general textbooks as it was by the Brelands themselves in their paper aptly headed 'The misbehaviour of organisms'. Outside the laboratory they found that animals misbehave themselves in that they do not always follow the rules of conditioning which were found to be adequate in the controlled conditions of the laboratory. With more freedom, animals display differences in behaviour from species to species and show how 'learned behaviour drifts toward instinctive behaviour'. The notion of instinct had returned to psychology and the hunt was on again for genetically organised patterns. At this point psychologists began to take note of the ethologists' observations of different species in natural environments. There was a 'realization by psychologists that perhaps the white rat cannot reveal everything there is to know about behaviour' (Breland and Breland, 1961).

About the same time, ethology entered child psychology. The first enthusiast was John Bowlby. The inspirations for Bowlby's work on the interactions of mother and infant derive from two of the three founders of contemporary development psychology, Freud and Darwin. The third founder, Piaget, is less important in Bowlby's approach. A review of developmental psychology since World War II can therefore begin with the important influences of psychoanalytic theory and ethology on the topic of maternal care, which, it could be argued, *is* the developmental psychology of the 1950s and 1960s.

Maternal care is another of those topics which divides us before we begin. For some it is *the* determinant of development. Others are at once keen to argue that maternal influences need not be permanent. Why do we so readily take sides? It is tempting to suggest that those of us who admire the mother-care given to us in infancy will readily see the influence as an important determinant of our development, while those of us who do not will reject the idea. But further reflection soon suggests that this is too simple an explanation. It is quite possible to derive satisfaction from believing that one has carried the burden of a bad start in life. The blame for failures in development can then be shifted from oneself to others. But the ramifications are numerous.

Contemporary developmental psychology owes a great deal to the Child Guidance movement of the 1930s and 1940s. Child guidance relied on psychoanalytic theory. Clinical practitioners saw family relationships as the principle determinants of emotional and social development. Freud first drew attention to the establishment of sexual identity as an outcome of the toddler's coming to terms with masculinity and femininity in himself (or herself) and in his mother and father, and then others. Melanie Klein then emphasised how much the nursling invested in his transactions .with his maternal environment. Adler described the struggle to assert in competition with siblings. Three sets of relationships were thus identified. In the order in which they occur in the child, they are: (1) the nursling and his mother, (2) the infant and his mother and father and (3) the child and his siblings. In the first relationship, it was assumed, the general foundations of sociability are laid, with the danger of psychosis when there are severe distortions. In the set of second relationships, sexual gender is established with consequent neurosis if persistent confusions prevail. In the third set lie the child's determining pattern of competence as a contender in competitive activities at school and elsewhere. In adolescence all three components are involved as the child emancipates himself from the dependence on the nuclear family which generates this intense sequence of events. The majority of clinicians viewed the child in this manner but were slow to formulate and publish their theories, partly through fear of criticism by tough-minded experimental psychologists but also because clinical flair and scientific competence are rarely combined. Explicit formulation of this kind of approach can, however, be seen in Guntrip (1971).

Bowlby was working in child guidance when he first wrote about maternal care. What caught his eye in the children who had been referred for stealing was that they struck him as 'affectionless' (Bowlby, 1946). Complete and prolonged separation of a child from his mother in his first five years appeared to stunt his sociability. In other words, deprivation of the primary, maternal relationship was followed by a failure to make relationships with others. Bowlby's WHO review (Bowlby, 1952) deals with maternal care and mental health. Child-guidance practitioners in accordance with the theory outlined above, value the capacity to make personal relationships. Indeed, as Guntrip has made clear, the psychoanalytic description of development, following the work of Klein and Fairbairn, has become a relationship theory of personality. Freud had begun with an instinct theory, where the neonate's instinctual impulses are inevitably seen to conflict with social norms. The only possible resolutions are (1) repression with consequent neurosis, (2) expression as delinquency or (3) some form of transformation of the impulses into socially acceptable forms. This is the pessimistic, biological Freudian theory which has its counterparts in some forms of popular ethology. But it should be noted that when Freud formulated his explanation of the development of conscience, as the internalisation of parental images, he shifted from instincts to relationships as the primary determinants of development. Klein and Fairbairn have made this explicit but Freud did not.

Bowlby's first hypothesis is a clear consequence of a relationship theory of personality development: ' . . . prolonged separation of a child from his mother stands foremost among the causes of delinquent character development' (Bowlby, 1944, 1946). What is not always recognised is that as early as 1956, Bowlby had himself abandoned the search for a specific link between maternal deprivation and particular personality characteristics and had chosen to concentrate instead on a careful analysis of mother–child interactions, still interested in personality rather than cognitive abilities. We will see in a moment that ethology, i.e. the comparative study of animal behaviour in natural settings, became more of a source of inspiration in Bowlby's quest than did his earlier contact with psychoanalytic theory. In the meanwhile we can note that maternal deprivation studies extended into cognitive development. Goldfarb (1943) had discovered that institutionalised children differed from fostered children in scholastic skills and language as well as in their capacity for relationships. With these findings the attention of psychologists was alerted to the possibility that the pre-school years determine the boundaries of all aspects of a child's subsequent development. Together with the neurological deprivation theories of Hebb, these findings became the basis of the compensatory education programmes.

It is the comprehensive nature of his theory of the consequences of early experience which has so provoked Bowlby's critics. For many critics the theory is a dangerously pessimistic outcome of male chauvinism: pessimistic because children who are deprived of continual loving, maternal care would be seen as disadvantaged forever, and male chauvinist because an implication of the theory would seem to bind mothers to domesticity. The social and political implications of a general belief in the importance of early experience will be discussed later. At present we will continue with a review of Bowlby's influence within developmental psychology.

It is arguable that Bowlby's main influence has been very much in the revival of an evolutionary perspective. From the late 1950s many researchers in studying mother–infant interactions observed animals, as well as human infants, and especially cats and monkeys. Some of the most useful observations came from ethologists working in the field rather than in the laboratory. The ethologists' concept of imprinting, sporadically referred to before by Lorenz (1935), was well established as a topic in contemporary ethology by the time psychologists chose to concentrate on analyses of maternal care. Any discussion of imprinting soon leads to talk about its survival value for the young and for the species: 'It is learning without which the species in question would not survive' (Hess, 1973). Thus in discussing infant behaviour psychologists began to ask 'why?' rather than 'how?' questions. 'How questions' are about the mechanisms of behaviour. 'Why questions' are about evolutionary functions (Alcock, 1975). If we ask why does an infant smile rather than how does he smile we immediately shift from a study of the infant as an isolated learner to the infant in relation to his natural environment. We can see then how Bowlby came to formulate his theory of the evolutionary adaptedness of man, in common with other species.

Man evolved, adapted by selection pressures, to survive and reproduce in wide, tree-less plains as a hunter-gatherer. By the time of Christ, half of mankind was still living in this way. In the three million years or so of cultural man's total existence he has been a hunter-gatherer for 99 per cent of the time. Agriculture only began about 10 000 years ago (Devore and Konner, 1974). Adapted to life in the savannah, with prolonged dependence in infancy as another characteristic of the species, it was assumed that infants of man would not survive if they lost the protection of their adults. Those that readily formed attachments with their mothers stood the best chance of living to reproduce. Attachment behaviours, therefore, which bring mothers and infants together, and keep them there, are the activities of infancy studied by Bowlby. The Kung San live today as hunter-gatherers in Botswana. Bowlby must have been excited to hear of the observations of mother–infant interactions made by Devore and Konner who list the following characteristics: (1) the Kung neonate's repertoire of reflexes is the same as a European's, (2) the infants are carried in a sling on the mother's side for at least the first year, (3) this continual contact promotes awareness of the infant's needs and the mother's habituation to urination and defecation, (4) when the infant is not asleep or in the sling he and the mother are in active face-to-face exchanges, (5) the infant eventually initiates separation and the mother does not leave him until the birth of her next infant in the fourth year, (6) weaning does not start until the mother is pregnant again in the third year and (7) by 15 months the infant is learning with his mother to gather by digging with a stick.

What are we to make of the fact that hunter-gatherer mothers give to their infants the kind of continual, loving care which Bowlby's clinical work suggested was essential for mental health in modern man? Do the Kung studies tell us what 'human infancy was meant to do and be'? In an evolutionary sense this must be what can be learned from the observations; but, of course, modern infants have to adapt themselves to modern demands. So although the Kung may be able to tell us what the biology of human infancy was meant to do and be, they cannot help us to prepare our children for the very different demands of our modern social world. They can, perhaps, remind us of the biological dispositions of infants and thus warn us when contemporary social fashions are disturbingly incompatible with the innate tendencies of mothers and infants. With this awareness we should be better prepared if we decide to reject the nuclear family and introduce alternative forms of infant care.

Bowlby's debt to Freud and Darwin is clear enough in the theories of attachment described in the preceding paragraphs and the bulk of the research in developmental psychology from the mid 1950s to the mid 1960s, related to his focus on mother–infant interactions. Is research derived from Piaget a separate strand? For many years it was indeed separate, but the merging of the three founders can now just be seen. To bring this account of the child in psychology up to date we must first go back to some earlier glimpses of Piagetian influences before attempting an assessment of his current dominance.

Between 1911 and 1916, Piaget (who was born in 1896) overcame an adolescent crisis and began to see how he would apply himself in the same kind of quest for an understanding of man which had seized Stanley Hall. He read Spencer, Comte, Darwin and William James (Gardner, 1972) and was thus influenced in much the same way as Hall had been by the biologists and philosophers of the late nineteenth century. Piaget has remained true to this early influence and has lived to see his biological approach to psychological development become fashionable once again. Working in Geneva, protected geographically and intellectually from the pressures of academic psychology in Europe and America, Piaget has gone his own way while psychologists elsewhere have interpreted him according to their changing needs. His theories have been drawn from biology but his techniques owe something to other movements in child psychology. The lesson from intelligence testing is well known. Piaget soon found, when standardising intelligence tests for Dr Simon in Binet's laboratory, that explaining the wrong answers given by children was much more exciting than totting up the scores of the ones they got right. His debt to psychoanalysis is also fortuitous: watching psychiatric interviews at Bleuler's clinic taught him the value of persistent delving until the thinking of the patient (or child) is established in its own right, no matter how odd it appears at first. If one is to understand someone else's thinking one must first pay attention to its idiosyncrasies and then have the patience and skill to explore them.

Piaget's work has been viewed in various ways over the years. The work itself has been in three stages (Elkind, 1970): (1) from 1922–29, in exploring the funny ideas children have about the world and themselves, Piaget described children's development from their initial animism and ego-centrism, (2) from 1922–40 he accumulated his detailed findings about the origins of intelligence in the activities of infancy, observing his own three children, (3) from 1940, and still continuing, he and his assistants have studied all the stages in cognitive growth from infancy to the formal thinking of adults. The work in the first and last periods appealed to some educationists immediately on publication but his emphasis on the origins of intelligence in the gropings of infants had to wait for our current interest in infancy before its significance became apparent to psychologists.

Throughout the years from 1922, however, the steady output of books and articles was noted somewhat uneasily by psychologists unable either to accept or dismiss them because they were not sure that they understood. This was partly Piaget's fault: he is long-winded, repetitious and cavalier in his inconsistent use of terms and in his attitude to the conventions of scientific psychology. A general appreciation of his view of development probably began about 1950 with the publication in English of *The Psychology of Intelligence* and with visits to Geneva by British and American psychologists after the War. From the early 1960s there was a growing recognition among developmental psychologists that they had a saviour in their midst who would lead them away from the over-worked concepts and methods of behaviourism and intelligence testing. We must now examine whether developmental psychology has found in Piaget's work a sound and comprehensive theory on which it can build without fear of the need for later demolition or evacuation.

The first thing to note is that Piaget recognises a variety of determinants of development. These he classifies into three groups with the following descriptions: (1) 'organic growth and especially the maturation of the nervous system and the endocrine systems', (2) 'experience in the actions performed upon objects' and (3) 'social interaction and transmission' (Piaget and Inhelder, 1966). For convenience we can use the terms (1) maturation, (2) behaviour and (3) socialisation in order to bring out the differences and similarities between Piaget and other psychologists. Some of the latter have been content to explain development by means of haphazard combinations, e.g. development occurs as the result of learning arranged for the child by adults (Skinner); or development is the outcome of the clash between instincts and culture (early Freud). But a further finding of Piaget's is the apparent universality of stages of development. Haphazard combinations of environmental experiences are unlikely to produce similar patterns of growth in different children. Even in a relatively homogenous urban England, children are not socialised with sufficient consistency. For Piaget the organisation determining universality comes from the child himself. It is (4) self-regulation which integrates the varied influences of maturation and experience to produce co-ordinated developnient.

We must now try to see the general shape of Piaget's biological theory of development. It is tempting to say that what Piaget has given us does not yet amount to more than a biological theory of the growth of knowledge, a biological genetic epistemology. Maturation and socialisation have been treated as somewhat arbitrary determinants by Piaget. Why be side-tracked by individual differences in heredity, or social fortunes or misfortunes, when what is required is a description of the principles of growth? Some children may be constitutionally more active than others and some may have mothers at hand to make more subtle adjustments to experience. If such differences could be shown to affect the child's progress in terms of the order or general pattern of growth, then no doubt Piaget would have attended to them earlier. Cross-cultural differences have not as yet, however, revealed significant departures from the general trends found in the children of Geneva.

To find universals in cognitive growth despite differences in maturation and socialisation may seem surprising. It is customary to attribute the causes of universals either to biological growth or to uniformity in training. How can there be universals in self-regulation? Piaget's answer appears to lie in what can only be described as his belief that intellectual growth is like organic growth: ' . . . it seems obvious that internal co-ordinations of the necessary and constant type, which make possible the integration of exterior cognitive aliment, give rise to the same biological problems of collaboration between the genome and the environment as do all the other forms of organization which occur in the course of development' (Piaget, 1971, p. 23). It is a belief which has paid off. In assuming that there are general patterns of growth, Piaget does not differ from other scientific psychologists. His particular contribution has been his assumption that these general patterns can be found in the apparently haphazard quirks of children's thinking and that cognitive organisation is comparable to embryological organisation. In this, of course, he follows other structuralists in their assumptions about generality, 'otherwise there would be as many structures as behaviours and little point in spelling them out' (Gardner, 1972, p. 10).

Developmental psychologists are now post-Piagetians, just as they are post-Darwinians and post-Freudians. Piaget started as a genetic epistemologist in that he set out to observe, explore and describe the development of knowledge manifested in individual children. As a result we now see the child as his own socialising agent. This does not mean that the custodians of culture—parents, teachers and other adults—are no longer seen as determiners of development: they are the instruments of Piaget's third category. What it does mean is that if the child is viewed as an active organiser of his interactions with his environment, rather than as a passive reactor, we are more likely as psychologists to be interested in the child's operating principles than in his reactions to isolated events. The approach has already influenced studies of intelligence, where there is a shift from what a child can do to how he does it. It has also influenced studies of language acquisition, where the shift is from the construction of plausible grammars to explorations of strategies in the comprehension of adult language.

If we look now at the ways in which Darwinian, Freudian and Piagetian influences are merging we see a concentration on infancy. An evolutionary perspective inevitably encourages us to begin at the beginning. Freud's patients always ended up in their associations by linking present problems to the memories of early childhood. Piaget starts with the spontaneous movements and reflexes of infancy as the point of departure for later perceptual and intellectual activity. For him, as for the ethologists, the foundations are there at birth. Early experience has become the principle topic and the amount of research in this area in the past decade is overwhelming. There is, to be sure, a danger of developmental psychologists falling into the same trap as the learning theorists. Behaviourists assumed that if they could only achieve a full understanding of the simplest learning they would soon take off into a rapid understanding of all learning. They are now less optimistic about ever achieving the first objective. The lesson for developmental psychologists may be that they should sink other shafts along the developmental course even before they have answered outstanding questions about infancy. Understanding the strategies of the 8 year old may open up new possibilities for research for general use. What the adolescent does in organising his modes of functioning may suggest what went on before. An additional danger from too much emphasis on early experience is that developmental psychologists may become alienated from policy-makers and the public.

The popular view of the child psychologist is that he believes that one's life is settled in infancy, especially as a result of maternal care. For some, this view should be rejected even if it were true because the consequences of general acceptance are not socially desirable. Among other things, the objectors argue, the view leads to pessimism in the rehabilitation of children who have had a bad start in life, an assignment of responsibility to mothers which is incompatible with concepts of sex equality and, as we have seen, a relative neglect by developmental psychologists of other stages in the total life-span. For these reasons, and especially the last, the explicit and meticulous critique by Clarke and Clarke (1976) is timely and should help developmental psychologists to avoid the mistake, which occurs repeatedly in the history of psychology, of stagnation and frustration through trying in vain to make the perfect brick before getting on with the building. The analogy cannot be pushed too far but it is surely true that we need more than an understanding of early childhood in order to construct a description of development. The comprehensive description may be reached sooner by working simultaneously at different levels rather than by striving to lay the perfect foundations.

The Search for a Human Psychology

This chapter began, however, not with conflicts within child psychology but with tensions between child psychology and general psychology. The majority of psychologists today would not describe themselves as developmental psychologists. How does their work relate to developmental psychology? Not for the first time since Wundt psychologists today are in an identity crisis. Psychology has always been best defined as what psychologists do. The stipulative definition of Wundt has been followed by other stipulative definitions, accepted by the majority of psychologists, so that text-books and courses have been in agreement in their choice of topics and methods. From Watson onwards there was very little change, but uncertainty has now crept in. For the first time in an important introductory text (Brown and Hernstein, 1975) it is conceded that 'psychology' cannot be defined and that it should be described as a 'coalition of enterprises'. Does this free psychologists from agreed essential components in their discipline and allow a greater variety of acceptable topics and methods? The essential distinctions between social anthropologists, ethologists and psychologists, are not easily drawn today. The concept of human development may provide the common theme for all these workers and suggest a particularly promising 'coalition of enterprises'. In this sense it will be argued in conclusion that developmental psychology could replace the former experimental psychology as the new orthodoxy. It does after all combine the respectability of scientific rigour with the human relevance so much sought after by Hall and others who look to psychology for personal as well as professional fulfilment. But we should first note the increasing number of psychologists who in recent years have found psychology unsatisfying as a science of human nature and who have succeeded in establishing themselves as recognised dissenters. Their objections and proposals give a convenient focus for a final discussion of the place of child psychology within general psychology and for a concluding assessment of prospects in developmental psychology.

As yet, the radical psychologists have been more concerned with the shortcomings of orthodox psychology (Shotter, 1975 and Heather, 1976) than with precise working proposals for an alternative psychology. They begin with a critique of psychology as a natural science of behaviour. With this definition, they argue, man is studied—from the outside—in order to discover his essential nature by the objective methods of experimental science. But this method, it is argued further, will never uncover the distinctive aspects of human nature because man is not explicable as a mechanism but only as a self-determining agent in a culture for which he is responsible. Shotter calls for a new psychology which is a 'moral science of action' rather than 'a natural science of behaviour'. By adhering to a natural science of behaviour, psychologists have not only failed to get to grips with what is distinct in human nature, they have helped to support the image of man as at worst mechanical, at best organic, but never personal, social and responsible. Heather also objects to psychology's treating persons as things but goes on to argue that its methods are put to use to bolster the prevailing values of society and to maintain the *status quo* in the management of industrial relations, mental health and education. In claiming that psychology is both inadequate and effective (but harmful) as an instrument of control, Heather advances the ingenious argument that it can be both inadequate and effective because by claiming to be objective, psychologists mask the values which they serve and thus block awareness of alternatives. From these two different criticisms of contemporary psychology we can see something of current unrests among a growing number of psychologists. What they have in common is an objection to the constraints of a Wundtian psychology which fails to come to terms with the distinctive characteristics of social man. The explanations of Shotter and Heather of the origins and consequences of a positivist psychology differ, but they both envisage benefits from escaping into a more human psychology. Can a psychology be found which is both human and free of bias?

The new developmental psychology is a promising contender. Firstly, it need not be vulnerable to the criticism that it does not study the self-determining, social human. The child as agent of his own development is a central theme in Piagetian theory. It is true that Piaget's research initially set on one side the ramifications of socialisation, though not because Piaget wished to settle the question of human nature as a biological isolate, but because a child organises his social experiences, with other perturbations from maturation and behaviour, in terms of the cognitive capacities available to him. For this reason a description of cognitive processes was a justifiable first objective. Recent work in developmental psychology, however, has sought to get to grips with analyses of social contexts (Richards, 1974). Nevertheless there is some force in the criticism that developmental psychologists have been unaware of the social biases in their work, particularly perhaps in their principal topic of maternal care. Yet is a sympathetic attitude to Bowlby's work evidence of a sexist bias? And, if so, will the bias permanently impede the progress of science? To answer these questions we have to look a little more carefully at what goes on in research.

There are at least four distinct aspects in a research process which really has no precise beginning or end: (1) the personal motives of the researcher in choosing the topic, (2) what he does, (3) his methods and data and (4) his interpretations of the data and then society's reception of his interpretations. This sequence is sandwiched between a larger social process so that to explain fully (1) and (4) we would have to extend backwards and forwards into a still larger slice of cultural history. The question we are concerned with is the detection of bias and the worry is that some biases may remain undetected. The bias in (1) need not worry us too much. It can usually be guessed without difficulty: research into social class and educational opportunity is unlikely (except in reaction) to be undertaken by a psychologist in favour of class divisions. What the psychologist chooses to do (2 and 3) is more troublesome: there is some evidence that psychologists get the results they want and the choice of hypothesis, sample and method may be implicated in these effects. But all these details are described in what is published so that if these biases are present they are, in principle, detectable. Bias sometimes causes statistical errors in the calculation of the data, but again these faults are detectable even though in some cases they have remained undetected for many years. It is, however, in interpretation of the data that hidden biases may remain undetected. For one thing, readers of journals are apt to look to the conclusions rather than scrutinise the complete paper. Furthermore, alternative interpretations usually require a freedom from current assumptions, requiring a flexibility of attitudes few of us possess. Society's reception of the researcher's interpretation is puzzlingly unpredictable but once given prominence in textbooks and the media the 'objectivity' of the results is difficult to dispel. Yet even here, as we see from time to time in the history of psychology, it is possible to distinguish results from values. A safeguard in a scientific psychology is that the whole process must be published in a form which enables others to engage in this very exercise of exposing the sequence to scrutiny. In the long run, biases need not survive. Perhaps the hardest to remove are those which determine choice of topics in that they are controlled by senior members of the profession whose flexibilities do not increase with advancing age.

The question of values in psychology has been dealt with at some length because it has been a fear of contamination by prejudice which has kept most psychologists devoted to the objective precisions of the laboratory experiment.

The methods prescribed and demonstrated in the laboratories of Fechner and Wundt over a century ago have guided the scientific psychology from which the majority of psychologists have taken their inspiration and their sense of professional unity. A history of experimental psychology could be described as the history of the use of laboratory instruments. The young researcher has only too often hit upon his hypothesis by getting a bright idea about how to use the set-up in his department's laboratory. A problem in human affairs may be interesting but if it cannot be tackled within the constraints of the available techniques it has been left unexplored. All this has been said before by humanist critics but the laboratory approach has served well enough until recently; it is just that an analysis of cognitive abilities within the constraints of the laboratory has lost its impetus. Many years ago Bartlett showed in his studies of memory how a more imaginative exploratory investigator could open up new avenues. His example has rarely been followed in experimental psychology. The method, however, which is essentially aimed at tracing the development of a process, has been more acceptable to child psychologists.

Psychologists when they founded their subject were faced with the alternatives of the laboratory studies of cognition demonstrated by Wundt or the exploratory genetic psychology inspired by Darwinism. They preferred the precision of the former. They have less reason now to fear loss of scientific respectability if they take the study of psychological development as their unifying theme. What are the alternatives? The psychology of animal learning which came into psychology from the Darwinian camp, to become constrained by the limitations of the laboratory, has now returned to the biology of animal behaviour. Perception and motivation, the other dominant topics, are now more neurophysiology than psychology. Social psychology has shown some movement away from its traditional analysis of attitudes but its most promising advances have been in the development of social interactions. If there is any scope at all for further formulations of mechanistic models of thinking we must wait for the results from computer specialists. The study of human development, the 'attempt to resolve the problems of psychogenesis', encompassing cross-cultural, animal and child psychology, was seen even by Wundt as an alternative to laboratory studies of cognition. It is ironic that

Wundt should have given such an impressive demonstration of laboratory methods that few have followed his later interests in psychogenesis 'at the very point where the experimental method fails us' (Wundt, 1904, p. 5). The Wundtian laboratory studies of adult cognition firmly captured the organisations of psychology departments and are tenaciously perpetuated. There is now a growing awareness among psychologists that their subject needs a new direction. They may once again reject the obvious alternative of genetic psychology if the barriers to studying children prove insurmountable by the majority. We end the chapter with an interesting, additional hazard. There is

'another obstacle to the serious study of the child. In the study of genesis, the first man and woman make their appearances as fully formed and functioning adults. Whether on the level of species or of individual evolution, the scientist is prepared to undertake developmental inquiry only when he divests himself of creationist mythology. This Darwin had done shortly before undertaking his first and in a real sense only investigation of human psychology, his brief study of the mind of an infant. How fitting it was for him to begin with a baby' (Gruber, 1974, p. 227).

Acknowledgements

Drafts of this chapter were read by Nicholas Tucker and Barbara Lloyd, my colleagues and friends at the University of Sussex. The reader will not know how much he owes to them but I do.

References

Alcock, J. (1975). *Animal Behavior: An Evolutionary Approach*, Sinauer Associates, Inc., Massachusetts

Allen, G. W. (1967). *William James: A Biography*, Hart-Davis, London

Ausubel, D. P. and Sullivan, E. V. (1970). *Theory and Problems of Child Development*, Grune & Stratton, New York

Baldwin (1961). In *A History of Psychology in Autobiography*, Vol. 1, (ed. C. Murchison) Russell & Russell, New York

Beach, A. (1955). *Psychol. Rev.*, **62,** 401

Bowlby, J. (1944). *Int. J. Psycho-Anal.*, **25,** 19

Bowlby, J. (1946). *Forty-Four Juvenile Thieves: Their Characters and Home Life*, Ballière, Tindall & Cassell, London

Bowlby, J. (1952). *Maternal Care and Mental Health*, W.H.O., Geneva

Breland, K. and Breland, M. (1961). *Amer. Psychol.*, **16,** 681

Brown, R. (1965). *Social Psychology*, Free Press, New York

Brown, R. and Hernstein, R. J. (1975). *Psychology*, Methuen, London

Bruner, J. (1976). Nature and uses of immaturity, in *Play—Its Role in Development and Evolution* (eds. Bruner, J. S., Jolly, A. and Sylva, K.), Penguin Books, London

Burt, C. (1952). In *A History of Psychology in Autobiography*, Vol. IV, (eds. Boring, E. G., Langfield, H. S., Werner, H. and Yerkes, R. M.) Russell & Russell, New York

Clarke, A. M. and Clarke, A. D. B. (1976). *Early Experience: Myth and Evidence*, Open Books, London

Dennis, W. (1972). *Historical Readings in Developmental Psychology*, Appleton-Century-Crofts, New York

Devore, I. and Konmer, M. J. (1974). In *Ethology and Psychiatry*, (ed. N. F. White) University of Toronto Press, Toronto

Elkind, D. (1970). *Children and Adolescents: Interpretive Essays on Jean Piaget*, Oxford University Press, New York

Erikson, E. H. (1965). *Childhood and Society*, Penguin Books, London

Flugel, J. C. (1955). *Man, Morals and Society*, Penguin Books, London

Gardner, H. (1972). *The Quest for Mind*, Coventure, London

Gessell, A. (1928). *Infancy and Human Growth*, Macmillan, New York (reprinted in Kessen, W. (1965) *The Child*, John Wiley and Sons, Inc., New York)

Gessell, A. (1952). In *A History of Psychology in Autobiography*, Vol. IV, (eds. Boring, E. G., Langfield, H. S., Werner, H. and Yerkes, R. M.) Russell & Russell, New York

Goldfarb, W. (1943). *J. Exp. Educ.*, **12**, 106

Grinder, R. E. (1967). *A History of Genetic Psychology*, John Wiley and Sons, New York

Gruber, H. E. (1974). *Darwin on Man*, Wildwood House, London

Guntrip, H. J. S. (1971). *Psychoanalytic Theory, Therapy, and the Self*, Hogarth Press, London

Hall, G. S. (1904). *Adolescence*, Appleton, New York

Hall, G. S. (1927). *Life and Confessions of a Psychologist*, D. Appleton and Company, New York

Heather, N. (1976). *Radical Perspectives in Psychology*, Methuen, London

Hebb, D. O. (1958). *A Textbook of Psychology*, W. B. Saunders Company, Philadelphia and London

Hess, E. N. (1973). *Imprinting: Early Experience and the Developmental Psychobiology of Attachment*, Van Nostrand Reinhold Company, New York

Jastrow, J. (1961). In *A History of Psychology in Autobiography*, Vol. I, (ed. C. Murchison) Russell & Russell, New York

Kamin, L. J. (1977). *The Science and Politics of I.Q.*, Penguin Books, London

Klein, M. (1960). *Our Adult World and Its Roots in Infancy*, Tavistock Publications, London

Kuo, Z. Y. (1924). *Psychol. Rev.*, **31**, 427

Le Bon, G. (1960). *The Crowd: A Study of the Popular Mind*, Viking, New York. First published in 1895 and quoted in J. Schellenberg (1970) *An Introduction to Social Psychology*, Random House, New York

Lorenz, K. (1935). *Journal für Ornithologie*, **83**, 137. In translation in Lorenz, K. (1970) *Studies in Animal and Human Behaviour*, Harvard University Press, Cambridge, Mass.

Newson, J. and Newson, E. (1963). *Patterns of Infant Care in an Urban Community*, Penguin Books, London

Newson, J. and Newson, E. (1976). *Seven Years Old in the Home Environment*, Allen & Unwin, London

Piaget, J. (1950). *The Psychology of Intelligence*, Routledge and Kegan Paul, London

Piaget, J. (1971). *Biology and Knowledge*, Edinburgh University Press, Edinburgh

Piaget, J. and Inhelder, B. (1966). *The Psychology of the Child*, Routledge and Kegan Paul, London

Richards, M. P. M. (1974). *The Integration of a Child into a Social World*, Cambridge University Press, Cambridge

Ross, D. (1972). *G. Stanley Hall: The Psychologist as Prophet*, University of Chicago Press, Chicago

Spearman, C. (1961). In *A History of Psychology in Autobiography*, Vol. I, (ed. C. Murchison) Russell & Russell, New York

Shotter, J. (1975). *Images of Man in Psychological Research*, Methuen, London

Stolz, L. M. (1958). Youth: the Gessell Institute and its latest study. *Contemp. Psychol.*, **3**, 10–15

Terman, L. M. (1961). In *A History of Psychology in Autobiography*, Vol. II, (ed. C. Murchison) Russell & Russell, New York

Watson, J. B. (1926). Quoted in Marx, M. H. and Hillix, W. A. (1963). *Systems and Theories in Psychology*, McGraw-Hill, New York, 63

Watson, J. B. (1961). In *A History of Psychology in Autobiography*, Vol. III, (ed. C. Murchison) Russell & Russell, New York

Wiseman, S. (1967). *Intelligence and Ability. Selected Readings*, Penguin Books, London

Wundt, W. (1904). Quoted in Marx, M. H. and Hillix, W. A. (1963). *Systems and Theories in Psychology*, McGraw-Hill, New York, 63

Zigler, E. F. and Child, I. L. (1973). *Socialization and Personality Development*, Addison-Wesley Publishing Company, Reading, Mass.

2 Neurological Development and the Growth of Psychological Functions

COLWYN TREVARTHEN

(Department of Psychology, University of Edinburgh, Edinburgh, Scotland)

Introduction

In this chapter I will try to show how knowledge about growth of the brain is increasingly important for psychology. I will take up-to-date ideas of brain embryology, and see if they will fit a working picture of what seems to be the essential strategy of human mental growth.

Luckily, recent findings in both neurobiology and developmental psychology brighten the prospect of this difficult task considerably. They also force a new look at too simple concepts of development that have held psychologists under a spell of reductionism and misplaced concreteness. In consequence, the human infant begins to have a different and larger meaning. The new evidence is fully accessible to only a few specialists, researchers who have equipment to see details of brain tissue and its activities, or who can analyse details of behaviour with esoteric techniques, but the resulting picture fits with common experience in interesting ways. It seems to free us from artificial concepts of genes, neurones, reflexes and learning that, by being used to explain too much, have obscured how the brain works and how it develops.

The discovery of infant human nature is not just of academic interest. Every gain in understanding about what motivates the human spirit is likely to have social and political consequences, which explains why statements about infant psychology become embroiled in political, as well as philosophical, controversy. Cultivation, treatment, control and prediction of the development of boys and girls to men and women are practised in all human societies, and, in the absence of more direct knowledge, people invent and defend notions about the causes of development, or of how and why it can fail. They make up mechanisms and so-called laws of growth to bolster their prejudices. Dogmatic principles defining humanity and its limitations are used to justify policies of social management, by the head of a band of desert nomads, and by officials of all kinds in the modern state. Therefore, every new item of information about the sources of human nature has potentiality to change, for good or bad, the governing principles of society. That is why discussion of what we know about the origins of infant intelligence, and especially what, after all, we do not know quite as well as we thought we did, is of real significance in human affairs. I believe that a more enlightened view of how the human brain develops will help us to be more appreciative of human diversity of intelligence and personality, and more optimistic about the motives of humans for co-operative social life.

However, it is important to admit, at the outset, that linking mental development to brain biology involves some awkward assumptions. We must take pains to avoid overconfidence. The gap between mental living, being a consciously active person with complex feelings and understanding of other persons, and the materialistic logic of evolutionary biology does not become smaller as we learn about the anatomy and the physiology of the brain. This is frustrating to a modern scientist, who is likely to become a dualist, looking for different explanations of physiological and mental or spiritual events. For people who are not biologists, and not committed to simplifying human behaviour, man's inherited biological nature seems irrelevant, a subordinate instrument of the mind, or a source of troublesome drives and urges in personal life of 'the self'. I believe we must confront this paradox of mind and biological matter if we are to understand the infant as a human being, for an infant is a young mind in biological matter. But I admit that it is easy to fall into a very crude explanation of the mind in terms of bits of structure in the brain. I sympathise with those who ask: can we really know enough, ever, about the colourless intricacies of the brain to say what it contributes to human mental life, and to the way people behave? More particularly, what has talk about the brain got to do with the development of conciousness, intentions and personal relations in a child?

Let us begin, where modern biology begins, with the gene. Can we pick up a useful thread of explanation in the unit to which physico-chemical analysis of life has led: the molecular mechanism of hereditary transmission called the 'code of life'? Psychologists often seem to believe that human characteristics at birth are genetically determined, and that thereafter they are modified and increased by influences from the environment. Is this what a developmental biologist would predict?

What is Biological Development?

Every human being begins life as one cell in which gene-carrying chromosomes of one egg and one sperm are combined. Through thousands of cycles of cell division, gene molecules manufacture images of themselves and pass them on equally to each cell. Their unique chemistry explains how chromosomes transmit nearly indestructible information to form the same species of organism, over and over, indefinitely (Crick 1962, 1963, 1966;

Watson, 1965). Gene molecules also generate and define the other molecules of life, but some of the products act in reverse to exercise control over the genes' fate. As soon as transcription of the gene code begins, the significant processes of development are moved rapidly from the molecular level to include the supramolecular, where interactions of folded cell membranes and fibres, of clusters and sheets of cells, become the code of life, complementing the genes.

In this remarkable story, which is modern biology's proudest achievement and a stirring justification of the scientific method, there is no doubt that the gene code has fundamental control over what the starting materials of an organism will be. Since this code is reproduced like a newspaper, one issue per cell, the transmission of living functions is assured with great reliability down long lineages of cells. But it is quite wrong to conclude that this explains the formation of complex multicellular organisms with elaborate living functions. The reason is that the genes, though essential, do not, in themselves, have living functions. Their 'code' has to be interpreted in cell chemistry, and in the physiology and life habits of the whole organism (Srb, Owen and Edgar, 1965; Waddington, 1966). Genes have different significance in different forms of life. They are like domesticated animals in a farm of cell structures, and they certainly change, becoming adapted to intracellular 'cultivation', as evolution proceeds (Grant, 1977). It has been suggested that evolution of social animals works with genes for 'selfishness' or 'altruism' (Dawkins, 1976), but these are concepts relating to human personality, and any selfishness or altruism the gene may have is conferred on it by the person it is in. In this respect the person causes the hereditary or genetic trait. Adaptation of genes to the cellular and organismic environment is made obvious very early in development by the phenomenon of cell differentiation.

In spite of starting with the same genes, body cells become very varied: they differentiate (Waddington, 1966). A muscle cell, for example, is full of contractile protein while a blood cell contains haemoglobin, a different protein. The haemoglobin molecule circulating in the human fetus before birth is different from the one that makes respiration possible after birth. Cells also have different shapes. Liver cells are like blocks, blood includes non-motile discs lacking nuclei, and active amoeba-like white cells, nerve cells branch and send extensions far within the body. These effects show that decoding the genes is a very elaborate process. The kinds of cells might be created by nuclei leaving behind different parts of their gene information selectively as they divide, but the nuclei of some highly specialised cells can (in tissue culture) reverse differentiation to remake unspecialised cells, and then be redirected to form another kind of cell. This reorganising of gene action proves that even specialised cells retain nuclei with unused or 'silent' parts of the DNA code. Research with bacteria indicates that genes are turned on or off in different combinations under control of external conditions, including the gene's own products, and a gene's activity may be regulated by other genes. This helps explain how the genetic information is activated selectively in development. It is even possible that, in bacteria at least, the cytoplasm may respond to the environment, change, then cause a reverse transcription and change the genes. How far this makes inheritance of acquired characteristics possible is not known.

The Formation of a Body

The great mystery of cell differentiation is how the body knows which part of the gene code to use at a given time and place (Waddington, 1966). The answer to this lies somewhere in the forces that group the highly structured cells of the embryo into an overall structure, the body. As soon as an assembly of cells is formed each one has its own environment, and the neighbourhood or adjacency of cells determines how their biochemistry will develop, because it determines the entry and exit of critical substances into each cell through its walls. Cells on the surface exchange substances with the outside, inside cells exchange with their neighbours. They may be linked to form tissues and organs that communicate preferentially together, and they may break contacts to follow isolated paths of development.

Gene activity is soon powerfully governed by this kind of communication system between cells in patterned arrays. In the early embryo, about one millimetre long, intercellular junctions tie the whole aggregate into a web of pathways, the contact points acting like doorways with highly selective rules for passage of molecules and ions in the living economy (Loewenstein, 1968). Hormones, messenger substances with power to direct development, may be routed along these pathways and controlled in their passage. In time some contacts are broken down and new ones are formed, and this switchboard of communication links fixes the early differentiations of cells and tissues in embryos. Then, contingents of embryo cells migrate along specific routes between other cells to create new arrangements. Sheets of cells buckle and fold, and all these obvious patterns of cell displacement open and close the interlocking communication channels for substances that may turn genes on and off.

These facts about how cells of embryos interact are important to our enquiry because nervous systems use all the kinds of cell communication and cell rearrangement more powerfully than any other kind of tissue. Moreover, we can see that the creation of a body of particular shape can no more be explained by describing the genes than can differentiation of cells. We must trace the history of cell interactions as the body grows, and add this to the gene story. The process by which cells in an embryo regulate each other's readings of gene information in the body is named *epigenesis*. Its importance in understanding the roles of genes in inheritance and in evolution was underlined by Edinburgh's late Professor of Genetics, C. H. Waddington

(1957, 1966). We may never know enough biochemistry or biophysics to trace the epigenetics of the nerve net for any behaviour of even a simple animal, though some are trying to do this with easily and quickly reproduced organisms like roundworms and fruit flies (Benzer, 1973). Experiments with embryos reveal complex developmental mechanics far beyond the sub-microscopic world of molecules or the single cell of a bacterium (Wolpert, 1971). They show up the strategies that form the body.

The processes of epigenetics are selective, producing a pattern of 'survival of the fittest' like high-speed evolution. Genes are activated in select combinations, most being inactive at one time, thus a six-sided cell may choose to interact closely with its neighbours by only three or four surfaces, or lobes or projections of a cell may grow in one or two directions at the expense of others and these may orient in a patterned medium. A flat sheet of cells may contract over its upper surface and remain elastic below, causing the whole sheet to curl into a pocket or tube. Many cells die and disappear, usually in picked groups to create gaps or holes, only those of particular constitution or location being left. Selective death of cells or parts of cells causes form-building much as a sculptor removes what he does not want from a block of stone to 'release' the form he desires. Indeed, the hand of man starts as a paddle-shaped lobe, then cells die in four patches to punch out spaces between five fingers: in this way the embryo sculptor is sculpted. Simple sets of choices like these, made in sequence with precise control, may generate complex and seemingly improbable shapes, as the embryologist Lewis Wolpert has illustrated by folding and cutting paper sheets.

At any one point in time, a given tissue in a developing embryo may have open to it many different 'fates'. As large numbers of components of the body make their choices, some may part company in the developing system so that, by differentiation, an increasingly elaborate diversity of elements is formed. The parts of a body may temporarily break up or disorganise to form a more plastic arrangement, or even melt into a liquid tissue as they do in the pupa of a butterfly. But, the products of differentiation continue to interact, and they hang together enough to keep the original pattern, or to re-establish the general form of the whole ensemble, or chosen parts of it. A butterfly is very different from its caterpillar, but it still has the same head and tail: the scaffold of the body and nervous system is the same (Benzer, 1973). Powerful integrative forces, the reverse of the forces of differentiation, cause reintegrations, and the constant re-construction of a coherent, polarised individual is called individuation.

Evidence for these organism-holding-together functions comes from effects of injury. Gaps in the embryo body tend to be repaired and the excess pieces to be eliminated as if some invisible craftsman were keeping an eye on the process (Russell, 1945; Waddington, 1966). However, the potentiality for recovery or survival of a part depends on the state of balance between differentiation, which multiplies diversity of form, and reintegration, which usually involves loss of parts. Integrity of structure has to be reasserted periodically against separate anarchic proliferation of parts. The effects produced are like cycles of expansion and recession in an economy, but much more time-tested, and much more dependable. The whole cycle of body-building results in the unique or little varied sequence of phases and processes, a life history, each step of which is both reintegrative with respect to the last, and a take-off point for the next differentiation. Life histories prove that development is self-regulated. That is a very special and powerful feature of living things.

All these principles apply to the developing nervous system. Brains are immensely differentiated, with millions of distinct components; yet they are intensely integrated. No point in the brain is free of relationship to all the other points. Some far separated points may act closely together after their integrative nerve connections have been developed. Developing brains are more powerful than most tissues at repairing the effects of injury or loss. But in the end the brain is a finely coherent system, all parts of which have a function. Finally, brain growth has a long and highly patterned life history, and our task is to find where the stage of infancy fits in this plan.

A Need for Reintegrative Theory

Modern molecular biology has achieved a breathtaking advance in discovery of the fine details of life processes, linking them with the chemistry and physics of non-life. But, when it comes to understanding how the body of an embryo is formed, our ideas are not much in advance of those obtained a century ago, with the low-powered optical microscope and a few simple but ingenious surgical experiments with the embryos of sea urchins and frogs (Spemann, 1938; Needham, 1942). Long before that, Aristotle, who knew nothing about cells, and Spinoza, who lived when the microscope was newly invented but who knew nothing about chromosomes, understood that development of organisms is a unique and self-directing activity that resists analysis into elements. Both of these philosophers believed that specific, essential form and function is determined by an inviolable sequence of forward-looking stages of matter with potentiality (Needham, 1942; Arber, 1950). They knew that the life history has form, as well as the adult end product.

In the last decade, biology has been concentrating on the elements, analysing the determining role of gene molecules and cell biochemistry (Crick, 1962, 1963, 1966; Watson, 1965). At the same time psychology, following the other Watson (1913), has come through a period in which it was divorced from the principles of biological determination, taking the position that psychological development is regulated principally by external contingencies of experience, with limits imposed by three or four physiological drives.

To avoid being misled by the elan of these two powerfully useful simplifications of scientific thinking, we need to turn to the full epigenetics of behaviour and the embryological processes by which psychological functions are controlled, and which are, in turn, controlled by these functions (Gottlieb, 1973). Facts about how the human brain grows guide us on the first steps back to a more coherent view of the meaning of human psychological growth. They help us perceive how mental processes may regulate their own growth in a mental life history, like the cells of an embryo regulate, choice by choice, their partnership of controlled gene action in growth of a body.

The Origin of the Brain: How it Comes to Represent Forms of Behaviour

Organisms, in differing degrees of intricacy, have size and shape with specific symmetry. From this we identify different species. A fixed body form or organization is especially critical for a large animal which controls its life by moving about and choosing where to go. Indeed, adaptation of behaviour means adaptation of body form, and the more complex the range of behaviour, the more accurately specified the body shape and its means of changing must be. That is why animals have more complex symmetry of form than plants.

Measured contraction of muscles on an incompressible, jointed skeleton causes predictable movements. But behaviour can only be adapted to external circumstances with some form of excitation-conducting system that coordinates contractions and picks up guiding information about their effects on the body, and on its situation in the environment. Nervous systems have evolved to increase the power and delicacy of behaviour. The forces that fit the central nervous system to a species' body and to that body's possible forms of action are, therefore, the primary determinants of behavioural development (Trevarthen, 1973, 1974a, 1978a). In fact, the brain becomes an image of what the body cells might do together, and then, after birth, having gained the capacities for imagination and memory of experiences, it employs the body as an instrument. Psychological functions depend on the extraordinary forward-looking embryology of nerve tissue that specifies body-centred elements of action and ways of perceiving.

At just $2\frac{1}{2}$ weeks after conception a human embryo has body symmetry (Figure 2.1A). One may easily identify anterior and posterior, dorsal and ventral, interior and exterior, left and right. There are no nerve cells, but a situation in the upper of the embryo's two layers of cells is fated to become the central nervous system. Surgical experiments with amphibian embryos show that a key group of cells from one spot on the zygote surface triggers formation of embryo brain cells (neurectoderm), but all the cells of the surface still look alike. The polarity of the body is fixed in relation to this organiser which takes

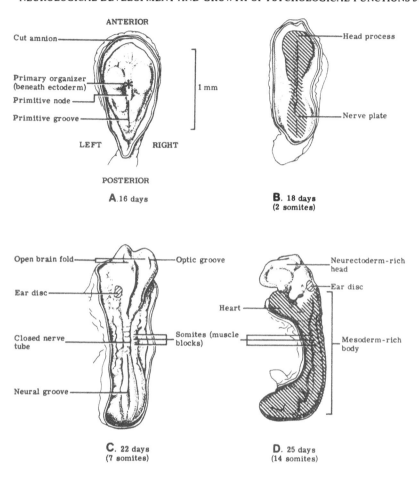

Figure 2.1 Early human embryos

the place of a capital city in the body's fate map.

The neurectoderm soon forms into a mid-dorsal nerve plate, shaped like the sole of a slipper (Figure 2.1B; neurectoderm cross-hatched). It becomes invisibly polarised so that the front is different from the rear (anterior-posterior axis), then shortly afterwards the midline cells become distinct from those at the edges (medio-lateral axis). Unbalanced forces in the cell walls cause the margins of the plate to roll over the top, then the two folds close up like a zip fastener and fuse to form a tubular central nervous system. The embryo elongates rapidly while the nerve plate is being formed and by three weeks it has a distinct head. As the tube closes, mesoderm cells multiplying along the midline of the back creep downwards and forwards, like amoebae, between ectoderm and endoderm. They form clumps either side of the embryo backbone (notochord) and spread forwards past the end of the notochord and round the place where the mouth will form (Figure 2.1C and D). The head, which will be the sensory and intellectual centre, then consists mostly of a large brain sac and ectoderm, with small patches of mesoderm. In the trunk, however, which will be the motor powerhouse of the body, the smaller nerve tube is flanked by large mesoderm masses that form the muscle plates of trunk and limbs. There is thus a gradient of increasing muscularity towards the trunk and tail (Figure 2.1D). Remarkable experiments with frog embryos, in which the cells were unstuck from each other then stirred up in mixtures of different composition, suggest that the ratio of muscle to skin and nerve is linked to what determines which nerve tube segments will become spinal cord and which brain (Toivonen and Saxen, 1968). Each part of the central nervous system (CNS) is fitted to the segment of the body it is in.

Next the embryo becomes divided into segments. These seem to be units of motor action. Primitive animals like earthworms are built of a chain of segments each capable of some local reflex response, the whole assembly being lined up in register and integrated by long connections between nerve cells of the central nervous system, so that the segments can act like a team. Body segments still form the basis of the early embryo, but the shape of the whole system is reintegrated to have a new design.

Most significant for mammalian psychological adaptations is the differentiation of the separate satellite mechanisms of the head on a flexible neck, with mobile eyes and ears, and the separation at the sides of two pairs of limbs with sensitive digits (Figure 2.3). For man, eyes, mouth and tongue and hands are psychological tools of a superior mind that can selectively perceive and act on the world in new ways. Subsequent developments indicate that the segments of the nervous system form mutually compatible building blocks each impressed with its own miniature, polarized, body-like map or system. The maps—images of the body—can be linked by formation of nerve fibre connections into equivalent sub-systems, each capable, when excited, of acting as an agent for the body or as one of a small group of agents in a hierarchical set. Selective attention and cooperative movement of body parts, essential functions of the complete brain, depend on the segmental units that originate by differentiation in one body field in the embryo. No psychological theory of the origins of space and object perception or the coordination of movements in intentions and selective attending can afford to neglect these basic embryological facts (Trevarthen, 1974a, 1978a).

In the month-old embryo of man the perceptive organs of the head (eyes, nostrils, ears, mouth and tongue) are easily identified. All begin as paired pockets or swellings of the skin near the brain. The eyes form as outpushings from the edge of the brain plate just after the latter closes over dorsally. In the second 30 days, each of the special head receptors achieves its peculiar adaptive design, with appropriately placed sensory cells and accessory structures: lens and eye chamber, semicircular canals, sacculus, cochlear,

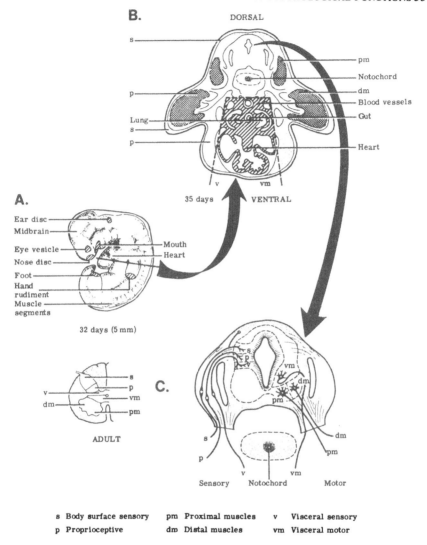

Figure 2.2   Primordia of sensory and motor organs in the late human embryo (A), sections of the trunk and spinal cord (B) and mapping of body territories into the brain (C)

nasal cavity, muscular tongue and lips. At the same moment hands and feet appear. They are just dense thickenings of tissue at the end of the limb buds at 30 days and miniature fingers and toes develop in the next 20 days. By day 60 all the special organs of perception and exploratory action are like scale models of the adult organs (Figure 2.3C).

All these remarkable preparations for an active, intelligent life take place before nerve fibres contact either the receptors or the muscles. The potentiality of the body to effect forms of action in a polarized, bilateral field of movement, and to be selectively sensitive to different forms of information about the patterns of structure in the world surrounding the body, is specified before any part of the nerve net has been formed (Figure 2.3).

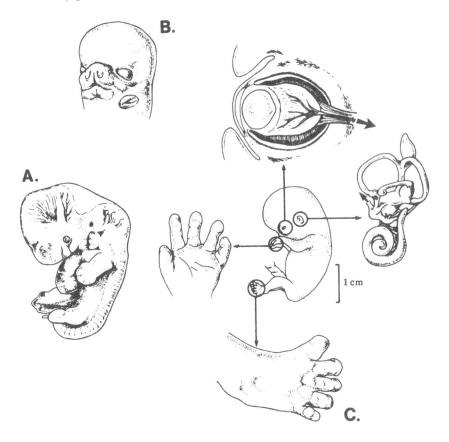

Figure 2.3   The last 20 days of the human embryo. (A) 40 days (hands, eyes, outer ear and foot begin development), (B) 50 days (the face) and (C) 60 days (well-formed special sense organs of the foetus)

The Nerve Net

The paths taken by the first nerve fibres in the body of a 1-month-old human embryo show that the brain in which the nerve cells germinate already contains an invisible image of the body in cell microstructure, and this governs the affinities of nerve cells for body parts, and their selective affinities for each other as well (Figure 2.4). It thereby defines a preadaptive and generative map of behaviour in a variety of modes. Cells of different parts of the eye, for example, have to distinguish brain cells that, in turn, command body movements to different points round the body.

A first step in defining visual circuits is the pegging out of the polarity of the retina, while the embryo cells are closely connected in a sheet. Later, when each cell is isolated by walls, an elaborate sorting process enables fibre tips from synchronously active neighbouring retina cells to occupy neighbouring spots in the visual cortex of the mid-brain, but the main up-down, front-back orientation of the map is decided long before. Delicate and ingenious surgical experiments with early embryos of newts and frogs have plotted the polarisation of the eye rudiments and of the visual field in the brain (Figure 2.4A) (Jacobson and Hunt, 1973). Apparently a small group of cells in the centre of the anterior brain segment (diencephalon) acts as polariser for these rudiments (Chung and Cooke, 1975). This organiser region must be a close cousin of the nearby primary organiser at the notochord tip of the earliest embryo phase, which determined the symmetry of the whole body (Spemann, 1938) (Figure 2.1A). Thus the first step in mapping of the retina occurs when the optic vesicle contacts the embryo ectoderm, and when its cells are in tight communication together, well before nerve cells appear.

At about $3\frac{1}{2}$ weeks, as the polarity of the human eye becomes irreversible, the first crop of nerve cells ceases to divide, in preparation for germinating like seeds to grow a feltwork of nerve connections (Figure 2.4A and C). This first human nervous system (Windle, 1970) corresponds to the CNS in lower vertebrates that controls the behaviour of the tiny larva when it starts swimming freely about for the first time. In the human embryo the primary nervous system has no function because the embryo is inert and has no use for behaviour. Indeed, many of its nerve cells are lost later. Nevertheless, pathways of interneuronal connections in the human brain in the second month are like those of the salamander tadpole studied brilliantly by two American anatomists, Coghill and Herrick, in the 1930s and 1940s, and this outline is certainly a basic framework for later developments (Coghill, 1929; Herrick, 1948). It is the ground plan of an actively swimming, robot-like being with the beginnings of power to perceive surroundings and move in relation to them, but, of course, it has no mechanisms for higher, specifically human intelligence.

How do embryo nerve cells start to build the CNS as they move vigorously about to form a regular pattern of layers and clusters? When axon filaments suddenly grow out from day 30 on, their choice of pathways, interweaving yet segregating to form distinct tracts, shows that their growth is guided. When fibres from the eye make contact with visual territories of the midbrain and diencephalon and not elsewhere, they must be making choices in the medium through which they grow, or must have selections imposed on them. Advancing nerve fibres have highly active membranous tips from which motile threads (filipodia) extend like tentacles of an octopus (Figure 2.5A).

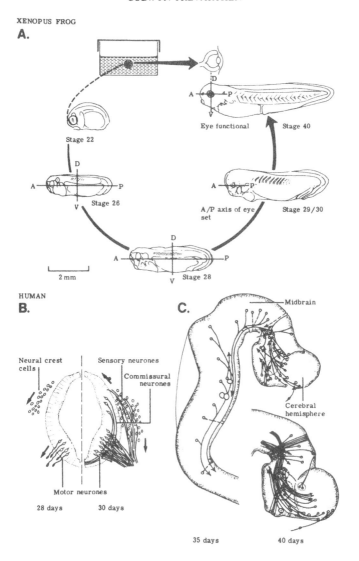

Figure 2.4   (A) *Xenopus* eye development. A Stage 22 eye can develop in culture to a complete
Stage 40 eye. If put anywhere in the body of a Stage 26 or older tadpole, it will be
polarised to fit the body's polarity. At Stage 30 the anterior–posterior (A–P) axis of
the eye becomes fixed. At Stage 40 the eye is no longer influenced by the polarity of
its surroundings. (B) First outgrowth of nerve axons in the human spinal cord
(compare with Figure 2.2). (C) First nerve pathways in the human brainstem

This 'growth cone' mechanism guides growth, the threads with nerve cell
exoplasm flowing in and out of them, acting in exploratory manner, poking
about and reacting to tissue membranes and the surfaces of other nerve cells.

This seeking process, still little understood, fashions the first outline of an integrative nervous system and sorts enormous populations of nerve connections (Harrison, 1907; Jacobson, 1970; Oppenheim, 1975).

In the busy cycles of migration, axon formation and nerve cell interconnection, vast numbers of cells, axon branches, dendrites, and so on, die and their remains are removed. The losses obey an intricate set of rules that emerge among the interacting cells, mediated by hormones and by nerve activities that control secretion of these hormones. They partly explain the formation of ever more complex structures (Jacobson, 1970). Competitive interaction appears to be the driving force for the sorting of specific nerve circuits that will conduct nerve impulses where they will be needed to control behaviour. The creative power of these processes is the secret of intelligence in its first preadaptive phase. They also control the wonderful power of the brain to take information from experience. Neurobiological studies show that brain embryology and learning are related kinds of process, intergrading with each other (Mark, 1974).

Refining the Brain with the Aid of Stimuli

By far the best known simple sensory-motor network is the one linking the eye to the brain field of fish or frogs, from which orienting movements of the animal as a whole are directed, and this system has been studied to determine if light patterns assist the development of seeing (Figure 2.5B) (Gaze, 1970). In man the first visual nerve fibres of the same system grow out at about day 35, when the embryo is 12 mm long. The nerves grow to the midbrain roof, the structure much studied in fish and tadpoles, but this linkage has no possible visual function in the sightless, parasitic embryo of man.

The frog rebuilds his visual system at metamorphosis from a tadpole, to fit a change of life style (Figure 2.6). Mammals, and birds, too, add large new forebrain components in the fetus, especially a visual cortex of revolutionary design that serves a new power in the seeing of detail and colour, as well as perception of meaningful objects, after birth. By the time a human baby is born, midbrain vision is relegated to a secondary role in seeing with discrimination. Nevertheless, it retains throughout life a key place in orienting and aiming of attention and action to events in space round the body (Trevarthen, 1968, 1970).

Experiments with visual circuits in fish, tadpoles and chick embryos show that much of the complex and delicate nerve circuitry is wired up to high precision without influence from light, in complete independence of practice in orienting, and without using sensory feedback from behaviour by trial and error (Figure 2.5B and D). Largely as a result of experiments with regenerative nerve connection begun 40 years ago by Roger Sperry, the eye-midbrain system (Figure 2.5C) has become the prototype of a neural circuit in

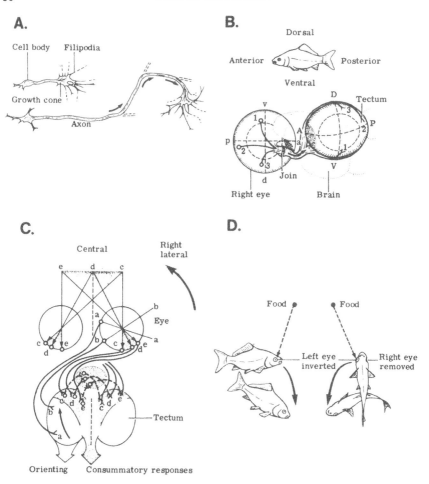

Figure 2.5 (A) Growth of a nerve axon. (B) The visual map of a goldfish; in regeneration studies the optic nerve is cut, joined and allowed to regrow from retinal cells to the optic tectum of the midbrain. (C) The basic map of visual space on the midbrain of vertebrates. (D) Abnormal behaviour of a fish with left eye inverted and nerve connections regenerated

which anatomy may determine behaviour before the behaviour can be practised; that is, without benefit of learning (Sperry, 1959, 1963, 1965).

Recently, a controversy has developed because it has been found that the first optic nerve endings are not tidy, but are diffusely spread out and mixed up. Their patterning becomes progressively more refined after the terminals have had a chance to 'talk' at the target site. The sorting out and revision, eliminating misfit elements or redirecting growing axons and adjusting contacts they make with central cells, is probably influenced by the synchronous beat of spontaneous electrical signals that come from adjacent retinal cells (Willshaw and von der Malsburg, 1976). The spontaneous firing of retinal cells in groups might regulate distribution of hormone-like substances, especially neurotransmitters, and so control sorting of links in the nerve net. According to this theory, accurate mapping is the result of a very elaborate democratic negotiation between cells signalling to each other, not a consequence of each nerve fibre being tagged with a private biochemical address to which it is sent by guided delivery (Figure 2.6).

This new epigenetic way of looking at the mechanism of nerve circuit formation helps bridge the gap to the still unknown neural processes of learning (Mark, 1974). Work done by Michael Gaze and his colleagues with the South American Clawed Toad, *Xenopus*, shows that parts of the visual system where inputs from both eyes converge may be wired up with help from synchronising information when the two eyes are stimulated by the same patterns of light at the same time (Figure 2.6) (Gaze, 1974). Pairing off input fibres from both eyes for one point in visual space is helped by reinforcing those nerve contacts that are excited together. This happens after the primary monocular visual maps, and an orderly motor mechanism for orienting the body left and right, are complete and functioning. The binocular parts of the visual system grow at the time the tadpole changes to a frog, when the eyes move to the front and top of the head as the animal changes feeding, locomotor habits and use of the visual field. Evidently the main orienting system is wired up without benefit of patterned stimuli.

The important point is that the process is aided by the pattern of visual stimuli coming from outside the animal, and this gives it significance in the nature–nurture controversy (Lewin, 1975; Oppenheim, 1975). If the binocular registration is decided by synchronisation of stimuli, then the structure of the projection is not written out as a chemical prescription by gene action in the nerve cells. On the other hand, it is not clear that the pattern and orientation of the basic map really is changed by stimuli, since the primary projection seems to be set up properly when the animal is kept in the dark. Moreover, the known effect in the binocular territory of the brain records neither the specific details of patterns of light in the eyes at any one time, nor the unique experience of any one frog. All frogs that get a reasonable amount of experience end up with about the same detailed binocular mapping. Light stimulation must simply be sufficiently textured and change enough during the critical period, when the new links between brain halves are being laid down.

The story is further complicated by the finding that in *Rana*, a more highly evolved frog, the binocular map is at least partly grown without benefit of visual stimulation. It seems to be a rule that more visually intelligent and active species have more prewiring of nerve circuits. But, the smarter frog also has a greatly increased capacity for learning in more complex levels of its behaviour. Evidently the later evolved circuits of the brain just extend a principle of brain formation worked out in the elementary brainstem circuits

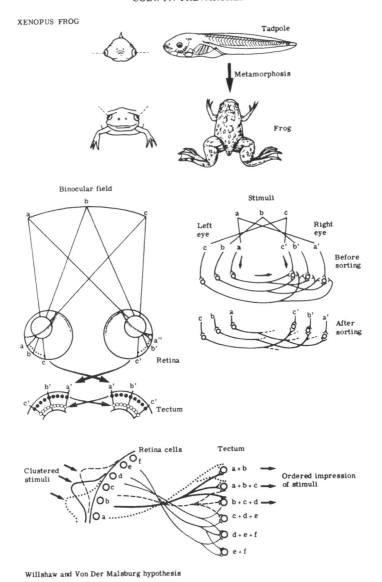

Figure 2.6   The binocular system of *Xenopus* is rebuilt after metamorphosis. Experiments show
that registration of the two eyes together in the midbrain depends upon stimulation,
which sorts the connections. See text

of lower vertebrates, to capitalise on the ability of growing nerve circuits to
use patterning of stimuli to sort out connections.

Microneurophysiological studies suggest that the cortical fields of vision in cat and monkey are mapped by the same principle as the binocular map of the frog (Figures 2.8 and 2.9) (Blakemore, 1974; Barlow, 1975; Hubel and Wiesel, 1977). Central nuclei, tracts and cortical fields are all linked in body-shaped (somatotopic) arrays, like those of the primitive visual system, though bigger and more elaborate, but circuits finished after birth may use stimulus information to polish or refine their connections.

In the series of vertebrate brains there seems to be a basic circuit design which is elaborated in evolution by inserting and expanding a multiplicity of regions without loss of its original polarised arrangement based on the form of the embryo body. Some of these new regions of brain maps need textured input to complete their morphogenesis. In man, eye-globe, retina, optic projection and brainstem visual field are all there in the embryo, but brain circuits are not finally connected until the fetus. The fetal circuits are not stimulated by light patterns as they will be after birth, because the receptor is inside the mother and thoroughly cut off from stimulation by fusion of the eye lids. The only possible experience is diffuse, low level, red intrauterine light. But, more advanced features of the retina and visual cortex, that mature in the infant after birth, are certainly refined and stabilised with the benefit of information from patterned light, and they become deformed if there are optical defects in the eye (Barlow, 1975).

Developmental plasticity of nerve circuit formation must apply to the other senses as well. It could be called 'selective stimulated neural induction of nerve patterns', a modified version of 'selective spontaneous induction' which we saw operating in the nervous system of embryo and fetus, when growing parts engage in cross-talk and sorting through biochemical information transported with the assistance of nerve impulses triggered spontaneously.

There is good reason to regard the brain growth before birth as related to what happens after birth when the brain picks up structure from experience. As far as we know the process of memory formation is physically, biochemically and microanatomically like the process that forms nerve nets in embryos. Richard Mark (1974) has explored this new way of looking at memory in terms of neuroembryology in an attractive synthesis of recent research in the two fields. But, putting together and refining the primary circuits for perception in early infancy does not seem quite the same as learning an entirely new kind of image or a new idea, because the outcome of a reasonable richness of stimulus information in the first case does not reflect the stimulation so much as a predetermined scheme, or limit of refinement, in the nerve net. Spreading of patterns from part to part of the nervous system and refinement in the arrangement of connections is aided, not created, by the excitation of neurones in groups. So, the gain in specificity of circuits is not quite the same as gaining knowledge of new things in detail. To understand how knowledge and consciousness of a world full of meaning comes about, we need to look further into the prenatal formation of the higher mechanisms of the mind and especially the motivations that drive curiosity and creativity, because it is these that define what knowledge may be about. They depend on the form of prewired nerve systems.

Development of Intention and Motives for Consciousness in the Fetus

To discover what happens in the human fetus experimenters turn to birds or mammals. Work by Hamburger, Oppenheim, and others with chicks in the egg bridges the gap from embryo to fetus (Oppenheim, 1974). Hamsters are born at a stage corresponding with the early fetal stages of humans, and experiments by Schneider (1973) show that the visual system in the newborn hamster, still being formed, is highly plastic, like the embryo body is at an earlier stage. Re-arrangements and removals of pieces of brain lead to compensatory branching of nerve fibre side shoots, or formation of new short-circuit connections, and these may result in patching up of a new, abnormal visual function to replace one which would have been irretrievably lost if the same operations had been done on an adult. From research with fetuses of rats, mice, cats and sheep we gain a glimpse of a brain undergoing a dramatic change (Trevarthen, 1978a).

The fetus is a life stage in which a new kind of intelligence, of bird or mammal, is created by transforming the basic lower vertebrate brain, Cinderella fashion, while an inactive larva is carried in the mother. The change recalls metamorphosis in the pupa of a butterfly. The larva and adult of the insect have been shown to be determined by somewhat independent sets of genes. Indeed it has long been realised that both larval and adult stages may separately undergo evolutionary change, and it seems to be the same with the higher kinds of brain. The human fetal brain has evolved out of the primate fetal brain to grow a new form of intelligence, one in which youthfulness has far greater meaning and far greater adaptive potentiality than may be found in any other species.

Loss of the adult, or slowing of adult evolution, with elaboration of wider potentialities of the less-committed juvenile, has been an evolutionary tactic for the start of many major new groups of animals. It is called neoteny (De Beer, 1940). Some think humans to be evolved neotenically out of the young of ape-like ancestors by extending juvenile curiosity and playful adaptability so that it occupies a larger part of the life span. One possibility is that human co-operative intelligence, man's greatest asset, may have evolved out of the instinct of young apes to share skills with their peers and elders.

The infant perceives the world and explores it in intimate dependence on maternal care. He gains the ability to walk about and fend for himself, but psychologically he remains dependent on parents or on peers for the rest of his life. The brain that governs these developments is outlined before birth. The extraordinary wisdom of infants and children for discovering the world of objects within the world of people depends on the pattern of fetal brain growth. In describing this growth, however inadequately, we come closer to the origin of human psychic functions. They cannot be fully explained by what happens after birth.

From two months after conception to adulthood the human body increases twenty times in length, but the brain only half as much. This difference hides the fact that the brain undergoes a unique change in complexity of structure. Body strength or physiological output increases with size, but brain power depends on minute structures that take up little more room as they are totally transformed. The principal new structures are the cerebral neocortex and cerebellum. The first of these two complementary brains is concerned with perceptual, cognitive and volitional aspects of conscious life and with memory; the second regulates the flow of forces of a complex and agile body in action and the programming of refined motor skills (Eccles, 1977).

We have seen in the middle stage human embryo that nerve cells first multiplied and dispersed themselves through the layers and clusters of a pattern close to that of the basic vertebrate brain. Receptor and effector primordia were mapped with a common code of positions, all oriented with respect to an 'organiser' for the body, and these maps were echoed in a paired chain of embryonic nerve centres in the brainstem, all of which 'represent' the body in the common code. These steps were completed in the first month. Then, in the second month, the nerve cells germinate fibres that link up to make a coherent net of conducting pathways. This was accompanied by production of myriad non-neural glia cells that fill up the expanding spaces between the branches and regulate the conditions of chemical communication and excitatory action among the nerve cells. Electrical activity generated in this net a few weeks later was expressed in shadowy forms of co-ordinated behaviour, but its main function is probably to remain latent and regulate the developmental process itself.

In the fetus, in a great wave of multiplication, a thousand million new cells are created, and the brain expands several times in bulk (Figures 2.7 and 2.9). It is transformed by the differentiation of many new and varied maps of the body's field of action, some specialised for one modality of perception or refined action of one body part, others integrating them together. The cerebral hemispheres and the cerebellum which were tiny rudiments in the embryo then become the main tissue of the brain.

Biochemical estimates of the gene DNA content of the human brain, a measure of the number of nerve cell nuclei, show up several bursts of nerve cell division in months three to five of gestation (Dobbing and Smart, 1974; Sidman and Rakic, 1973). Use of radioactive tracers in nucleotides, out of which chromosomes of the new nerve cells are synthesised, has made possible tracing of nerve cell 'birthdays' and the routes of migration of cells in the fetal mouse brain (Angevine, 1970). Exceedingly refined and highly regulated patterns of cell movement are found. Cells migrate into the neocortex from a germinal zone lining the cavity of each cerebral hemisphere and these

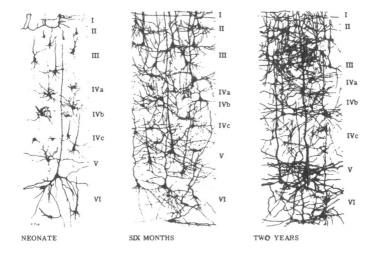

NEONATE   SIX MONTHS   TWO YEARS

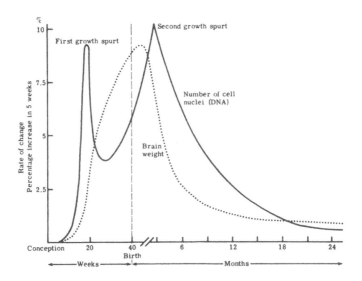

Figure 2.7   Human brain growth. (*above*) Dendrites in the visual cortex of an infant (from Conel, 1939–63). (*below*) Two peak periods of cell production in the brain. The first reflects nerve cell multiplication, the second dendrite growth and glia cell multiplication. Brain weight increases most rapidly early in the second growth spurt (after Dobbing and Smart, 1974)

assemble in orderly radiating columns packed side-by-side in a layer many cells deep. This cortical cell plate is of extremely precise organisation, becoming more detailed in its design as its cells meet and interact. It is mapped, as the embryo brain was, in invisible microscopic territories which represent the body over and over again in relation to the different fields of experience and of action that the body will enter months or years later. Genetical deformity of brain developments during this first fetal brain growth spurt (Figure 2.7), or poisoning, radiation damage or a virus infection of the mother and fetus have drastic effects on the future mind. Sometimes the whole cerebrum is degenerate. Like all periods of intense differentiation, this one is critically sensitive. Confusion of the process of rapid nerve cell multiplication in the cortex may cause serious stunting of intelligence or idiocy. On the other hand, some defects that begin at this stage may be concealed in subsequent brain development (Sperry, 1969). The reintegrative forces are very powerful, conferring great plasticity of anatomical organization.

A second jump in brain size, a fourfold increase from about 100 cm³ to 400 cm³, takes place in the last months of gestation (Figure 2.7); but this growth spurt reveals differentiation, not multiplication, of nerve cells. As nerve cells elaborate projections, the cerebral cortex thickens and develops the rumpled appearance characteristic of the brain of a highly intelligent animal, and soon it looks unquestionably human (Larroche, 1966) (Figure 2.9). Inside, dendrites are extending to form a thicket of enormous delicacy and complexity. Neurones are also growing in the cerebellum, and in the brainstem nuclei and reticular formations directly involved with the two ' higher structures. The DNA assay technique reveals that glia cells are multiplying in vast numbers in the second 'brain growth spurt'. They penetrate the spaces between the nerve cells as the tissue swells and spreads out like an omelette cooking. The glia surround neurones, changing their conduction of nerve impulses, and regulate the pattern of tree-like growth and formation of nerve cell contacts (synapses) upon which all integrative functions depend.

Synapses are the currency of information exchange in the nervous system and the elements of memory. Their arrangements depend on nerve cell form. Axons growing into the cortex from other parts of the brain and from within the cortex itself develop synaptic buttons on minute spines on the dendrites. A mature cortical neurone may have upwards of 10 000 synapses from the numerous axons that end on it, so there are an astronomical number, some 10^{15}, a thousand million million, in one human cortex. For comparison, the population of humans on the Earth is less than 5000 million. There is a major synapse-forming period when most contacts are formed in main cortical circuits. This event has been followed painstakingly by Cragg (1975) in the visual system of newborn kittens (Figure 2.8). It takes place from just before birth through the first two weeks after birth when the eyes are still closed, and it coincides with a critical period of maturation of the inborn ability to see shapes. The last stages of circuit formation are adjusted by the influence of patterned stimulation of the eyes and final refinements depend on this stimulation (Blakemore, 1974) (Figure 2.8), but the early phase is protected by closure of the eyes and anatomical developments proceed automatically.

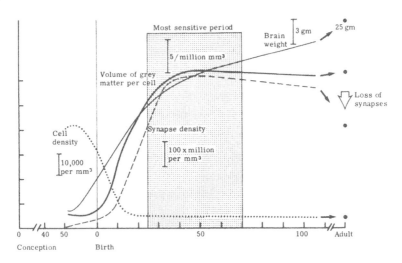

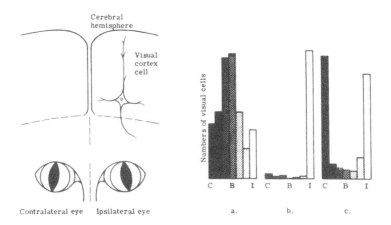

Figure 2.8   (*above*) Formation of synapses and separation of nerve cells in the developing visual
cortex of a kitten (after Cragg). (*below left*) Projection of the eyes of a cat to the
cortex. (*below right*) Numbers of visual cortex with 100 per cent contralateral
eye connections (black), 100 per cent ipsilateral eye connections (white) and graded
amounts of mixed, binocular connections; (a) normal cat, (b) after closure of the
contralateral eye in the critical weeks of development and (c) after alternating monocular exposure of the kitten's eyes to vision (after Hubel and Wiesel)

Nerve net formation is a much longer process in man than in most other
animals, and it is far from complete at birth. The rapid phase of cell separation
continues for three months after this, and, indeed, synapses patterning occurs
in some regions for many years. These developments can be traced by plotting
the formation, by glia cells, of fatty myelin sheaths round the nerve axons, and

this refinement of the conducting lines of the brain coincides with maturation of the synaptic arrays at the ends of each nerve cell. The brain doubles its volume (to 800 cm^3) in the first year of infancy, reaching in a three-year-old about 90 per cent of its adult volume of about 1400 cm^3 but , once more, this obvious increase hides a far greater change in complexity of circuit structure.

Behaviours of newborns show that the outline of the main functions for co-ordinating the body and picking up experience are laid down in the womb, including generators for command functions of intelligence in different forms: looking with the eyes, listening with the ears and handling objects with the hands. The brain is ready to guide its further differentiations in infancy by these forms of action. Malnutrition of the mother in the last two months of pregnancy and poor feeding of the infant in the early months after birth can wreck this process and cause defects of active intelligence that become more serious later in life. This is the stage of development that starvation may hit hardest in a destitute human community, affecting the minds of children more than their bodies, in spite of a natural protection in favour of saving the brain. Blindness, limblessness or deafness in infancy, disorders that may lie at first outside the brain, also lead to permanent loss in psychological development, in spite of powerful compensatory forces to rebuild a workable system in the common, supramodal appetitive machinery of the brain. Finally, deprivation of affectionate care from other humans in early life is terribly destructive (Curtiss et al., 1974). Thus, for normal development of human nature the rapidly differentiating brain mechanisms of infancy and early childhood are dependent on good nutrition in an appropriately rich, humanly regulated and affectionate environment. These exacting requirements are specified in developments before birth.

The cerebellum lags behind the primary mechanisms of the cerebral hemispheres (Figure 2.9). In the early fetus it is an almost invisible ridge of tissue on the hindbrain roof, and even at five months it is very rudimentary (Larroche, 1966). Its giant co-ordinating Purkinje neurones reach their final position in the late fetus, and the main structure of the tissue round these cells is added from just before birth until six months after birth (Jacobson, 1970; Sidman and Rakic, 1973; Eccles, 1977). Cerebellar conducting circuits mature as the infant perfects locomotion in a cycle of growth that matches development in the muscular power of the body. In early infancy, perception, communication and manipulation outstrip locomotion or other forms of powerful action. A baby sees and understands before it can move things and walk about to explore the world. The developments of motor skills, even the instinctive ones for walking and manipulation, continue throughout childhood and they benefit from practice, as cerebellar circuits undergo their final differentiation.

Small cycles of nerve cell production occur long after birth in certain parts of the cerebral hemispheres as well as in the cerebellum. Micro-neurones invade the cortical tissues and form into small star-shaped cells with short local connections, ideally fitted to modulate the functions of the main prewired circuits as their synaptic constellations are formed (Jacobson, 1974). Star cells are thought to be inhibitory and highly sensitive to selective effects of stimulation. They appear to be part of the intricate mechanism of learning, whereby the innate structures of the brain are differentiated to fit specific conditions in the world.

The patterns of formation of myelin in the human brain, revealing maturation of axons, indicate that the cerebral systems concerned with emotional and instinctual functions undergo elaborate development over childhood and adolescence (Yakovlev and Lecours, 1967). The parts of the cortex essential to higher forms of mental activity (the frontal and temporo-parietal 'association' or 'command' cortices), together with the giant interhemispheric bridge (corpus callosum, which unites the mechanism of awareness and memory), and the reticular formation of the brainstem (which governs central states of activation of the brain), differentiate throughout adulthood in step with continuing increase of knowledge, understanding, and the practised skills of decision-making (Figure 2.9). The infant and child, though well-equipped with basic tools for intelligent behaviour, is apprentice to these late maturing functions that progressively enrich the motivations of his mental life from within.

Behaviour in the Womb

We know from studies of lower vertebrates and the embryos of birds and mammals that intricate motor programmes may be prewired in the spinal cord and brainstem, even before the sensory nerves make contact with them (Oppenheim, 1974, 1975). Human behaviour, too, begins in this way in the embryo. The first movements have been observed in aborted embryos of less than two months. But these distressed organisms show only elementary orientations and twitches, of uncertain importance in brain differentiation. A three-month-old fetus will respond to touching on various parts of the face and body with slow 'reflex' movements (Hooker, 1952; Humphrey, 1969), indicating that co-ordinating structures are being built, and spontaneous electrical activity of nerve cells can be picked up from the brainstem. By five months, the cell groups at the base of the cerebral hemispheres join in, but there is no cortical electrical activity (EEG) before the sixth month.

By month four, fine face and hand movements show beyond doubt that the motor circuits for these highly specialised and very human organs are beginning to be formed. The human hand and the human face have motor abilities and muscles possessed by no other species, and these organs develop a complete outline of the adult anatomy in the early fetus. After birth, the highest levels of perception in vision, hearing, touch, taste and smell will be governed by movements of the muscles in head and hands. Human visual

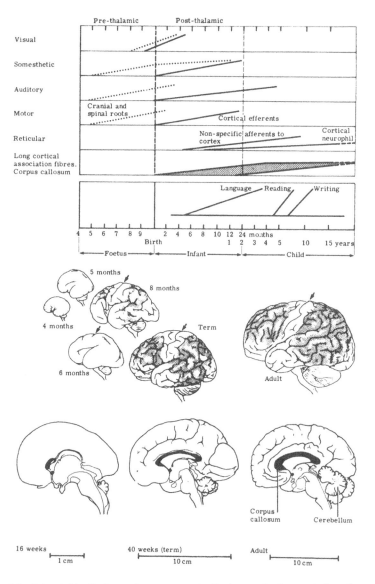

Figure 2.9 (*above*) Myelin formation on axons in the human brain—an index of nerve cell maturation. Higher cerebral systems develop throughout childhood, as do psychological functions. (*middle*) Human brains at the same scale of magnification. The arrow marks the central sulcus, a landmark. Association cortex is stippled. (*below*) Development of the corpus callosum linking the hemispheres, and of the cerebellum

reception requires delicate orientations and focalisations, and the muscles of the eye are completed in miniature four to six months before birth, at the same time as those of face and hand. A four-month fetus will move eyes, lids, eyebrows, limbs and hands, tongue and lips in outlines of purposive orienting, looking, grasping and mouthing, and also begin to show grimaces of facial expression. Later these 'preview' acts fade until they re-emerge clearly nearer birth. Once again, they give evidence of elaborate preparations for human intentions, well in advance of mature function.

But, like a hibernating bear, the early fetus moves little and is cut off from its surroundings. The eyelids and nostrils are fused shut and the inner ear is closed with a plug. The sense organs of the skin are just beginning to form in the fifth month. A few highly specialised behaviours appear in the last four or five months of gestation, as if vital survival tactics were being practised in preparation for life after birth. A six-month fetus can adjust its posture in the womb, react to accelerations or shocks caused by the mother's activity, and nourish itself by swallowing amino-acid-rich amniotic fluid, eliminating excess water through the skin. At seven months, a premature infant can breathe and be kept alive in air in an incubator, as long as it is protected against water loss in a controlled temperature, and artificially fed. Yet, these behaviours have no particular relation to the extraordinary manifestations of perception and intention relative to the outside world of a newborn baby, behaviours that show amazing development in two or three months after a full-term birth.

Altogether, the late fetus is in a mysterious, waiting state of restless sleep, the cerebral hemispheres expectant but strangely ineffectual. The last three months are the period of most rapid development in the EEG and this correlates with accelerating growth of cortical circuits. Prematurely born babies of this period are more alert to changes in light, sounds or touching, and their muscles are less flabby than those at an earlier developmental stage (Saint-Anne Dargassies, 1966). Their eyes open and their ear ossicles are free to transmit air-borne sound waves. Body movements, heart beat or respiration show habituation to a repeated stimulus, so a learning mechanism is already functional. They are getting ready for birth.

All the evidence suggests that at term, 40 weeks from conception, the human being is a highly specialised creature ready to be born, extremely weak and inactive considering the elaborate brain he has, but quite capable of contributing actively to the physiologically and athletically demanding process of birth itself. Indeed, it has recently been discovered that a special form of hormone, prostaglandin, allows the fetus to direct the mother's uterus and other birth organs to prepare for birth and the same hormone readies the infant's lungs for breathing air. A newborn is adapted to a range of essential activities immediately after birth. These activities for survival are not reflex automatisms. They respond in close association with the mother's movements of holding and feeling. Artificial induction of birth that short-circuits the cerebral control leads to a complex chain of difficulties and compensations (Chard and Richards, 1977). At the present time medical practice, having learnt brilliant techniques of keeping the 'at risk' or premature infant alive, protecting it as a 'biological' (eating, breathing, metabolising and responding) being, is becoming concerned with fetus brain states; and also more human or psychological aspects of newborn behaviour and the matching behaviour of new mothers, both of which may be interfered with by anaesthetics and other medical tactics to aid birth (Brazelton and Robey, 1965; Brimblecombe *et al.*, 1978; Richards, 1978). Paediatricians find that mother and infant are ready for close contact immediately after a normal birth, and that the quality of this first meeting is important for the establishment of their relationship of care and affection.

The State of the Newborn Brain

At birth the brain looks near complete, all but a negligible proportion of its cells in their final positions and all the nuclei, tracts and cortices finely arranged in the adult pattern. It has virtually the same external appearance as a half-sized adult brain (Larroche, 1966) (Figure 2.9). Obviously the fundamental plan of human psychological functions is determined before birth. But, from the point of view of what the brain can do, this appearance is obviously misleading. It does not fit the psychological immaturity of infants, and it conceals an immense unfinished complexity of nerve circuits, which in some regions take several decades to reach full maturity and refinement of function. This is why brain damage at or soon after birth has different consequences from the same damage at a later stage of life.

Recent research confirms that the fine nerve-cell arrangements and intercellular connections that are essential to higher mental functions are sketched in considerable detail in the newborn brain. But it also shows that they are left with a great redundancy of possible links, most of which are suppressed. Final sorting and commission for active expression takes place after birth, as information about the world is admitted under control of rapidly maturing movements of exploratory stimulus-seeking. The communications between nerve cells inside the fetal brain, by spontaneous impulse production through the net and by excitation from stimuli impinging on already active receptors like those for touch, limb displacement, acceleration of the head or water-transmitted sound in the womb, are not enough to complete morphogenesis of the perceiving brain before birth (Trevarthen, 1978b).

In the last couple of years, anatomical details of the visual system of the monkey just before and soon after birth have been seen for the first time (Hubel and Wiesel, 1977) (Figure 2.10). The intricate cell structures that 'process' the input, segregate information about colours, brightnesses, contours or edges, textures, binocular disparity, velocity of displacement over the retina and direction in the visual field, all appear to be prenatally 'wired in', or to develop quickly inside the first month or two with little instruction from the environment. Their formation obviously depends on intense interactions between nerve cell components in a pattern of closed competitions. A superabundance of axo-dendritic links between neurones allows selective removal on a large scale and separation of distinctive elements that become units of perceptual resolution. This sorting, while not depending passively on the chance form of stimulation received, needs to be nourished by a sufficient variety of forms of stimuli in generally significant categories. The necessary perceptual alimentations are picked up by the young monkey's constantly active gaze as he explores his early world. If the experiences of the two eyes are experimentally dissociated, or if one eye is deprived of light over the critical postnatal weeks of synapse completion, then large anatomical deformations occur in the brain (Figure 2.10). The effects prove that when the details of neural interconnections are being sorted out, they are sensitive to crude derangement of excitation among the competing parts. In the case of kittens, born much less mature than monkeys or humans, the effects of redundant patterning of stimulation or unbalanced stimulus deprivation are even more extensive (Figure 2.8). It has been shown that receptor elements in the visual cortex can be moulded by the spatial and temporal coincidence of excitation among them. Extreme distortions cause long-lasting anatomical peculiarities, but recovery effects are also strong.

In man, visual acuity and binocular steropsis develop quickly after birth, and they are affected by defects like squint or eye deformity (Barlow, 1975). There is also a dynamic adjustment between the changing specifications of the eye (refractory properties and geometry of cornea, lens, posterior chamber and retina) and the neural mechanism of pattern and motion detection. The eye grows for several years after birth and its structural development is under neuro-hormonal control. It has been found, too, that the visual circuits of infants may adapt to a distorted image, either to compensate for the distortion or to lose function of one deformed eye in competition with a normal eye. Nevertheless, this plasticity of response in the eye and brain does not appear to be a major factor in the creation of a perceptual mechanism of a normal child in a normal environment (Trevarthen, 1978b).

In agreement with the anatomical facts, recent psychological research shows that infants are far better endowed for awareness of their surroundings than had been supposed. Even the clear deficiencies of the neonate, like poor discrimination, and the limited attentive or exploratory powers of infants less than four months old, may not represent absence of a preformed mechanism so much as incompleteness or inhibition of certain necessary bits. These and other kinds of perception are finished or resolved with information from stimuli, under control of the innate movements for selective attention that choose particular constituents out of the stimuli reflected in the natural world.

Most remarkable of all the evidence about development of mental

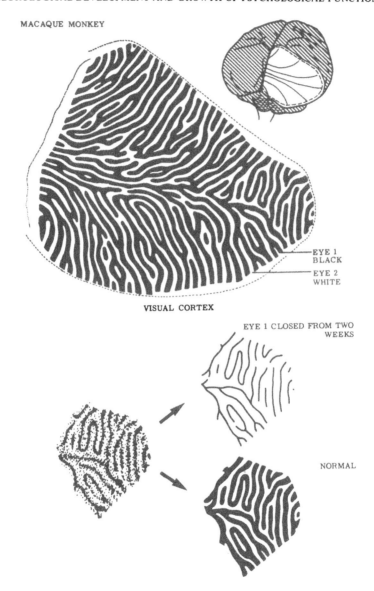

Figure 2.10   The pattern of left and right eye connections on cells in the right visual cortex of the monkey. It is present at birth, but develops in sharpness in early months. It is deformed if one eye is closed soon after birth (after Hubel, Wiesel and Le Vay)

mechanisms before birth comes from the discovery of anatomical asymmetries in the cortices of the two cerebral hemispheres. The lop-sided tissue areas correlate with the lateralisation of speech control to the left side of the brain, and their development fits with the growth of language. The sidedness of the basic language mechanism is an inherited trait, special to man and related to, but sometimes separate from, right-handedness. Left-hemisphere language control is a characteristic of about 90 per cent of adults and it grows progressively stronger through childhood to adolescence. Over the past century, brain territories responsible have been located in adults by testing the effects on speech and understanding of language of localised brain injury in hundreds of patients in hospital, then comparing results with direct anatomical data on the brain tissues of individuals who die. In the last ten years one-sided speech and language structures have been seen in a majority of adults' brains and the same structures are found in fetuses (Galaburda *et al.*, 1978). Children do not speak until their second year, and language takes decades to attain maturity, but the cerebral mechanism for control of speaking and learning words begins to develop long before birth (Trevarthen, 1978a). Man, though he learns a vocabulary, is certainly an innate speaker and listener to speech.

Intelligence in Infant Behaviour

In the recent past it has been easier to collect accurate data about the powerful mechanisms for ensuring basic survival in a newborn: the ability to begin breathing air, a ferocious ability to cry for, orient to and suckle from the mother's breast, defensive movements that protect the skin from irritation, or the face from covering. But the newborn also has a complex array of more subtle responses to being held close or spoken to. Though weak and shaky, with crude proprioceptive control against the new forces of gravity, the body is far from unco-ordinated or unresponsive. More remarkable are recently described acts that foreshadow seeking of experience from the world, manipulating it or looking for companionship and communication from other persons, at a distance. Now we may shake off prejudices about the rudimentary cerebral state of newborns. We notice, for example, that eye movements are regulated against the new patterns of visual stimulation in a highly systematic manner from birth. Newborns also orient to sounds and move the hands and feet in patterns that specify reaching and grasping and locomotion. They smile and make many other evocative grimaces, and they react by calming and snuggling to contact with persons who treat them gently. There are good grounds in these behaviours for expecting the newborn to have a sensitive and subtle regulation of awareness.

A wonderful phenomenon, which impressed Charles Darwin and influenced all his thinking on human evolution, is the expressiveness of the human face (Darwin, 1872, 1877). Even a premature baby has the muscles and peripheral neural machinery for almost all human facial expressions (Oster and Ekman, 1977). Highly refined patterns as of distress, happiness, puzzlement, annoyance pass like patches of coloured light over a sleeping baby's features. Likewise the neonate's hands make many beautifully articulated gestures and indications. Even the neuromotor mechanism of vocalisation and speaking is present in outline. But these forms of action adapted to human communication are still weakly, unpredictably motivated as in a dream. They give the moods of a neonate a mysterious human quality that is attractive but very difficult to describe, a shadowy sign of what will develop into active life within a few weeks.

Developments of Infant Psychology

Early in the present century, psychology was taken up by a school of pragmatic democrats who did not believe in inborn talents or faculties. Unlike Darwin, these men, for whom John B. Watson (1913) became the dominant spokesman, rejected introspection about experiences and recollections as a source of knowledge about the mind. For the behaviourists, the infant possesses only a handful of essential reflexes, including three reflex emotions of affection, fear and anger. It is random in most of its movements, and it is ready to be moulded by experience.

Insistence on experimentation with formal conditioning techniques helped reduce infant psychology to measurement of the attainment of skills by trial-and-error under reward or punishment. All that remained of the biologically based psychology of Darwin, and of his great near contemporary the brain embryologist Prayer, who also made a classic study of infants, was the painstaking description by Gesell and his associates of the emergence of physical capacities and the attainment of such milestones in motor development as visual tracking, reaching for a standard object or walking without support (Gesell *et al.*, 1934). The mental functions of infants were only slightly more studied by the followers of the Gesell school than they were by their detractors, the followers of Watson.

Infant psychology has resurrected itself in the past decade from this long period when all the emphasis was on finding a very simple explanation of infant behaviour. In the English-speaking scientific world, the 50 years' work of Jean Piaget suddenly gained a dominant place in the 1960s. Piaget's main preoccupation is with the attainment of knowledge in the form of abstract ideas (Piaget, 1970). Although he does not consider how the formation of brain structures may cause the ideas, his description of how infants perceive objects, gain knowledge of their properties by using them, and build a representation of a constant set of properties that inheres in each object in spite of changing information in perception, shows his firm conviction that psychological activities require an elaborate structural foundation. He demonstrates that exceedingly complex basic mental capacities are achieved in the first two years of life before words are learned. He believes that mental images begin in automatic relation to events, and that infants are unable, at first, to distinguish themselves in the world. They are egocentric. The emergent ability of the mind to represent a separate world with objects in it comes about, somehow, from interaction between conflicting actions and experiences that integrate together, or 'equilibrate'.

New successes in the discovery of what infants perceive and understand have come in the past 10 years essentially from a new way of looking at them. The difference is not due simply to the application of more exact methods of research, but it comes from allowing the infant more freedom to express preferences, feelings, interest and recognition while being observed. The experiments which have yielded most are ones in which the infant chooses an object while performing a complete mental act, like seeking familiar or interesting things, or trying to communicate with a person. To do these tasks, even young infants will organise their search to overcome obstacles which, as the infant becomes older, may last longer or be more complex. The errors they make reveal their limitations of memory or understanding and their involvement in immediate perceptions. However, the most striking attribute of infants at all ages is their ability to generate coherent purposes or states of motivation. They are not at the mercy of stimuli, nor are they in constant conflict of impulses. Gradually, we learn of a systematic growth of more and more powerful strategies for knowing the world and acting on it. And it becomes more and more obvious that the main psychological functions are outlined at birth, though in very immature form.

Inborn Patterns of Experiencing

A few examples will show how acts of infants have been made to show up the world a baby actively seeks to understand.

Piaget, in the 1930s, noticed that sucking stops, or is inhibited, during visual exploration (Piaget, 1953). This has been used recently to study interest in visual and auditory stimuli, and loss of interest with presentation of the same stimulus over and over again. Inhibition of sucking when the infant notices novel events shows that newly born infants hear some speech sounds as adults do, in syllables, and so some of the mechanism of auditory perception best suited to understanding talking is probably inborn (Eimas et al., 1971; Trehub, 1973). Instruments have been made to allow infants to control projected pictures by sucking. The results prove that they perform this instinctive act in co-ordination with movements that are able to control the intake of experience.Looking and sucking interact strongly. Bower used the degree to which infants stop sucking to measure 'surprise' caused by visual perception of unexpected events (Bower, 1966, 1974).

Though infants one or two weeks of age are frequently unresponsive and usually slow to react, they do turn to look at stimuli, and they may follow moving objects by rotation of eye and head (Haith, 1977). They turn their heads quickly and effectively to align the mouth to the touch or odour of the breast and, also, to direct their ears and eyes to sounds. Fantz, in the early 1960s, was the first to show that by watching the eye movements of infants a few days old, when the baby had only two things to look at, one could determine inborn preferences for looking (Fantz, 1961). By swapping the positions of the objects, by varying their appearance, and by counting the number of eye fixations, he proved a hitherto unsuspected ability to tell the difference between volumes, textures and forms, and a preference for face-like patterns. This activity of looking does not tell us how much of the difference between objects infants perceive, or if they rapidly acquired the power to discriminate in the course of the repeated trials of the test. But it has been used in many studies since to prove that young infants may distinguish a large number of features of paired objects, and that, up to a point, they have a built-in preference for more intricate patterns; they avoid the very plain ones when there is a choice, as if they need to drink up visual texture.

At two months, infants are clearly more deliberate in their selection of what to look at. They have begun to build and regulate refined images of surroundings. They look less and less at something repeatedly presented, and more at something new and different. It has recently been found, using this habituation behaviour, that infants group things as the same or different in ways that resemble basic perceptual categories long thought to be learned. Bornstein (1975) has used looking behaviour, recorded by television, to show that four-month-olds sort colours perceptually into blue, green, yellow and red as adults do. Since he has also shown that the brain circuits of monkeys (which have essentially the same colour vision as humans) use the same hue categories, these categories are definitely inbuilt structures of the primate brain, not creations of language, as has been proposed. Looking has also been used by McKenzie and Day (1972) in Australia as a measure of interest in a novel event in a study of the sensitivity of young infants to shifts of an object in depth and to show that infants do not see a rotated object as a changed one. Although such perceptual distinctions find useful application to the natural world, they are evidently not formed by learning what the world offers.

The looking of infants, its rate regulated from birth, has an element of purpose in it, and it can be conditioned so that the movement anticipates a reward. Papousek (1961) showed that infants a few weeks old could learn to make a controlled head turning to left or right to a sound of bell or buzzer. When they made the 'correct' movement, they received a drink of milk from a nipple. At four months, babies acquired patterns of head turning, making two or three small movements in quick succession to one side, or alternating between left and right, in order to obtain stimulation from a flashing coloured light. Papousek observed that the manner in which the movements were made and the facial expressions of the infants indicate that there was a complex, emotion-charged purposiveness in the act. It could not be described as a simple consequence of a link being formed by conditioning or learning between the light and the arrival of milk in a nipple. It seems to be a kind of communication (Papousek, 1967).

In any conditioning experiment, the relationship established between certain responses and artificial stimuli makes it appear as if the subject is passively recording and storing certain external chains of events. However, this is not the way adult learning normally takes place. Learning involves active mental exploration of alternatives and prediction of events. It is regulated by a plan of behaviour. Close observation of the learning of infants shows that even in the first few days of life, a human being actively adjusts or accommodates his acts to stimuli associated with the performance. Although the conditioning ability of infants has been described as very great (Lipsitt, 1969), they learn more readily when free to choose responses themselves, and are easiest conditioned when there is a close relation in time and space between the reward they seek and the stimulus.

As has been mentioned, infants express pleasure when they predict successfully and sadness when they fail to fulfil their expectations. When he observed this, Papousek (1969) drew two important conclusions. First, that 'the infant is able to analyse and categorise the informational input, to detect simple structural relations, schemes or rules in the input, and to adapt his behaviour to them', and second, that 'congruence between the infant's plan or expectation and the real events seemed to please him'. Papousek considered that this pleasure proved the infant to be making a 'specific human patterning of response'.

What are called, in careful, mechanistic language, 'state variables' in the conditioning behaviour of infants, reflect not just fluctuations in physiological control, but also functional changes in a central regulator of experience and generator of movement. Indications of state change include, not only electrical signs of brain activity and changes in respiration and heart beat, but also spontaneous body movements and local movements of hands, eyes, mouth, etc. Alertness in adults means steadiness of focus in attention, as well as sharp or highly resolved awareness, and intelligent selection of experiences by moving receptors. Even newborn infants alert or orient by stopping competing acts and concentrating movement to aim the appropriate organs of reception. If they are sucking and a light comes on, they usually stop sucking and rotate and fix the eyes to the stimulus, if it is not too far from the centre of the field. If a sound occurs, they stop other movements and turn their head, directing not only the ears but also the eyes in precise co-ordination to the place of the sound. Quietening and turning-towards movements may be used to observe the strong sensitivity of newborns for persons, and particularly their alertness to their mother's presence when they are hungry.

The reactions of young infants to objects and persons moving about them indicate that they are aware of direction and distance in a three-dimensional space before they can effectively reach and grasp objects. They are relatively indifferent to events more than a few feet from their bodies, but show numerous accommodations to things close by. Early experimenters assumed infants could not see in three dimensions before they could move themselves in the world or reach and grasp objects. Then Gibson and Walk (1960) demonstrated that crawling babies (older than six months) showed an 'instinctive' fear or avoidance of heights when the only information about a drop near them was a checkerboard patterned surface seen through a sheet of glass on which the baby could crawl. Bower (1966) applied the learned head-turning technique to demonstrate that three-month-old infants perceived rectangular blocks in three dimensions, or at least did not confuse them with similar two-dimensional shapes. In this experiment, a social experience was used as the 'reward' for a discriminatory response. The mother smiled when the infant was 'correct', saying 'peek-a-boo', and came close to the infant. The infant was, in fact, engaged in a communication game.

In a large series of subsequent experiments, Bower (1974) has employed the following forms of action: arrest of sucking and heart-rate change to measure surprise (under four months), visual tracking of object movement from side to side and behind screens (from eight weeks), defensive reactions of face, head, arm and hand to objects threatening to collide with the infant's face (two weeks) and early attempts at grasping objects (from two weeks). He has sought to answer questions concerning the development of perception of the displacement, location, separation from surroundings, size and form of objects, and cognitive functions permitting awareness of the continuation of object existence in spite of their disappearance behind screens or into hollows in other objects.

All of these studies benefit from ingenious use of the spontaneous and highly organised patterns of action which infants perform. They accept that infants strive to perform movements which are purposeful. I believe that much may be gained by investigating the organisation of purposeful movements of infants for their own sake, to determine their intrinsic antenatally specified design. I think the experimental studies of perception and cognition have exaggerated the retentive awareness or imagery of the infant. Act-formulating or intentional functions may be relatively independent from perception of the external world, especially in an infant, and be generated more from within the infant as part of the strategy of mental growth (Trevarthen, 1978b). Very likely, the trend to more descriptive methods will lead, in the near future, to considerable further advances towards understanding of the generation of purposeful acts by infants. We may then hope to relate these acts to development of parts of the brain that make them and that react to the forms of excitation which the acts control.

Communication of Infants with Persons

The social communications of infants were long treated as reflex-like responses to a set of signals from others. The signals were thought to be few in number at the start of life, and subsequently increased by learning of quite new combinations. This belief has engendered attempts to discover the most effective or most simplified stimuli for certain responses such as crying, the smile, laughter, 'vocalisation'. At the same time, there have been many indications that social stimuli are the most important in the real world of the infant. In some studies, like those of Piaget, social rewards of voice, touch or smile by the observer, and social responses by the infant (smiles, laughs, coos, crying) have been employed to gain information about some other perceptual or cognitive function, but, as a rule, the communication function itself is then not further considered. However, it has been clear for at least 100 years that infants produce many different social signals which resemble the expressions by which adults communicate with each other. Gradually, the complex psychological significance of such acts as looking into the eyes of another person, avoiding gaze, or smiling, by infants only a few weeks of age, has become appreciated. At the same time, many equally common acts of communication have been passed over.

   Newly born infants adapt their activities to the personal style and conduct of the mothers in the first days; they signal a variety of states of need or distress by different patterns of crying. By two months, they may smile when approached and spoken to, and then take an active part in a complex social exchange (Schaffer, 1977; Trevarthen, 1974b, 1977, 1978c). Infants communicate best when both they and their partners are free to regulate the pattern of behaviour mutually. When the timing of acts is observed precisely, it is found that both the infant and the adult in an exchange are detecting and predicting (Condon and Sander, 1974). That is, true communication takes place very early after birth. Inside one year, it creates a sharing of ideas through transmission of information about the goals and the stimuli to which both infant and partner attend (Trevarthen, 1978d; Trevarthen and Hubley, 1978).

   Interest in the learning abilities of infants has led to studies of the degree to which social acts can be learned. Infants may learn quickly their behaviour when social rewards are varied (Gewirtz, 1961; Rheingold, 1961). Usually, experimenters assume that this gives evidence for the formation of communication skills, such as turn taking in conversation, by learning from others, rather than by growth of in-built structures. On the other hand, preoccupation with cognitive abilities and their growth have given a somewhat unreal bias to experimental studies attempting to determine when infants first are able to recognise their most frequent companions as different from strangers. Such approaches reveal no more than an outline of the complexity of infant expression, and they leave unclear the mechanisms by which personal relationships come into existence and grow.

The issue of imitation, long a puzzle to psychologists, has been brought to the fore again by careful analysis of film or video records of infants as young as one month. Accurate imitation by the infant of actions repeatedly made by the experimenter, including voice sounds, tongue protrusion, hand movements, show that children are born with a template or image-forming mechanism which links the infant's perception of acts of expression with their performance (Meltzoff and Moore, 1977). Rather than fulfilling the expectations of those who wish to explain growth of social communication by learning, these facts prove that learning alone does not establish awareness of persons. Moreover, proof that newborn infants may imitate leaves the place of imitation in the growth of communication uncertain. Under normal circumstances, two-month-old infants are more likely to generate expressions from their own repertoire when excited socially. When this happens while mother and infant are attending to one another, it is usually the mother who imitates (Trevarthen, 1977). Evidently, her simplified and imitative behaviour extends the communicative powers of the infant and contributes to their control, but it does not create them.

In film studies in my own laboratories of infants from four weeks of age through the first year, we have obtained evidence of many forms of expression which include, besides the usually accepted emotions of joy, sadness, anger, fear, surprise, etc., gestures of recognition or indicating (e.g., hand-waving in greeting, index-finger pointing), and lip-and-tongue movements that resemble elements of speaking (Trevarthen, 1978c) (Figure 2.11). Associated with the latter activity, which we name 'pre-speech', but not necessarily accompanying it, is a cooing vocalisation that is quite distinct from either crying of distress or loud shouts of excitement. Towards six months it develops into babbling.

It is of capital importance that this complex array of expressions, representing almost the full range of human communication, is not produced formlessly and unrelated to the acts of persons who are present and responding to it. Acts of young infants in communication are frequently fragmentary, disjointed or indistinct, and they may, like all acts infants perform, be made with cavalier indifference of external stimuli. But, again like the other acts of infants on their own (e.g., looking and reaching), communication acts are capable, from the start, of accommodation to circumstances to which they are inherently adapted. Infants smile, gesture, grimace, pre-speak and vocalise to persons, often tuning and grading their expressions to fit closely with the pattern expression of their partners. Disruption of the partner's acts, caused by inattention, emotional withdrawal or external interference is, we have found, capable of producing strong indications of distress and withdrawal in an infant of two months who has been in communication just before. This proves both that infants are capable of close involvement in the complexity

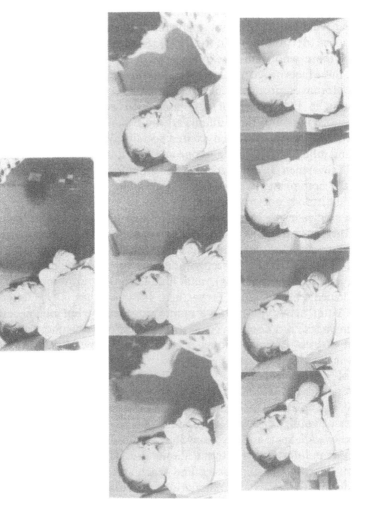

Figure 2.11   Expressive movements of a two-month-old when confronted with an object held by her mother (top) and when interacting with her mother face-to-face

and variety of normal 'baby talk', and that they are emotionally dependent on its progress in a certain manner. Human emotions, rather than causing expression, and thence communication, reflect the success or failure of communication, and they are expressed to aid in maintaining communication (Brazelton *et al.*, 1975; Papousek and Papousek, 1975). It seems likely, from observations made on film and television, that the cognitive achievements of young infants are emotion-charged because infants are inclined to treat the experimental situation as part of communication with other persons. That is, they may treat the experiments, even very mechanical and unnatural ones, as games with social significance. Experimental psychology with human subjects may always be a form of interpersonal exchange, even when the subject is only one or two months of age, and when the experimenter's theory expressly excludes such communication.

The Task for Infancy, Set by the Growing Brain, is to Build a Social Mind

In the embryo the rudiments of tissues and organs drive development of structures towards formation of the body of a particular species of animal, a human. Epigenetic regulations orchestrate the activities of genes and respond to their changing control. In the fetus the nervous system elaborates a hierarchy of maps for behaviour based on an impress in the nerve circuits of the body's symmetry. In the infant a powerful set of rudimentary mental operations guide the mind in the formation of the first steps for understanding a world for behaviour. Thus, broadly speaking, a human being goes through body morphogenesis, neurogenesis of the brain and then psychogenesis of a mental state in the brain. Since the brain of a newborn person is embryonic in all its higher, most psychological functions, its means of growth involve formation of ever more differentiated purposeful acts: acts that specify consequences for the brain of stimuli from the world. That is what psychological development means.

Of all the foresightful explorations of experience made by the infant brain, those directed to an emotion-charged social life are by far the most powerful. Before beginning to explore objects by hand and before walking about in the world, an infant communicates. He alerts to, seeks out and regulates communication from other humans. A baby of two months is a complex personality distinguishing persons from other 'physical' objects and treating them as a category of developmental influence in primary position (Trevarthen, 1974b). After stating a clear preference for human care and human understanding, after establishing an outline of conversational interaction in the first three months, there is a period of several months in which curiosity about what can be seen and heard, and then what can be manipulated and so be seen, felt and heard better, competes with social life.

This exploring of objects and effects within movement is fostered by responsive companions in play, and by the discovery of infant-centred games that easily resolve conflicts in the developing images and purposes of the infant mind (Trevarthen and Hubley, 1978) (Figure 2.12). Undoubtedly, the interlocking cerebral structures needed to formulate voluntary and conscious control of acts of exploration and performance by eye, ear, hand and mouth are undergoing enormous anatomical differentiation in this epoch of games. Essential differences between personalities may have their beginnings in the individual patterns that balance attentions to persons and things in the minds of six-month-old babies. The sexes may differ in the way they communicate and explore from early infancy.

Research on the effects of the separation of infants from their mothers has led to the conclusion that the formation of a bond of affection in the first six months of life is both normal and necessary to further psychological growth (Bowlby, 1969; Ainsworth, 1973). When separated from a mother or other affectionate caretaker, to be taken to hospital, or when the mother is absent or dies, or when cared for without affection, an infant becomes emotionally insecure and develops into a socially maladjusted child, without remorse. But, even the effects of extreme cruelty and almost total deprivation of human contact may be partly reversed if loving attention is given (Curtiss *et al.*, 1974). Curiosity about surroundings and adaptation to unfamiliar situations or strange persons towards the end of the first year are measures of the security of an infant's relation to the mother. Ainsworth describes types of mothering, which she believes to be responsible for the differing patterns of attachment (Ainsworth *et al.*, 1972). Other workers emphasise that most infants develop attachments to several persons, not just to the mother. In some cases, the main relationship is with someone else, and success seems to be determined by the closeness and co-operativeness of companionship (Schaffer, 1971; Rutter, 1972).

We still have no clear idea of the mechanism or function of this common motivation called 'attachment', and research on bonds of immature animals to their parents has not provided an adequate explanation. There is little information on what affectionate mothers or others do to foster attachment, and less on what the infant contributes. The assumption usually made is that, at the start, the infant possesses only a few instinctive demands, but this is not tested by adequate observation. Security in the exploration of objects is described as a by-product of a relationship to a person, when it could equally be a goal of the growing communication.

The methods used in work on attachment focus on the emotional and behavioural effects of strange and disturbing events. They, therefore, tell us little of what goes on between infants and others in 'happy' situations. Recent work on the development of language skills before speech opens a wealth of possibilities, and suggests that the relationship of infants to their best companions is an incubator for the growth of understanding. Bruner (1976),

Bates *et al.* (1975) and others have emphasised that the social play of infants from about four months on allows them to practise and develop patterns of sharing at nine months. That is when they begin systematically to seek instructions and co-operation from older playmates. Quite suddenly, at about 40 weeks after birth, when the infant has grown into and learned a special relationship with the mother and a group of intimate companions and has become dependent on their interest and presentations of the world, the interpersonal behaviour is transformed. Now, instead of making communication subservient to the immediate guidance of organs for picking up experience and regulating body movement, the infant seeks to share and co-operate with other persons, to accept their ideas openly (Figure 2.13). For the first time acts of meaning, instructions, declarations, greetings, recognitions, are performed for their own sake (Trevarthen and Hubley, 1978). The child begins to co-operate with his companions in a world of agreed interests. A one-year-old child cannot speak but can explicitly make ideas about the world common property with others. Every act is a potential display or demonstration, and what a partner does, or shows, or offers is immediately interesting for that reason.

I believe that this protolanguage behaviour, as Halliday, the linguist, calls it, is the germ of culture and civilisation in man (Halliday, 1975, 1978). It is an invention of the baby, something synthesised in his young brain. When a baby, too young to say a word, is able to understand the name of a familiar person or thing, he is already part of his society's culture and its language. When, at the same age, he co-operatively learns how to increase his skill in play with a toy, by watching what another does to vary the possibilities, he is starting on the way to cumulative technology. He also has suddenly found the trick of showing something or giving it to another with obvious pleasure in their acceptance. He shares his growing body of understanding while he learns new ideas from others (Figure 2.13).

All these behaviours, outlining the syntax and semantics of language, as well as its mood and prosody, foreshadowing co-operative work of all kinds and co-operative search for knowledge, are manifestations of the state of his human brain mechanisms in a physically helpless organism so immature that it must be fed, carried about and protected from environmental stresses and extremes. The strategy of this life history is a remarkable inversion of evolution. Being human in essence, the brain can begin the process of human communication before learning any object concept or how to locomote about the world, and can begin involvement in assimilating and extending cultural use of experience before talking about it. The human brain is thus an organ of culture that intuitively stimulates the getting of education from other humans who know the details of the world better. The transfer of wisdom is a response to a request by the child (Trevarthen, 1978d).

Having found clear evidence that infants possess the germ of cultural co-operation, we are led to explore the life of toddlers and school children to see

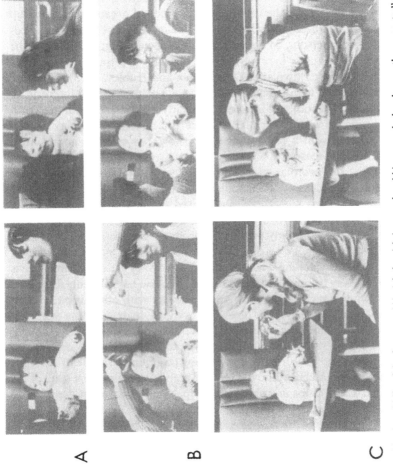

Figure 2.12   Games played in the middle of the first year. (A) A baby girl six-months-old is amused when her mother repeatedly throws her head back then comes quickly in to blow at the baby's chest. (B) The same little girl enjoys a game in which her mother carries a ball high in jerks then suddenly drops to touch the baby's chin. The climax is anticipated excitedly. (C) An eight-month-old watches her mother blow in a plastic globe in a turn-taking game. She anticipates being touched by her mother's fingers as they creep over the table (a variant of 'round-and-round-the-garden'). (Photographs courtesy of Penelope Hubley)

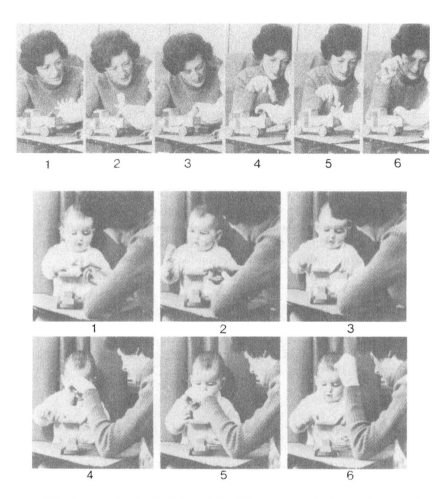

Figure 2.13   Just after her first birthday a baby girl co-operates with her mother in putting wooden dolls in to a truck. (1, 2 and 3) The mother gives her one man and points to the truck asking her to put it in, which she does. (4, 5 and 6) The mother asks her to put in a second man, she points, takes the man and puts it in. (Photographs courtesy of Penelope Hubley)

how they control their life in community with others. I have no doubt that we will find the growing brain to be just as rich in strategy and resource in control of psychological life, even beyond childhood to adolescence, indeed through all the seven ages of man. The humanness firmly established in the brain of the infant, which has enormous influence over the life of all the infant's close companions, remains basic to all that persons learn to do together.

Conclusion: The Value of Infancy

I think this summary of what we know about brain growth and the psychology of infants teaches respect for the vital generative force of biological development. It is not just physical and chemical. It is epiphysical and epichemical, with a great chain of downward causation from cultures, to families, to minds, to brains, to bodies, to cells, to genes.

The twin value of an infant's nature is thus to remind psychologists that we are innately human in the widest possible sense of that word, and, more importantly, to invite parents, teachers and all other companions of children to join in' the task of handing on to them whatever human cleverness has achieved. While amazingly retentive of details of experience, the human brain is also innately regulated to develop into a member of a community of brains that govern co-operative actions of the bodies they are in. No science fiction could be more exciting or mystifying than this statement of newly perceived facts of human nature and its cultivation.

Acknowledgements

Grateful acknowledgement is given to the Social Science Research Council for support of research on infant communication discussed in this paper.

I also wish to thank Penelope Hubley for use of her photographs in Figures 2.12 and 2.13.

References

* These are introductory articles or classical papers on topics of primary importance. Other references are more specialised.

* Ainsworth, M. D. S. (1973). The development of infant-mother attachment. In, *Review of Child Development Research* (ed. B. Caldwell and H. Ricciuti) University of Chicago Press, Chicago, Vol. 3, pp. 1–94

Ainsworth, M. D. S., Bell, S. M. and Staydon, D. J. (1972). Individual differences in strange situation behaviour of one-year-olds. In *The Origins of Human Social Relations* (ed. H. R. Schaffer), Academic Press, London

Angevine, J. B. (1970). Critical cellular events in the shaping of neural centers. In *The Neuro-Sciences. Second Study Program* (ed. F. O. Schmitt and T. Melnechuk). Rockefeller University Press, New York, pp. 62–72

Arber, A. (1950). *The Natural Philosophy of Plant Form*. Cambridge University Press, London

* Barlow, H. B. (1975). Visual experience and cortical development. *Nature*, **258**, 199–204

Bates, E., Camaioni, L. and Volterra, V. (1975). The acquisition of performatives prior to speech. *Merrill-Palmer Quarterly*, **21**, 205–226

* Benzer, S. (1973). Genetic dissection of behavior. *Scientific American*, **229**, 24–37
* Blakemore, C. (1974). Development of functional connexions in the mammalian visual system. *British Medical Bulletin*, **30**, 152–157
Bornstein, M. H., 1975. Qualities of color vision in infancy. *Journal of Experimental Child Psychology*, **19**, 401–419
* Bower, T. G. R., 1966. The visual world of infants. *Scientific American*, **215**, 80–92
* Bower, T. G. R. (1974). *Development in Infancy*. Freeman and Co., San Francisco
* Bowlby, J. (1969). *Attachment and Loss: Vol. I – Attachment*. Hogarth Press, London
Brazelton, T. B. and Robey, J. S. (1965). Observations of neonatal behavior: the effect of prenatal variables, in particular that of maternal medication. *Journal of the American Academy of Child Psychiatry*, **4**, 613
* Brazelton, T. B., Tronick, E., Adamson, L., Als, H. and Wise, S. (1975). Early mother–infant reciprocity. In *Parent–Infant Interaction* (ed. M. O'Connor), pp. 137–154. Elsevier-Exerpta Medica-North Holland, New York
Brimblecombe, F. S. W., Richards, M. P. M. and Robertson, N. C. R. (eds) (1978). *Early Separation and Special Care Nurseries*. Clinics in Developmental Medicine, Spastics Publications
* Bruner, J. S. (1976). From communication to language – a psychological perspective. *Cognition*, **3**, 255–287
Chard, T. and Richards, M. P. M. (eds) (1977). *Hazards and Benefits of the New Obstetrics*. Clinics in Developmental Medicine, Spastics Publications, no. 64
Chung, S. H. and Cooke, J. (1975). Polarity of structure and of ordered nerve connections in the developing amphibian brain. *Nature*, **258**, 126–132
* Coghill, E. G. (1929). *Anatomy and the Problem of Behavior*. Cambridge University Press, Cambridge
Condon, W. S. and Sander, L. W. (1974). Neonate movement is synchronized with adult speech. Interactional participation and language acquisition. *Science*, **183**, 99–101
Conel, J. LeRoy (1939–63). *The Post Natal Development of the Human Cerebral Cortex*, Vols. I to VI, Harvard University Press, Cambridge, USA
Cragg, B. G. (1975). The development of synapses in the visual system of the cat. *Journal of Comparative Neurology*, **160**, 147–166
* Crick, F. H. C. (1962). The genetic code. *Scientific American*, **207**, 66–74
Crick, F. H. C. (1963). On the genetic code. *Science*, **139**, 461–464
Crick, F. H. C. (1966). The genetic code III. *Scientific American*, **215**, 55–62
Curtiss, S., Fromkin, V., Kraschen, S., Rigler, D. and Rigler, M. (1974). The linguistic development of Genie. *Language*, **50**, 528–555
* Darwin, C. (1892). *The Expression of Emotions in Animals and Man*. Appleton and Co., New York (Reprinted: University of Chicago Press: Chicago, 1965)
Darwin, C. (1877). A biographical sketch of an infant. *Mind: Quaterly Review of Psychology and Philosophy*, **2**, 285–294
Dawkins, C. (1976). *The Selfish Gene*. Oxford University Press, Oxford
De Beer, G. R. (1940). *Embryos and Ancestors*. Oxford University Press, Oxford
* Dobbing, J. and Smart, J. L. (1974). Vulnerability of the developing brain and behaviour. *British Medical Bulletin*, **30**, 164–168
* Eccles, J. C. (1977). *The Understanding of the Brain*. McGraw-Hill, New York
Eimas, P. D., Sequeland, E. R., Jusczyk, P. and Vigorito, J. (1971). Speech perception in infants. *Science*, **171**, 303–306
Fantz, R. L. (1961). The origin of form perception. *Scientific American*, **204**, 66–72
Galaburda, A. M., LeMay, M., Kemper, T. L. and Geschwind, N. (1978). Right-left asymmetries in the brain. *Science*, **199**, 852–856

* Gaze, R. M. (1970). *Formation of Nerve Connections*. Academic Press, New York

Gaze, R. M. (1974). Neuronal specificity. *British Medical Bulletin*, **30**, 116–121

Gessell, A. L., Thompson, H. and Amatruda, C. S. (1934). *Infant Behavior: Its Genesis and Growth*. McGraw-Hill, New York

Gewirtz, J. L. (1961). A learning analysis of the effects of normal stimulation, privation and deprivation on the acquisition of social motivation and attachment. In *Determinants of Infant Behavior* (ed. B. M. Foss), Wiley, New York

Gibson, E. J. and Walk, R. D. (1960). The 'Visual Cliff'. *Scientific American*, **202**, 64–71

* Gottlieb, G. (1973). Introduction to behavioral embryology. In *Studies on the Development of Behavior and the Nervous System, Volume I, Behavioral Embryology* (ed. G. Gottlieb), pp. 3–45. Academic Press, New York

Grant, V. (1977). *Organismic Evolution*. Freeman, San Francisco

Halliday, M. A. K. (1975). *Learning How to Mean*. Arnold, London

* Halliday, M. A. K. (1978). Meaning and the construction of reality in early childhood. In *Modes of Perceiving and Processing Information* (ed. H. L. Pick and E. Saltzman), pp. 67–96. Erlbaum, Hillsdale, N.J.

Haith, M. M. (1977). Visual competence in early infancy. In *Handbook of Sensory Physiology*, Vol. VIII (ed. R. Held, R. Leibowitz and H-L. Teuber) Springer-Verlag, Berlin

Harrison, R. G. (1907). Observations on the living developing nerve fiber. *Anatomical Record*, **1**, 116–118

Herrick, C. J. (1948). *The Brain of the Tiger Salamander*. University of Chicago Press, Chicago

Hooker, D. (1952). *The Prenatal Origin of Behaviour*. University of Kansas Press, Lawrence, Kansas

* Hubel, D. H. and Wiesel, T. N. (1977). The Ferrier Lecture: Functional architecture of macaque monkey visual cortex. *Proceedings of the Royal Society, Series B*, **198**, 1–59

Humphrey, T. (1969). Postnatal repetition of human prenatal activity sequences with some suggestions of their neuroanatomical basis. In *Brain and Early Behaviour: Development in the Fetus and Infant* (ed. Robinson, R. J.), Academic Press, New York, 43–84

Jacobson, M. (1970). *Developmental Neurobiology*. Holt, New York

* Jacobson, M. (1974). A plenitude of neurones. In *Aspects of Neurogenesis* (ed. G. Gottlieb), pp. 151–166. Academic Press, New York

Jacobson, M. and Hunt, R. K. (1973). The origins of nerve cell specificity. *Scientific American*, **228**, 126–135

* Larroche, J-G. (1966). The development of the central nervous system during intrauterine life. In *Human Development* (ed. F. Falkner) pp. 257–276. Saunders, Philadelphia

Leboyer, F. (1975). *Birth Without Violence*. Wildwood House, London

* Lewin, R. (1975). Cats' brains are controversial. *New Scientist*, 20 Nov., pp. 457–458

Lipsitt, L. P. (1969). Learning capacities of the human infant. In, *Brain and Early Behaviour: Development in the Fetus and Infant*. (ed. R. J. Robinson) Academic Press, New York

Loewenstein, W. R. (1968). Communication through cell junctions. Implications in growth and control and differentiation. *Developmental Biology Supplements*, **2**, 151–183

* Mark, R. F. (1974). *Memory and Nerve-Cell Connections*. Oxford University Press, London

McKenzie, B. F. and Day, R. H. (1972). Object distance as a determinant of visual fixation in early infancy. *Science*, **178**, 1108–1110

Meltzoff, A. N. and Moore, M. K. (1977). Imitation of facial and manual gestures by human neonates. *Science*, **198**, 75–78

Needham, J. (1942). *Biochemistry and Morphogenesis*. Cambridge University Press, London

Oppenheim, R. W. (1974). The ontogeny of behavior in the chick embryo. In, *Advances in the Study of Behavior*, Vol. 5. (ed. D. H. Lehrman *et al.*) pp. 133–172. Academic Press, New York

* Oppenheim, R. W. (1975). Progress and challenges in neuroembryology. *Bioscience*, **25**, 28–36

Oster, H. and Ekman, P., (1977). Facial behaviour in child development. In *Minnesota Symposium on Child Development* (ed. A. Collins). Thomas A. Crowell, New York

Papousek, H. (1961). Conditioned head rotation reflexes in the first six months of life. *Acta Pediatrica*, **50**, 565–576

Papousek, H. (1967). Experimental studies of appetitional behavior in human newborns and infants. In *Early Behavior* (ed. H. W. Stevenson, E. H. Hess and H. L. Rheingold) Wiley, New York

Papousek, H. (1969). Individual variability in learned responses in human infants. In *Brain and Early Behaviour: Development in Fetus and Infant* (ed. R. J. Robinson), pp. 251–266. Academic Press, New York

* Papousek, H. and Papousek, M. (1975). Cognitive aspects of preverbal social interaction between human infants and adults. In *Parent–Infant Interaction* (ed. M. O'Connor). Elsevier, Amsterdam

Piaget, J. (1953). *The Origins of Intelligence in Children*. Routledge and Kegan Paul, London (Original French Edition, 1936)

* Piaget, J. (1970). Piaget's Theory. In *Carmichael's Manual of Child Psychology* (ed. P. H. Mussen), Vol. I, 3rd edition, pp. 703–732, Wiley, New York

* Rheingold, H. L. (1961). The effect of environmental stimulation upon social and exploratory behaviour in the human infant. In *Determinants of Infant Behaviour*, (ed. B. M. Foss). Wiley, New York

* Richards, M. P. M. (1978). A place of safety? An examination of the risks of hospital deliver. In *The Place of Birth* (ed. S. Kitzinger and J. Davis) Oxford University Press, London

Russell, E. S. (1945). *The Directedness of Organic Activities*. Cambridge University Press, Cambridge

Rutter, M. (1972). *Maternal Deprivation Reassessed*. Penguin, Harmondsworth

Saint-Anne Dargassies, S. (1966). Neurological maturation of the premature infant of 28–41 weeks gestation age. In *Human Development* (ed. Falkner, F.), Saunders, Philadelphia, 306–325

* Schaffer, H. R. (1971). *The Growth of Sociability*. Penguin, Harmondsworth

Schaffer, H. R. (ed.) (1977). *Studies in Mother–Infant Interaction*, Academic Press, London

Schneider, G. E. (1973). Early lesions of the superior colliculus: factors affecting the formation of abnormal retinal projections. *Brain Behaviour and Evolution*, **8**, 73–109

* Sidman, R. L. and Rakic, P. (1973). Neuronal migration, with special reference to developing human brain. A review. *Brain Research*, **62**, 1–35

Spemann, H. (1938). *Embryonic Development and Induction*. Yale University Press, New Haven

* Sperry, R. W. (1959). The growth of nerve circuits. *Scientific American*, **201**, 68–75

Sperry, R. W. (1963). Chemoaffinity in the orderly growth of nerve fiber patterns and connections. *Proceedings of the U.S. Academy of Sciences*, **50**, 703–710

Sperry, R. W. (1969). Plasticity of neural maturation. In *The Emergence of Order in Developing Systems* (ed. M. Locke), pp. 306–327, Academic Press, New York

* Sperry, R. W. (1965). Embryogenesis of behavioral nerve nets. In *Organogenesis* (ed. R. L. Dehaan and H. Ursprung), pp. 161–186, Holt, New York

* Srb, A. M., Owen, R. D. and Edgar, R. S. (1965). *General Genetics*, Freeman, San Francisco

Toivonen, S. and Saxen, L. (1968). Morphogenetic interaction of presumptive neural and mesodermal cells mixed in different ratios. *Science*, **159**, 539–540

Trehub, S. E. (1973). Infants' sensitivity to vowel and tonal contrasts. *Developmental Psychology*, **9**, 91–96

Trevarthen, C. (1968). Two mechanisms of vision in primates. *Psychologische Forschung*, **31**, 299–337

Trevarthen, C. (1970). Experimental evidence for a brain-stem contribution to visual perception in man. *Brain, Behavior and Evolution*, **3**, 338–352

* Trevarthen, C. (1973). Behavioral embryology. In *Handbook of Perception, 3* (ed. E. C. Carterette and M. P. Friedman), pp. 89–117, Academic Press, New York

Trevarthen, C. (1974a). Cerebral embryology and the split brain. In *Hemispheric Disconnection and Cerebral Function* (ed. M. Kinsbourne and W. L. Smith), pp. 208–236, Charles C. Thomas, Springfield, Illinois

* Trevarthen, C. (1974b). Conversations with a two-month-old. *New Scientist*, 2 May, 230–235

* Trevarthen, C. (1977). Descriptive analyses of infant communication behaviour. In *Studies in Mother–Infant Interaction* (ed. H. R. Schaffer), pp. 227–270, Academic Press, London

Trevarthen, C. (1978a). Modes of perceiving and modes of acting. In *Psychological Modes of Perceiving and Processing Information* (ed. H. J. Pick and E. Saltzman), pp. 99–136, Lawrence Erlbaum, Hillsdale, N.J.

Trevarthen, C. (1978b). Neuroembryology and the development of perception. In *Human Growth: A Comprehensive Treatise*, Vol. III, (ed. E. Falkner and J. M. Tanner) Plenum, New York

Trevarthen, C. (1978c). Communication and cooperation in early infancy. A description of primary intersubjectivity. In *Before Speech: The Beginnings of Human Communication* (ed. M. Bullowa) Cambridge University Press, London

* Trevarthen, C. (1978d). Instincts for human understanding and for cultural cooperation: Their development in infancy. In *Human Ethology* (ed. M. von Cranach and J. Aschoff). Springer, Berlin (In press)

* Trevarthen, C. and Hubley, P. (1978). Secondary intersubjectivity: Confidence confiding and acts of meaning in the first year. In *Action Gesture and Symbol: The Emergence of Language* (ed. A. Lock) Academic Press, London (In press)

Waddington, C. H. (1957). *The Strategy of the Genes*. Allen and Unwin, London

* Waddington, C. H. (1961). *The Nature of Life*. Allen and Unwin, London

* Waddington, C. H. (1966). *Principles of Development and Differentiation*. Macmillan, New York

Watson, J. B. (1913). Psychology as the behaviorist views it. *Psychological Review*, **20**, 158–177

Watson, J. D. (1965). *Molecular Biology of the Gene*. Benjamin, New York

Willshaw, D. J. and von der Malsburg, C. (1976). How patterned neural connections can be set up by self-organization. *Proceedings of the Royal Society of London, Series B*, **194**, 431–445

Windle, W. F. (1970). Development of neural elements in human embryos of four to seven weeks gestation. *Experimental Neurology Supplement*, **5**, 44–83

Wolpert, L. (1971). Positional information and pattern formation. *Current Topics in Developmental Biology*, **6**, 183–224

* Yakovlev, P. I., and Lecours, A. R. (1967). The myelogenetic cycles of regional maturation of the brain. In *Regional Development of the Brain in Early Life* (A. Minkowski, ed.), pp. 3–70, Blackwell, Oxford and Edinburgh

3 The Relevance of Ethology

P. J. B. SLATER

(*Ethology and Neurophysiology Group, School of Biological Sciences, University of Sussex, Falmer, Brighton, Sussex, England*)

Introduction

Tinbergen (1963) defined ethology as 'the biological study of behaviour' and, as such, its subject matter is much the same as that of psychology, though its perspective is rather different. From time to time this has led to sharp divisions of opinion between proponents of the two approaches, and the extent to which ethology is relevant to psychology and, in particular, to human behaviour is still a matter of debate. Before considering some of these issues in greater detail, I should like to make a few general comments on changing ideas within ethology and how these relate to the approaches and thinking of psychologists.

Interest in the naturalistic observation of animal behaviour can be traced back several centuries (Crook, 1970) but, as with so much else in biology, it took the theoretical framework and observations of Darwin (1859, 1872) to point the way to more systematic work in this area. A few pioneers took up the challenge, but it was not until the writings of Lorenz in the 1930s (see Lorenz, 1970) that a comprehensive theory of instinctive behaviour began to emerge. The change was exciting and revolutionary. Prior to this, the closest to a biological theory of behaviour had been provided by concepts such as 'kinesis' and 'taxis' (Fraenkel and Gunn, 1940), which went a long way towards explaining the behaviour of invertebrates, but were clearly inadequate for that of more complex animals. When ideas such as 'releaser' and 'fixed action pattern' were put forward, it seemed that at last a theory was available which could account for the bewildering complexities of the behaviour of vertebrates. The culmination of this era came when these ideas were clearly and fully expressed in English for the first time (Lorenz, 1950; Tinbergen, 1951).

Initial criticism of these theories came most strongly from comparative psychologists in America, rather than from within ethology, and centred on the nature–nurture issue. While some ethologists were reluctant to accept such criticisms, the majority modified their views, so that it is now unusual to find an ethologist who believes in rigidly determined 'instincts' or 'innate behaviour patterns'. The question of nature–nurture is still to some degree a controversial one, however, and I shall return to some of the problems it presents in the next section. Many of the other ideas of Lorenz and Tinbergen have also been modified or abandoned in the past 25 years: as Blurton Jones (1972, pp. 3–33) comments, 'ethological theory has diminished at a rate that some find alarming'. In retrospect this is less surprising than the fact that such a sweeping general theory ever existed. Given the ethologist's belief in detailed observation as a basis for hypothesis, his sense of wonder at the diversity of animal behaviour and his training in evolution, it is odd that a theory was constructed which took little account of species differences in phylogenetic level and way of life. While natural selection was seen as a moulding force which produced behaviour patterns beautifully adapted to the requirements of the animal, the underlying instincts were somehow seen as immutable. For a drive theorist or behaviourist to believe in commonality of mechanism between animal species and between behaviours is unremarkable; it is more curious for a biologist, with his knowledge of evolutionary theory, to do so. Nevertheless, these theories provided hypotheses on which subsequent work could be based and attracted many biologists into the study of behaviour. Ethology grew and, as the number of species studied increased, it became clear that the requirements of different species vary considerably and that evolution has adapted motivational systems as well as individual behaviour patterns to fit them. Despite their popular image, ethologists have become extremely cautious about generalising.

The theory of instinctive behaviour was largely concerned with causation (the mechanisms underlying it, seen in this particular theory as the way in which instincts worked or were discharged), but it also had implications for development. As interest in these two areas was shared by psychologists, some of whom occupied extreme environmentalist positions, an argument between the two schools of thought was only to be expected. Fortunately, both fields have gained from the interchange, and today only subtle differences in emphasis can be used to discriminate between many ethologists and experimental psychologists working in these areas. But ethologists also work on two other topics which have not, until recently, been considered of relevance or interest to psychologists: function and evolution, two key questions in modern biology. It is in its stress on natural selection as the prime force leading to species differences in behaviour, and on the idea that these differences arise because they are functional (in the biological sense of having survival value), that ethology has made its widest impact. Not all of this attention has been welcomed by ethologists themselves. Popular books on human behaviour from an evolutionary viewpoint appear at an alarming rate and, although few are by trained ethologists, they tend to be regarded as so. Some of these books contain fascinating ideas and hypotheses, untested (and sometimes untestable) but dressed up as if they were scientifically established facts rather than fantasies on the part of their authors. Wilson (1975), in his important recent book, labels this route to discovery as the 'advocacy method': evidence is gathered in favour of a particular case and it is argued as persuasively as possible without regard to contrary possibilities. Although, as we shall see, his own discussion of human behaviour does not altogether avoid this pitfall, he argues for the more conventional, if more laborious, routes used by scientists, as does Martin (1974) in a detailed critique of some of these writings. The problem is not, however, a simple one, as questions about function and evolution are difficult to put to the experimental test. But evolutionary thinking within biology has advanced immensely in the past few years, and this is a topic to which we shall return in some detail for it has clearly had an influence on developmental psychology, both through the theory put forward by Bowlby (1969) and through the influx of ethologists into the field.

There are perhaps three main ways in which developmental psychology may benefit from ethology. One of these, which has led several ethologists to study child development, is the feeling that an evolutionary approach has advantages in this area. After all, it is only about 10000 years since man first developed an agricultural economy and cultural evolution became a major force leading to the very different societies in which most humans now live. Prior to that time there was little to separate the behaviour of man from that of his mammalian relatives, yet now there is plenty. The crucial point here is that the time between, is, in evolutionary terms, extremely short: at birth a child now is much as a child was then, its abilities and potentialities very much the product of evolution. From the moment of birth it starts to interact with an environment very different from that in which man spent most of his evolutionary history; an evolutionary perspective may help towards under-standing features of this interaction, why some abilities are present at birth, yet others develop only slowly and in certain circumstances. The importance of this contribution must not be over-rated, however. It is, perhaps, only a matter of time before our knowledge of ethology and of human evolution will lead someone to propose a natural child rearing strategy, recommending that humans should adopt once more those practices with which evolution endowed early man. This would, of course, be naive, for evolution is a process of adaptation to an environment and, while our genes may not have changed much in the last few millenia, our environment certainly has. Given that the two are now out of step with each other, the task is to understand their interaction as it is and what constraints and limitations evolution has put upon us so that we can modify our own behaviour as far as possible to fit the changed circumstances.

A second contribution that ethology can make comes from those who have remained with their animals. As with experimental psychologists, those ethologists who study animals hope to be able to make generalisations which apply beyond the bounds of a single species. This process has, of course, proved its usefulness in pharmacology where man has, in general, benefited greatly from the use of drugs which have first been tested on monkeys or rodents. With animals one can carry out experiments which would be unethical on man, and one can also gain understanding of basic processes by studying them using the much simpler systems which animals provide for us. Nevertheless, as the results of ethology have increasingly shown, the hazards of generalising between species are great when it comes to behaviour, so that conclusions from animal studies can do little more than provide hypotheses about human behaviour. Where these ideas cannot be tested on humans, the answer perhaps lies in the succinct statement by Harlow *et al.* (1972): 'one cannot generalise, but one must'. However, on certain issues one may be on a firmer footing as, for example, where animals turn out to be more complicated than one previously thought. Thus the discovery that drive theories are inadequate to account for the complexities of motivation in animals immediately suggests that they will fall short in the human case.

A final reason why the ethological approach may be valuable is a methodological one. Ethologists have long experience of observing the behaviour of unconstrained animals, of categorising the actions involved, and of studying the situations in which they occur and the associations between them in a reasonably quantitative manner. Of course, ethology has had to become proficient at this, in a way that human psychology has not, because its subjects cannot answer questions. But perhaps psychology has become too dependent on the existence of this ability in those whom it studies. For all its limitations, the ethological approach has a hardness and objectivity which is difficult to achieve with the use of questionnaires or rating scales (see Blurton Jones, 1972, pp. 3–33), and it also provides a methodology which can usefully be applied to humans, particularly in the pre-verbal stage.

This final point is one which has been covered extensively by ethologists working on human behaviour, as for example in the books edited by Blurton Jones (1972) and by Richards (1974), and the article by Smith (1974). We will not therefore consider it further here, but instead go on to discuss two topics related to the previous, more controversial, points: first, changing ideas within ethology about the development of behaviour and, second, evolution theory and its possible relevance to human behaviour.

Ethology and Development

For a long time ethologists tended to avoid detailed study of development, although imprinting in birds is an obvious exception: Lorenz (1935) himself did more than anyone else to focus attention on this phenomenon. Nevertheless, the wider area was relatively neglected. The reason for this is simple: their interest was in studying fixed action patterns, elements of behaviour which are stereotyped and species typical, and were originally considered to have a number of other characteristics, one of which was that they were innate. Innate behaviours were thought of as wired into the system from the outset so that, at the appropriate time, when the animal encountered the correct combination of stimuli, they appeared fully formed with no slow process of development being required.

This idea was based on a variety of observations and lines of argument, at the heart of which lay the assumption that a given pattern of behaviour could arise in two very different ways: through instinct and through learning. Fixed action patterns were considered to be innate or instinctive because they appeared even in animals reared by hand or in isolation which had had no opportunity to copy them from others (the so-called deprivation experiment). They were sometimes shown to crude models of the appropriate stimulus, and they sometimes 'misfired', as in the case of the goose which continues with the movement of rolling its egg towards the nest even after the egg itself has slipped away: these characteristics were not what one would expect of 'intelligent' behaviour, so that it was thought reasonable to label the patterns involved as 'instinctive'. Furthermore, these acts were extremely constant and stereotyped, contrasting with the flexibility which was the hallmark of learned behaviour. To these general points can be added striking specific examples of behaviours which seem to arise rather than develop. Take the newborn lamb, for instance: with a few false starts and a little wobbling it can walk within a few minutes of birth and, as it shows a marked liking for nuzzling under its mother's body, it soon finds a nipple. Examples of such abilities have even more impact when they indicate adaptive differences between closely related species, as is the case with a study of hand-reared ducklings by Kear (1967). She found that the young of ground-nesting ducks tended to move to the shallow side of a visual cliff. By contrast, those of species which nest in trees moved at random but, if they chose the deep side, they leapt off it as they normally would when leaving the nest. In those few cases where ground-nesters did choose the deep side they pushed off with both feet as if leaving the edge of a pond. Such experiments leave little doubt that genetic influences have a strong part to play in moulding the behaviour of animals. Why then is it no longer fashionable to call such behaviour innate and be done with it?

The first types of objection to be raised were theoretical and methodological. Amongst many such critiques, that of Lehrman (1953) was the most persuasive and strongly worded; Lorenz (1965) replied in kind by referring to his critics as behaviourists, which they were not, and to behavioural development as a subject for embryologists. Lehrman (1970) produced a rejoinder, but by now he was largely preaching to the converted, though there remain a few notable exceptions (for example the text by Eibl-Eibesfeldt, 1971, is written very much from a Lorenzian viewpoint).

A major problem with calling a pattern of behaviour innate stems from the fact that this word can have so many meanings: 'present at birth', 'appearing the first time the animal encounters the appropriate stimulus', 'not copied from others', 'not learnt'. All these are possible, and it is not often clear which is meant. The deprivation experiment usually excludes copying from others, though more extreme forms of deprivation may attempt to remove any possibility of learning. For instance, Eibl-Eibesfeldt (1963) considered hoarding by squirrels to be innate because animals reared in isolation on a plentiful liquid diet and without material on the floors of their cages in which to dig, still hoarded when given solid food and a substrate in which it could be buried. To this type of evidence Lehrman (1953, 1970) objects that innateness is being defined purely by exclusion to mean 'not learnt'. Even so, he points out that only certain of the most obvious opportunities for learning have been removed and, on the basis of such evidence, all one can say with certainty is that 'we have not yet found a manipulation which will modify the development of this behaviour': hardly a suitable definition on which to build a useful dichotomy. Furthermore, even if it were possible to exclude all forms of learning, this would not mean that the behaviour is entirely genetic, for genes can only act to produce behaviour in an environment, and presumably there are limits to the range of environments which will give the appropriate outcome. At an extreme, the absence of gravity or of an adequate food supply is likely to have widespread effects on behavioural development, and more minor environmental differences, which have nothing to do with learning, may also lead to changes. Each species has what Bowlby (1969) refers to as its environment of evolutionary adaptedness, and it is in this that the genes have been selected to operate. Take the genes out of this environment and natural selection has nothing to say about what the outcome should be: the situation has never been encountered before. Lehrman (1970) cites a particularly clear example of this discovered by Stockard (1909). A species of fish which normally has two eyes will, if kept in magnesium chloride solution, sometimes develop with a single centrally located one. Natural selection has evolved an animal with two eyes, but what it has not done is to encounter magnesium chloride: if it had, presumably some genetic changes would have been instituted (those with one eye would have been selected out) so that the outcome would remain the advantageous one despite the environmental change. This example is a morphological one, but the same arguments apply to behaviour, except that the particular class of interaction between the animal and its environment called learning may make behaviour even more susceptible to environmental change. As Hebb (1953) put it, both heredity and environment are 100 per cent important for behaviour: no genes, no behaviour; no environment, no behaviour. Development is a continual interaction between the two and they cannot be simply teased apart.

It is crucial to realise that arguments such as these do nothing to play down the importance of genetic effects on behaviour; they are as much a counter to extreme environmentalist views as to those of traditional ethology. It is impossible to conceive of a behaviour, no matter how clearly learning plays a role in its development, which does not have some genetic basis which would allow it to be modified by natural selection. The success of artificial selection for maze-bright and maze-dull rats (e.g. Thompson, 1954) is but a single case in point.

These theoretical considerations led ethologists to a closer study of the development of behaviour. Some surprises were in store and some very fixed behaviours turned out to depend a great deal on environmental factors. The 'innate' alarm response of young birds to an overhead hawk was found to be given also to a wide variety of other stimuli they had never encountered before (Schleidt, 1961). In the original experiments the birds had apparently failed to respond to goose-like models because they were already fully habituated to this shape. Likewise the pecking response of young gulls, which was studied by Tinbergen and Perdeck (1950), was thought at that stage to be an innate response to the particular configuration of the parent's head and beak. Hailman (1967) found that the newly hatched chick does indeed peck more at some stimuli than at others, but the stimulus characteristics they can discriminate between are much less detailed than originally thought; for example, they prefer red objects to those of other colours, but will peck as much at the beaks of other gull species as at those of their own. It is only after some days of exposure to their parents, or to a model gull's head which presents them with food, that they come to prefer this stimulus to all others even when these are very similar to it. In this way a young herring gull can be trained to peck at a model of an adult laughing gull more than at one of its own species.

Birds have also provided us with what must surely be one of the clearest demonstrations of how different developmental strategies can give rise to what, on the face of it, appear to be very similar outcomes. This is the case of bird song, the study of which continues to have implications for development far beyond its own restricted area. At one extreme, some birds produce their own species song if fostered by other species or reared in isolation; at the other there are species which will, if trained, incorporate a wide variety of different sounds into their songs. Numerous intermediates also exist: the chaffinch, for instance, produces a very poor semblance of its own species song when raised in isolation, yet it will not readily mimic other species. It appears to be constrained from the outset to learn chaffinch song. Each of these modes of development can be said to fall on a continuum between the environmentally stable, which develop the same in a wide range of environments, and the labile, which are easily modified during ontogeny. It is convenient to think in these terms, even if the description is something of an oversimplification. We understand a lot about the mechanisms underlying these different strategies of development, but an important question, to which there is as yet no clear answer, is what the function or selective advantage of each strategy is for each species. Why is development so stable in some and so labile in others? When the answer to this question is known it may shed light on why man, alone amongst the primates, first developed his marked capacity for vocal mimicry. But it may tell us more than this, for it may also indicate the sorts of circumstances in which stable and labile patterns of ontogeny are likely to be found elsewhere in behaviour, where modifiability is advantageous and where it is not.

Nottebohm (1972) makes several suggestions as to why song development, which he considers originally to have been stable, might have become modifiable through copying during the course of evolution. He argues against the possibility that learning might be advantageous because it makes individual recognition possible, on the grounds that learning from other individuals leads to similarities not differences. Nevertheless, learning does lead to local dialects, cultural lineages of song types, suggesting that it is more likely to lead to differences between individuals than would be an ontogeny which does not involve copying. In complex social groups, being able to distinguish between different individuals, between group members and outsiders, and between relatives and non-relatives may all be advantageous. We will see in the next section that current evolutionary theory suggests, in particular, that the last of these should certainly be selected for. All are made more feasible where learning has a part to play.

Another likely reason for song learning is that it makes a large repertoire of different noises possible. Although there are exceptions, in general, species the songs of which develop normally without copying have simple songs, while copying is essential where songs are complex. There seem to be two main reasons why selection may have favoured complexity. First, if song is to embody such detailed information as individual or group characteristics it cannot be a brief or simple utterance. Second, if females for some reason prefer to mate with males having more elaborate songs, then sexual selection will favour maximum complexity for its own sake. Why must learning be involved in this? A probable explanation is that there are limits to what can be encoded in the genotype (Immelmann, 1976). To produce an animal with a few simple learning mechanisms which will, during the course of its ontogeny, acquire a complex song is likely to involve many fewer genes than the construction of one which develops a complex song without learning being involved. The latter strategy requires more detailed information to be carried in the genes and less to be extracted from the environment. This may also be a reason why young birds have to learn the characteristics of their own species through imprinting. The necessity to recognise the mother from many different angles and distances again requires a lot of information: Bateson and his collaborators (Bateson and Chantrey, 1972; Chantrey, 1972, 1974; Jackson and Bateson, 1974) have shown how young chicks possess a few simple learning mechanisms which, combined with their initial preference for following large moving objects, probably ensure this outcome given the predictability of the environment into which they are born. In addition, selection may have favoured learning in this situation as it enables the young bird to recognise the individual characteristics of the mother and so follow her in preference to other females.

So far we have discussed only cases where ontogeny involves a good deal of environmental input and, in particular, a larger contribution from learning than ethologists originally supposed. What about the other side of the coin: the constraints on learning which have recently attracted a good deal of attention (Shettleworth, 1972; Hinde and Stevenson-Hinde, 1972)? At a gross level, such constraints are obvious and trivial: in general the higher their phyletic level, the more complex the tasks that animals will learn and the more sophisticated their approach to a problem. There are, however, some striking exceptions. For example, ants trained in a T maze in which one arm is rewarded with water 70 per cent of the time and the other 30 per cent consistently choose the more productive arm (Fleer, cited by Garcia *et al.*, 1972). This strategy is also found in humans and yields reward on 70 per cent of trials. Fish, on the other hand, go to the arms in the ratio that each is rewarded which gives only 50 per cent success (Bitterman, 1965). Such exceptions are presumably related to the particular way of life of the species concerned, selection having favoured those abilities necessary for the animal to cope with its natural environment, and not others which are unnecessary or deleterious. Indeed there are convincing cases where animals have been found to cope with one task more easily than another despite the fact that the two seem, on the face of it, to be very much equivalent. Thus rats can be trained with ease to run from the centre of an arena to its edge to escape shock, but not from the edge to the centre, a response incompatible with their natural alarm reaction (Grossen and Kelley, 1972). When frightened, rats usually freeze or flee: they can be induced to press a bar to avoid shock, but only by persuading them initially to freeze on top of the bar and then shaping the response from there (Bolles, 1970). Yet again, rats can be trained to avoid a sweet solution which is followed by nausea, and to avoid water associated with a noise when this is followed by shock. But, after a similar amount of training, they do not avoid noisy water which is followed by nausea or sweet water which is followed by shock (Domjan and Wilson, 1972). Doubtless, in the natural environment (if the white rat can be thought of as having one), noises tend to be followed by pain and tastes by nausea rather than the other way round, so that the rat has evolved a bias towards making one association rather than the other. Results such as these indicate that constraints on learning stem from the adaptation which each species has to its particular way of life as well as from its phylogeny. This is a point to which we shall return later when discussing ways of comparing between species, but it is worth noting here that the rat, being a nocturnal rodent, is not an easy species from which to generalise, as many comparative psychologists now recognise (Beach, 1950; Hodos and Campbell, 1969; Lockard, 1971).

Does this recent work allow any general conclusions to be made about behavioural development? It is clear that all behaviour depends upon both genes and environment. Selection favours those animals which survive and produce as many offspring as possible which in turn survive to breed. At each stage of its life an individual is therefore selected to behave in such a way as to maximise its chances of doing so. Sometimes this will involve lability, such as moving to a new area when the old becomes uninhabitable or changing food sources when the supply of one becomes depleted. Sometimes stability of development will be selected for, and here courtship signals and anti-predator reactions are the most obvious examples. Animals which mate with the wrong species waste their effort, so selection is likely to favour signals which are highly stereotyped and resistant to change when the environment changes; the animal that does not respond appropriately to a predator on the first occasion that one is encountered will be rapidly selected out. This fixity does not, however, mean that no learning is involved: if the environment of evolutionary adaptedness is predictable enough it may, combined with some constraints on what is learnt, produce a very fixed outcome without requiring an enormous increase in the size of the gene complement. We have seen how imprinting and song development in birds fit in with this picture, and earlier we had an example of how anti-predator behaviour is initially shown to a wide variety of novel stimuli, then habituates to those which are frequently seen and innocuous so that it is finally a response to a very specific stimulus configuration.

All these experimental results demonstrate the subtlety of the interplay between heredity and environment leading to behaviour. But they also teach us another important lesson. Behaviours labelled as innate are easily thought of as totally fixed, regardless of any environmental variation, so that no conceivable manipulation could alter them. As we have seen, this is unjustified: however fixed development normally is, changing the environment from the natural one may alter its course. Lorenz (1966) does not seem to recognise this when he argues, in his widely quoted book *On Aggression*, that man has an aggressive drive or instinct which, being innate, cannot be got rid of, but must be side-tracked into harmless activities such as sport. This view is not shared by many other ethologists. With the realisation that motivational systems can differ markedly between behaviours and between species depending on their particular requirements, most would not now refer to any behaviour as under the control of a drive. The term suggests a specific motivational arrangement, with expenditure during performance and re-covery during non-performance, and this model, while a rough approxi-mation for some behaviours, is especially misleading in the case of aggression (see Hinde, 1970). Quite apart from this, there seems to be no justification for the view that levels of aggression cannot be changed either during develop-ment or later (and a good deal for the contrary opinion). Fortunately for our own species, one of the recent lessons of ethology is that behaviour is not fixed and inescapable like this: some behaviours may be more easily modified than others, and the search for the appropriate manipulation may be arduous, but it would be silly to give up on the supposition that genetic constraints make the task an impossible one. The evolutionary history of all species is one of continuing adaptation to keep pace with a changing environment. Man has succeeded in modifying his surroundings more rapidly than genetic change could keep pace with; by reducing mortality so that less well adapted individuals are more likely to survive and breed, he has also buffered himself against natural selection producing adaptive changes in his genotype. As selection will no longer help him, he must himself adapt his behavioural development to the new environment he has created.

Finally, on the subject of development, is it possible to decide where on the stability – lability continuum a particular behaviour should be placed? It has been argued by some (e.g. Jensen, 1969) that the heritability measure used by geneticists can give one a guide to how fixed or flexible development is in a quantitative manner: thus high heritability is taken to indicate a strong genetic basis, low heritability a strong environmental one. This is a misunderstanding of the concept and has been refuted by many (e.g. Hirsch, 1970; Layzer, 1974; Feldman and Lewontin, 1975). The heritability concept was originally developed as a measure of the susceptibility to selection of, for example, a given characteristic in a strain of wheat. It was based upon the extent to which the variance of the character stemmed from genetic variance, rather than environmental variance, a high proportion of the former being essential if selection is to bring about change. This is a very different matter from arguing that behaviour is more or less genetically based. Take, for example, two strains of mice, each of which has been inbred until it is assumed to be genetically homogeneous, and which are reared in the same environment. All within-strain variance in a trait is then environmental, while between-strain variance is genetic in origin. But this is only relative to a particular environment. Strain A may score better on a test when reared in one environment to which it is well adapted, while B does better in another; in an impoverished environment both may score equally badly. Thus the heritability scores obtained will vary considerably depending on the exact environment used for the experiment and the way in which the genes of each strain interact with it.[1] What if the two strains have a characteristic which is only affected by a single gene which both possess? Individual differences can then be entirely attributed to the environment, there being no genetic variance. The zero heritability score which results indicates that selection will not modify the character, and this is correct: selection can only be based on genetic differences. The score does not, however, indicate that the character has no genetic basis. We return, yet again, to the conclusion that the interactions between heredity and environment are too complex and subtle to allow a simple partitioning of their effects.

The Evolutionary Perspective

The previous section was largely concerned with behavioural development but, being from an ethological standpoint, it contained frequent references to evolution and function, two issues central to ethology, but of little note to psychologists. Because of this, and because their relevance to human behaviour is either overstated, as in some popular books, or ignored, it may be helpful to explore these areas a little further. This will also provide a basis for the final section, which will deal more specifically with human behaviour.

Let us take what is meant by function first. The word, in its everyday sense, refers to the consequences of something or what it achieves. A biologist would call this the immediate function of a particular behaviour pattern or other characteristic; that of grooming, for example, is keeping the body clean. But evolutionary theory has taught us that for a behaviour to evolve it must confer upon the individual that possesses it selective advantage. More precisely, though selection acts on the outcome, in this case a behaviour pattern, it is the genes affecting it which are selected for or against. Only genes which are beneficial from the point of view of natural selection will spread through the population; those which are not will be selected against to an extent depending on how deleterious they are, and will eventually disappear. The reason why a behaviour gives selective advantage to those animals possessing it is known as its ultimate or biological function. This is not as simple as it might seem, however, for any behaviour is likely to have both positive and negative effects on survival and reproduction. To take grooming again, two probable advantages are that it removes parasites and that it preserves the insulating capacity of the body covering. But it may also occupy time which could be spent in searching for food or a mate and distracts the attention from looking for predators. For a behaviour to have evolved, one must assume that its benefits, in terms of enhanced survival and reproduction, outweigh its costs.

It is relatively easy to study the immediate functions of behaviour patterns: one can simply watch and see what they lead to. Unfortunately, it is much harder to discover the ultimate functions of a behaviour and, while suggestions have been made for many patterns, most of these are somewhat speculative. The main problem is that behaviour patterns which are species typical are present in all members of the species of a particular age and sex, yet to discover their selective advantage experimentally would require two populations, one with and one without the behaviour, but otherwise identical. As this is not possible, one has to resort to less direct means. Correlating between species is the most commonly used method. If two closely related species differ in behaviour, in what other ways do they differ and can these differences be attributed to their ecology and way of life since separating? Conversely, perhaps a particular behaviour occurs in a number of widely divergent species, like vocal mimicry in birds and man: if there are other similarities between the species these may help to indicate the probable function of the behaviour.

Though each of these types of comparison has its limitations, both may contribute to our understanding of the evolutionary basis of human behaviour if the species compared are chosen carefully. For example, attempts to reconstruct the behaviour of early man, and to understand the selective forces acting on him when he moved from the forest into the savannah, may be helped as much by studies of animals such as hyaenas (Kruuk, 1972) and baboons (Altmann and Altmann, 1970), which live in this type of habitat, as by those of his closest living relatives, the chimpanzee (Goodall, 1968) or gorilla (Schaller, 1963). Studies of chimpanzees and gorillas are relevant because they share more of their evolutionary history with man than do any other living species; the points which they have in common with man can give an impression of how the common ancestor must have behaved and indicate those aspects of human behaviour which are recent acquisitions. But these species are no closer to the common ancestor than is man himself: they too have evolved since diverging from the human line and this evolution has been shaped by very different environments. This makes comparison between close relatives tricky because, as mentioned in the last section, it is now apparent that similarities due to common descent are overlaid by differences due to ecological pressures since divergence, and it is also clear that minor differences in behaviour can have profound effects on such features as social organisation (e.g. Kummer, 1971). This is where comparison with species such as hyaenas and baboons may be helpful, for they have had to face some of the same pressures as those encountered by early man, the hyaena as a plains dwelling carnivore and the baboon as a primate which has moved out of the forests. The main problem here is that these species, while sharing some features with man, differ from him in many others: this makes it important not to push comparison too far and not to consider one species to the exclusion of others. The most fruitful comparisons of this sort are likely to be those which search for orderly relationships between ecological variables and behavioural ones over a wide range of species. Nevertheless, the interpretation of correlations of this sort is a difficult matter, and it remains the case that the majority of functional reasoning depends more upon the preconceptions, ability and imagination of the reasoner than on solid data. But, as we shall see, the situation is likely to improve, because notable theoretical advances have recently been made in this area: even where experiment cannot help, advance is often possible by observation alone when it is aimed at testing the predictions of a theory.

This revolution in functional thinking takes as its origin a controversy hinging on the level at which natural selection acts: does it affect the individual, the group to which it belongs or the whole species? Selection is usually regarded as acting on the individual, with every animal in competition with every other, each trying to get as big a share of the next generation as possible. However, Wynne-Edwards (1962) set the ball rolling in another direction when he built up a theory of social behaviour based on the idea that selection acts at the group or population level. He argued that animal populations remain at an optimum size and thereby avoid eating out their food supply and becoming extinct. One mechanism he suggests for this is that certain individuals do not breed, group organisation being geared to ensure this. This theory highlighted the possibility that selection might act at a level above that of the individual, but it has a major obstacle. An animal which disobeys the rule to forgo breeding will pass more of its disobeying genes to the next generation, so that these genes will increase in frequency and the system will break down. The effects of individual selection will thus over-ride those at the level of the group. The selfish will flourish and the altruistic will die out.

It is relevant to discuss this particular point here because, although the theory of Wynne-Edwards has received little support, it led to changes in thinking about selection. One major problem was to understand cases where altruism appears to exist despite the fact that selection at the individual level might be expected to rule it out. It is worth considering this in some detail for two reasons. First, altruism, though relatively rare amongst animals, is common in our own species. Second, Bowlby (1969), in his major attempt to put human development in an evolutionary perspective, discussed the topic only briefly because he supposed selection to act at the group or species level, which we now realise is rarely if ever the case.

Trivers (1971) suggests one way in which altruism may arise within the framework of natural selection acting on the individual. This proposal is referred to as reciprocal altruism and the case for it is argued as follows. If the altruistic act costs the donor very little and benefits the recipient greatly it may be worth giving as long as the recipient is likely to repay the 'kindness' at some future date, even if the two animals involved are unrelated. Thus hurling a rope to a drowning man involves little risk, but may benefit him considerably. Nevertheless, in terms of natural selection it is only advantageous if such risks as are incurred are likely to be offset by a future benefit. With this type of argument 'cheating' is always a problem: what is to stop some individuals from accepting altruism without giving it in return? Trivers argues that others may withhold altruistic acts from such animals and thereby put them at a disadvantage, an explanation which depends on individual recognition and may account for the rarity of altruism amongst animals. On the other hand, this seems a reasonable explanation for the existence of altruism in human societies, remembering that man evolved in small groups in which each individual was likely to know all others. On a speculative level it might also account for reduced altruism towards strangers in, for example, large cities where the chances of meeting again are slight.

Another way in which apparently altruistic behaviour may evolve makes it necessary to consider a complication to the idea that natural selection takes place at the individual level rather than that of the group. Selection acts on animals, but it is through changes in genes that it has its effect. In fact it can be argued that animals are slaves to their genes: merely vehicles which they use to reproduce themselves. Obviously, the most direct way to get as many of one's genes as possible into the next generation is to survive, produce the maximum number of young and care for them well. There is, however, another way, as Hamilton (1964) has shown. An animal shares $\frac{1}{2}$ of its genes with each full brother or sister, $\frac{1}{8}$ with each first cousin and so on in decreasing proportion as the relationship gets weaker. As well as reproducing itself, it may therefore pay it to assist others to do so, the amount of assistance rendered depending on the extent to which genes are shared. Of course, the costs and benefits of such behaviour are not consciously worked out by the animal: natural selection will produce the most beneficial behaviour simply because the genes promoting it are favoured and so spread through the population. This process, known as kin selection, can explain a number of instances of apparent altruism in animals. In the future, knowledge of its effects may also be able to give us a fuller understanding of why animal societies have the structures that they do, though at present this is hindered in many cases by lack of information on the extent of the relationship between their members and on the extent to which their relationships are known to the individuals concerned. Once these are discovered, a more exact appraisal of the costs and benefits of helping others becomes feasible. If the costs are very slight, it may be advantageous to behave altruistically towards some remote cousin. If they are great, as for instance when one lays down one's life for another, this should only be done when several close relatives (e.g. at least two brothers or eight first cousins) will thereby survive, or for lesser gain by older animals which have a low potential for further reproduction. These are the sort of predictions made by the theory. It is also likely that the ability to recognise other individuals, or at least their degree of relatedness to itself, will be selected for so that the individual can behave appropriately towards them: otherwise behaviour towards them can only be based on their probable degree of relatedness. In the absence of cues, all others would have to be treated equally, even though it would be advantageous to treat cousins better and strangers worse.

In two further important papers, Trivers (1972, 1974) has applied Hamilton's theory, and analysis in terms of costs and benefits, to the relationship between the sexes and to that between a parent and its offspring. We can only summarise a few of the major points here. It is assumed that the two members of a breeding pair are not closely related to one another, and this is probably reasonable as inbreeding is disadvantageous and something equivalent to an incest taboo has been found in a number of animal species (e.g. Lindzey, 1967). This means that they should only help each other to the extent that this benefits their mutual offspring. In fact each should try to push the other into taking on a greater share of the parental burden. The willingness of one parent to accept an increased share will depend on what Trivers calls its previous 'investment'.[2] Thus, at the time of birth in a mammal, the female has invested considerably in the prospective progeny, not only in the form of an egg but in the time and physiological strain involved in pregnancy, while the male may have done little except to copulate with her.

Because of this prior investment, if the male takes little part in parental care, or even deserts her, it may be advantageous for her to increase her contribution, rather than cutting her losses and starting again. The male, with his lesser investment, is more likely to give up and seek another mate elsewhere rather than boost his share if the female deserts or contributes little. For a male, Trivers suggests that cuckolding other males may be a good reproductive strategy in those species where the male helps with parental care. Thus an animal which succeeds in mating with another's female while his back is turned makes little investment himself, as he avoids parental care and can spend the time and effort that he would devote to this mating with yet other females or rearing a family with his own mate. Yet he leaves more progeny and his genes are therefore at an advantage. On the other hand, mechanisms are likely to exist in females (or in either sex at a stage when it has invested more) to avoid being deserted, and in males to avoid being cuckolded by others and thus put in a position of inadvertently rearing their offspring. In the latter case, Trivers points to the long courtship period commonly found before mating as being advantageous because this enables the male to be sure that his female has not been inseminated by another before him, and also to the widespread existence of female guarding by the male in animals where the male assists in rearing the young.

This sort of conflict of interests which probably exists between mates may also be a feature of the relationship between a female and her offspring (Trivers, 1974). Suckling often delays the time when a female can have another young one. Early in lactation the costs of suckling are likely to be slight, little milk being required by a small infant, and the benefits great: the infant would probably die without it and thus the previous investment would be wasted. As lactation proceeds, however, the costs are likely to rise and the benefits to fall. When the former exceed the latter, it is advantageous to wean the young one, which will probably survive, and start investing in further offspring. From the point of view of the infant, the cost-benefit ratio of receiving parental care is likely to change differently from that of the mother. It has all of its own genes, whereas it has only half of hers: the young one's genes will thus benefit if it persists in demanding parental care at a time when it would be best for the mother to move on to the next infant. This argument predicts what has in fact been documented (e.g. Hinde and Spencer-Booth, 1967): that a conflict will occur at weaning because the mother rejects the attempts of the young one to continue feeding. It also predicts differences between species in which females mate with the same and with different males for successive offspring. The female gives half of her genes to each of her progeny and should therefore wean all at the same time. But the infant should try to delay weaning more, leading to greater conflict, where the next born will be a half-sib, with which it shares $\frac{1}{4}$ of its genes, than a full sib, with which it shares $\frac{1}{2}$.

I have included this account of recent changes in thinking about function and natural selection for several reasons. First, it illustrates the fact that thought in these areas has changed considerably over the last few years, and has become much more rigorous and quantitative in outlook. Second, it shows that a theory is emerging which makes strong predictions, and this will undoubtedly add direction and force to research in this area, which has previously been largely descriptive and speculative. But third comes my most important point. These theories are general, and will be applied increasingly to human beings (Trivers, 1974, cites man as a good example of some of the points he makes about parent–offspring conflict) yet, while the actual behaviour of humans fits in with many of the points they make, these very aspects of behaviour often run counter to ethics and morality. Desertion, cuckoldry and promiscuous mating by males all occur in human societies, but are usually regarded as failings rather than virtues. There is a possibility that a biological theory that accounts for them, and sets out the circumstances in which they are selectively advantageous, may be taken to give them a stamp of approval, so that a new brand of social Darwinism will arise. This is very dangerous ground, which deserves careful consideration before the inevitable popular accounts promote such ideas further.

The nearest to a popular book on this subject to appear so far is that by Dawkins (1976), but it is a relatively uncontroversial and scholarly treatment of the relevance of new ideas in evolution theory to the behaviour of animals. Dawkins is careful to keep his speculations within limits and, when he turns to man, his discussion skips to the established processes of cultural evolution rather than considering the more difficult question of the extent to which genetic evolution places constraints on human behaviour. He argues that the passage of ideas, or 'memes' as he calls them, between people overshadows in importance that of genes. But, as the rest of his book makes a strong case for the behaviour of animals being geared to the good of their genes, it is not clear why cultural evolution amongst humans should be regarded as on a totally different plane. In other words, to borrow his terminology, are not our genes likely to set limits to the memes which we can have, restricting them to those which are selectively advantageous? As the next section will show, views differ considerably on this sort of question.

Constraints on Man

In the previous sections we have considered two topics which are closely interrelated: the extent to which behaviour has a genetic basis and the way in which it is constrained by evolution. The problem we must now face is how well human behaviour fits in with the principles we have been discussing. Just how labile or stable is human behaviour and, allied to this, to what extent does our evolutionary heritage set limits to its modifiability?

Perhaps the leading proponent of applying evolutionary ideas to man is

Wilson (1975), who concludes his otherwise excellent book with a highly controversial chapter on human behaviour. In common with a number of other evolutionary biologists, and particularly those who work on invertebrates, he sees little objection to calling behaviours innate and places great emphasis on their genetic basis. In the case of man he supports his arguments by reference to heritability scores, without any consideration of their limitations. Though he pays lip-service to flexibility of behaviour in man, the gist of his argument is very much nativist. The extent to which this is so is illustrated by his suggestion that 'scientists and humanists should consider together the possibility that the time has come for ethics to be removed temporarily from the hands of philosophers and biologicized': an alarming idea when one has seen the prospect that this might afford. It is also surprising for a critic of advocacy in science to state baldly, without evidence, that 'deception and hypocrisy . . . are very human devices for conducting the complex daily business of social life'. One is left to wonder whether these traits are others which a biological ethic would condone.

Wilson's views are extreme and the tenets on which they are based run counter to much that we have discussed. Where it is possible to explain man's behaviour in terms of evolution theory, this is more likely to be because he has had the flexibility to adapt his environment to suit himself and his behaviour to suit his environment, rather than because his behaviour is genetically fixed to operate within narrow limits pre-set by evolution. Our knowledge of human evolution suggests that man evolved in the tropics, living there in small groups of hunter-gatherers (see for example Pilbeam, 1972). Not only has he now spread throughout the globe, but many humans now live in much larger social units and most neither hunt nor gather. Natural selection preadapted man for these changes, but during their course he has moved increasingly outside its ambit. He has become post-evolutionary, the changes between one generation and the next being more due to cultural than genetic influences. As we have previously noted, the same genes in a changed environment may give a changed outcome: cultural evolution over generations and learning within the individual lifetime make it possible for adaptation to continue without genetic change. That man continues to behave in a selectively advantageous manner is then due to the ultimate trump-card of evolution: a preadaptation to work out solutions for himself, the perfect answer for an unpredictable environment or one with which genetic evolution cannot keep pace. To illustrate this, take the example of reciprocal altruism mentioned earlier, a mechanism suggested by Trivers (1971) as important in human social relationships. Perhaps this mode of behaviour has evolved over millions of years because it is selectively advantageous; alternatively, perhaps someone with the appropriate genetic prerequisites hit upon it as a good way to run social relations and it has been passed on culturally since then. Either way genetic factors are of importance and adaptation is achieved since learning, as defined by most biologists, is an adaptive process, as is evolution. The main difference between these routes to adaptation lies not in the adaptiveness of the outcome, but in the fact that in the first case the behaviour is likely to be stable, even appearing in environmental circumstances where it is inappropriate, whereas in the second different environments are likely to lead to different solutions. Behaviour which is selectively advantageous need not therefore be stable and unmodifiable.

Despite the fact that much of human behaviour does seem to fit in with evolution theory, some features suggest that a change in the rules is taking place. Institutions and structures have been generated which cannot simply be attributed to natural selection acting at the individual or kin level. Ethics have been developed which place more value on the individual human life and less on procreation than evolution theory would predict. Animal societies can legitimately be regarded as collections of individuals each seeking the furtherance of its genes. While it is generally true that humans enjoy doing what is good for their genes, they are subject to other constraints, primarily educational and legal, which limit their freedom to do so in such a way that the group as a whole does not suffer. That such constraints as these can override evolutionary ones is best illustrated by the fact that so many human societies have succeeded in breaking the most fundamental rule of natural selection: that each individual should endeavour to produce as many surviving children as possible. To escape from this evolutionary dictum, human behaviour must indeed be flexible.

The important question for the future is not so much whether human behaviour can be fitted into an evolutionary framework, but whether particular aspects of it are stable or labile. Put differently, does our evolutionary history limit the possibilities as far as modifiability is concerned? There can be no doubt that some constraints of this sort do exist and that, as is the case with animals, some elements of human behaviour are more labile than others. Though it is hard to think of stable behaviours in man, there are several elements which show cross-cultural similarities, such as laughing, crying and blushing (Darwin, 1872), eye-brow raising in greeting (Eibl-Eibesfeldt, 1971) and some features of language (Chomsky, 1972), and these therefore develop similarly in a variety of environments. The fact that these behaviours are widespread does not, however, imply either a strong genetic basis or an ancient evolutionary history. Another possibility is that there is a single best way of organising a particular behaviour and that patterns which were originally diverse have converged upon this optimum form. In the case of language it is also possible that this form of communication arose only once and that all current languages are derived from this single original. Though they have changed considerably as cultures have separated and merged, they retain certain basic features in common. Recent cultural evolution which, though analogous, has little to do with either Darwinian evolution or genetics, could account for both these types of influence. Nevertheless, however it is achieved, some elements of behaviour do show great stability, perhaps because they are involved in communication, a category of behaviour which must be stereotyped because it must be understood by other individuals.

As well as in individual behaviour patterns such as these, stability of development undoubtedly also exists in motivational systems. Some of these effects are rather obvious: given the evolutionary importance of self preservation and reproduction it is clear why pain should be unpleasant and eating and mating enjoyable. Yet again, however, this stability does not imply that any modification is out of the question. Melzack and Scott (1957) found that dogs raised in isolation chambers were slow to learn to avoid an object which gave them an electric shock: while normally reared animals ran away squealing, the isolated ones would investigate it without apparent signs of pain. Although the effect was a temporary one, this does illustrate that rearing conditions can modify a response as basic as that to pain. Evolutionary constraints may also have a strong influence on sleep. On the basis of comparative evidence, which shows species to vary enormously in their daily requirement for sleep, Meddis (1975) argues convincingly that this behaviour evolved as a mechanism for immobilising animals at times of day to which they were ill-adapted. He suggests that the recuperative role of sleep is a later development, various regenerative functions having subsequently become tied to the period of immobility. Even though humans no longer require to sleep at night to avoid predators, these later developments may make sleep a physiological necessity. On the other hand, it may simply be a legacy from the past. It is certainly true that some humans sleep very little, and it will be interesting to see whether ways can be found of drastically reducing the daily requirement of others.

The area of development is one in which some evolutionary constraints are likely to exist because, as mentioned earlier, the behaviour of the newborn human is more the product of evolution than is that of the adult. Indeed in such a species, where adults vary greatly in both experience and behaviour, making it possible and likely that they will try to adopt a variety of different child-rearing strategies, it would not be surprising if a system had evolved whereby the child played a large part in controlling the upbringing given to it. This is, however, a speculation of the sort with which evolutionary thinking is generous, and hypotheses do not further understanding without being tested. We have already discussed the difficulty of testing evolutionary hypotheses, the dangers of generalising between species and the risks of jumping to conclusions on the basis of selected or inadequate evidence. These difficulties are particularly great in the case of man and, as human behaviour is a matter of practical as well as academic importance, it is imperative not to assume the existence of constraints where none may exist. Given the changed environment in which development takes place and the modifiability of human behaviour, it is safer to assume that evolutionary constraints have a relatively small part to play, unless it can be proved otherwise. Whether or not particular aspects of human behaviour are easily modified is a matter for empirical testing rather than armchair speculation based on the comparative evidence.

In support of this last point, it is noteworthy that little has come of much of the evolutionary speculation about human behaviour which has taken place in the past few years because of the difficulties of testing hypotheses of this nature. The clearest case of a hypothesis from evolution being tested on man is that on lactation patterns described by Blurton Jones (1972, pp. 305–328). Some mammals leave their young in caches and give them infrequent feeds with milk of high protein and fat content; others carry them and feed them 'on demand' with milk which is much weaker in these constituents. Both the composition of human milk and other comparative evidence suggest that man belongs to the latter category: a conclusion with clear relevance to those who advise on child-rearing because it involves a physiological constraint as well as possible behavioural ones. While few can now doubt that human milk is that to which babies are adapted, if one must feed on schedule, then it is probably more likely to succeed with the nutritionally richer bottled milk. Some other constraints are more obvious than this: clearly babies, unlike lambs, cannot walk at birth, and a sensitive period exists for achieving this capability, as for others such as language development. The timing of these sensitive periods can doubtless be modified to some extent by sophisticated educational techniques from that originally determined by evolution, but limits to this are likely. So much of development consists of building one stage upon the last that a major change of schedule is probably impossible.

Despite these examples, to invoke evolutionary constraints to explain aspects of human behaviour is, in most cases, like attributing them to instinct: it is a cloak for ignorance with little explanatory power. Each case must be taken on its merits, but one must not forget that the behaviour of man is more modifiable than that of any other species and that he has escaped from the forces of evolution to a greater degree. Wilson looks forward to what he calls 'a genetically accurate and hence completely fair code of ethics'. This is surely a *non sequitur*: while genetic accuracy will set broad limits, the problem will be to define fairness.

Acknowledgements

I am grateful to Professor R. J. Andrew, Dr P. Clifton, Dr J. H. Mackintosh and Mr J. Sants for their comments on an earlier draft of this article.

Notes

1. The same may be said of I.Q. differences in humans, except that here there is also the question of whether the measure itself is an appropriate one.

2. For the purposes of illustration the term investment is used rather loosely here. In fact Trivers defines parental investment as 'any investment by the parent in an individual offspring that increases the offspring's chance of surviving (and hence reproductive success) at the cost of the parent's ability to invest in other offspring'.

References

Altmann, S. A. and Altmann, J. (1970). *Baboon Ecology: African Field Research*, University of Chicago Press, Chicago

Bateson, P. P. G. and Chantrey, D. F. (1972). Retardation of discrimination learning in monkeys and chicks previously exposed to both stimuli. *Nature*, **237**, 173–174

Beach, F. A. (1950). The snark was a boojum. *Amer. Psychol.*, **5**, 115–124

Bitterman, M. E. (1965). The evolution of intelligence. *Sci. Amer.*, **212**, 92–100

Blurton Jones, N. (ed.) (1972). *Ethological Studies of Child Behaviour*, Cambridge University Press, London

Bolles, R. C. (1970). Species-specific defence reactions and avoidance learning. *Psychol. Rev.*, **77**, 32–48

Bowlby, J. (1969). *Attachment*. Hogarth Press, London.

Chantrey, D. F. (1972). Enhancement and retardation of discrimination learning in chicks after exposure to the discriminanda. *J. comp. physiol. Psychol.*, **81**, 256–261

Chantrey, D. F. (1974). Stimulus preexposure and discrimination learning by domestic chicks: effect of varying interstimulus time. *J. comp. physiol. Psychol.*, **87**, 517–525

Chomsky, N. (1972). *Language and Mind*, Harcourt, Brace, Jovanovich, New York

Crook, J. H. (1970). Social organisation and the environment: aspects of contemporary social ethology. *Anim. Behav.*, **18**, 197–209

Darwin, C. (1859). *The Origin of Species by Means of Natural Selection*, Murray, London

Darwin, C. (1872). *The Expression of the Emotions in Man and Animals*, Murray, London

Dawkins, R. (1976). *The Selfish Gene*. Oxford University Press, Oxford

Domjan, M. and Wilson, N. E. (1972). Specificity of cue to consequence in aversion learning in the rat. *Psychon. Sci.*, **26**, 143–145

Eibl-Eibesfeldt, I. (1963). Angeborenes und Erworbenes im Verhalten einiger Sauger. *Z. Tierpsychol.*, **20**, 705–754

Eibl-Eibesfeldt, I. (1971). *Ethology: The Biology of Behavior*. Holt, Rinehart & Winston, New York

Feldman, M. W. and Lewontin, R. C. (1975). The heritability hang-up. *Science*, **190**, 1163–1168

Fraenkel, G. S. and Gunn, D. L. (1940). *The Orientation of Animals*. Clarendon Press, Oxford

Garcia, J., Clarke, J. C. and Hankins, W. G. (1972). Natural responses to scheduled rewards. In *Perspectives in Ethology*, (ed. P. P. G. Bateson and P. H. Klopfer) Plenum Press, New York

Goodall, J. (1968). Behaviour of free-living chimpanzees of the Gombe stream area. *Anim. Behav. Monogr.*, **1**, 161–311

Grossen, N. E. and Kelley, M. J. (1972). Species-specific behavior acquisition of avoidance behavior in rats. *J. comp. physiol. Psychol.*, **81**, 307–310

Hailman, J. P. (1967). The ontogeny of an instinct. *Behaviour Suppl.*, **15**, 1–159

Hamilton, W. D. (1964). The genetical theory of social behaviour. *J. theoret. Biol.*, **7**, 1–52

Harlow, H. F., Gluck, J. P. and Suomi, S. J. (1972). Generalization of behavioral data between nonhuman and human animals. *Amer. Psychol.*, **27**, 709–716

Hebb, D. O. (1953). Heredity and environment in mammalian behaviour. *Brit. J. Anim. Behav.*, **1**, 43–47

Hinde, R. A. (1970). *Animal Behaviour.* McGraw-Hill, New York

Hinde, R. A. and Spencer-Booth, Y. (1967). The behaviour of socially living rhesus monkeys in their first two and a half years. *Anim. Behav.*, **15**, 169–196

Hinde, R. A. and Stevenson-Hinde, J. (eds.) (1972). *Constraints on Learning.* Academic Press, London

Hirsch, J. (1970). Behavior-genetic analysis and its biosocial consequences. *Seminars in Psychiatry*, **2**, 89–105

Hodos, W. and Campbell, C. B. G. (1969). *Scala naturae*: Why there is no theory in comparative psychology. *Psychol. Rev.*, **76**, 337–350

Immelmann, K. (1976). The evolutionary significance of early experience. In *Function and Evolution in Behaviour*, (ed. G. Baerends, C. Beer and A. Manning) Clarendon Press, Oxford

Jackson, P. S. and Bateson, P. P. G. (1974). Imprinting and exploration of slight novelty in chicks. *Nature*, **251**, 609–610

Jensen, A. R. (1969). How much can we boost I.Q. and scholastic achievement? *Harvard Educ. Rev.*, **39**, 1–123

Kear, J. (1967). Experiments with young nidifugous birds on a visual cliff. *Wildfowl Trust Annual Report*, **18**, 122–124

Kruuk, H. (1972). *The Spotted Hyena.* University of Chicago Press, Chicago

Kummer, H. (1971). *Primate Societies: Group Techniques of Ecological Adaptation.* Aldine-Atherton, Chicago

Layzer, D. (1974). Heritability analyses of I.Q. scores: science or numerology? *Science*, **183**, 1259–1266

Lehrman, D. S. (1953). A critique of Konrad Lorenz's theory of instinctive behavior. *Quart. Rev. Biol.*, **28**, 337–363

Lehrman, D. S. (1970). Semantic and conceptual issues in the nature-nurture problem. In *Development and Evolution of Behavior*, (ed. L. R. Aronson, E. Tobach, D. S. Lehrman and J. S. Rosenblatt) Freeman, San Francisco

Lindzey, G. (1967). Some remarks concerning incest, the incest taboo and psychoanalytic theory. *Amer. Psychol.*, **22**, 1051–1059

Lockard, R. B. (1971). Reflections on the fall of comparative psychology: is there a message for us all? *Amer. Psychol.*, **26**, 168–179

Lorenz, K. (1935). Der Kumpan in der Umwelt des Vogels. *J. f. Ornith.*, **83**, 137–213, 289–413

Lorenz, K. (1950). The comparative method in studying innate behaviour patterns. *Sym. Soc. exp. Biol.*, **4**, 221–268

Lorenz, K. (1965). *Evolution and Modification of Behavior*, University of Chicago Press, Chicago

Lorenz, K. (1966). *On Aggression*, Methuen, London

Lorenz, K (1970). *Studies in Animal and Human Behaviour*, Vol. 1, Methuen, London

Martin, R. D. (1974). The biological basis of human behaviour. In *The Biology of Brains*, (ed. W. B. Broughton) Blackwells, Oxford

Meddis, R. (1975). On the function of sleep. *Anim. Behav.*, **23**, 676–691

Melzack, R. and Scott, T. H. (1957). The effects of early experience on the response to pain. *J. comp. physiol. Psychol.*, **50**, 155–161

Nottebohm, F. (1972). The origins of vocal learning. *Am. Nat.*, **106**, 116–140

Pilbeam, D. (1972). *The Ascent of Man*, Macmillan, New York

Richards, M. P. M. (ed.) (1974). *The Integration of a Child into a Social World.* Cambridge University Press, London

Schaller, G. B. (1963). *The Mountain Gorilla: Ecology and Behavior.* University of Chicago Press, Chicago

Schleidt, W. M. (1961). Reaktionen von Truthuhnern auf fliegende Raubvogel und Versuche zur Analyse ihrer AAM's. *Z. Tierpsychol.*, **18**, 534–560

Shettleworth, S. J. (1972). Constraints on learning. *Advances in the Study of Behavior*, **4**, 1–68

Smith, P. K. (1974). Ethological methods. In *New Perspectives in Child Development* (ed. B. Foss), Penguin Education, Harmondsworth

Stockard, C. R. (1909). The development of artificially produced cyclopean fish – 'the magnesium embryo'. *J. exp. Zool.*, **6**, 285–337

Thompson, W. R. (1954). Development and inheritance of integrated neurological and psychiatric patterns. *Proceedings of the Association for Research in Nervous and Mental Diseases*, **33**, 209–231

Tinbergen, N. (1951). *The Study of Instinct*, Clarendon Press, Oxford

Tinbergen, N. (1963). On aims and methods of ethology. *Z. Tierpsychol.*, **20**, 410–433

Tinbergen, N. and Perdeck, A. C. (1950). On the stimulus situation releasing the begging response in the newly hatched herring gull chick. *Behaviour*, **3**, 1–39

Trivers, R. L. (1971). The evolution of reciprocal altruism. *Quart. Rev. Biol.*, **46**, 35–57

Trivers, R. L. (1972). Parental investment and sexual selection. In *Sexual Selection and the Descent of Man, 1871–1971*, (ed. B. Campbell) Aldine-Atherton, Chicago

Trivers, R. L. (1974). Parent-offspring conflict. *Amer. Zool.*, **14**, 249–264

Wilson, E. O. (1975). *Sociobiology: The New Synthesis*, Harvard University Press, Cambridge, Massachusetts

Wynne-Edwards, V. C. (1962). *Animal Dispersion in Relation to Social Behaviour*, Oliver & Boyd, Edinburgh

4 Some Methodological Issues in Developmental Research

HARRY McGURK

(Department of Psychology, University of Surrey, Guildford, Surrey, England)

Introduction: A Four-Dimensional Model of Developmental Research Methods

Developmental psychology can be defined as the systematic study of mental and behavioural development in humans. Its concern is to understand those changes in ability and behaviour which are associated with increasing age. The task of the developmental psychologist, therefore, is to specify the nature of the psychological processes underlying age-related changes in ability and behaviour. The task, in effect, is a twofold one: firstly, to identify and describe developmental phenomena—changes in behaviour occurring along the dimension of age—and, secondly, to provide an explanatory account of the phenomena thus identified. It bears stressing in this context that age itself cannot be regarded as an explanatory variable; growing older does not cause behavioural change. Ten-year-old children can do many things that five-year-olds cannot, but the explanation for this does not lie in the fact that the former are five years older than the latter. Chronological age is simply a convenient way of measuring the passage of time since birth, but the mere passage of time does not explain behavioural change. It is for this reason that age is sometimes referred to as a carrier or index variable, a dimension within which the processes which do cause behavioural development may be located. These processes—experiential, maturational, physiological—co-vary with increasing age simply because they require time in which to occur. Ultimately, however, explanations for developmental phenomena are sought in terms of the variables which moderate the course of the changes in ability and behaviour that are observed to take place with increasing age. It is with some of the methodological issues which arise in the study of age-related changes in behaviour that this chapter is concerned.

McCandless (1967, 1970), following Spiker (1966), has advanced a four-dimensional model within which any research study in developmental psychology may be precisely located in terms of its objectives and methodology. The dimensions, or continua in question are (1) normative (descriptive)–explanatory; (2) atheoretical–theoretical; (3) naturalistic–manipulative; (4) ahistorical–historical. It should perhaps be pointed out that this is a different sequence of presentation than that offered by McCandless who discusses these dimensions in the sequence (1), (4), (3), (2). However, it appears to the writer that the present sequence is a more logical arrangement; dimensions (1) and (2), broadly speaking, refer to research objectives whereas dimensions (3) and (4) have more specific methodological connotations. However, the sequencing is relatively arbitrary and it is clear that, although logically and conceptually distinct, values on the dimensions are likely to vary interdependently rather than independently for any given research project. For example, a researcher with a disposition toward a learning theory account of human development is likely to conceptualize his research problems in stimulus–response–reinforcement terms, to operate towards the explanatory end of the normative–explanatory dimension and to engage in manipulative, laboratory-based investigations rather than conduct his observations within naturalistic settings. Nevertheless, the McCandless model does provide a useful framework within which to consider methodological issues arising in research on psychological development.

The Normative (Descriptive)–Explanatory Dimension

The investigator operating at the normative descriptive end of this dimension seeks to establish the average behaviour or the frequency of occurrence of particular types of behaviour, to describe behavioural norms for children at different ages. The systematic study of child development blossomed during the first half of this century and much of the initial research effort was directed towards detailed, descriptive investigation of behavioural development. Large scale, normative data were collected to determine the sequence of physical and motor development: when the infant first sits unaided, when walking can first be observed, the onset of visually guided reaching and grasping, when small objects are first retrieved by thumb and forefinger in opposition as opposed to the scrabbling, palmar grasping of early infancy. It became fashionable to publish behavioural schedules describing when particular developmental milestones are reached and illustrating the motor behaviour typical of children at different ages and stages of development (see, for example, Shirley, 1933; Gesell and Amatruda, 1941).

Careful and detailed description of the phenomena under investigation represents an essential phase in the development of any discipline and is a necessary precursor to the elaboration of explanatory accounts for the phenomena of interest. Moreover, normative data provide a valuable rule-of-thumb against which to compare individual performance. On the basis of normative data we know that there is little cause for concern on the part of parents of a twelve-month-old who is yet to take his first unaided step, though by the same token they may be justly concerned if he is still not walking at twenty months. On the other hand, norms do not provide explanations, though they may sometimes be disguised as such. Parent: 'Why is my two-year-old, who was previously such a nice, attractive, amenable child now so bloody-minded and difficult to control?' 'Expert': 'Oh, but all two-year-olds go through a negative phase.' The parent may feel relieved and the expert relatively satisfied that he has given an explanation for a commonly occurring experience. In fact, nothing has been explained, for norms can never be explanations. Normative research may establish the what of behaviour but cannot provide answers to how or why questions.

Developmental research has other goals than mere description. Explanation of the phenomena described is an important aim and for explanation we need to go beyond the compilation of frequencies and averages. Accordingly, research located towards the explanatory pole of the normative–explanatory dimension has as its goal the identification of the processes which have a causal relationship to the phenomena observed. Usually, though not necessarily, such research will be guided by theory, testifying again to the interdependency between the four dimensions specified by McCandless.

The Atheoretical–Theoretical Dimension

The role of theory in developmental psychology, as in any other discipline, is to provide a coherent set of principles which will serve to account adequately for already established observations and, either inductively or deductively, to yield predictions leading to new observations. A good theory serves to organise and integrate existing knowledge. In addition, it acts as a guide to research and, in consequence, leads to the discovery of new knowledge and understanding.

Theories serve to reflect reality. They are not descriptions of reality. Rather, they are representations which assist comprehension of reality. Theory-based research, therefore, always has at least the potentiality of providing information which will expand the understanding of development. If the data from such research are commensurate with theoretically derived predictions, then the theory is to that extent validated and our confidence in it as an adequate reflection of reality is increased. However, even negative results from theory-guided research are useful in that they provide the impetus for clarification and refinement of the theory. Theory-based research, therefore, enables one to go beyond the information given in facts or descriptions to the reasons why the facts or descriptions turn out to be as they are.

Suppose the fictional expert in the previous example, instead of invoking the norm (or the myth!) of the 'terrible twos' as an explanation for the fractiousness of a particular two-year-old, had reasoned along the following lines. The literature on language development (e.g. Brown, 1973; Halliday, 1975) illustrates the extent to which two-year-old children have the capacity to generate socially relevant meanings and intentions but are deficient in the ability to communicate these meanings and intentions in the conventional meaning system represented by the language of their adult caretakers. During the period of holophrastic speech, for example, the young child is restricted to using one or two words to convey his meanings; the single word hole may be used by the child to mean variously 'look, there's a hole'; 'make a hole'; 'put (object) into the hole', depending upon context. Parental expansion of children's utterances into conventional language represents an active search after their meaning and it is clear from such interactions that the child means more than he says. On the basis of our theoretical understanding of language development, it might be hypothesised that much of the parent–child conflict said to be typical of the two-year-old has its origins in the frustration the child experiences as a consequence of the discrepancy between his competence (i.e. his capacity to generate socially relevant meanings and intentions) on the one hand, and his performance (i.e. ability to communicate in language) on the other. This formulation, albeit only crudely based upon the competence–performance distinction, leads to a set of interrelated predictions each of which is testable: (i) that as the child develops proficiency in language, so should negative behaviour decline; (ii) that individual differences in language development during the period in question should be related to individual differences in child–parent conflict; (iii) that, similarly, individual differences in parental understanding of the protostructure of the child's language or in parental ability to gain access to the child's meaning system should be related to individual differences in child–parent conflict. Investigations designed to test such predictions would facilitate evaluation of the original hypothesis and might enhance understanding of language development and of the relationships between language development and social behaviour.

Data derived from research located towards the theoretical pole of the atheoretical–theoretical dimension are more readily integrated with existing findings and serve to enhance theoretical understanding of developmental processes. However, research is frequently carried out for purposes other than theoretical ones. Research may be required to solve a particular practical problem. McGurk (1977), for example, conducted a series of experiments as part of a preventative programme aimed at reducing the risk of infants and young children being poisoned in the home by their spontaneous ingestion of small objects containing harmful chemicals. For example, many household chemical products come in solid form and a significant proportion of accidental poisonings occur during periods when these products are in legitimate use but the infant is momentarily unsupervised (e.g. the mother is about to use the product, removes it from its container and then is distracted by a telephone call or other minor emergency); at such moments, nothing stands between the young child's ability to put the object into his mouth and the danger of his being injured thereby. Both Freudian and Piagetean theory address the issues of infant oral behaviour but neither offer much guidance in the present context. The aims of McGurk's research, therefore, were entirely empirical: to develop a shape for small solids which infants and toddlers would find difficulty in grasping, which, if grasped successfully, would entail a high probability of being dropped and which, if successfully held and transported to the mouth, would present a minimum surface area for insertion into the oral cavity.

Other atheoretical research may be conducted to confirm at a formal level some observation which the investigator has previously made in an informal context. Alternatively, research may be carried out to answer empirical questions of the type, 'Of methods a and b, which is the more efficient to use to teach children aged x years to perform task y?' and so on. Well conducted empirical research can provide meaningful answers to clearly formulated empirical questions. Such answers may even be found to have theoretical relevance *ex post facto*, but until such relevance is predictively tested then its validity is assumed rather than demonstrated. At the end of the day, empirically oriented research may result merely in another fact without a theoretical home. Well established facts are a challenge to understanding, but they do not represent understanding in themselves.

The Naturalistic–Manipulative Dimension

The location of a given research study on this dimension is dependent upon the extent to which the particular method of data collection employed interferes with the normally occurring behaviour of the subject and or with the environment within which the behaviour is displayed. At one pole of the dimension lie those studies employing the methods of naturalistic observation. Naturalistic observation involves the study of the spontaneous behaviour of unrestrained organisms (babies, children, adolescents, etc.) in the naturally occurring settings of everyday life. A researcher using this technique, having decided upon the behaviour of interest and the method of recording, in no way attempts to manipulate his subjects' environment or to interfere with the range of behaviour displayed; the focus is upon behaviour as it freely occurs. A little more toward the manipulative pole are located those studies employing the methods of controlled observation. Here, either to observe the effect of environmental manipulation upon the manifestation of a particular behaviour, or to increase the probability that the behaviour of interest will actually occur, the observer conducts his observations within a controlled setting. However, focus is still upon the spontaneous display of behaviour within that setting and there is no restriction upon the range of behaviours in which the subject engages. At the manipulative extreme of the dimension lie those studies employing the methods of controlled experimentation. Here control is exercised over all environmental and organismic variables likely to influence the behaviour of interest in a significant way and the subject is restricted to emitting behaviour (frequently referred to in this context as responses) from within a circumscribed range.

Detailed discussion of the data-collection techniques available to developmental researchers and of research methodology can be found in Mussen (1960), Hutt and Hutt (1970) and Wohlwill (1973); McGurk (1975) provides a brief overview. However, although a wide variety of specific procedures are employed in the investigation of developmental phenomena, the vast majority can be regarded as variations or adaptations of four basic types of procedure. Three—naturalistic observation, controlled observation and experimentation—have already been mentioned. The fourth is standardised testing. Published versions of standard tests contain relatively precise instructions for the administration and scoring of each item. Accordingly, standardised testing has many of the characteristics of experimental investigation. Each subject is presented with an identical series of stimuli—test items—under controlled conditions; the acceptable range of responses is limited. Thus, investigations employing standardised testing are located toward the manipulatory pole of the naturalistic–manipulatory dimension.

During the earlier part of the century, much child-psychological research was concerned with socialisation processes, social and personality development. The principal methods were those of naturalistic and controlled observation. Much of the work was atheoretical and dealt with complex variables which are difficult to define or control. Through to the late 1930s the emphasis was upon descriptive studies. Perhaps inevitably, therefore, there was a decline of interest in developmental psychology around this time. As Stevenson (1968) points out, the allure of describing the behaviour of children could not sustain the interest of researchers in the face of the challenges being presented in other areas of the rapidly expanding science of psychology. In consequence, the number of new researchers entering the developmental field trailed off as did the number of publications on developmental topics; the latter halved between 1938 and 1949.

Around the early 1950s, however, developmental psychology itself entered a new phase of development and expansion, one that continues to the present. A number of factors have contributed to this revitalization of the field. In the first place, there occurred what Wohlwill (1973) has called the 'invasion of the experimentalists' into developmental psychology. Disillusioned perhaps, with the relevance of the rodent orientation of the behaviourist tradition, an increasing number of researchers trained in the rigours of experimental psychology turned their attention to the analysis of psychological aspects of human development. In consequence, techniques of measurement and control that had proved effective in the field of general experimental psychology were applied to the study of developmental topics. Moreover, there was a commensurate shift in focus from studies of general behavioural development to experimental investigation of clearly defined problems in such areas as perceptual, learning and attentional development. As a result, developmental psychology has become more fully integrated within the general discipline of psychology than it perhaps was in an earlier era.

A second major factor contributing to the resurgence of interest in developmental psychology was the discovery, or rather rediscovery, of the work of Piaget. Piaget has been continuously active in the study of the growth of knowledge and understanding in children for more than half a century. However, he published in complex and difficult French and it was not until the mid-1950s, when his work became more widely available in English translation, that his ideas had a profound effect upon developmental psychologists in Britain and the USA. From then on, however, his influence has dominated the field of cognitive development. Much initial effort was devoted to replicating the various findings reported by Piaget, for in his work on cognition he had employed the older methods of observation and clinical interview. It was necessary to establish, therefore, that his results could also be obtained under more controlled conditions and that his findings could be verified by rigorous statistical analysis. On the whole, Piaget's original observations have been reproduced with remarkable consistency and in contemporary times Piaget-oriented research, the bulk of it experimentally based, accounts for one of the largest single entries in the annual abstracts of psychological research.

A third factor responsible for the revitalization of developmental psychology has been a renewal of interest in the very origins of behaviour. During the past several years, there has been a marked increase in the number of research studies involving very young infants as subjects with the aim of determining precisely the repertoire of skills and behaviours available to the infant from birth. How functional are the newborn's auditory and visual systems and how are they interrelated? What kinds of perceptual discrimination is the newborn capable of? How soon after birth is the infant's behavioural repertoire, however limited it may be, modified by the procedures of conditioning and reinforcement? These are among the kinds of question toward which much recent and current research is directed with the goals of tracing development from the point of origin in ontogeny and of identifying the variables which influence development. Although some of this work is essentially observational, the predominant trend in infancy research has been toward experimentally based methodologies.

The combined effect of these three influences—the invasion of the experimentalists, the rediscovery of Piaget and the renewed interest in infant behaviour—has been to shift the bias of developmental research away from the naturalistic and towards the manipulative pole of naturalistic–manipulative dimension. An entire journal, *The Journal of Experimental Child Psychology* is now exclusively devoted to the publication of manipulative research. Moreover, the papers published in contemporary issues of the more general journals, for example *Child Development*, are predominantly experimental–manipulative in orientation, and these papers report studies which are more likely to have been conducted in child development laboratories than in the homes, streets, shops, playgrounds or schoolrooms where young children spend much of their waking lives. It is this feature of contemporary research that has led Bronfenbrenner (1974, 1977) to protest that most of our present knowledge of developmental processes is derived from studies of children doing strange things in strange situations in the presence of strange adults! Bronfenbrenner's stricture is heavy with the implication that knowledge so derived is of little relevance to the understanding of the child's spontaneous behaviour in its natural environment.

There are two aspects of Bronfenbrenner's criticism of laboratory-based, manipulative research which are worthy of consideration. The first of these refers to the apparently atypical, highly artificial nature of much behaviour that is made the object of laboratory study. The second relates to the fact that the process of manipulation, whether in terms of environmental or behavioural constraint, may frequently distort the measurements or observations being made. These two points will be illustrated by examples drawn, respectively, from studies of infant sucking behaviour and from the study of linguistic communication in preschool and older children.

Over the past decade a voluminous research literature has emerged based upon the study of infant sucking behaviour (see Crook, 1978 for a recent review). The sucking response is one of the most highly organised behaviours with which the neonate is endowed at birth and it has the distinct advantage, from the experimental psychologist's view point, of being readily and reliably measurable. An impressive technology has developed around this behaviour whereby, by means of specially adapted teats connected to pressure transducers, such parameters of sucking behaviour as number of sucks per sucking burst, duration of bursts, duration of pauses, rate of sucking, amplitude of sucking can all be automatically recorded and measured. On the basis of research employing such apparatus we have come to understand a great deal about the temporal and structural organization of sucking and about its co-ordination with other behaviours such as swallowing or looking and listening. In addition, because it can be so conveniently measured and is readily brought under operant control, the sucking response has frequently been employed as a dependent variable in studies of infant learning and perception. In this respect, as Crook (1978) points out, the sucking response has served psychologists in much the same way as the lever-pressing response of the laboratory rat.

This kind of experimental investigation of sucking behaviour, however, entirely ignores the context in which sucking normally occurs. In the experimental laboratory, the infant is alone with his teat; in the natural situation there is invariably another person, the caretaker, present. In other words, sucking normally occurs in a social context. Thus, while laboratory study of the isolated infant may provide much information about the organisation of sucking behaviour and about its plasticity, it has little to contribute to our understanding of the function of sucking behaviour in the social context to which it is presumably adapted. It is only relatively recently that developmental psychologists have begun to investigate the significance for social development of sucking activity in the natural context and already the harvest has been a rich one. For example, Kaye (1977), in an observational study of mothers feeding their infants during the latter's first month of life, has demonstrated how, in this context, mother–infant interaction is organised around the pattern of infant sucking. Mothers tend to be relatively passive during sucking bouts and to talk to, or stroke or jiggle the baby primarily during pauses between sucking bursts. Duration of the latter is related to the duration of maternal activity. Thus, while mothers may believe that they engage in such activity in order to stimulate the baby into sucking again, their behaviour has the opposite effect of prolonging the pause! The resultant pattern of interaction is one in which baby sucks and mother is passive, baby stops sucking and mother talks to and or strokes the baby, mother stops this activity and baby starts sucking again. Kaye sees in this elementary turn-taking behaviour the foundations of social dialogue. This aspect of the significance of sucking activity could not have been illuminated by the kinds of experimental–manipulative investigations referred to earlier.

In studies of cognitive development, much is frequently made of the egocentrism of the young child's linguistic communications. For example, a five-year-old is asked if he has any brothers or sisters. He replies that he has a brother called William. If he is asked if William has any brothers, there is a very high probability that he will answer negatively (Piaget, 1951). The child is thus held to be incapable of departing from his own point of view and of recognising that the fraternal relationship is a reciprocal one, that he is also a brother to his brother. Failure to take the needs and perspective of another into account has also been frequently reported in studies of communication by older children. For example, Flavell et al. (1968) required two groups of children, one aged approximately seven years, the other approximately thirteen years, to learn how to play a simple board game. Each child learned the game by playing it with one of the experimenters under conditions of silence. The children were then instructed to inform in turn, two apparently naive adults how to play the game; one of the adults wore a blindfold over his eyes. In their explanations, the thirteen-year-olds took into account the fact that the latter adult was unable to see and provided longer and more detailed descriptions than for the sighted adults. The younger children failed to discriminate in this way and provided the same kind of description for blindfolded as for sighted adults. The seven-year-olds were just as aware as the older children of the difference between the two adults, but did not seem to be capable of taking this into account when formulating their explanations.

By contrast, Maratsos (1973) found that three-year-old children provided an adult with quite different instructions when they had to tell her how to carry out a simple task under sighted and unsighted conditions. The procedure was presented to the children as a game in which they had to tell the experimenter which of several toys was to be put into a model car before it was rolled down a slope toward the child. When the adult's eyes were uncovered, the children tended to point mutely to the toy of their choice. On the other hand, when the adult covered her eyes with her hands, the children would verbally label the toy of their choice, perhaps also describing its colour: 'The red duck'. Thus, these young children adapted their instructions to the needs of the listener so that, once her hands were removed from her eyes, the adult was able unambiguously to identify the toy intended by the child.

There are many possible explanations as to why the three-year-olds in the Maratsos study behaved less egocentrically than the seven-year-olds in the experiment by Flavell *et al.* For one thing, the Flavell procedure required a greater memory and information-processing load than the simple naming task involved in Maratsos' study and the sheer difficulty of the former may have influenced the performance of the seven-year-olds, causing them to display an immature mode of functioning. On the other hand, as Flavell (1977) acknowledges, the Maratsos procedure is more natural and has a greater spontaneity to it than does the rather formal, somewhat contrived process of one adult silently playing a game with a school-child and then requiring the child to explain the game to another adult who happens to be wearing a blindfold! It is highly probable that such unnatural procedures lead to underestimation of abilities under investigation as in the examples illustrated here.

These criticisms of the contrived, artificial nature of much manipulative research are not new. They are defended by those committed to such research as the method of choice on the grounds that the laboratory provides the best environment in which to study behaviour under controlled conditions. To the argument that most normally occurring behaviour is too complex to be brought meaningfully under experimental control, a researcher with this orientation would respond that the complexity of naturally occurring behaviour results primarily from the large number of factors involved, but that each factor by itself may operate in a relatively simple manner, readily and completely understandable in a laboratory setting. This posture is adopted particularly forcibly by researchers who take a learning theory approach to the study of behaviour development (e.g. Bijou and Baer, 1960).

The strategy of the learning theorist in attempting to account for the development of a particular behaviour involves three distinct stages. The first stage is to devise a history of learning experience which would result in the behaviour to be explained. The second is to construct a simulation of the hypothesised acquisition process under the controlled conditions of the laboratory, thereby demonstrating (a) that the presumed learning history can be reproduced and (b) that it results in the behaviour in question. The third stage involves generalisation of laboratory results to the outside world, entailing the assumption that children who display the behaviour in question under natural conditions have been exposed to experiences analogous to the hypothesised learning history.

As Baldwin (1967) indicates, such reasoning entails the critical fallacy of judging that because A is a sufficient cause of B, the occurrence of B necessarily implies the prior occurrence of A. There may be many routes to B of which A is only one. It follows, therefore, that if laboratory studies are to contribute to the understanding of the development of naturally occurring behaviour, it is incumbent upon those engaged in laboratory-based research to demonstrate, neither by conjecture nor by analogy, but by direct observation, that the experience of the child in the natural environment approximates to the hypothesised acquisition process created under laboratory conditions. McCall (1977) makes a similar point when he argues that, although laboratory manipulations may demonstrate how behaviours can be acquired under particular conditions, the critical question for the developmentalist is not, 'How *can* this behaviour be produced?' but, 'How *does* this behaviour typically develop in natural life circumstances?'

These criticisms are not intended as a blanket condemnation of all experimental–manipulative research. They are to be regarded, rather, as an appeal for a greater degree of cross-fertilisation between naturalistic and manipulative methodologies. It is frequently argued, with justification, that naturalistic, observational data are inadequate as evidence for casual relationships and that only experiments with clearly defined treatment and control conditions can provide this evidence. At the same time, it must be acknowledged that the ultimate goal of developmental research is to provide the basis for a comprehensive and systematic understanding of the nature of developmental processes in their natural context. In terms of their validity with respect to this goal, borrowing from Hillman (1976), potential data sources might be hierarchically listed as follows: (i) observations or measurements of the unrestrained behaviour of organisms in their normal environment, not significantly affected by being observed or measured; (ii) observations or measurements of the unrestrained behaviour of organisms in their normal environments, significantly affected by being observed or measured; (iii) observations or measurements of unrestrained behaviour in unusual or abnormal environments, the abnormality of which might significantly affect the observations or measurements; (iv) observations or measurements of the behaviour of organisms in normal or abnormal environments such that there is restriction on the range of behaviours which might otherwise be displayed.[1]

Note that both experimental and observational procedures can be applied at any or all of the levels indicated. However, the bulk of contemporary developmental research, whether experimental or observational, is located within levels iii–iv. If developmental research is to provide valid understanding of the nature of development within the individual's total enduring environment then much thought will need to be devoted to redressing this imbalance. Recent papers by Bronfenbrenner (1976) and McCall (1977) are specifically addressed to this issue, and reflect increasing concern among many developmentalists that the discipline should free itself from excessive reliance on laboratory-based, manipulative research.

The Ahistorical–Historical Dimension

In identifying this dimension of classification of research methodologies, McCandless had in mind the distinction between those studies which have and those which do not have a concern with a temporal parameter. In the child-development literature there are many reports of investigations which are ahistorical in nature, studies in which there is no concern to relate the behaviour of the subject now to experience or to behaviour at earlier or later ages. Such investigations are frequently concerned with the relationship between two or more variables at one particular age point. For example, McCall *et al.* (1977) studied the deployment of visual attention toward novel stimuli by 10-week-old infants following repeated exposure to a familiar standard stimulus. They found that duration of infant fixation toward the novel stimuli was an inverted U-function of the magnitude of discrepancy between the new and the standard stimulus and interpreted these results as supporting the predictions of the so-called discrepancy hypothesis (Hebb, 1949; Hunt, 1963). Studies which examine differences in the behaviour of same-age children as a function of sex (e.g. Douvan, 1960), social class or intelligence (e.g. Golden *et al.*, 1977) also lie toward the ahistorical pole of the ahistorical–historical dimension.

Ahistorical research can and does provide a great deal of empirical information about the variables which influence the behaviour of children at particular ages. Such research can also be of theoretical relevance, as evidenced by the McCall *et al.* (1977) study. Further, such studies may provide the basis for the elaboration of hypotheses about the antecedents, say, of observed social class or sex differences in behaviour which can then be tested in more historically orientated research (see below). Note, however, that by itself ahistorical research can contribute comparatively little to the understanding of behavioural development, either in terms of how a particular behaviour changes with age or in terms of how particular experiences at one stage of development may influence behavioural outcomes at a later stage. These are the issues which, *par excellence*, are the concern of the developmentalist and their investigation requires research strategies which involve observation and measurement of behaviour at more than one age level.

Those changes in behaviour which vary as a function of age are the primary interest of the developmental psychologist, but the developmental researcher suffers from the distinct disadvantage that he can exercise no control over the ageing process (to be understood here as the passage of time during which developmental processes occur). Since he cannot manipulate age directly, he must rely upon nature doing or having done this for him. Until relatively recently, developmental psychologists have relied upon two broad strategies in their study of age-related changes in behaviour and it is to consideration of these that we now turn.

In the cross-sectional approach, the investigator obtains representative samples of children at different ages, applies his experimental treatments, observational or measurement procedures to them and then analyses the resulting data for differences in behaviour between subjects of different ages. For example, applied to the study of language acquisition, such a procedure might involve assessment of the average length (i.e. number of words) of spontaneous utterance in different groups of two, three, four, and five-year-old children. Once the data are collected, length of utterance could be plotted against age to yield information on the developmental function (change with age) for this variable. A more sophisticated analysis of the developmental function might result in its precise mathematical description.

In the longitudinal approach, the investigator obtains a single sample of children at some specific age point and then follows up that sample, obtaining measurements on the same group of subjects at successive age points. As before, data are subsequently analysed for differences in behaviour at different ages and, again, developmental functions may be identified (see McGurk, 1975 for an extended contrast of cross-sectional and longitudinal methodologies).

It should be apparent that, in terms of amount of time required to yield a developmental function for any particular behaviour, the cross-sectional strategy is more efficient than the longitudinal approach. The cross-sectional researcher does not have to wait for ageing to occur; within a relatively short period of time he can make observations on subjects at a number of different age levels. The longitudinal researcher, by contrast, can only operate at the rate at which time itself passes. In the language-development example quoted above, the cross-sectional strategy would allow the data to be collected within a few days or weeks, depending on the size of the samples and number of staff available. However, regardless of sample size or the personnel involved, a longitudinal design would occupy an absolute minimum of three years before data collection was complete. Since ageing of subjects proceeds on the same time scale as ageing in investigators, it should come as no surprise to recognise that cross-sectional designs are employed by developmental psychologists with much greater frequency that longitudinal designs. Correspondingly, the bulk of present knowledge of age-related changes in behaviour is derived from cross-sectional studies in which subjects are seen on only one occasion.

Now, there is little doubt that the broad sweep of developmental change in psychological functioning can be assessed relatively efficiently by well designed cross-sectional investigations. Particularly in exploratory investigations of new research areas, the cross-sectional approach has much to commend it. Within a relatively short time span it is possible to determine general trends and to identify those periods during which change appears to be occurring most rapidly and which might be worthy, therefore, of more intensive study. The fact that age trends in behaviour are readily identified in this way is at once the strength and weakness of the cross-sectional approach. At the end of such a study the nature of the differences between groups of children at different age levels can be described and to that extent the approach is historical, within the context being discussed here: the behaviour of children at one stage can be compared with that of children at earlier and later stages. Referring to a previous point, cross-sectional procedures can also be used to establish age-norms for particular developmental phenomena and these norms can provide a base-line against which to compare the performance of an individual with that of his peers.

It should be obvious, however, that while cross-sectional studies can yield information about the magnitude of age-related differences in behaviour between children from different age groups, they cannot inform us of the nature of the age-related changes, or of patterns of growth and development in individual children. Of individual differences in growth and change, cross-sectional approaches are also uninformative. From cross-sectional data it cannot be determined whether the individual child shows the same developmental progress as that reflected by age-group differences, nor can it be known whether the child who manifests developmental precocity at one age point maintains that precocity at later age points. To address such issues, a longitudinal approach is essential. Only by comparing each child with himself at earlier and later points in development is it possible to uncover individual differences in developmental progress. Similarly, only the longitudinal approach can yield data which permits assessment of the influence of antecedent conditions on the form of the developmental function and on the nature of individual differences.

Longitudinal research, therefore, clearly belongs towards the historical pole of the methodological dimension presently under consideration. Cross-sectional research affords description of how children at one age differ in behaviour from children at another. Longitudinal designs yield information of this quality also. In addition, however, longitudinal data provide information on rate of development: whether development is slow or rapid and whether the developmental function is smooth and continuous or discrete and discontinuous, and on the stability or instability of individual differences; whether development of particular behaviours or skills is such that the individual's ranking with respect to his peers is constant or variable with increasing age. Moreover, only longitudinal designs enable the evaluation of the influence of particular life experiences on subsequent developmental progress.

On the face of it, only a longitudinal strategy can provide truly developmental data (i.e. data which address issues related to change with age than merely age group differences) and, on this basis one would expect the more historically oriented, longitudinal approach to be favoured by developmental researchers. In fact, as noted above, studies based upon cross-sectional designs far outnumber longitudinal investigations in the contemporary research scene and, indeed, they have always done so. Moreover, 'developmental' studies in which age does not feature as a variable are carried out at about the same frequency as cross-sectional projects and, of course, much more frequently than longitudinal studies. For example, the most recent issue (at time of writing) of a most prestigious and highly respected journal exclusively devoted to the publication of developmental research contains 56 research reports. Of these, 35 were concerned with single age studies and 30 were reports of cross-sectional investigations; only one report was based on a longitudinal design and it encompassed a period of six months in the lives of two groups of toddlers!

One reason for the paucity of longitudinal research has already been hinted at. Longitudinal research is exceedingly expensive in the demands it makes upon the investigator's time and, particularly if the age span covered is at all extended, long periods of time must elapse between the initiation of a study and the evaluation of results. Young research workers at the beginning of their careers are understandably reluctant to make this kind of commitment. Because academic advancement is so closely tied to publication record, there is considerable pressure on workers to engage in research which will rapidly produce career-development papers rather than result in significant contribution to the understanding of child development. The one-shot, ahistorical approach and the cross-sectional methodology serve this end more parsimoniously than does the longitudinal strategy! We have seen, however, that if research is to make a worthwhile contribution to knowledge of developmental processes, then the longitudinal method must come more to the fore.

It is important, when longitudinal methodology is being advocated, to give consideration to arguments which have been advanced in recent years against this approach to developmental research and, indeed, against the research strategies generally employed by developmentalists. For example, over the past decade, Schaie and his colleagues (Schaie, 1965; Baltes and Schaie, 1973; Nesselroade and Baltes, 1974) have consistently argued that data from simple longitudinal or cross-sectional designs cannot avoid being contaminated by the inherent confusion between subjects' age, the year of birth and the time of measurement. Year of birth establishes a subject's cohort and, since different cohorts grow up during different periods of historical time and are therefore exposed to different environmental conditions of growth, data derived from the study of one cohort will reflect the particular historical or secular experience of that cohort. Accordingly, differences between different age groups (different cohorts), or differences between measurements obtained from one cohort at different points in time may merely reflect the influence of secular changes rather than demonstrate truly developmental progression. Since age at measurement is defined jointly by year of birth and year of measurement there is no simple way of isolating age changes *per se*. Further, with particular reference to longitudinal designs, it can be argued that differences between measurements of performance at successive points in time may merely reflect the cummulative effects of repeated measurement rather than attest to any truly developmental change.[2]

To illustrate some of these points, consider the hypothetical case depicted in Figure 4.1. Assume that a contemporary researcher is interested to assess differences in measured intelligence at intervals across a large portion of the human life-span and chooses to adopt a cross-sectional strategy. He therefore, assembles samples of subjects at 10 year intervals between 10 and 60 years, obtains his measurements and plots mean data points for each age level, resulting in the function described by the solid line in Figure 4.1.

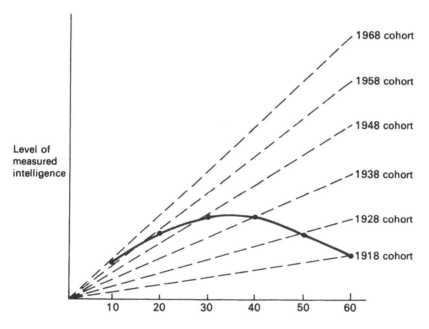

Figure 4.1   Hypothetical data illustrating the confounding of age and cohort differences in traditional cross-sectional designs. (—) cross-sectional function; (---) hypothesised cohort-specific age functions (adapted from Nesselroade and Baltes, 1974)

The cross-sectional data thus obtained suggest that measured intelligence increases during childhood and adolescence to a plateau in early adulthood and thereafter shows decline. Note, however, that each data point on the cross-sectional curve is based on a once only measurement of groups of subjects from different cohorts; thus, age and cohort differences are confounded. Note also that such cross-sectional data can be derived from cohorts in each of which measured intelligence increases monotonically with increasing age (hypothesised longitudinal functions are shown in Figure 4.1 by broken lines), nicely illustrating the point that the age differences revealed by cross-sectional study may bear little correspondence to age changes in developmental function. Finally, note that the longitudinal functions for each cohort reveal different rates of development and different developmental end points; thus, longitudinal data derived from only one cohort may yield a misleading picture of the nature of the developmental function. It should not go unmentioned either that the practice effects introduced by repeated testing of longitudinal samples can distort the form of the developmental function and may, indeed, give rise to apparent age changes in performance where none, in fact, exist.

Although illustrated here by hypothetical data, these weaknesses and shortcomings of traditional cross-sectional and longitudinal designs have been demonstrated in a number of empirical investigations. For example, in a study of personality and cognitive development during adolescence, Nesselroade and Baltes (1974) found that changes in performance were influenced less by age than by the cohort to which subjects belonged and by retest effects. Similarly, Labouvie *et al.* (1974) found that retest effects contributed more to improved intelligence test scores than did increased age in a group of adolescents who had been followed up longitudinally over a period of one year.

To overcome the limitations and to permit evaluation of possible sources of confounding in the designs traditionally employed in developmental research, Schaie and his colleagues have urged workers in the field to adopt what have become known as sequential strategies of data collection and analysis. These involve the simultaneous deployment of longitudinal and cross-sectional procedures on samples drawn from successive cohorts according to the age span to be covered and the number of measurement points anticipated. By these procedures, it is argued, it becomes possible to assess the extent to which the performance of subjects at different ages is influenced by age changes *per se*, by time of measurement and by cohort differences. In addition, with appropriate control samples, it is possible to assess the effects due to repeated measurement.

A variety of sequential designs are discussed in the relevant literature (e.g. Buss, 1973; Nesselroade and Baltes, 1974; Schaie, 1965; Wohwill, 1973). However, for illustrative purposes, consider how the implementation of these proposals would influence the design of a study in the limiting case where a researcher is interested in change in some set of variables (e.g. attributes of personality development) across two age points (e.g. 3 and 6 years). The design is presented in Table 4.1, where the cell entries refer to year of testing.

TABLE 4.1. SEQUENTIAL CROSS-SECTIONAL AND LONGITUDINAL DESIGN

| | | Age at testing (years) | |
		3	6
	1972	—	1978
Cohort	1975	1978	1981
	1978	1981	1984

As is apparent from Table 4.1, the design involves measurement of three cohorts and includes replication of cross-sectional and longitudinal sequences. The statistical models employed to assess the influence of particular factors (age, cohort, time of testing) are discussed fully in the references quoted above. However, it can be appreciated from the table that comparison of the two longitudinal samples will reveal whether developmental changes are similar or different for the 1975 and 1978 cohorts. Similarly, the design makes it possible to determine whether, at 1984, the six-year-olds from the 1978 cohort show the same level of performance as six-year-olds from the 1972 and 1975 cohorts when they were assessed in 1978 and 1981 respectively, thus enabling evaluation of historical differences between cohorts. The inclusion of further independent samples from 1975 and 1978 cohorts who are assessed once only at 1981 and 1984 respectively would make it possible, by comparison with subjects from the longitudinal samples, to identify any effects due to repeated testing of the latter.

Of the various research strategies discussed in this section, the sequential designs are the most truly historical. They alone make it possible to examine ontogenetic change in behaviour—the primary focus of the developmental psychologist—within the context of generational change and secular change. Alas, however, they are unlikely to find favour among the main body of developmental researchers. The reasons for this are obvious. If traditional longitudinal research is expensive in terms of its demands upon researchers' time and resources then the sequential methodologies are, literally, doubly so. A standard longitudinal investigation in the example discussed above would occupy a research team for three years. The sequential alternative quoted would require twice as long and would vastly increase the number of subjects involved. Quite simply, such commitment is beyond the resources normally available to individual research workers, especially where the developmental span to be encompassed in a particular project is at all extended.

According to this analysis developmental research methodology has, on the face of it, reached something of an impasse. Cross-sectional designs are demonstrably inadequate to provide anything but the crudest index of age differences in performance and on occasion, as we have seen, can yield results that are downright misleading due to the confounding influence of cohort differences. Simple longitudinal designs are also frequently suspect, due to their restriction to single cohorts and to the contaminating influence of repeated testing effects. Yet, the alternative of successive sequential methodology is beyond the financial resources and the time available to the vast majority of individual research workers; and it is upon the shoulders of the latter that the primary burden for advancing developmental research has rested and will continue to rest.

What, then, of the future for a significant psychology of human development? For reasons already indicated, it is unlikely that the profession is about to abandon traditional cross-sectional and longitudinal designs. However, in the light of what is now known of the distorted picture of development which can result from reliance on cross-sectional data, continued excessive dependence on this strategy by developmentalists can hardly be justified. The longitudinal approach, despite its acknowledged limitations, is more defensible and the pressure is upon us now to make it the method of choice. With respect to the previously elaborated criticisms of this method, McCall (1977), in an important paper referred to earlier, has pointed out that the available literature on cohort, time of testing and repeated testing effects indicates that these have their primary influence upon average levels of performance, that is upon average increases or decreases in developmental function. However, with respect to individual differences or developmental stability (i.e. the extent to which the relative standing of an individual on a given attribute at one point in time compares with his standing at earlier or later points in development), cohort, time of testing and retesting effects may have relatively little influence.[3] Individual differences, their antecedents and consequents are of enduring interest to developmental researchers and in this respect the longitudinal strategy is the method of choice. McCall (1977), however, makes a spirited defence of its application to the study of developmental functions also.

At the same time, the limitations inherent in simple longitudinal methodology cannot be gainsaid. Research reports of studies based upon sequential methodologies have clearly demonstrated cohort and time of testing effects upon the average level of performance on tests of mental ability and various aspects of personality functioning, even across time spans of only a few years (e.g. Nesselroade and Baltes, 1974). It is not unlikely that such influences also effect performance in other areas of psychological development. In an era of rapid social and environmental change, such as the present one, it is critical that research methodologies are employed which are sensitive to these influences on developmental function, both for their relevance in constructing adequate theoretical models of development and for their contribution to the social validity of research findings. Simple cross-sectional and longitudinal designs are demonstrably limited in this respect. In this context, thought needs to be given to ensuring that future generations of researchers do not remain as uninformed as contemporary workers of the potential influence of cohort, time of testing and retesting effects upon developmental function. Identification of the problem is one thing, its solution another. Certainly, the work involved could not be undertaken by one researcher or one team of researchers. It is more an institutional task and probably calls for the creation of one or more independent but nationally funded developmental research institutions charged with the continuing responsibility for conducting successive cohort studies across fairly wide age spans and across a fairly extended domain of psychological development. Periodic publication of data from such continuing investigations would serve a variety of important purposes. Firstly, with extensive commitment to longitudinal research on the part of individual workers, the availability of data from sequential studies would provide a valuable backcloth against which to interpret findings from smaller scale investigations. Secondly, analysis of data from sequential studies would serve to identify those aspects of psychological development where cohort (or generational) and time-of-testing (or secular) effects are most marked; information on the latter would be of particular relevance in the planning and evaluation of social policy as it influences the lives of children. In addition, data from such studies would serve also to identify aspects of development where cohort and other effects are negligible and whose detailed investigation could therefore be prosecuted by alternative research strategies. This is not the place to advance detailed proposals on how such integrated programmes might be established, but the issues involved are of sufficient importance to merit the urgent consideration of all concerned with the study of human psychological development.

Notes

1. This listing is neither as exhaustive nor as exclusive as the classification system developed by Hillman, but it is sufficient for present purposes.
2. Throughout this discussion it is assumed that the longitudinal strategy is applied to intact samples. Non-random drop-out of subjects is a further source of contamination of longitudinal data. For discussion of this problem, see McGurk (1975).
3. Individual differences in development are usually assessed by correlation coefficients. The value of a correlation coefficient is independent of the means of the distributions involved in its calculation. Thus, factors which influence the latter need have no necessary influence upon the former.

References

Baldwin, A. L. (1967). *Theories of Child Development*, New York, Wiley
Baltes, P. B. and Schaie, K. W. (1973). On life-span developmental research paradigms: retrospects and prospects. In *Life Span Developmental Psychology: Personality and Socialization* (ed. P. B. Baltes and K. W. Schaie), New York, Academic Press

Bijou, S. W. and Baer, D. M. (1960). The laboratory-experimental study of child behaviour. In *Handbook of Research Methods in Child Development* (ed. P. H. Mussen) New York, Wiley

Bronfenbrenner, U. (1974). Developmental research, public policy and the ecology of childhood. *Child Development*, **45**, 1–5

Bronfenbrenner, U. (1976). Ecological factors in human development in retrospect and prospect. In *Ecological Factors in Human Development* (ed. H. McGurk), Amsterdam, North-Holland

Brown, R. (1973). *A First Language*. Harmondsworth, Penguin Books

Buss, A. R. (1973). An extension of developmental models that separate ontogenetic changes and cohort differences. *Phychological Bulletin*, **80**, 466–479

Crook, C. K. (1978). The organization and control of infant sucking. *Advances in Child Behaviour and Development* (in the press)

Douvan, E. (1960). Sex differences in adolescent character processes. *Merrill-Palmer Quarterly of Behaviour and Development*, **6**, 203–211

Flavell, J. H. (1977). *Cognitive Development*. Englewood Cliffs, Prentice Hall

Flavell, J. H., Botkin, P. T., Fry, C. L., Wright, J. W. and Jarvis, P. E. (1968). *The Development of Communication and Role-taking Skills in Children*. New York, Wiley

Gesell, A. and Amatrude, C. (1941). *Developmental Diagnosis*. New York, Hoeber

Golden, M., Montare, A. and Bridger, W. (1977). Verbal control of delay behaviour in two-year-old boys as a function of social class. *Child Development*, **48**, 1107–1111

Halliday, M. A. K. (1975). *Learning How to Mean: Explorations in the Development of Language*. London, Edward Arnold

Hebb, D. O. (1949). *The Organization of Behaviour*. New York, Wiley

Hillman, H. (1976). Towards a classification of evidence in biological and medical research in respect of its validity. *Acta Biotheoretica*, **25**, 153–162

Hunt, J. McV. (1963). Motivation inherent in information processing and action. In *Motivation and Social Interaction*. (ed. O. J. Harvey) New York, Ronald

Hutt, S. J. and Hutt, C. (1970). *Direct Observation and Measurement of Behaviour*. London, Thomas

Kaye, K. (1977). Towards the origin of dialogue. In *Studies in Mother-Infant Interaction* (ed. H. R. Schaffer), London, Academic Press

Labouvie, E. W., Bartsch, T. W., Nesselroade, J. R. and Baltes, P. B. (1974). On the internal and external validity of simple longitudinal designs. *Child Development*, **45**, 282–290

McCall, R. B. (1977). Challenges to a science of developmental psychology. *Child Development*, **48**, 333–344

McCall, R. B., Kennedy, C. B. and Appelbaum, M. I. (1977). Magnitude of discrepancy and the distribution of attention in infants. *Child Development*, **48**, 772–785

McCandless, B. R. (1967). *Children: Behaviour and Development*. New York, Holt, Rinehart and Winston

McCandless, B. R. (1970). *Adolescents*. Hinsdale, Illinois, Dryden Press

McGurk, H. (1975). *Growing and Changing*. London, Methuen

McGurk, H. (1977). A developmental study of behavioural factors influencing ingestion of small solids by infants and young children. Unpublished manuscript, University of Surrey

Maratsos, M. P. (1973). Nonegocentric communication abilities in preschool children. *Child Development*, **44**, 697–700

Mussen, P. H. (1960). *Handbook of Research Methods in Child Development*, New York, Wiley

Nesselroade, J. R. and Baltes, P. B. (1974). Adolescent personality development and historical change: 1970–1972. *Monographs of the Society for Research in Child Development*, **39** (1, Serial No. 154)

Piaget, J. (1951). *Judgement and Reasoning in the Child*. London, Routledge and Kegan Paul

Schaie, K. W. (1965). A general model for the study of developmental problems. *Psychological Bulletin*, **64**, 94–107

Shirley, M. M. (1933). *The First Two Years of Life*, Vol. 2, Minneapolis, University of Minnesota Press

Spiker, C. C. (1966). The concept of development: Relevant and irrelevant issues. *Monographs of the Society for Research in Child Development*, **31** (5)

Stevenson, H. W. (1968). Developmental psychology. In *International Encyclopaedia of the Social Sciences* (ed. Sills), New York, Macmillan

Wohlwill, J. F. (1973). *The Study of Behavioural Development*. London, Academic Press

5 Piagetian Perspectives

HANS FURTH

(*The Catholic University of America, Washington, USA*)

It would be right to call Piaget's theory an epistemology since he set out to investigate the nature and limits of knowledge from a perspective which had hitherto been peculiar to philosophers. But he added the qualifying adjective genetic to indicate that his method of investigation would differ from the philosopher's. From the philosopher's viewpoint, Piaget's preoccupation with developmental observations was unheard of, and from the scientist's point of view his willingness to allow the search for answers to theoretical questions to be emphasised rather than the 'scientific method' seemed equally disturbing.

But in fact what can be more theoretical than questioning the objectivity of sense data or what is more indecisive than children's responses to questions about the wind and the clouds? Even more puzzling is Piaget's seeming reluctance to become involved in bona fide psychological issues, not merely those apparently removed from his preoccupation, such as individual differences or motivation, but precisely those which he seems to study in their own right. Memory, image, learning, symbol, and other familiar topics become something entirely different when they are subject matter of the Piagetian perspective. When the American Psychological Association bestowed on him its gold medal, for the first time to a non-American, it referred to his seminal psychological contributions 'almost as a by-product' of his primary work. And he himself, when asked questions about sundry psychological issues, often replies, 'If I were a psychologist this would be an interesting enterprise. . . .'

There can be no doubt that the substance and justification of Piaget's work is epistemology and that our understanding of his contribution is proportionate to our willingness to grant that epistemological concerns cannot be separated from the scientific study of knowing and of man, the knower. Indeed the epistemological perspective may be of primary importance despite the widespread opinion that one can pursue cognitive psychology without bothering about philosophical issues. It is generally admitted that once a scientific question has been asked the range of possible responses is already severely curtailed by the question itself. To pretend that we can have questions unbiased by epistemological concerns is an illusion that becomes all the more seductive the closer the problem bears on the nature and the underlying purpose of questioning itself.

However, it would be equally futile merely to theorise on the nature of knowledge and expect psychologists to share this belief. First, a theory is useless for psychology unless its concrete application can be spelled out in sufficient detail to allow one to appreciate its empirical relevance and its logical cogency. Second and most important, the function of a theory is not to legislate but to guide, and provide a perspective to the empirical investigator. Accordingly there is little merit in arguing *in abstracto* about the validity of Piaget's epistemological theory: the proof of the pudding is in the eating. In other words, does the Piagetian perspective lead to empirical observations that are new, reliable and psychologically relevant? This is the main criterion on which the theory should be evaluated.

What is it that Piaget has observed? It is neither knowledge as understood by the philosopher nor is it the child as studied by the psychological investigator; hence, strictly speaking, Piaget is neither a philosopher nor a psychologist. Rather, Piaget's object was to describe the development of the intelligence that made science possible as observed in and interpreted from children's spontaneous construction of their knowledge structures. What is unobservable in itself and in its adult form is largely hidden from conscious re-construction becomes amenable to empirical observation when studied in its genesis. The procedure of describing developmental stages in the child's knowledge structure is therefore more than a convenient methodology. For Piaget it is the necessary perspective that turns an insolvable epistemological quest into a solvable empirical enterprise. It is here that Piaget himself sees his principal scientific contribution. His aim was nothing less than to establish a science in its own right, straddling philosophy and psychology, without being either: genetic epistemology.

The Objective Environment

From a biological viewpoint the environment is that on which an organism acts and with which it interacts. To do this adaptively to the furtherance of its species means that the organism 'knows' how to organise its behaviour in its environment. The use of the term 'to know' may appear objectionable to some who would like to reserve it for something closer to scientific and critical knowledge. Suffice it to say that Piaget recognises different ways of knowing something. At the same time, as a biologist he deals with knowledge in an evolutionary context and thereby can perceive basic continuities in all forms of knowing. The most fundamental characteristic of knowledge is precisely that it underlies all adaptive behaviour. This capacity distinguishes a living from a non-living structure, a living from a physical reaction.

This living response is implied in Piaget's terminology relative to knowing: schemes, assimilation and accommodation. Schemes refer to he structure of knowledge within the organism, while assimilation refers to the incoming pro-cess of taking in environmental data and transforming them according to these schemes: schemes being instruments of assimilation. Accommodation on the other hand means the outgoing process of applying general schemes to particular data. It is a common misinterpretation to equate accommodation with a change of schemes in response to environmental pressure. That crucial change of structure which Piaget calls development will be discussed in detail shortly. The basic meaning of accommodation, however, is just the opposite: an invariant scheme applied to a variety of changing situations.

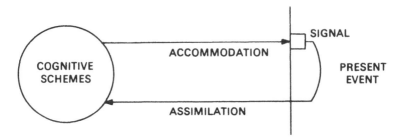

Figure 5.1   Piaget's basic knowledge circle

The basic 'knowledge circle' outlined in Figure 5.1 puts an organism into knowing contact with its environment or, conversely, turns a physical situation into a living, i.e. known, environment. Schemes, assimilation and accommodation are three perspectives of the same thing: as a psychological *capacity* one speaks of schemes and as a psychological *process* one speaks of assimilation or accommodation depending on the inward or outward direction one wishes to emphasise. In any case, knowledge is thereby conceptualised as an internal, subjective capacity for a two-way multilevel activity between what eventually comes to be known as subject and object.

What type of activity is knowledge? You cannot point to it in a body's behaviour, rather it is an inferred activity of organisation and co-ordination without which there would be no living body or behaviour. It is a cognitive activity *sui generis* involved in all biological functioning at any evolutionary stage whether physiological, instinctual or psychological. In the latter case knowledge itself can attain different degrees of consciousness and become an 'object' of knowledge.

The cognitive schemes are called instruments of assimilation and determine what stages of knowing give structure to a particular activity. Note further that an event is never known in its totality, rather we know present events as a function of what are variously called perceptual features, recognitory cues or sign releasers. All these are part components of present events and can be called by the generic term signals. The box labelled SIGNAL indicates that the accommodation of schemes involves being in contact with signals.

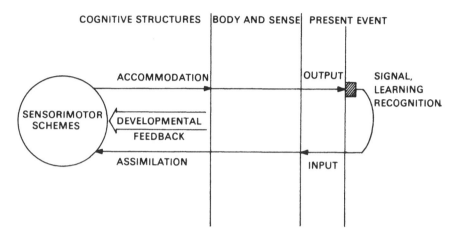

COGNITIVE STRUCTURES   BODY AND SENSE   PRESENT EVENT

Figure 5.2   Sensorimotor functioning

We can enlarge Figure 5.1 by inclusion of several new parts to enrich the
basic conception of Piaget's knowledge circle (see Figure 5.2). First, we
include between the psychological structures and the known event the
intermediary of body and sense to make clear that the functioning of schemes
requires an intact body. Schemes are first and foremost co-ordinations of
external actions and actions are executed by means of motor and sense
systems. Second, since body and sense activities are observable, it seems
legitimate to call the observable part of assimilation 'input' and the
observable part of accommodation 'output'. Third, by limiting our consideration to schemes of acquired action co-ordinations—co-ordinations not
present at birth and requiring lived experience for their acquisition—we are
effectively focusing on what Piaget calls sensorimotor functioning. This
coincides with the knowledge underlying the external actions of higher
animals, including humans.

Having said that accommodation is not the source of developmental
changes, how should we describe the process of developmental acquisition of
schemes? Piaget conceives of it as an internal feedback from the cognitive
experience itself. Development is indicated in Figure 5.2 as a double arrow
emanating from the interplay between assimilation and accommodation. It
leads to growth and differentiation of schemes, that is, the growing child
becomes 'more intelligent'. While development has its source internally
within the cognitive structure, the content component of knowing is found in
the outward directed process of accommodation with its output and signal. In
distinction from 'development' this can be called 'learning in the strict sense' if
we understand by learning the acquisition of new cognitive signals or content
and by development the acquisition of new cognitive structures.

This distinction between development and learning parallels the distinction between cognitive structure and content; it makes explicit what is implied by assimilation of a scheme and accommodation to a specific event. Piaget's theory is therefore structuralist but at the same time it is developmental in that it attempts to explain the genesis of the structure. It follows that in any particular behaviour of a person one could, from a cognitive viewpoint, distinguish four aspects: (1) the present schemes of assimilation, (2) their application to present signals (= accommodation), (3) development or the genesis of the schemes, (4) learning or the genesis of the signals.

To make this theoretical distinction concrete and show the essential interrelatedness of these aspects, consider a five-month-old infant who is beginning to be successful in opening and closing a particular box. First, the infant assimilates the present box event to a variety of available general schemes, primarily sensorimotor schemes or ways of co-ordinating physical activities such as those of handling and of seeing, the infant having already developed what Piaget calls the scheme of hand–eye co-ordination. Second, he adjusts or accommodates to the event by focusing on and recognising particular signals—this rather than another box—in addition to sundry perceptual cues. Third, this event can be viewed as part of a sequence that has led to the infant's practical knowledge of opening and closing not just this, but any box: the child develops a new general scheme. If need be, it could be called a sensorimotor scheme of understanding how a lid works. Fourth, we can certainly assert that the infant is learning the handling of this one particular box and can predict that as a consequence a future handling and recognition of it will be more adequate in comparison with earlier handling or other boxes. This trivial example illustrates that psychological observers describing human behaviour can legitimately limit their interests to some aspects rather than others. While Piaget focuses on aspects (1) and (3) above and to a certain extent and more recently on (2), learning theorists are more interested in (4). By itself this should cause no conflict. But when certain aspects are peremptorily exaggerated or excluded by psychological theorising, then it becomes necessary to analyse the philosophical foundations of the theory in order to discover what is a legitimate inference from empirical observation and what is unanalysed philosophical preconception.

We should spell out more clearly what type of psychological actions are included in sensorimotor functioning as schematically shown in Figure 5.2. It is important to realise adequately the richness of sensorimotor intelligence, otherwise we shall fail to appreciate the continuity of earlier and later stages of knowledge and be tempted to project into sensorimotor functioning what is a characteristic achievement of later stages. In Piaget's conception, sensori-motor activity does not involve (1) a concept of a theoretical object of knowing distinct from the practical doing (object concept), or (2) a representation distinct from the present signal (representative symbol). But it does include perception, discrimination, recognitory memory, co-ordinated action in space and in time, particularly the most typical means–end action of sensorimotor intelligence: an action to reach a certain goal. There is also proprioception of bodily states and signal communication, both receiving and giving, as well as co-ordination of affective tendencies. All these may have innate (instinctual and maturational), in addition to behaviourally acquired, components and the co-ordination of the acquired and the biological is also part of sensorimotor functioning. Along with all these there is learning, if we focus on the acquisition of particular content, and there is development, if we focus on restructuring of cognitive schemes which co-ordinate, relate and transform the content in the service of a successful ('intelligent') present action.

Sensorimotor functioning can therefore be inferred from a rich variety of behaviours organised in the context of a situation that is perceptually (or proprioceptually, e.g., hunger) present to the organism. Hence it is theoretically and empirically warranted to infer schemes of co-ordination that give structure to the action of the subject on the object, but it is unwarranted to postulate an initial distinction of subject and object. The biological matrix of knowledge is adaptive behaviour of an organism that does not know—and does not need to know—the differentiation between self, action and external fact. In modern times 'objective' means factually true and unbiased by subjective idiosyncratic consideration. For the sensorimotor infant the environment is anything but objective. The infant's world does not differentiate between self, action and object and has no objective framework of space, time or causality. Piaget describes the first two years of an infant as a gradual development of increasingly differentiated sensorimotor schemes.

However, around the age of one-and-a-half years the infant reaches a substantial degree of sensorimotor know-how in the activities listed two paragraphs above and the child's behaviour is beginning to show that the environment is no longer merely the occasion for doing something, but has become something that is known in its own right. This new quality of behaviour is the first glimmer of objectivity—a tendency that leads toward logical-scientific thinking—and is demonstrated primarily by the child's systematic search for a hidden object and, more indirectly, by the insightful invention of appropriate means to reach certain ends. Piaget observed the slow developmental acquisition of these behaviours in various sensorimotor substages. He concluded that earlier limitations in object searching or means-invention argued for the lack of an adequately elaborated object concept ('permanent object'), just as behavioural success proved its presence.

What does the object concept imply? Principally it establishes a differentiation of the subject of the action and the object of action. It means that children know that things exist, located in time and space, independently of their present action toward them, and they themselves have a separate existence from, and are one among other 'objects' in this world (where the word object means 'object of knowledge' including things and persons). From this time on it makes sense to refer to knowing as being theoretical in the sense of beginning to understand the theory of action, while at the sensorimotor stage knowing is accurately conceived as a practical know-how or understanding how to do an action. The differentiation of action and object brought about by theoretical knowing has its fateful consequence in the traditional split between 'action' and 'knowledge'. For an understanding of Piaget's theory it is, however, important to keep in mind that the change from practical to theoretical knowing, from doing to thinking, does not change the action character of knowing. To underline this fact Figure 5.3 presents by means of broken lines the functioning of schemes of thinking of which the earliest manifestation is the object concept and which culminate in Piaget's concrete and formal operations.

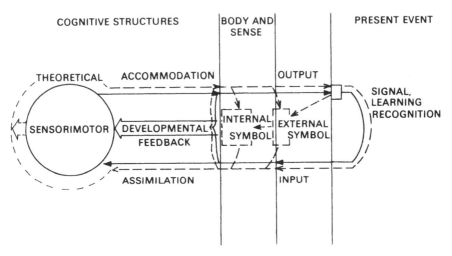

Figure 5.3   Sensorimotor and theoretical functioning

The broken double arrow in Figure 5.3 indicates the origin of thinking schemes by means of internal developmental feedback, just as is the case with doing schemes. Note that the presence of theoretical schemes does not substitute or eliminate sensorimotor schemes. The latter remain the underlying cognitive structures of all practical 'doing' and they function in part in conjunction with the child's schemes of theoretical knowing or 'thinking'. To think of an external thing as a permanent object, as a 'theoretical thing', has been shown to be the beginning of this new capacity. The operations which are developed during the subsequent four to eight years are direct elaborations of this beginning in terms of internally consistent logical systems of which the following three are most prominent: quantification, classification and seriation. These are called 'concrete operations' since they are logical structures that bear on concrete physical (or imaginable) things. A further development that begins to take place in pre-adolescence is the stage of 'formal operations' where the content of thinking is no longer a concrete event but a theoretical event that can only be expressed as a formal proposition. Formal operations create the base of fully independent logical reasoning and make scientific thinking possible. The development from the object concept to fully elaborated formal schemes takes about 15 years and is implicitly included in the broken circle of the thinking schemes.

The formation of the symbol is an immediate consequence of the object concept. To know a thing theoretically implies the capacity to think of it in its absence. This function is called symbol formation and is indicated by the broken arrow from the signal towards the person. If need be, the child who knows something theoretically can make present (re-present) what is absent. Figure 5.3 indicates schematically this new capacity to close the knowing circle within the confines of the person. Instead of accommodating to the external present event, the accommodation-output stops short at a symbolic representation in the form of a motoric quasi-imitation of the event. This imitation derives from the signalling features of the event and constitutes the material component of the symbol, whereas the *meaning* component of the symbol resides in the identical thinking schemes to which the original event is assimilated.

As an illustration, a child may imitate driving a car and use this imitative behaviour to symbolise cars. This is an externally observable symbol and is constantly encountered in children's symbolic play and spontaneous gestures. Subsequently the symbolic movements become diminished and eventually unobservable. This 'internalisation' of a symbol is shown by the broken arrow within the person and leads to what is experienced as an internal image. Images form part of dreams, mental anticipation and recall memory. All these phenomena are internal symbols in the sense of deriving their meaning from the schemes of theoretical knowing and their material component from the internalisation of external features.

What is fundamental in this conception of knowledge and distinguishes Piaget's from other theories can now be summarised in two points. (1) Objective knowledge is not a suitable starting point for a scientific or philosophical consideration of knowledge. For environmental events do not present themselves to organisms as objects to know but as undifferentiated parts of action co-ordinations. It is only toward the end of the second year that the human child constructs the first glimmer of an 'objective' view and only with the construction of a system of logical operations a dozen years later that the ideal of an objective and scientific knowledge is somewhat approached. Knowledge is and derives from a constructive activity, whether it gives structure to external actions (doing) or internal actions (thinking). Through its internal tendency toward objectivity, knowledge, once fully developed, becomes the source of 'objective' facts and logical consistency.

(2) Symbols (= representations) are derivatives and essential products but never the source of knowledge. This statement encompasses not only personal symbols, such as gestures or images, but also the socially vastly important conventional symbol system which is society's language. Since society and its language are traditionally linked to knowledge and its development, the next section will be devoted to the factors that contribute to a child's intellectual development among which society and its products looms prominently.

The Social Environment

The preceding section focused on the structural component of knowledge as it develops in the child's doing and thinking and leads to the system of logical operations that are the basis of objective, scientific knowledge. Here we shall first ask which factors contribute to the development of intelligence and what in particular is the place of biological and social factors. Figure 5.4 presents the interplay between these factors in relation to intellectual development.

Box I shows the psychological structure of intelligence and its cognitive function of doing or thinking. Above is box B which stands for biological factors, such as the anatomy and physiology of the organism as well as maturational processes of biological structures which may continue for many years after birth. These factors undoubtedly influence intellectual functioning as a necessary precondition. Below are boxes S and O encompassing all behavioural experiences. Piaget distinguishes two components of cognitive experiences, a distinction similar to the one mentioned above between development and learning: those experiences that result in subjective co-ordinations and those that lead to knowledge of environmental objects. The first, labelled S, deals with subjective experiences involved in the acquisition of schemes, schemes of doing at the sensorimotor stage and of thinking at more advanced stages. These experiences through developmental feedback lead to the restructuring of intelligence, so that Piaget can define intelligence as being the totality of available cognitive structures. The second component, labelled O, deals with the objective experience of environmental objects, in other words, the totality of particular content that is learned and known in any way: persons, things, symbols, etc.

Even though one can distinguish conceptually the two components of cognitive experience, they are closely interwoven in that the environment provides the indispensable occasion and the content of all subjective co-ordinations. In fact, the most fundamental relation implicit in all cognitive activity is precisely the subject–object relation. Piaget gives it the name of equilibration in order to stress the self-regulatory balance relation inherent in knowing. It is an open balance between subjective and objective factors and by its own intrinsic working leads to intellectual

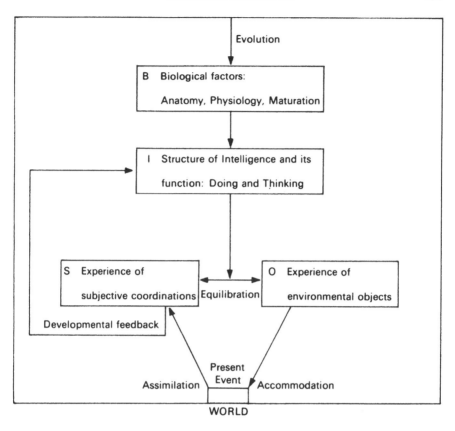

Figure 5.4   Factors contributing to the development of intelligence

development. More will be said on equilibration later. Suffice it to note that for Piaget three factors influence intellectual development: the first factor S, acquired 'subjective' co-ordinations, contributes directly to the structure of intelligence by means of developmental feedback; intelligence itself is the source of, and is responsive to, equilibration between factor S and the second factor O, acquired environmental or 'objective' experience; moreover, equilibration is constantly dependent on the third factor B, the biology of the body's physiology and its maturation. The two components S and O can be called the framework through which intelligence makes contact with its 'real' world: it assimilates the world through S and accommodates to it through O. Since the biological factor B, and in fact the rest of the entire model of intelligence, are integral parts of this world, the encompassing square labelled WORLD includes the three factors and, in particular, through evolution and heredity, feeds back into B.

   In describing the content of knowledge, which we called environmental experience, it makes sense to stress its eminently social character. To know an object is merely the converse of knowing the self and this self is first and foremost experienced in relation to other persons. These other persons, including the self, are part of a social group which beyond the narrow confines of the family involves society at large, its language, culture and all that it implies. There are physical things, to be sure, but the majority are artefacts produced by society and used according to cultural norms, such as houses, clothes or toys. Artistic products, such as songs or pictures, symbolic institutions embodied in customs and myth and the symbolic instrument *par excellence*, society's language, are all closely tied up with social or societal relations. Then there are natural phenomena embodied in animals and nature, but here too the social significance seems to be of paramount importance. This is quite clear in the case of pets, flowers or food which serve human-social needs.

But what about physical things in themselves, the experience of physical dimensions, such as weight or number? Or the activity of one's body and senses, such as a child's experience of running or throwing? These things, while they do not seem to be in themselves social, are precisely what subjective experiences of co-ordinations are. When we know spinach as something to grow, cook and eat, we know it as content in relation to social customs and norms. But when we study the plant as a biologist, we attempt to know it within an objective framework which is given by the subject's co-ordinations. In a word, an event receives meaning either in relation to social interactions as belonging to the human world-society, or in relation to practical or logical co-ordinations, as belonging to the more limited realm of the structure of intelligence.

It goes without saying that the two types of knowing and experience constantly interact, not merely successively but above all simultaneously, as does assimilation and accommodation to which the respective experience components relate directly. It remains, however, to spell out more clearly how in Piaget's theory the content functions and for the purpose we shall discuss in turn, (a) symbolic representation and how it relates to content and consciousness, (b) the concept of social interaction, and (c) the function of communication and language.

(a) The primary content to which intelligence gives cognitive structure is interaction with the world, particularly other people. This appears on the surface less a world of knowing than of doing. There is some truth in this statement as long as we realise that doing occurs within multiform levels of knowing: for instance, driving a nail into the wall may be primarily sensorimotor doing, but this practical know-how, as any carpenter knows, contains a generous portion of theoretical know-how in connection with strength, direction and attack of the stroke, none of which is possible as mere sensorimotor skill.

But the most conspicuous feat of theoretical knowing, as was outlined in

Figure 5.3, is the capacity to represent, so that for many the concepts of representation and theoretical knowledge are synonymous. In a Piagetian perspective, theoretical knowing and representation are different psychological processes; however, there is a functional relation between knowing and representation, such that knowing is the cognitive structure and representation is the symbolic content that receives meaning from the structure. In order to clarify this perspective further, one has to introduce consciousness. Referring to Figure 5.3, one may readily admit that what is on the left side, the cognitive schemes and the inward processes of assimilation and developmental feedback, are unobservable and unconscious. However, this is not the case with the right side of the knowing circle. After all, it is the event that is known and a known event is as a rule something the knower is conscious of. Here also the distinction between sensorimotor and theoretical knowing must be made. For while one cannot deny to a sensorimotor means–end action the quality of intentionality and attentive awareness, the concept of consciousness seems to imply at least the possibility of knowing the self in a more differentiated way than that of which sensorimotor functioning is capable. Hence, limiting ourselves to theoretical knowing, we can assert that as a rule—and exceptions to the rule are very important psychologically—personal consciousness in various degrees accompanies knowing. This psychological quality is founded on two characteristics of theoretical knowing: first, the concept of self as an active person, distinct not only from the object of the act but from the act itself; second, symbolic representation. In order to know something, to be conscious of something, the knowing circle must close by means of accommodation. When the known content is present there is no problem and no need for a representation, but when it is absent, the representation is psychologically required to give content to the structure of knowing.

Thus symbolic representation as used here is not an inferred theoretical concept; it is a psychologically 'real' event, observable to an outsider if it is an external representation, as is so often the case with young children and shown in the right symbol of Figure 5.3. When the representation is fully internalised—the left symbol—it is still a psychological event which the knower can experience. Consequently representation (= symbol) is used by Piaget in the sense of something that a person experiences. Frequently, representation is used in a different sense, e.g., it is said that the visual system has a representation of three-dimensional space. In that case representation is no longer a psychological phenomenon rather it is something that at best belongs to the physiological functioning of a person. Similarly the knowledge of calculus that describes accurately some of my motor functioning, is not something that I as a person can claim as knowing; this is biological knowledge which remained hidden in the wisdom of evolution for generations until a Newton came along and turned it for those who have studied calculus into personal knowledge. In brief, for the Piagetian system representation is a symbolic instrument for making present to the person absent cognitive

content and since it is a symbol it derives its meaning from post-sensorimotor
(= theoretical) schemes.

(b) The content proper to which cognitive schemes accommodate, as was
suggested above, is chiefly the world of human interaction, primarily with
other persons and secondarily with products, both artifacts and symbols. The
child's long-term dependency on others makes the task of relating to others
biologically imperative and it would seem strange indeed if the development
of intelligence were not geared in this direction. Smiling, fear of strangers,
recognition of and search for others, making adults do something to attain a
certain end, communicating, these and other behaviours are integral
components of sensorimotor development. The behaviour of small children
beyond that stage is characterised by its almost constant interaction with
others, adults and increasingly peers. Add to it what is called affective
relations of a positive or negative kind, moral values in relation to what is
experienced as right or wrong, not to mention the highly significant fact of
communication for its own sake—which is probably the main function of
language—and the entire field of motivation to please and to be observed by
others, all this underscores the social nature of the child's behaviour. When
the young child engages in symbolic play, it is mostly to act out social events
or roles and from this fact alone one can justifiably conclude that the child's
internal symbol world, the dreams, the imaginings, the phantasies are related
to experiences of the social world.

If the environment with which a child is interacting is chiefly social, the co-
ordinations that derive from these interactions should also be primarily
social. And indeed, what is first discriminated on the sensorimotor stage? The
face of a person. What is first remembered as familiar? A particular person.
What at the threshold of theoretical knowing becomes the first object? A
person. Why does it then take years before the child takes serious notice of
'objective' physical dimensions? Probably because children's thinking is
preoccupied with co-ordinating their own emotions and the relations between
self and others. When children make their own the language, the customs and
the values of their society, that means in Piaget's perspective that they
assimilate these things to internal schemes and in so doing gradually reconstruct by differentiation and integration more advanced schemes. In other
words, they become socially and emotionally more mature.

Since object formation implies a separation of self and action, it is therefore
also the beginning of the self-concept. That the self-concept is derived from
the experience of personal interaction is today universally accepted. What is
less readily appreciated is that the self, like any other object, can only become
something known when the child's intelligence has developed to the point
where it can construct an adequate framework. The child needs theoretical
schemes to which the self's interaction can be assimilated and through which
a more or less conscious representation—the self image—can be formed. In
turn, concepts of other persons are acquired in a corresponding fashion from

the matrix of self–other interactions. The third social element which has its experiential source in personal interaction is the society, first starting with the smaller group of the family but eventually extending to society-at-large. It makes sense to assume that the development of the self-concept, of relating to others and of becoming a part of society are three interrelated components of the same process which could be called 'getting to know one's society' or simply 'socialisation'.

The point to stress here is that, contrary to appearances, the Piagetian perspective is quite open to the realities of the social world and is by no means limited to scientific thinking about physical dimensions. Having discovered biological and sensorimotor co-ordinations as the genetic pre-forms of logical co-ordinations and positing them as organising schemes within the most primitive manifestation of life, Piaget's theory is certainly applicable to the social, affective and moral aspects of human behaviour. It is as legitimate to talk of schemes in these areas as one talks of perceptual schemes for co-ordinating perceptual processes. Even more to the point, Piaget as a theorist holds to a unitary and all-pervading conception of intelligence. What gives structure to social relation, to emotional balance, to moral values is the same intelligence that also gives structure to physical dimensions. A logical-mathematical framework is not merely good for scientific thinking, it is also at work in those other fields. Some components of logic are found in all human activities—this means really no more than that some knowledge is present in all behaviours—but note also that logic alone cannot adequately describe any human activity.

Piaget's favourite alternative word for schemes is 'co-ordinations'. He calls fully organised logical schemes 'operations' which in the social field takes the form of 'co-operation'. This is not a mere playing with words. Even though one does not customarily associate interpersonal relations with knowledge, instead one refers to them as behaviours, attitudes, emotions, motivations, they imply co-ordinations. With Piaget we broaden the meaning of the knowledge concept and then have no difficulty discovering aspects of knowledge, including knowledge of self, of others and of society, in all relating. This knowledge would be at different stages of development, consciousness and verbalisation, not unlike knowledge of physical things: even fully developed operations are not things the child can easily be conscious of or verbalise. Fully formed operations are instruments of organising something, like solving a problem, understanding a situation, according to an internal criterion that derives from the operations themselves. Analogously, mature co-operations in the social field are schemes of relating, of understanding a social situation according to a criterion that recognises both self and others as autonomous persons.

(c) Concerning the language of society—speech—the child assimilates it as soon as it serves a functional purpose, that is, toward the time of object formation which ushers in the capacity to symbolise. This by itself shows the dependency of speech on theoretical thinking. What is even more important is the concomitant qualitative change from signal to symbol communication. Signal communication as part of sensorimotor functioning refers to present events or demands, while symbolic communication is free to refer to events absent and unconnected with immediate demands, hence it was called above communication for its own sake.

It is usual to select two aspects in which speech seems to be unique and different from other forms of representation, particularly, spontaneous gestures and mental images: its arbitrariness and internal grammar. Now it is true enough that the word 'moon' appears to be an arbitrary human product, whereas the half-moon shape of an image is apparently imposed by the shape of the moon itself. However, for the young child in an English-speaking community the sound sequence 'moon' is experienced as much a part of the moon event as is its visual shape. Moreover, the adult may still use a visual image of a half-moon without thereby failing to know that a moon can appear full or be completely hidden in darkness or behind clouds. In other words, what counts in symbol use is the underlying knowledge to which the symbol is assimilated, not whether the symbol has or does not have a pictorial likeness. If by opposite of arbitrary one means imposed by, and undifferentiated from, the external event, then to no symbol can one assign a non-arbitrary origin— as one can, for instance, to a conditioned signal—since the source of symbolic meaning resides in internal theroretical schemes on which all differentiated (= arbitrary) knowledge depends. Recent studies of the gestural sign language of deaf people confirm this proposition unequivocally. Gestures that an observer can readily associate as pictorial imitations, when habitually used, lose for the deaf persons the pictorial quality and are treated as conventional, that is, arbitrary combinations of gestural elements (Klima and Bellugi, 1977). Even the spontaneously acquired gestures of those deaf children who are not exposed to the sign language of other deaf persons are clearly used as symbols and not merely as signals; more to the point, studies of these deaf children also indicate that they employ grammatical frames without any external model. If these initial results become further confirmed and expanded, we shall have empirical evidence for what otherwise would remain a theoretical position, namely, that crucial parts of so-called linguistic universals have their source within the developing intelligence of the child rather than being primarily due to the environmental language.

In effect language acquisition can be described as follows. Children who have reached the developmental stage of symbol formation and symbolic communication construct a system of arbitrary symbols and grammatical rules in conformity with the given speech model, not unlike how, for social relations, they construct general schemes that conform to society's model. The very instrument which was supposed to carry the burden of explaining acquisition from outside, and was singled out as arbitrarily imposed by external convention, can no longer be seen in this light. Rather, acquisition of language seems to conform much better to the general developmental model of Piaget where the main thrust is an internal construction of rules on the part of the subject with the environmental contribution limited to specific content.

In concluding this section we note the three factors contributing to the growth of intelligence, one internal to this intelligence which is variously referred to as developmental feedback, co-ordination experience or equilibration, and two others, one as the biological base, the other as the content component to which intelligence gives structure. This content is chiefly the personal self which interacts with events within a social world. Through equilibration these interactions create the subjective co-ordinations (=intelligence) of sensorimotor and theoretical schemes, which include understanding of self, relating to others and society, and dealing with the symbolic and physical products of society. The environmental component of the equilibration leads to the learning of specific content with respect to the entire gamut of life experiences. Symbolic representation was described as the psychological function through which absent content of knowledge is conserved and society's language was shown to derive its formal quality of arbitrariness of grammar from its being symbolic communication, with the environmental model providing the specific linguistic content.

The Developing Person

Concerning Piaget's conception of stages, one would do well to ascribe to them a mobile rather than a rigid or all-encompassing status which would militate against the very model of Piaget's structural development. Stages refer to characteristic structural properties of behaviour in contrast to levels in the sense of observable performance criteria. They are simply cross-sections of a continuous developmental process and, like the divisions of the colour continuum, have something arbitrary about them, albeit only to a certain extent. For this reason one should focus first on the most convincing and most fundamental stage differences, namely those between sensorimotor and theoretical schemes on the one hand and those between instinctual and acquired sensorimotor schemes on the other hand. Next in importance are the substages Piaget proposes within sensorimotor functioning and the definition of an achieved operation in contrast to pre-operations. Finally, there is the proposed stage distinction between formal and concrete operations. So we have three or four stages for humans: sensorimotor, pre-operatory, concrete and formal operations with the corresponding chronological onset at birth, and then around two, six and thirteen years respectively.

Operations are strictly defined as logical-mathematical systems which form a structured whole and thereby assure invariance (=the conservation of the whole) and reversibility (=the transformation of single parts within the whole). Operations are most clearly observed in the fields of natural sciences.

Their application in other fields, where other than cognitive components take on a more predominant role, is less literal but still quite meaningful, such as in the field of moral and social relation. The problem with formal thinking is its abstract, field-independent nature. For that reason it is, on the one hand, less readily observable and, on the other hand, its application to any specific area, while theoretically always possible, is in practice severely limited by cultural and personal contingencies.

Piaget's substages of sensorimotor functioning, which he inferred from observing his own three children, have been repeatedly confirmed. It would be erroneous to assume that around age two sensorimotor development is finished. Piaget's interest being the origin of scientific thinking, he searched for its root in the sensorimotor stage and followed it until the first appearance of theoretical thinking, after which he pursued the further development of theoretical thinking. In fact there are of course many facets of sensorimotor function which develop at a much later time. Further, the presence of theoretical thinking has continuous repercussion on the sensorimotor functioning as Piaget observed most clearly in perceptual processes. Finally, sensorimotor functioning remains not only the genetic root from which the co-ordinations of theoretical actions derive, but also a constant present concomitant of all human functioning, at the very least in relation to the material form of a symbolic image (e.g., the visual shape of the image) or the position and functioning of the body (sitting or reading).

Stages are as 'real' as is development, of which they are a temporary cross-section. In order to describe the developing child, Piaget as observer limits his investigation to particular concepts, e.g., quantity, speed, causality, space. When he then analyses the development of these concepts, he suggests a number of substages. In general, it will be found that it is the concepts that are in stages, not the children. In Piaget's perspective, as was pointed out earlier, the same concrete behaviour can be structured simultaneously by schemes of differing substages, or on a same task the same person can use different substages on repeated occasions. If development does not follow a cumulative linear model of reliable levels of performance, one should not expect that developmental stages have the psychometrically desirable qualities of reliability, individual predictability, normal distribution and age progression. This statement does not imply the end of psychology as empirical science, but it does suggest that the model of a standardised individual score of intelligence may be misleading and not fruitful as a scientific quest, even though it may have some practical and managerial utility.

While stages reflect and describe development, they do not explain it. They indicate the direction where the explanation has to be found, namely, within the structuring activity itself and not in the environment towards which accommodation is directed. This is so for two reasons. Stage differences are differences in structure, not in content, and living structure cannot arise or be imposed from outside the organism. But in this connection a profound problem arises. It involves the paradox implied in the saying, 'the more you know, the more you know what you don't know'. A structure is by definition a whole; and a living whole is characterised as being in a state of equilibration. But why should a whole change unless the balance characteristic of human intelligence carries within it the seed of dis-equilibration?

Equilibration is a concept for which everything about Piaget's theory should have prepared us and it remains to enlarge on its significance. Consider again Figure 5.4. There, equilibration is pictured as the essential behavioural manifestation of intelligence-in-action. It is an equilibration between general subjective co-ordinations and particular content. Equilibration means schemes to which content is assimilated and content to which schemes are accommodated. This is the knowing circle of Figures 5.1 to 5.3. However, knowing is not a uni-level affair and what is content is not absolute or simply given. Consequently we deal with a mobile equilibration which is open on both sides, on the subject side, the subject changes and on the content side, the object changes.

All behaviour, including knowing, implies the assimilation of events into a multiple network of schemes. This network of mutual relations of the schemes is itself a state of equilibration and it provides the person with the opportunity to focus on one or another content in relation to particular schemes. As an illustration, to a child a particular teacher may also be known as a football player and this can lead to a comparison of two overlapping social roles. As another example, the same physical event of expanding a line of blocks can be viewed from the perspective of spatial extension or whole numbers. Piaget observed that the very act of knowing tends to focus on what is positive (what the event is) and neglects the negative aspects of a situation (what it is not). A child moving 'n' elements from collection A to collection B quite readily focuses on the act of addition, that is, assimilates the action to the schemes of addition, but is less likely to assimilate it to the corresponding schemes of subtraction. As a consequence, this child will not easily answer the question about the just created difference between A and B with a judgement based on structural knowing (the difference $= 2n$), but rather may have to count and rely on empirical evidence. This preference for the positive is linked to sensorimotor functioning where the goal-directed action is of paramount biological importance, the goal being invariably what a thing is or does, and not what it is not. Thus, even though negative schemes are available, their active use is in part a function of the extent to which the structures have been adequately developed.

Piaget's general model of equilibration is shown in Figure 5.5. It represents his recent attempt (Piaget, 1975) to describe the concept in a more comprehensive way than before by the significant inclusion of the object of knowing and the use of two distinctions. First there is the familiar subject-object (S-O) distinction; in addition there is the distinction between what is observable and what is inferred. What is observable is usually referred to as an

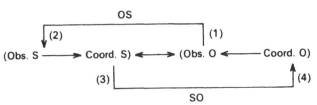

Figure 5.5 Piaget's model of equilibration. S, subject; O, object; Obs., observable ('facts');
Coord., co-ordination of Obs. The principal tendencies of equilibration are
indicated by the arrows, starting with Obs. O

observed fact and what is inferred is based on subjective co-ordinations. The
arrows indicate the principal directions in which the knowledge process
moves. The entire process is continually regulated by equilibration which in
Figure 5.5 connects the subject and the object and which in Piaget's
epistemology is equivalent to knowledge. This model dissects, if you like, the
multi-process nature of knowing and makes it possible to show how
restructuring is possible.

The process begins with becoming conscious of the results of actions, say,
the action of getting a chocolate from a machine. Here accommodation to the
external results prevails. Subsequently, the child may become conscious of the
subjective act of taking a coin, putting it in the particular slot in a particular
manner. We would say the child becomes aware of the assimilation of the
machine to the scheme of putting in a coin. Gradually the child begins to
interpret the subjective action as a lifting of the coin outside the machine
(which is observable) and a dropping of the coin inside the machine (which is
inferred). From this beginning the child may finally arrive at an understanding of the physical mechanism by which the machine operates. As a final
consequence an understanding of the machine's mechanism will now
influence the initial observation of various types of machines and their various
ways of displaying the product. With a new observation of O a new cycle of
equilibration commences and theoretically the process can go on *ad infinitum*.

Admittedly we have here a conception of knowledge as a multi-directional
and continuous process that covers a number of disparate components in a
most unaccustomed fashion, which merely goes to show why of all of Piaget's
concepts equilibration is universally singled out as most mysterious.
Consider: knowledge is equilibration and thus the entire process is implicitly
contained in any one act of knowing. Yet the entire process may take years to
come to completion. Putting a coin in the box and expecting a chocolate can
be as early as sensorimotor co-ordination or as advanced as formal
understanding of mechanical laws. What the model underscores is the
impossibility of treating knowledge as a given state that can be transmitted as
a neat package of given objects, to be registered as known. Knowing
'what a vending machine is' just is not one piece of information or knowing a

fact: it covers all possible developmental stages. Each stage represents this knowing in a qualitatively different manner and some disparate stage characteristics may work simultaneously while others are subsumed in higher stages. Equilibration makes explicit the four aspects of the knowledge component of any behaviour that were mentioned in the beginning: the cognitive structure and its development, the object content and its learning. In so far as the concept of equilibration relates these aspects, it goes far toward explaining why intelligence and development are correlative terms. We begin to understand Piaget's claim that the structure of development and the structure of intelligence are two sides of the same coin: they are both regulated by the same process of equilibration. This process, however, is more readily observed in developmental changes than in the habitual acts of equilibrated intelligence.

Clearly then, not every act of behaving or knowing fits the model of equilibration in its entirety. Sometimes one, sometimes another component comes to the fore. In habitual behaviour, for example, the equilibration between S and O is well established and the act merely reinforces the established habit. When appropriate schemes are unavailable to the child there is no choice but to transform a spontaneously arising or imposed problem into something entirely different which the child can assimilate. Thus to a four-year-old child the creation of Lake Geneva is understood in the manner of the making of a puddle in a sand box. Between these two extreme cases, however, there is a vast array of situations the understanding of which is, first, adequate for present functioning, but second, is in potential discrepancy with an otherwise established knowing. This then can be the origin of a state of conflict, a disturbance which disrupts the psychological equilibrium. I say 'psychological' because a conflict situation can make the workings of equilibration conscious, if only by the half-unconscious awareness of a question that sooner or later requires an answer (I am using the words questions and answers in their formal, not literal sense). These occasions of intellectual challenge and of vigorous intellectual activity on the theoretical stage can aptly be likened to the strenuous actions of the sensorimotor stage which indicates the health and the growth of physical co-ordinations. Similarly these challenging occasions are symptoms of the health and the growth of theoretical intelligence.

All intellectual progress is at the same time compensation and reconstruction, compensation with respect to a previous disequilibrium, reconstruction with respect to change in the cognitive structure. Frequently this change does not abolish the external occasion of the disequilibrium, but on the contrary subsumes it into a transformation explainable and, therefore, predictable by the restructured whole. Thus the flying of planes may be seen as a disturbing factor vis-à-vis gravity. When, however, properly understood it is not only not contrary to, but actually confirms the system of gravity and mutual attraction.

In concluding this section we realise why Piaget proposes equilibration as the intrinsic motor of intellectual development, whatever role extrinsic motivation may play. The developmental process is multi-directional, from subject to object, and vice-versa; from observable to inference, and vice-versa; and multi-linear, that is, simultaneously at different stages. A particular child's graph of intellectual growth would not resemble a straight ascending line, rather a fuzzy zig-zag with spurts and starts, including temporary recessions, but in the long run inexorably rising. But since development is a restructuring, a more appropriate picture, a favourite of Piaget, is the upside-down pyramid; or better, a spiral ascending and getting larger, but returning to earlier positions which are now subsumed in a higher and more general synthesis.

Status of Piagetian Psychology

That Piaget's theory is popular is beyond dispute; however, whether this popularity is matched by an adequate understanding of his theory is very doubtful. He is best known in a field that engaged only his marginal interest, namely, education; he is least known in the field closest to his heart, namely, philosophical epistemology. Psychologists in general are somewhat puzzled by the tremendous scope of the Piagetian work, the philosophical depth and the uncertain empirical base. Why this ambivalent reaction?

Social scientists are probably quite unaccustomed to be serious about epistemological considerations. The traditional emphasis on stimuli, performance and physiological states provides scant points of reference into which to fit questions about the process of knowledge, its acquisition and its multiple components. They are justifiably suspicious of dogmatic pronouncements. Even where they have no choice but to accept the psychological data which Piagetian research has made available, their first inclination is to explain the data within a different epistemological perspective, quite unaware that by so doing the very data change. An early illustration of this state of affairs were the psychologists who claimed to disprove Piaget's notion of egocentrism by counting the frequency of 'I' and 'me' in children's speech as an index of egocentricity; more recently, psychologists (Bryant, 1974) claimed to observe operations of number or transitivity in very young children—again as a disconfirmation of Piaget's theory—without taking into account that for Piaget operation is a precisely defined term which cannot be equated with an isolated performance. Moreover, pre-forms of operations can always be discovered at much earlier, even sensorimotor stages. If Piaget refuses to equate intelligence with performance measures, this is not because he objects to them in principle, witness his countless observations that have permanently enriched the psychological literature. Controlled data are clearly a prerequisite of any science that claims to be empirical. But adequate interpretation of these 'facts' is just as crucial and this depends on the underlying theory according to which these facts were observed.

Yet in spite of the fact that much psychological research of Piagetian data reveals more about basic misunderstandings of the theory on the part of the researchers than about the adequacy and further elaborations of the theory, there is a sufficient momentum of serious research, both within the field as well as in allied areas, that Piaget's lasting contribution to psychological thinking is assured. At the very least concepts such as development, structure and cognition have become respectable topics of psychological discussion whether or not they are seen in Piaget's peculiar perspective where they form three aspects of the same thing.

The least controversial of Piaget's discoveries are the observations of his three children on which he founded the theory of sensorimotor functioning. Another body of research, much more controversial, deals with the pre-operatory period, or more precisely, the question whether or not children functioning in a pre-operatory manner can be taught to acquire concrete operations. The literature is by now quite vast. The conclusion, as one could expect, is certainly not an outright rejection of Piaget's claim that the development of schemes and the learning of performances are two different things and that, strictly speaking, schemes cannot be 'taught.' On the other hand, Piaget has become more supple and incorporated the objective, observable situation as well as subjective conflict within his newer model of equilibration and also taken more seriously the notion that in some situations development and learning are two perspectives of the same behaviour. In this sense the Genevans themselves (Inhelder *et al.*, 1974) have now published a series of studies in which children, pre-operatory on certain tasks, are induced to engage in behavioural activities to bring about operatory functioning.

A third area of research deals with cultural differences and with purported claims of universality in Piaget's theory (Dasen, 1976). This research is frequently concerned with standardised norms, as for instance when the attempt is made to compare the chronological onset or the presence of certain operations in particular cultures. Leaving the discussion of Piagetian test-norms for later, we can come to similar conclusions here as in the training studies. No clear case of reversal of main stages has been observed; which in my opinion is really a logical impossibility needing no empirical proof. The observed infrequency or absence of formal thinking—if one can accept the facts—would only be a serious challenge to Piaget's theory, if he postulated a development entirely directed from within the person and if more were known about the occasions and distribution of formal operations. The claim that some cultures have no concrete operations seems to me to reflect more the difficulties encountered by the observers than the inconceivable state of a society without any stable concepts. On the other hand, Piagetian theory has become more cautious in its claims of universality even though these claims were never more than implicit at the most. Concrete and, particularly, formal operations are stages of physical and scientific thinking and their counterparts in other areas of life are far from clear. Moreover, a theory like Piaget's that stresses the required equilibration between subjective and environmental components, can hardly propose that the cultural environment plays a negligible role. By definition, Piaget's conception of intelligence includes a cultural bias: this refers first to the conception of intelligence in general and then, as a particular case, to Piaget's own conception. It is not a Piagetian who would dream of a culturally unbiased intelligence test. As one consequence of studies in different cultures Piagetians have become more aware of the culture-dependent pressures that direct the application of a child's intelligence in one field more than in another.

As a special case of environmental variations there is the case of persons deficient in some part of body or sense. As a result they are deprived of a whole segment of what is otherwise included in the natural human environment. Profound deafness, blindness and total paralysis at birth are three conditions which preclude auditory or visual input or moving around respectively. Without auditory input the acquisition of society's language is impossible except by laborious industry of formal teaching through which a limited number of deaf persons acquire language competence. But the great majority of persons born profoundly deaf hardly ever, if at all, arrive at a comfortable knowledge of society's language. In contrast, they become eventually adept at a sign language of gestures. In any case, most deaf children during the first six to ten years are literally children without a convention language provided by society. If language is theorised as a crucial contributor to the development of intelligence, one would easily expect to discover wide-spread intellectual deficiencies in these deaf children. That extensive research (Furth, 1973) has not confirmed these expectations is a clear case where empirical observations prove a particular theory wrong. Moreover, the evidence strongly, albeit indirectly, confirms Piaget's theory for which conventional language is in no respect a source or a necessary ingredient of logical operations. In the case of children born totally blind, they cannot possibly have visual images. In so far as one observes in them good orientation in space and quite adequate recall for past events, this observation argues against a theory of spatial knowledge and of recall memory which is based on storage of visual images. Finally, the relatively normal intellectual development of persons body-paralysed from birth indicates that the occasions for developmental feedback need not necessarily extend to strenuous external activity, even though for healthy children this activity will be a normal part of their functioning and developing. In general these special conditions point to the relative independence of the development of human intelligence from specific sense or body modalities and indirectly are proof for an epistemology such as Piaget's, that posits the source of intellectual growth within the organising core of the person rather than in specific input or output.

It is rather remarkable that close to twenty years' effort at establishing standardised norms for Piagetian tasks has not created even half-way satisfactory instruments or norms that could be used for purposes of individual testing or group comparisons. Some reasons for this have been mentioned earlier and they all can be reduced to the one factor that Piaget appears assiduously to have disregarded: individual differences. It is true that he has never studied differences between individuals since his aim was to discover what is common and invariant in human development. But it is also true that the theory is quite tolerant of individual differences to a degree that would make test and measurement people quite uncomfortable. Concerning stages, Piaget has never propounded any age norms and is merely insisting on regular succession. Concerning variability of personal inclinations and the effects of motivational components, Piaget's theory has nothing special to offer except to take away the need to explain intellectual growth fully by means of factors external to intelligence: this is taken care of by the intrinsic component of equilibration.

This quest for what is common rather than for individual differences lies also at the core of Piaget's method for gathering evidence. He is out to discover the spontaneous tendencies of a person's thinking in the form of samples of verbal and non-verbal behaviour from which he can infer the underlying structure of thinking. Now this is a precarious enterprise and open to all kinds of obstacles. Piaget is the first to admit this and puts down rigorous safeguards to make the psychological observations and subsequent interpretations less open to ambiguity. But when all is said and done, Piaget's method of the clinical interview can never achieve the impersonal exactitude of a standardised test. However, for Piaget's epistemological purpose the method suffices and in any case constitutes a radical shift from all previous epistemological endeavours which proceeded *more philosophico*.

What are some current research implications of Piaget's theory? First, the central concept of equilibration, only recently worked out theoretically in sufficient detail, requires a great deal of empirical underpinning. His recent monographs on this topic, including Genevan research on cognitive conflict and grasp of consciousness, delineate some of the directions this research may take. Likewise, a new interest in individual strategies should clarify the concrete application of intellectual structures in the solving of given problems.

Second, in the area of early language acquisition there is now a widening of interest beyond the confines of vocabulary and syntax. With attention more on semantic meaning there is a concomitant switch toward studying the linguistic interaction. As a result the development of communication and symbolic representation has now come to be the focus of early language research and Piagetian theory is quite relevant and fruitful in this context.

A third large area where Piagetian research is having an increasing influence is the field of social interaction in the manifold aspects of a child's developing social cognition: moral judgement, role taking, understanding of personal interaction, self concept, societal understanding. This is a vast, as yet largely uncharted area, where a Piagetian perspective provides new and promising directions.

There have been as yet only a few Piagetian studies of developmental operations beyond adolescence to cover the life span including old age. In fact, there still remains an urgent need to study more carefully what Piaget calls formal operations, since his own research was limited to one selected sample of high-school students. In contrast to concrete operations the acquisition of which is assured by the presence of physical realities, the occasions for the acquisition of formal operations are obscure as is the theoretical question whether they should be considered part of normal development or comparable to a specialised interest or occupation (Piaget, 1972). This is clearly tied up with the broader problem of whether formal operations are directly applicable to scientific problems and only indirectly to other realms or whether there are different forms of formal operations depending on the field (e.g., in social relations, history, art).

Considering applied fields, Piaget's work is tremendously influential in educational circles and has been one of the main overarching theories to inspire new efforts in modern curricula, teaching methods, and new topics. In the field of mental health too, those interested in the well-being of children are beginning to overcome their strong bias against what they fear to be over-intellectualising and realise that the child's intelligence, if well used, can be a strong force for, indeed is part of, mental health. This seems particularly true for the age period of five to twelve which coincides with Freud's latency period and Piaget's period of concrete operations. At this stage children seem to have worked out their major emotional and social crises and at the same time they are beginning to experience themselves for the first time as authentic thinkers in possession of a stable cognitive framework, namely the achieved operations. Consequently the repercussions of a healthy intellectual functioning on overall mental health and ego strength makes the early school experience quite crucial. Piaget's theory is probably best applied in judging what activities are apt to challenge the child's intelligence and thus bring about an intellectually healthy school atmosphere (Furth and Wachs, 1974).

Conclusions

It will no doubt be noted as a curious historical fact that Piaget is the first psychological investigator who, a century and a half after the publication of the then revolutionary and universally acclaimed Kantian critique, took apparently so simple a step as to observe the biological and psychological base of the mind which the philosopher described. In the meantime the synthesis which Kant had constructed in order to bridge the gap between empiricism and idealism remained a philosophical speculation. As a consequence the 19th century with its tremendous expansion of the natural sciences and the birth of empirical psychology could afford to neglect the epistemological issue and continue for a while in the empiricist tradition. Philosophers, having been made aware through Kant of the untenable position of a pure empiricism, came up with two compromise solutions which initially satisfied both the scientist and the epistemologist.

On the one side, the pure empiricism of positivism (truth equals existing facts) was modified towards what came to be called logical positivism (truth equals scientific propositions about facts) with more and more emphasis on the way language is used in the verbal or mathematical statements that comprise the scientific corpus. Analytical philosophy became primarily an analysis of scientific language. This trend contributed to and was in turn supported, first, by linguistics—the first successful empirical social science— and second, the popular belief that tended to equate knowledge and language. Language, as an external conventional symbol system of the community, seemed to provide a convenient handle through which to get to the ephemeral nature of human knowledge.

On the other side and as a direct consequence of Kant's dictum that science deals with things as they appear, not as they are, philosophers were quick to dismantle the precarious bridge Kant had attempted to build and acclaimed two kinds of knowledge, one proper to science and given over to an empiricistic epistemology, the other of an existential kind and more akin to an idealistic epistemology. To make matters worse and create a veritable schism within man's knowledge structure, these two knowledges were proposed to be largely unrelated. In addition, physical scientists who appeared to be the staunchest supporters and witnesses of the success of the empiricist tradition, toward the end of the century and increasingly since then, started to question the very base of that tradition, namely the static physical reality itself.

Largely unperturbed by these epistemological upheavals, empirical psychology has stayed firmly in the empiricist tradition and searched assiduously for its 'facts' throughout its chequered history. Whether they were facts of consciousness, sensations, stimuli, performance criteria, environmental contingencies, physiological states, information, as long as they could be measured and adequately described, that sufficed. Consider the dilemma: what epistemology could psychology espouse, the science which was supposed to provide an empirical solution to psychological problems, including that of intelligence and knowledge? The only model psychologists could work with was the empiricistic one. What indeed can a scientist do with an idealistic or an existential epistemology that is conceived as opposed to scientific thinking?

Piaget recognised the dilemma which faces the psychological investigator of knowledge and took it by both horns. Rejecting with Kant as inadequate both extremes of the empiricist–idealist pole; he refused with equal conviction the compromise of two types of knowledges. Instead he modified the sense in which the *a priori* should be understood and analysed as an empirical investigator the apparent paradox contained in Kant's categories and the juxtaposition of experience and innate in Kant's synthetic *a priori*. By retaining the essential component of the *a priori* in the sense of an internal biological precondition and eliminating the irrelevant temporal sense of 'from the start', he constructed again the bridge that Kant had first conceived, but this time on the empirical base of observing the construction of the categories. Piaget's research attempts to provide empirical evidence that intelligence is neither innately pre-programmed nor merely a learning from without, but, as Kant had proposed, a process of structural acquisition from within. Kant's *a priori*, the philosophical base of logical necessity and universal judgements, instead of being a preconceived starting condition which eludes all explanation, becomes for Piaget the logical end product of the observable structural development.

In this manner, Piaget's epistemology is no longer a mere philosophical theorising; it is linked to biological evolution and open to empirical observation. With Piaget it has become 'genetic' and, as the preceding pages attempted to show, he has for the first time given substance to a psychology of 'pure reason' and its development. Only time will tell how psychology as a whole will ultimately respond to the challenge of Piaget's genetic epistemology.

References

Bryant, P. (1974). *Perception and Understanding in Young Children*, Methuen, London
Dasen, P. R. (ed.) (1976). *Piagetian Psychology: Cross-cultural Contributions*, Garden Press, New York
Furth, H. G. (1973). *Deafness and Learning: A Psycho-social Approach*, Wadsworth, Belmont, California
Furth, H. G. and Wachs, H. (1974). *Thinking Goes to School: Piaget's Theory in Practice*, Oxford, New York
Inhelder, B., Sinclair, H. and Bovet, M. (1974). *Learning and the Development of Cognition*, Harvard University, Cambridge, Mass
Klima, E. S. and Bellugi, U. (1977). *The Signs of Language*, Harvard University, Cambridge, Mass
Piaget, J. (1972). Intellectual evolution from adolescence to adulthood. *Human Development*, **15,** 1
Piaget, J. (1975). *Equilibration des Structures*, Presse Universitaire de France, Paris; English translation *The Development of Thought: Equilibration of Cognitive Structures*, Viking Press, New York (1977)

6 Two Decades of Research into Early Language

ROGER GOODWIN

(*School of Cultural and Community Studies, University of Sussex, Falmer, Brighton, Sussex, England*)

Introduction

It is one of the truisms of science that progress generally comes from simplifying the phenomena under study, and then proceeding step-by-step from the simple to the complex cases. The idea that complex behaviour could be understood as the outcome of many simple, experimentally isolable processes was a central tenet of behaviourism. More recently, psycholinguistics has provided a counter example to these beliefs. While our knowledge of such supposedly simple and basic processes as the learning of simple associations between words has scarcely advanced at all, the last 15 years have seen an exciting revival of research into the acquisition of language itself. This is undoubtedly one of the success stories of developmental psychology, since it has yielded a substantial body of observations which are proving to be reliably replicable in subsequent studies of different children, learning different and unrelated languages. Perhaps most impressive of all, many observations are even proving replicable with different observers. This chapter aims to tell something of the history of this research and the theories that have guided it, and to suggest some likely future directions that it may take.

Developmental psycholinguistics, besides being a fascinating subject in its own right, may well prove to have much to offer to cognitive psychology and to linguistics. For psychology, it can provide potentially a vital source of evidence on the course of cognitive development in children. Thus, after hearing a child correctly use some linguistic form such as, for example, the comparative, one can ask 'What cognitive abilities must the child possess in order to be able to say that?'

Conversely, a child's initial inaccuracies and omissions may provide helpful diagnostic clues to his cognitive organisation. The study of the spontaneous speech of children is a potentially valuable source of information which has scarcely been exploited by Piaget and his followers. Further, their use of the clinical method of interview often assumes that the child understands the question, even though he may lack all the means required to produce the correct answer. This assumption is unwarranted. It may well be that he has not understood the question and has simply not tried to find the solution to the problem which the interviewer believes he has posed.

One of the central concerns of linguistics has always been the study of the processes by which languages change. Since the last century, it has been argued that languages evolve because each successive generation of a speech community learns a slightly different language from that spoken by its parents. Hockett (1950) insists that the most important environmental influence on the emerging dialect of a child is the speech of other children. This fact is well understood by middle-class parents in England when they select a school for their children. Since linguistic evolution is primarily the work of successive generations of small children, it seems likely that knowledge of how they acquire their native language might tell us how and why they change it. This possibility has recently been explored by Antilla (1976), Baron (1974), and notably by Traugott (1974) in her discussion of spatial terms. Slobin (1977) has also drawn parallels between the ontogeny of language in children, and the phylogentic development of pidgin languages, as they emerge from their origins as auxilliary languages, used primarily for the restricted purposes of trade, into fully-fledged languages, with their own native speakers, called creoles.

The acquisition of language has been of perennial interest not only to linguists but also to philosophers, both speculative and natural, and there is a long tradition of careful observational study. Bar-Adon and Leopold (1971) have reprinted a selection of this work. Some of this research, notably the monumental study by Leopold (1939–49) of the development of English-German bilingualism, is of exceptional merit. The distinctive innovations of recent work come not in methodology, where there has sometimes been some regression, but in the linguistic and psychological theories which are used to organise and interpret observations.

The Influence of Chomsky

The new theories were provided by the great linguist Noam Chomsky. His enduring achievement can be summed up, in an outrageously oversimplified way, by the slogan 'Chomsky showed that languages are more than jigsaw puzzles'. His revolutionary book *Syntactic Structures*, published in 1957, is the original spark which set off the new wave of research into language acquisition. As we shall see, developments in linguistic theory, rather than psychology, have guided this research ever since.

Chomsky provided an explicit theory, or 'generative grammar', which precisely delineated and gave structural descriptions for a wide variety of the sentences of English. In doing this, he demonstrated that languages are not made up merely of separate and individually shaped components which somehow fit together to form a coherent whole (the 'jigsaw puzzle' metaphor), but are organised according to powerful and precisely specifiable rules, some of which control the form of almost every sentence of the language. Chomsky went further and claimed that some of these rules might be found, subject to essentially insignificant variation, in many, if not all, human natural languages. The common properties of languages would be reflected in 'linguistic universals', which specify the form of grammars needed to describe them.

The central working principle of Chomsky and his school is the 'autonomy of syntax': that the grammar of a language may be investigated without taking meaning into account. This principle has proved increasingly hard to maintain, and many younger linguists, of the so called 'generative semantics' persuasion, no longer adhere to it. Chomsky took as his data single isolated sentences abstracted from any linguistic or extralinguistic context. He thus confined his attention to the structural organisation of the sentence (the syntactic approach) and debarred himself from studying how language is used (the functional approach). He also, along with most other linguists, ruled out any unit of linguistic analysis larger than the sentence. He was therefore able to say nothing about how successive sentences, produced by one or more persons, link together to form a coherent text. An understanding of these processes of linguistic 'cohesion,' as Halliday and Hasan (1976) call it, is essential for any study of the use of language in social interaction (the conversational approach).

The history of theoretical linguistics in the years between the publication of Chomsky's first book, *Syntactic Structures*, in 1957 and that of his second book, *Aspects of the Theory of Syntax*, in 1965, consisted largely of the clarification and extension of his syntactic approach. The years since then have seen increasing efforts to escape from the grave, self-imposed limitations in Chomsky's methodology and discuss those aspects of language which he excluded from linguistics, while trying to maintain the standards of precision and logical rigour set by him. Despite these limitations of scope, Chomsky's theories provided the original intellectual stimulus for contemporary psycholinguistics.

On the basis of his theories about the language of adults, Chomsky put forward a number of provocative claims about how children acquire language. Thus he argued (Chomsky, 1971, p. 429):

'In formal terms, then, we can describe the child's acquisition of language as a kind of theory construction. The child discovers the theory of his language with only small amounts of data from that language. Not only does his "theory of the language" have an enormous predictive scope, but it also enables the child to reject a great deal of the very data on which the theory has been constructed. Normal speech consists, in large part, of fragments, false starts, blends, and other distortions of the underlying idealised forms. Nevertheless, as is evident from a study of the mature use of language, what the child learns is the underlying ideal theory. This is a remarkable fact. We must also bear in mind that the child constructs this ideal theory without explicit instruction, that he acquires this knowledge at a time when he is not capable of complex intellectual achievements in many other domains and that this achievement is relatively independent of intelligence or the particular course of experience. These are facts that a theory of learning must face.'

Chomsky's claims about language learning can be summarised as follows: (1) Every mature native speaker of a language has a precise and complete, though perhaps slightly idiosyncratic, knowledge of the syntax of his language, termed his 'linguistic competence'. The fundamental task in learning a language is the acquisition of this knowledge. (2) Language learning commences at about two years of age and is substantially complete by the age of five, before entry to school. (3) Children are able to learn the grammar of their language despite being exposed to a great deal of ungrammaticality in the speech of their caretakers. These adults give the children little, if any, specific language tuition.

On the basis of these premises, Chomsky concluded that language learning is only possible because every human infant has an innate faculty for the task, which is part of the genetic endowment of the human species. Human language is far too complex for any organism to acquire through a process of conditioning, as had been proposed by Skinner (1957) and others. As we shall see, the first of Chomsky's premises has now been rejected, since everyone has come to see that there is more to language than syntax. His second premise was disproved by Mrs Chomsky (1969), when she showed that children of up to ten years of age have still not fully mastered certain complex, but by no means obscure, grammatical constructions. The third premise is also in the process of being disproved. Nonetheless, Chomsky deserves our gratitude for having put forward such fruitful ideas and thereby rekindling scientific interest in language acquisition. Nor has the invalidation of his premises necessarily disproved his conclusion, which remains an interesting possibility.

History

In the 50 years B(efore) C(homsky), the 'jigsaw puzzle' metaphor of language held sway, and led to a concern with the acquisition of vocabulary. The results of this work are summarised by McCarthy (1954). Since the conceptual revolution brought about by Chomsky, research has been guided by a succession of theoretical viewpoints each of which can, in retrospect, be seen to have evolved from what went before. In the early 1960s, Roger Brown and his associates at Harvard, Martin Braine in Maryland, and Susan Ervin-Tripp and Wick Miller at Berkeley, independently inaugurated the syntactic approach to language development. In the later 1960s, Lois Bloom and I. M. Schlesinger, still working within an essentially linguistic framework, added meaning to grammar to develop a semantic approach. The introduction of meaning led, via the new grammatical theories of Charles Fillmore, to the exploration of relations between language development and cognitive development, by John MacNamara, Derek Edwards and others. In the early 1970s, the British linguist Michael Halliday adopted a functional approach by asking what purposes language served for the young child. Today, researchers such as Elinor Keenan and Catherine Garvey, are exploring the origins of conversation, and the role of dialogue in the learning of language.

The basic method of research has been a careful longitudinal study involving naturalistic observation of small numbers of children, usually no more than three or four. The psycholinguist visits the child about once a month and records everything said by the child and said to the child by its caretakers, together with everything they do together, over a period of one to two hours. He then transcribes this data and attempts to write a grammar, or set of rules, which will describe the child's linguistic competence. As research has progressed, the conception of linguistic competence has extended beyond Chomsky's narrow emphasis on syntax to the notion of 'communicative competence': the ability to use language appropriately for a purpose. As a result, information about the extra-linguistic activities of the child and its caretakers, which provides the context of their utterances, has become almost as important as records of the utterances themselves.

The developmental psycholinguist is at a disadvantage compared with the anthropological linguist because it is very hard to obtain metalinguistic judgements from children concerning the linguistic acceptability of sentences. It is not impossible, however, since Gleitman *et al.* (1972) have found that, by five years of age, children are able to give explicit judgements of the grammaticality of utterances while even two-year-olds implicitly display, through their verbal and other reactions, a rudimentary awareness of what is or is not linguistically acceptable. Unfortunately, most young children lack the patience needed to be really good native informants on their language, so that detailed questioning is quite impossible.

The Syntactic Approach

Syntax governs the combination of words into larger linguistic units such as phrases and sentences, so a single-word sentence has no syntactic structure. By adopting the syntactic approach, Brown and the others were therefore led into beginning their studies of language acquisition with the first two- and three-word utterances of their children, and largely ignoring all the developments leading up to that accomplishment. Typical examples of the sentences they recorded are the following (from Braine's children):

P1 + O	O + P2	O + O
see boy	push it	morning sleep
pretty boat	boot off	pants change
my milk	airplane by	two checker
bye-bye man	Mama come	find bear
hi Mommy	hot in there	milk cup
more melon	bitty down there	
I sit		
No bed		
other bib		
that Tommy		

Notice that the examples consist almost entirely of content words (nouns, verbs and adjectives) together with deictics ('pointing words'), some spatial prepositions, some pronouns and a quantifier (*more*). With the exception of the negative particle, the grammatical function words such as articles and non-spatial prepositions, together with auxiliary verbs, are almost entirely absent. In languages which express grammatical relations by morphological inflections (changes in the form of words, particularly their endings), these too will be absent from the initial speech of children (see Slobin, 1966 for the example of Russian). The abbreviated nature of these utterances led Brown and Fraser (1963) to describe them very aptly as 'telegraphic speech'.

Braine (1963) analysed such sentences in terms of two syntactic categories,* pivot and open words. Words in the open class could occur alone, as one-word sentences, or in pairs, while pivot words seldom if ever occurred except in combination with an open word. Some children do not follow any definite rules of word order in their initial two-word sentences, so that they have only a single class of pivot words. But in most cases, they soon develop and consistently adhere to such rules and thereby divide their pivot words into sub-classes, one of which (P1) always comes before an open word, while the other (P2) always follows one (see the examples we have cited).

The children's syntax can be described by the following miniature grammar:

Phase Structure Rule:

$$S(\text{entence}) \longrightarrow \begin{Bmatrix} (P1) + O \\ O + (P2) \\ O + O \end{Bmatrix}$$

---

* 'A syntactic category is a group of words in a given language than can replace one another in any sentence of the language whatsoever without affecting grammaticality.' (Culicover, P. W. (1976). *Syntax*, Academic Press, p. 9).

Lexical Insertion Rules:

P1 $\longrightarrow$ see, pretty, my, bye-bye, no, that, etc.

P2 $\longrightarrow$ it, off, by, come, in there, etc.

O $\longrightarrow$ Mommy, boy, sock boot, sleep, change, two, etc.

$\longrightarrow$ denotes 'is expressed as'; one item only is chosen from within { }, while items within ( ) are optional.

Thus, in their earliest structured utterances, in which pairs of words are pronounced together, with a single pitch contour, the children are able to employ the grammatical devices of syntactic categories and word order. They are also able to make expressive use of intonation, although this has received little attention in contemporary research. They are not, however, able to use the other grammatical signals of morphology, and adpositions (such as the English preposition 'by' which precedes the agent in a passive sentence, or the Japanese post-positions *wa* and *ga* which follow the subject of a sentence).

In the sentences we have listed, the pivot class includes verbs, adjectives, pronouns, deictics and a quantifier, while the open class consists of nouns and verbs. Other children have included adjectives in their open class and very few nouns within the pivot class. From the point of view of adult grammar, therefore, the pivot and open classes are made up of a mixture of words from different syntactic categories. Indeed McNeill (1966) has claimed that no child studied by Brown, Braine or Ervin-Tripp and Miller had pivot and open classes corresponding exactly with any sub-division between the syntactic categories of adult speech. Brown and Bellugi (1964) describe the subsequent differentiation of the pivot class in the speech of the children, as they master the structure of noun phrases.

The linguistic competence of these children is genuinely 'creative' in Chomsky's sense of the term, since they produce far too many different sentences for there to be any possibility that they have learnt them by rote. More evidence against any theory of parrot-like imitation comes from an examination of the sentences themselves. For example, Braine (1963) found the pivot word *allgone* in such sentences as *allgone shoe, allgone vitamins, allgone lettuce*, where the only plausible adult models would be 'the shoe is allgone', etc. The children showed semantic as well as syntactic productivity, with such sentences as *allgone sticky*, said after washing hands, *allgone outside*, said after the front door had been shut, and *more page*, a request to mother to continue reading. The late Ruth Weir (1962) recorded a series of monologues produced by her 2½-year-old son Anthony, as he lay in bed at night. These contain many fascinating examples of creative play with language in which he produced novel combinations of sounds and words and systematically varied his pronunciations of words, almost as if he were working through the exercises in a language textbook.

Such evidence leads us to a view of language acquisition as an active process of re-invention by the child, in which his linguistic competence evolves through a succession of stages toward the adult form. We therefore regard small children as speaking a language of their own, rather than a simplified dialect of adult language distorted by errors and omissions.

The pivot grammar we have described was derived from distributional information concerning which words combine to form sentences and the serial orders in which they combine. The most we can hope to derive from this methodology is a description of the syntactic competence of the children. We can learn nothing about their semantic competence. More recently doubts have arisen about the adequacy of pivot-grammars even for the restricted task of describing syntax. The inadequacies are summarised by Bloom (1971). In her own research (Bloom, 1970) she failed to find a pivot class in the speech of two of the three children she studied. She also found that particular pivot words in the speech of a given child combine with only some of the words in the open class. For example, Braine had noted that for one child the pivot word *it* was always preceded by verbs. Bloom took careful notes of the context of sentences. These gave clear evidence that the same sentence could be used to express different meanings. For example *Mommy sock* was uttered in two separate contexts: (1) the child picking up her mother's sock, and (2) the mother putting the child's sock on her foot. In the first instance the sentence was interpreted as expressing a possessive relation, while in the second it referred to the agent and object of an action, but omitted the verb naming the action. Clearly, there is more to children's speech than its surface structure.

The Semantic Approach

Around 1968, I. M. Schlesinger, in Jerusalem, and Lois Bloom, in New York, independently proposed a radically new way of interpreting children's earliest structured sentences. Schlesinger's (1971, 1974, 1975) proposals have remained largely programmatic and interpretive, but Bloom (1970) reported a highly original and interesting study of language acquisition in three children—Eric, Gia, and Kathryn—performed for her doctoral dissertation at Columbia University. Their new idea was to describe the children's sentences not just in terms of their syntactic organisation, but in terms of meanings inferred from the linguistic and extralinguistic context in which they were uttered. Thus Bloom and Schlesinger claimed that, although they lacked many of the linguistic devices used to encode such concepts in adult speech, the children, nonetheless, intended to express certain fundamental semantic roles and relations such as agent and action, action and object, possessor and object of possession, and so on. With this innovation, Bloom and Schlesinger inaugurated the semantic approach to child language.

The process of imputing meaning to children's utterances on the basis of linguistically unexpressed contextual information has come to be known as 'rich interpretation'. The only grammatical signals initially available to children are the serial order of words, word classes (defined in terms of their serial order), and intonation. These are not enough to render their sentences unambiguously interpretable without any supporting context and even when contextual information is taken into account many sentences still remain ambiguous. So the best we can hope for from 'rich interpretation' is at least one plausible meaning for each utterance. We can seldom, if ever, be wholly certain that we have correctly understood what a two-year-old child meant to say. Nor, in practice, can the rudiments of metalinguistic awareness, which Gleitman *et al.* (1972) and de Villiers and de Villiers (1974) have shown in young children, be brought to bear on this problem.

Clearly 'rich interpretation' is an uncertain business. Psychologists have been properly wary of it, and the fundamental tenet of behaviourism was an absolute refusal to indulge in any such practice. In attempting to describe children's early language, we must be continually alert to the risk that we are producing a theory of how adults interpret the speech of the children rather than describing what the children are actually trying to say. Howe (1976) draws attention to a number of weaknesses in the 'rich interpretations' offered by Bloom, Schlesinger, Brown and Slobin, and suggests that future research should make far more effort to ascertain, by studying conversations between adults and children, which adult interpretations of their utterances the children will accept. Obviously, any interpretation placed upon a child's utterance must be within the limits imposed by that child's cognitive capacities, since a child cannot mean what it cannot yet think.

Semantic Relations

In retrospect, Bloom now seems somewhat cautious in interpreting her results, so that Brown (1970, 1973) has provided the most widely accepted summary of her findings and of others related to them. He presents a classification which, he claims, will describe at least 75 per cent of the sentences of children during their first stage of structured speech. Brown divides early sentences into (1) operations of reference, and (2) relations. Within operations of reference, four sub-classes are distinguished, as shown in Table 6.1.

These operations of reference are expressed by pivot and open (Pl + O) constructions and refer to only a single object, property or action in the environment.

The nominations are always used in the presence of the object referred to and are often accompanied by pointing and other gestures drawing the listener's attention to that object. (Slobin (1972) calls them 'pointing and naming'.) Brown notes that 'Hi' is not really a greeting, as it is used with inanimate nouns, as in 'Hi spoon', often when a child first notices an object. Recurrence can refer either to the reappearance of a given object or to new exemplars of a given class of object. Non-existence refers to the disappearance of an object from view or to the absence of an object which the child

TABLE 6.1   OPERATIONS OF REFERENCE (adapted from Table 21 (p. 171) of Brown (1973) and Table 2.2 (p. 24) of Dale (1976))

Semantic class	Syntactic form	Example
Nomination	(Deictic) + (N) (Pronoun) (Adj)	that book, it green, there cat, --
Notice	hi + N	hi Mommy, hi cat, ---
Recurrence	(more) + (N) ('nother) (V)	more milk, more read, 'nother cookie, ----
Nonexistence	(allgone) + (N) (no more) (Adj)	allgone green, allgone dog, no more cookie, ---

had expected to find in some particular location.

The relations involve at least two objects, properties or actions and express the semantic relation between them. They are the basic 'building blocks' from which the complex sentences of adult speech are assembled. Brown divides the relations into seven sub-classes, shown in Table 6.2. Also shown in Table 6.2 are four further relations which have also been reported, although with a far lower frequency of occurrence. Both the initial and final words of relations are highly varied and so they are expressed by open and open constructions.

TABLE 6.2   RELATIONS (adapted from Table 2.2 (p. 24) of Dale (1976) and p. 179 of Brown (1973))

Semantic class	Case structure	Syntactic form	Examples
(A) The seven most frequently expressed semantic relations			
Attributive	O + Predicate	Adj + N	big train
Possessive	O + P	N + N	Mommy lunch
Static Locative	O + L	N + N	sweater chair
Dynamic Locative	Verb motion + G	V + N	go store, walk street
Agent and Action	A + Verb	N + V	Eve read
Action and Object	O + Verb	V + N	put book
Agent and Object	A + O	N + N	Mommy sock
(B) The four less frequently expressed semantic relations			
Action and Beneficiary	Verb + B	V + N	give Mommy
Action and Instrument	Verb + I	V + N	sweep broom, cut knife
Comitative	Verb + Com	V + N	Mommy go
Conjunction	O + O	N + N	umbrella boot

The attributive draws attention to a particular property of an object. Nelson (1976) reports that initially adjectives are used predicatively to comment on the transitory states of objects although, later, their attributive use, to distinguish particular objects or classes of objects, comes to predominate, as in 'I want the big apple' (not the small one) or 'Big girls don't cry'. The possessive identifies, for an object, the person who has special rights of use over that object. Thus 'Daddy television' refers to a receiver whose controls are operated by the father, but not the child. Edwards (1973, Section 3.2.2) reports that, in addition to permanent possessives of the sort just described, children also express inalienable possessives, referring to body parts, such as 'Daddy face', 'Helen thumb', and transitory possessives, involving the action of giving and the recipient. The static locative, normally lacking any preposition, names the location of a moving object, as in *book table*. The dynamic locative names the endpoint, or goal, of a movement. Very occasionally it may refer to the starting point, or source, of a movement, as in *soldier horse* said after a toy soldier had fallen from its horse. Locatives do not seem to be used to refer to the source of a movement by the child itself, so a child about to leave home on a shopping expedition will say *go store* but not *go home*. The possessive and the action and beneficiary relations are parallels, within the domain of possession, to the static and dynamic locatives, respectively.

The agent and action, and action and object relations are used in the obvious way, while the agent and object relations are distinguishable on contextual grounds from other relations expressed by a noun and noun structure, such as possessives. Unfortunately, little attention was paid to stress and intonation, although systematic study of these cues might well have helped to disambiguate many noun pair sentences, as Wieman (1976) has since noted.

The course of development runs from an initial predominance of operations of reference toward an increasing proportion of relational utterances, which are then expanded into full sentences of three elements and more. This is a re-statement, from the semantic viewpoint, of our previous syntactic observation that an initial preponderance of pivot + open sentences gave way to a greater and greater proportion of open + open sentences.

The semantic approach goes beyond the formal definitions, based on distributional information, which underlie the syntactic approach to language. Concepts such as agent, object, location and possessor are notionally defined on the basis of extra-linguistic contextual information. Bloom (1970) described her data by means of a grammar based on Chomsky's theories. Such grammars cannot readily represent the different types of semantic information expressed by the relational sentences. For this reason, Brown (1973) re-interpreted much of the available data on early speech using a Case grammar, invented by Charles Fillmore (1968). Case grammars are particularly suited to describing the findings of the semantic approach to child language since they too are based on a set of notionally defined semantic roles. Brown's interpretation is given in Table 6.2.

Case Grammar

According to Fillmore (1968), the meaning of a sentence comprises two parts: the modality, which includes its mood, polarity and tense, and the proposition, which includes all the other semantic information in the sentence. This propositional content is expressed by a predicator together with one or more noun phrases, each in a different semantic role or case relation to the predicator. Thus the central element in the syntactic and semantic organisation of a sentence is its predicator, which can be either a verb, or a copula (the verb *to be*) together with an adjective, noun, phrase or preposition phrase. The predicator determines which semantic roles or cases can be linked with it to make up a sentence; the possible combination(s) of cases that can occur with a predicator being called its 'case frame'. For example, the verb predicator *murder* requires an animate human object (O), a human agent (A), and may involve an inanimate instrument (I), so that it has the case frame (＿O + A + (I)) and appears in such sentences as *Punch murdered Judy with an axe*. If we do not wish to refer to the agent, then the sentence must be put into the passive voice, giving *Judy was murdered with an axe*. An active sentence must have an agent as subject, so *someone murdered Judy*. Thus, on hearing the verb *murder* in a sentence, one immediately knows that there must be a murder victim, a murderer, and maybe also a deadly weapon, regardless of whether or not any of these were specifically mentioned.

Fillmore (1968) states that 'The case notions comprise a set of universal, presumably innate, concepts which identify certain types of judgements which human beings are capable of making about the events going on around them, judgements about such matters as who did it, who it happened to, and what got changed' (p. 24). He hoped that a small set of cases could be specified which would be adequate to describe the basic semantic relations underlying the sentences of any language. Clearly, if this could be done it would tell us a great deal not only about the semantic structures of language but also about the organisation of thought itself. Unfortunately, there is, at present, no generally agreed set of such cases. The classification we shall describe is due to Edwards (1973) and is an extension of that used by Brown.

Sentences can convey two sorts of information. They can describe the actions, states, and changes of state of objects and persons and they may also contain information about the chain of causation leading to these actions, states and events. Thus, in our example given earlier, information is given about a change of state on the part of the object, *Judy*, from being alive to being dead, and we are also told that the causer of this sad event was the animate agent *Punch*, whose action involved an inanimate instrument, *an axe*. This is an example of a causative stative sentence, and it contrasts with dynamic stative sentences, such as *Judy died*, which describe changes of state by an object but include no information as to their cause. Unchanging states of an object are described by static sentences, such as *Judy was dead*. The central case role in any stative sentence, whether it be static, dynamic or causative, is the object, since the essential information in the sentence concerns the state(s) of its object. In contrast, other sentences, such as *Punch laughed*, involve no change of state on the part of an object and are classified as actional, since they focus on the behaviour of their agent. Edwards (1973) classified the cases according to the scheme shown in Table 6.3. Table 6.3 shows the strong distinction which is made between material and mental states and processes, affecting objects and experiencers, and between physical and animate causality, arising from instruments and agents. Animate agents are normally assumed, unless it is specifically stated to the contrary, to be acting intentionally when they perform actions or cause material or mental processes to occur. This distinction between animate beings acting intentionally, and able to undergo mental as well as material processes, and inanimate objects, incapable of purpose or intention and only able to perform or undergo material processes, seems to be fundamental to human cognition and is reflected throughout language, in both semantics and syntax.

TABLE 6.3   CASE ROLES PLAYED BY PERSONS AND OBJECTS
(originally Table 4 (p. 421) of Edwards (1973))

	Affected roles	*Relational roles*	*Causer roles*
Objects and persons inanimately involved	Object	Goal, source location	Instrument
Persons animately involved	Experiencer	Benificiary possessor	Agent

Fillmore (1968, pp. 24–5) offers a provisional list of cases and their definitions which includes the following:

Agentive (A): 'The case of the typically animate perceived instigator of the action identified by the verb.' (This case is now generally called 'Agent'.)

Instrument (I): 'The case of the inanimate force or object casually involved in the action or state identified by the verb.'

Objective (O): 'The case of anything representable by a noun whose role in the action or state identified by the verb is identified by the semantic interpretation of the verb itself; conceivably the concept should be limited to things which are affected by the action or state identified by the verb.' Edwards (1973, p. 400) defines it more clearly as '. . . the role of the entity said to be in a particular state or condition, or to undergo a change of state or position, or to be affected by an Agent and/or Instrument.' Thus *Judy* is the object in such sentences as: (1) *Punch struck Judy.* (2) *Judy died.* (3) *Judy was at home.*

Edwards (1973, pp. 401–2) defines the locative as referring to the location of a stationary object, while the source and goal cases refer to the start and end point of a movement, respectively. Owners of objects have the case role of possessor, while those who receive such objects are termed beneficiaries. We should add to this list the further cases of donor, one from whose possession an object passes, and comitative, the case role of one who accompanies another. Thus, in the sentence: (4) *Punch gave the baby to the crocodile. Punch* is both agent and donor, *the baby* is the object, and *the crocodile* is the beneficiary. While in: (5) *Punch went to hell with the crocodile. Punch* is the agent, *hell* is the goal, and *the crocodile*, has the comitative role.

So far, we have defined the case roles occurring in sentences referring to material processes taking place within the physical world. In order to describe mental states and processes, taking place within the minds of individuals, two further case roles are required:

Experiencer (E):' . . . . the case of the animate being who is said to be having some kind of mental experience. The type of "experience" involved is identified by the experiential verb.'

Phenomenon (Ph): The object or event perceived or reacted to, or the fact known or reacted to, by the experiencer.

Thus, in the sentences: (6) *Judy saw Punch kill the baby.* (7) *Judy disliked the crocodile. Judy* is the experiencer, while the phenomena are *Punch kill*(ing) *the baby* and *the crocodile*, respectively, and the verbs refer to mental processes of perception and reaction, respectively.

Cognitive Foundations

Semantic Relations

The observations we have described provide impressive evidence that, from the time they start to produce structured utterances, children are able to express many of the basic semantic roles, such as agent, instrument, object, locative, goal, and possessor, which are postulated by Case grammar. Are we therefore justified in analysing children's early sentences in terms of a Case grammar? Such grammars were intended to describe the language of adults and so it is a very strong claim to say that they can be applied to the speech of two-year-olds.

In order to claim that a child is expressing the concepts of agent and instrument, we must be sure that (1) the child can discriminate between animate and inanimate objects, and (2) that he has some concept of causality. To express the meanings of locative and goal, the child must have the concept of permanent objects existing at particular locations in the environment and of objects being able to move to a particular place.

Piaget (1953, 1954) (see Flavell, 1963, Chap. 6, for a summary) shows, on the basis of non-linguistic evidence, that, during the period of sensorimotor intelligence, children develop the concepts of permanent objects and space and time, together with basic notions of human and physical causality, termed 'efficacy' and 'phenomenalism', respectively. Edwards (1973) presents a detailed argument that this knowledge provides exactly the conceptual foundations which underlie the semantic organisation of Case grammar, thus justifying it as an account of children's early semantic competence. The sole exception to this is case of possessor. As we have seen, a person has the relation of permanent possessor to an object if he has rights of use over that object. Thus, the concept of permanent possession is socially defined and must be acquired through social interaction. It therefore falls outside sensorimotor intelligence. Edwards summarises his arguments by means of a table (Table 6.4).

TABLE 6.4   SUMMARY OF LINKS BETWEEN SENSORY-MOTION COGNITION AND LANGUAGE (originally Table 6, p. 432 of Edwards (1973)

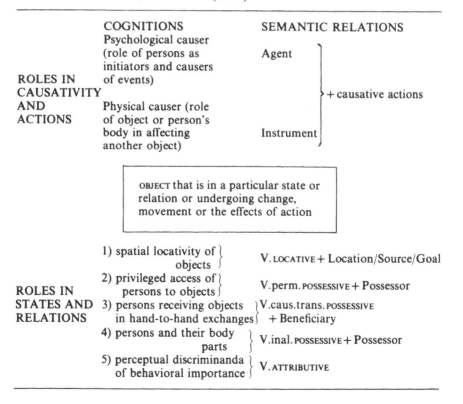

The Origins of Reference

Piaget's theory of sensorimotor intelligence throws light not only on the nature of early semantic relations but also on the origins of reference and the growth of vocabulary. The most insightful studies of initial vocabulary are due to Nelson (1973, 1974). She summarises her observations of the first fifty words learnt by a group of children, between one and two years of age, thus:

> 'They are personal and for the most part action related. It is apparent that children learn the names of the things they can act on, whether they are toys, shoes, scissors, money, keys, blankets, or bottles as well as things that act themselves such as dogs and cars. They do not learn the names of things in the house or outside that are simply "there" whether these are tables, plates, towels, grass or stones. With very few exceptions all the words listed are terms applying to manipulable or movable objects.' (1973, p. 31).

'Dog', 'cat', and 'ball' are the most common object names among the first ten words acquired by children. Among items of clothing named in their early vocabularies, two thirds are footwear and these are the things that children most frequently put on and take off.

Nelson argues that an object is first identified through the actions which it performs or through the actions which the child performs upon it, saying 'It seems likely . . . that the relations at the functional core of the child's first concepts will be actions, whether these are caused by the child himself or by others animate or inanimate' (1974, p. 279). Nelson claims that her theory goes beyond the broad generalisations of Piaget to give an account of how individual concepts are formed and related to words. Nonetheless, her approach is clearly related to that of Piaget.

Edwards (1978) draws attention to the importance of the context in which a word is first acquired. Many words and phrases are first used by a child in a very limited range of situations. For example, Edwards reports that one child, Mark, initially used the adjective *big* only in the context of his having difficulty in pushing his toy cars through narrow gaps. The word was used to describe both large and small objects if there was a physical constraint on their movement. Another child, Jamie, used the expression *too big* similarly, to describe a situation where one object would not fit inside another—such as a foot in a shoe—but, inappropriately, described the container as *too big* as well as the object which would not fit into it. It seems likely that careful observation will reveal many other words with a meaning differing considerably from their dictionary definition. For example, words such as 'dirty', 'sticky' and 'hot' are probably first understood as meaning 'don't touch' since, if mother's prohibitions have been effective, the child will have little direct experience of such physical properties. Such words are first used to refer to situations rather than properties of objects.

Barrett (1978), taking his cue from the logician Kotarbinska, draws attention to the importance of negative examplars in enabling a child to establish the ranges of reference of words. It is perfectly reasonable for a child who has acquired the single animal name 'doggie', as referring to dogs, to over-extend it to refer to other, physically somewhat similar, animals. Negative feedback from adults, when a word is misused, is essential to make clear to the child what class of objects it does refer to and to indicate to him that he must learn other names to refer to other objects falling outside that class. Barrett insists that acquiring the meaning of a referential word involves not just learning the common characteristics of the objects it refers to but also learning what characteristics distinguish them from objects in other classes. Thus, a child trying to establish the references of 'cat' and 'dog' will not be helped by learning that they have the common characteristics of four legs and a tail. He must learn to distinguish barking from meowing and paws from claws. Barrett's basic message is that nouns are used not just to refer to, but to distinguish among, objects of different classes.

Semantic Limitations

According to Piaget, sensorimotor intelligence derives from an individual's interaction with the physical world. We should, therefore, expect that children will first talk about what they can see going on around them. We can see that this is so if we examine the adjectives that they use. Bloom (1970, pp. 245–6) gives the following list for a twenty-one month old girl, Kathryn (here subclassified according to Edwards, 1973): (1) Physical properties: *big, little, tiny, heavy, sharp, sticky, fuzzy, hot, cold, pink*. (2) Reward-punishment: *dirty, funny, careful*. (3) Actional and reversible: *open, stuck*.

She also used one other adjective, *tired*, to describe her own state. Edwards (1973, p. 424) provides a remarkably similar list covering the adjectives produced by his daughter Helen up to the age of twenty-eight months.

The *physical property* adjectives all refer to directly perceivable properties of size, colour, shape, texture, weight, and temperature. As we suggested earlier, some of these, such as *heavy*, *sharp* and *sticky*, together with the *actional and reversible* adjectives are probably learnt in the context of physical or social constraints on the child's actions. The *reward and punishment* adjectives are applied by the child both to itself and to other people and also to offending objects. Here social constraints upon action are the crucial factor.

More 'abstract' adjectives, such as *clever*, *proud*, *true*, *false* either do not occur or are used with an idiosyncratic meaning. Thus Kathryn (see Bloom, 1970, pp. 47–53) said *Mommy busy* whenever her mother was unavailable to play with her, regardless of whether her mother had personally refused or was unavailable due to absence.

If we examine the first mental process verbs used by children, a similar picture emerges. Halliday (1970) divided these into: (1) Reaction: *like, please, envy*, etc. (2) Perception: *see, look, hear*, etc. (3) Cognition: *believe, think, know*, etc. (4) Verbalisation: *say, speak*, etc. Types (1), (2) and (3) are experiential verbs, referring to private mental processes and subjective states, while type (4) is a sub-class of the communication verbs. Of these, only types (1) and (2) seem likely to occur in early speech. The cognition verbs require subtle introspective judgements about the state of one's knowledge, while the verbalisation verbs involve the notion of communication as a distinct mode of behaviour, together with the concepts of direct and indirect speech.

Bloom (1970, pp. 103–5, 243–58) lists the mental process verbs of three children, aged 19–22 months as follows: *look, read, see, show, want, watch*. All of these, except *want* are not only perceptual but visual. Edwards (1973) confirms these observations and suggests that these verbs are not really being used with experiential meaning. Thus, if a child says '*See Teddy*' he usually tugs at one's sleeve, points to the stuffed bear and insists that it be thoroughly inspected from all angles. The stative verb *see*, usually referring to an involuntary process, is here being used with the active sense of 'look at'. The verb *want*, which is a reaction verb for adults, is best analysed as an imperative marker, requesting an object, in children's speech.

Limber (1973) (see table on p. 176) reports that by 30 months children use the verbalisation verbs *say* and *go* with direct speech, as in *Cows go moo*, and by 3 years of age, they can use the cognition verbs: *think, know, remember, forget*. Unfortunately his report does not give enough information to show whether or not the verbs are used with normal adult meanings.

Interpreted in terms of Case grammar, these findings indicate that children initially lack the concepts of experiencer and phenomenon. This is scarcely surprising, since their knowledge of mental processes must be very limited. Unlike physical events, which can be directly observed, mental states and events can often only be understood on the basis of complex and indirect inferences. However, Masangkay *et al.* (1974) report that children very soon become able to make inferences about the visual percepts of others and it seems likely that an understanding of visual perceptions as a mental process provides the key to knowledge of the other classes of mental activity.

Polarity

As all parents know, children very soon learn how to express negation. Indeed they can do so long before they master the intricacies of syntax. Bloom (1970) distinguishes three semantic classes of negative sentence, which appeared in the order (1) non-existence, (2) rejection and (3) denial; though pre-linguistic expressions of rejection would have appeared earlier. Initially, the grammatical form of a negative sentence consisted of a negative element placed before a phrase or clause, as in *No more lunch, No the sun shining, Not a teddy bear*. Non-existence was expressed by *No more* or *All gone* followed by a noun, as described earlier. Rejection was expressed by *No* or *Don't*, as in *No dirty soap* and *Don't wash me*. Denial was usually expressed by *No* or *not*, as in *That not lollipop* or *No truck*, said in denial of a statement that a car was a truck. The subsequent stages in the development of the syntax of negations in English are described by Klima and Bellugi (1966), while Wode (1977) attempts to provide a theory to account for its development both in English and other languages.

The denials and statements of non-existence, which refer to the absence of expected objects, follow the pragmatic rule governing the use of negation in adult speech: a negative is used to deny an incorrect statement or belief on the part of the audience. Wason and Johnson-Laird (1972) summarise the experimental psycholinguistic research demonstrating the reality of this principle, and de Villier's and Flusberg (1975) report an experiment, using two, three and four-year-old children as subjects, which replicates one of Wason's most important demonstrations.

Rejection of a visible object, expressed by the single word *No*, probably precedes the expression of non-existence which, by definition, refers to an invisible object. Non-existence and denial have symbolic referents, represented only in the minds of speaker and hearer, and cannot be expressed by a single word. They are therefore likely to develop later.

In addition to these distinctions of polarity, young children also distinguish grammatically between declarative, interrogative and imperative sentences. We shall examine the origins of these distinctions of mood when we consider the functional approach to language development.

A Universal Pattern of Development?

Dan Slobin, at the University of California at Berkeley, has directed a large programme of cross-cultural research on language acquisition, which pays particular attention to English, Italian, Serbo-Croatian, and Turkish. Studies of these and other languages have led him to conclude that the initial stages of language development follow the same pattern, no matter what language is being acquired (Slobin, 1970). Klima and Bellugi (1972) give a preliminary report on the development of American Sign Language (ASL), a language of manual gestures used by the deaf and dumb in the USA. The development of ASL as a first language, by the children of deaf and dumb parents, appears to follow the pattern described for spoken language by Brown and Slobin. Even more remarkably, Goldin-Meadow and Feldman (1977) report that the deaf children of hearing parents, who have been exposed neither to oral language nor a manual language such as ASL, develop a manual sign language of their own, which has many of the semantic properties of natural spoken language. Goldin-Meadow and Feldman believe that this communication system is largely the invention of the children rather than their parents.

There will of course be substantial individual differences between children in the ages at which they start to speak and pass through the various stages of development on the path to adult competence. There will also be substantial differences in the level of fluency and linguistic skill eventually attained. Nonetheless, all children appear to pass through very similar stages of development in the same order.

More recently, Nelson (1973, 1975) has suggested that there may be at least two different strategies for acquiring language. On the basis of her study of vocabulary development, Nelson (1973) distinguished two groups of children. One, which she called the referential group, initially acquired a relatively large number of nouns and rather few words from other classes, while the other, expressive, group acquired fewer nouns but more verbs, adjectives, grammatical function words and expressive phrases. This latter group produced more phrases and sentences during the early stages of language learning, while the referential group first concentrated on naming and showed a clear progression from an initial stage of single-word utterances to a later two-word stage. Observations similar to Nelson's have since been reported by Dore (1974), Bloom *et al.* (1975) and Ramer (1976).

Nelson (1975) reports that, while the referential group have larger vocabularies at twenty-four months, by thirty months this advantage has disappeared and nor is there any difference in mean length of utterance (MLU) between the two groups. This rapid convergence in performance suggests that the referential and expressive strategies represent more of a difference in emphasis than fundamentally different paths into language. So Nelson's observations should not be seen as a rebuttal of Slobin's claim of universality.

Syntactic Limitations on Production

So far we have been arguing that, by a very early age, children have much of the basic semantic knowledge needed to produce complex sentences. Nonetheless, they are unable to produce utterances of more than two or three words in length. The reason for this limitation is definitely not shortness of breath since many children, who cannot spontaneously link more than two words within a single breath, are capable of imitating the intonation patterns of extended phrases such as advertising jingles. They may also string successive two-word phrases together with a single intonation contour. For example, Derek Edwards' daughter, Helen, when aged twenty-six months, managed to say in a single breath, '*Read a book, Growly read a book, Growly read a book*'. (Growly is her teddy bear.)

Nor can the brevity of early sentences be blamed on slowness of mind since children will often produce strings of sentences in which a succession of different nouns are placed in a single sentence frame. For example, Weir (1962) reported a monologue by her son Anthony which included the sequence, '*What colour? What colour blanket? What colour mop? What colour*

glass?', together with alternations between affirmatives and negatives, such as
'*Not the yellow blanket, the white. It's not black; It's yellow. Not yellow. Red.*'
Examples like these lead us to the view that small children have plenty of ideas
ready to mind and that the limitations on their expression must have a
linguistic, rather than cognitive, origin.

The limitations seem to arise from problems with the syntactic organisation
of sentences. A child may show clear evidence of following the rules agent
precedes verb and object follows verb, leading him to produce *Mama eat* and
eat lunch respectively, but be unable to combine them to produce *Mama eat
lunch*. These difficulties seem to involve production rather than comprehension, since Shipley *et al.* (1969), Petretic and Tweney (1977) and Sachs and
Truswell (1978) report that children understand commands expressed in a
more advanced style than they are yet capable of producing better than if the
commands are expressed with child-like grammar.

Words are definitely not omitted at random to produce telegraphic speech.
Weisenburger (1976) studied the speech of a two-and-a-half-year-old girl, Jill,
with a mean length of utterance of less than three words. When examined in
context, her sentences were found to omit only those constituents which were
not absolutely necessary for unambiguous communication. Thus, in making a
request, the most important element to be named is the object being
requested, and children will leave one in no doubt of what it is they want.
Weisenburger concludes that, in general, new and non-redundant information is most likely to be expressed in words.

The Functional Approach

The Ideas of Halliday

A speaker of a language is able to understand and produce utterances that are
not just grammatical but also appropriate, in their context, to achieve his
communicative intentions. To understand the development of this 'communicative competence', we must explore the functions which language
serves in the lives of children at the various stages of their development. The
pioneer in this task of studying the development of language functions is
Michael Halliday, who gives a brief account of his approach in an article
entitled 'Learning how to mean' (Halliday, 1975a) and a fuller account in a
book with the same title (Halliday, 1975b). Halliday (1973) observes that

'. . . it is characteristic of young children's language that internal form
reflects rather directly the function that it is being used to serve. What the
child does with language tends to determine its structure. This relatively
close match between structure and function can be brought out by a
functional analysis of the system, in terms of its meaning potential. We

can see from this how the structures that the child has mastered are direct reflections of the functions that language serves for him' (p. 347).

In statements such as these, Halliday denies the Chomskyan doctrine of the 'autonomy of syntax' and forcefully asserts that language exists to serve the needs of communication. This leads him to make the following very important point:

'From the functional point of view, as soon as there are meaningful expressions there is language, and the investigation can begin at a time before sounds and structures have evolved. . . . It then emerges that the child has a linguistic system before he has any words or structures at all. He is capable of expressing a range of meanings . . . that become quite transparent when interpreted functionally, in the light of the question "What has the child learnt to do by means of language".' (1975a, p. 247).

As we noted earlier, the syntactic approach has led researchers to largely ignore one-word utterances, let alone the possible communicative skills of children who could not yet produce recognisable words.

Halliday distinguishes three stages in the acquisition of language: Phase I, the child's initial functional linguistic system, which is idiosyncratic to the child; Phase II, the transition from this system to that of adult language; and Phase III, the learning of the adult language, where the child acquires a communicative system defined by the speech community into which it is born.

Phase I

Halliday hypothesised, *a priori*, that language may serve seven basic communicative functions. These are: (1) The *instrumental* function of obtaining material goods and services. (2) The *regulatory* function for controlling the behaviour of others. (3) The *interactional* function for establishing contact with others. (4) The *personal* function, which expresses the feelings of an individual and thereby establishes his individuality. (5) The *heuristic* function in which language is used to explore the environment. (6) The *imaginative* function where language is used to create an environment. (7) The *informative* functions by which language is used to convey factual information to others.

Halliday predicted (a) that the functions would appear in the language systems of children roughly in the order that they have been listed, with the informative function definitely developing last, (b) that in Phase I they would occur discretely with any given utterance subserving only one function, and (c) that the mastery of all of them, except possibly the informative, would be a necessary prerequisite for the transition to the adult system. In support of his first prediction, Halliday (1975b) argues that

'All the other functions in the list (except the informative) are extrinsic to language. They are served by and realised through language, but they are not defined by language. They represent the use of language in contexts which exist independently of the linguistic system. But the informative function has no existence independent of language itself. It is an intrinsic function which the child cannot begin to master until he has grasped the principle of dialogue, which means until he has grasped the fundamental nature of the communication process' (p. 31).

Halliday's prediction that the imaginative use of language will precede its informative use is not as counter-intuitive as it might appear, since the earliest imaginative uses of language involve sound, with conceptual play—in story-telling and pretending—appearing later.

Halliday tested his hypotheses in an observational study of his son Nigel from the age of nine to twenty-four months. At the lower end of this age range, children produce a variety of sounds and it is necessary to have clear criteria for regarding some of their vocalisations as 'language'. Halliday's criterion was 'that there must be an observable and constant relation between the content and the expressions: that each particular expression must be observed in at least three unambiguous instances, and its content must be interpreted in functional terms' (1975b, p. 38). He claims that in practice, he had no difficulty in distinguishing systematic from random vocalisation and that he feels confident of his interpretations of the functions of Nigel's utterances. There is, however, no way in which one can check his very 'rich' interpretations though independent research, notably by Carter (1974) and Dore (1975), corroborates many of his observations.

On this basis, Nigel's vocalisations at nine months were pre-linguistic or on the borderline of language but by ten and a half months he had a linguistic system with a meaning potential including the first four functions hypothesised by Halliday. This system is shown in Table 6.5. Halliday (1975b, pp. 149–57) provides a similar set of tables covering Nigel's development up to the age of eighteen months, while Halliday (1973) provides further data on Nigel at the age of nineteen months).

Thus, by the age of about ten months, Nigel can use language to express his personal feelings, to establish contact with others, to control their behaviour, and to obtain his material wants. These observations accord with Halliday's predictions except for the absence of any developmental trend: all four functions seem to occur from the beginning. Later observations showed that they preceded the heuristic, which appeared at seventeen months and the imaginative, involving singing and pretending to sleep, which first appeared at nineteen months, with the informative function not occuring before twenty-one months.

TABLE 6.5 NIGEL AT THE START OF PHASE I (originally Figure 1, p. 148 of Halliday (1975b))

Function	Content systems	Expression: Articulation - - -	Tone	Gloss
Instrumental	demand, general	nà - - -	mid	give me that
	demand, specific (toy bird)	bø	mid	give me my bird
Regulatory	command, normal	ə̃	mid	do that (again)
	command, intensified	m̂nŋ	wide; ff	do that right now!
	initiation — normal (friendly)	= ø; dø; dɔ	narrow mid	nice to see you (& shall we look at this together?)
	intensified (impatient)	ennn	mid	nice to see you—at last!
Interactional	response	ɛ ; ə	low	yes it's me
	interest — general	= ø	low	that's interesting
	interest — specific (movement)	dɔ; bø; ø	low	look it's moving (? a dog, birds)
	participation — pleasure — general	a	low	that's nice
Personal	pleasure — specific (taste)	n̂ŋ	low	that tastes nice
	withdrawal	g̊ʷɒı - - -	narrow low	I'm sleepy

Note: All above on falling tone; mid = mid fall, narrow low = low fall over narrow interval, etc. - - - indicates syllable is repeated. At 0; 9, Nigel had two such meanings, both expressed as [ø] on mid or mid-low falling tone; one interactional, 'let's be together', the other (usually with the wider interval) personal, 'look, it's moving'. He also had another three meanings expressed gesturally; two instrumental, 'I want that', grasping object firmly, and 'I don't want that', touching object lightly; and one regulatory, 'do that again', touching person or relevant object firmly (e.g. 'make that jump in the air again'). The gestures disappeared during NL 1–2.

There is no grammar here in two senses. Firstly, there is no syntax because syntactic rules govern the combination of linguistic elements, but this does not yet occur. Secondly, the meanings of these utterances can be directly related to their forms, so there is no need for rules, such as those proposed by Chomsky (1957, 1965) to account for complex and indirect relations between the meanings of sentences and the forms of their expression.

With the exception of (bφ)—'I want my toy bird'—all of the sounds used by Nigel are spontaneous inventions on his part and not related to any English words. Nigel sometimes responded to the passage of an aeroplane overhead by producing a sound which seemed to imitate that of the plane. This is an example of what Piaget (1970) calls an 'index'. Halliday reports no other examples like this, and nor have many been described by other researchers.

The Role of Gesture

One crucial matter, somewhat neglected by Halliday, is the role of manual and other gestures in the early stages of communication. Ann Carter explored this problem for her doctoral thesis at the University of California, Berkeley in 1974. She was able to identify for one child, David, a set of gestural schema. These are given in Table 6.6.

The similarity of these functional categories to those identified by Halliday, for Nigel at a slightly younger age, is clear. Carter (1974) comments that 'The

TABLE 6.6 GESTURAL SCHEMATA EARLY IN THE SECOND YEAR (originally Table 2, p. 173 of Ervin-Tripp and Mitchell-Kernan (1977))

Schema	Gesture	Sound	Goal	Frequency*	Total
1. Request object	reach to object	'm'-initial	Get help to get object	298	342
2. Attention to object	point, hold out	'l'-initial 'd'-initial	Draw attention to object	245	334
3. Attention to self	vocalisation	*David Mommy*	Draw attention to self	142	142
4. Request transfer	reach to person	'h'-initial	Get from or give object to other	94	135
5. Dislike	falling tone	nasalised	Get help to change situation	82	82
6. Disappearance	slapping, waving	'b'-initial	Get help in removing	4	32
7. Rejection	negative headshake	[ə̃?-ʔə̃]	Get help to change situation	3	20
8. Pleasure–surprise–recognition	smile	breathy 'h' with vowels	Express pleasure	—	20

* Including only instances in which gesture and sound occurred together.

fact that gestures are usually clear in their communicative intent may be attributed perhaps to the functional origin of most gestures: they indicate their goals by attempting to accomplish their goals' (p. 8). This strongly suggests that the initial stages of communication by children are mediated by parental interpretations of their gestures, rather than the sounds they produce.

Carter (1975) describes, for David, the progression from an exclusive reliance on gesture, at twelve months, to the use of words 'move' and 'mine' as elements within multi-word utterances, at twenty-four months. This development is described in the Table 6.7.

TABLE 6.7 THE EVOLUTIONARY DIFFERENTIATION OF 'MORE' AND 'MY', 'MINE' (originally Figure 1, p. 236 of Carter (1975))

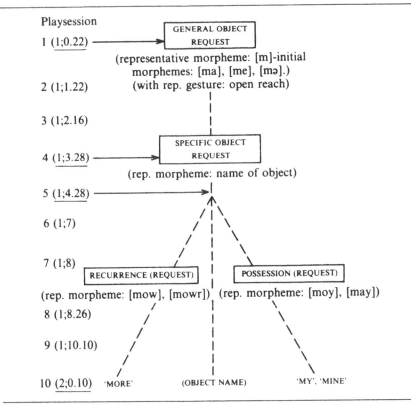

Initially, David's communication system can be defined by reference to his gestures, which are accompanied here by an m-initial sound. By sixteen months, he had mastered the procedure of asking for objects by name. One month later, he started to distinguish two m-initial forms which develop into an instrumental request to obtain an object ('more') and a separate regulatory request to be allowed to maintain possession ('mine'). With the acquisition of recognisable words, the occurrence and role of the accompanying gestures was greatly reduced.

Phase II

The second phase of language acquisition—that of transition to the adult system—began for Nigel at seventeen months and lasted until he was almost two years old. This stage involved two crucial developments: a shift in functional orientation and a very rapid advance in vocabulary, syntax and dialogue, involving the emergence of true grammar.

Nigel acquired about a hundred new meanings in a 'vocabulary explosion'. The great majority of these were expressed by recognisable approximations to adult words, mostly nouns. Thus Nigel went beyond his initial idiosyncratic system to acquire the externally-given code of English vocabulary. He appears to come within Nelson's (1975) nominal group, though it is likely that the start of Phase II is marked in almost all children by a rapid acquisition of referential vocabulary.

Initially, Nigel passed through a period in which single words constituted complete utterances. Although for Nigel this stage was brief, other children have been observed to remain at this level of development for several months. There has been considerable controversy over the interpretation of these one-word sentences, which receive detailed treatment in Bloom (1973) and Greenfield and Smith (1976). The so-called 'holophrastic hypothesis' claims that they are really full sentences. In effect, the case-grammar interpretation for two-word sentences is extrapolated backwards to claim that the children possess the semantic knowledge required for the conception of full sentences but their expression of them is constrained by a production limit of one item. If it could be demonstrated that the children could understand full sentences, spoken to them by adults, then the holophrastic hypothesis would gain credibility. Unfortunately our knowledge of children's comprehension abilities at this level of development is negligible and little support for this hypothesis can be got from their speech production.

Goldin-Meadow *et al.* (1976) report that initially children only produce nouns, and not verbs. Since case grammar asserts that verbs are the central elements in the structure of sentences, it is hard to claim that there are sentences if no verbs occur. Verbs, together with adjectives, are predicators, but it is not certain that predication occurs at this stage of language. Lyons (in press) comments that

'. . . as far as the early utterances of children are concerned, it is very often impossible to distinguish reference from predication: one cannot say that the child is referring to something in the situation and leaving implicit what he wants to say about it, or alternatively, that he is leaving implicit his references to some entity in the situation and making explicit what he wants to say about it. It is only later that reference and predication can be distinguished; and they may be thought of as developing ontogenetically from something, proto-reference or proto-predication, that is originally not clearly the one or the other.'

The Origins of Structure

Halliday reports that most of the words in Nigel's new vocabulary were initially used with only one function. For example *cat* had interactional function ('hullo cat') and *syrup* was used instrumentally ('give me some syrup'). But there were also the first signs of utterances serving two functions, as in *cake* meaning 'look there's a cake, and I want some'. (1975b, p. 42). Unfortunately Halliday provides no contextual information to clarify or justify these rich interpretations.

Nigel produced two types of proto-structure. These consisted of a specific word, with a definite function, combined with either (i) a gesture or (ii) a general expression of the same function. Examples of the first included: [dà:bi] *Dvořak* + beating time, 'I want the Dvořak record on' (instrumental) (he also asks for Bartok); [ndà] *star* + shaking head (negation) 'I can't see the star' (personal), and [ù æyì] excitement + *egg* (personal). Nigel's first truly structured utterances—two words phrased as a single unit, as opposed to being separately pronounced, as if in a list—came at nineteen months, just one month after the first major growth in vocabulary. Shortly afterwards, two main classes of structure could be distinguished, as in these examples (Halliday, 1975b, p. 46):

(1) *mummy come, more meat, butter on, squeeze orange, mend train, help juice* ('help me with the juice'), *come over there, now room* ('now let's go to the room'), *star for you* ('make a star for me'), *more meat please*.

(2) *green car, two book, mummy book, bee flower* ('there's a bee on the flower'), *bubble round-round* ('the bubbles are going round and round'), *tiny red light, two fast train*.

The utterances listed under (1) are classified as *pragmatic*, and involve the regulatory and instrumental functions, which seek control events in the world. The utterances listed under (2) are classified as *mathetic*, since they involve the use of language for learning about the world. This new function arises, so Halliday claims, from a synthesis of the personal and heuristic functions. Initially, it is realised through verbal labelling but later, with the development of structured multi-word utterances, it depends upon predication. The elaboration of the mathetic function requires the development of vocabulary, to refer to objects properties of objects and processes, and linguistic structures, to express semantic relations.

The distinction in function between pragmatic and mathetic utterances was expressed by intonation. Within the span of one week, Nigel, then aged nineteen months, introduced a systematic opposition between utterances spoken with rising and falling pitch, which he retained throughout the rest of Phase II. Pragmatic utterances, which require a fairly specific response from the hearer, were marked by a rising tone, while mathetic utterances, which do not request a definite response, were pronounced with a falling tone.

The Beginning of Dialogue

Nigel learnt to engage in genuine verbal dialogue just before eighteen months of age. Previously, there had been signs of 'proto dialogue'. By about one year, he gave separate response to calls, greetings, and gifts, while three months later, he could implicitly answer questions of the form 'Do you want . . . ?', 'Shall I . . . ?', where the answers required were of instrumental, regulatory, or interactional function. But he could not yet initiate a dialogue. His responses were constrained within the range of functions available to him. Thus, he could express the meanings 'yes' and 'no' in the instrumental senses of 'yes, I want that' or 'no, I don't want that', or the regulatory senses of 'yes, do that' and 'no, don't do that', but he could not respond to any questions seeking factual information, such as 'Did you see a car?' or 'What did you see?'.

Dialogue involves the adoption by oneself and the assignment to others of social roles. These communicative roles, such as questioner and respondent, exist only in and through the use of language. For efficient dialogue, the assignment of these roles has to be specific: not just the 'pay attention to me' of the interactional function in Phase I, but 'I am asking specific information from' or 'I want you to carry out the following instructions or give me the reason why not'.

Halliday reports that Nigel grasped the essentials of verbal dialogue in a two-week period. By the end of this brief span, he was able to do five things: (1) Reply to a Wh-question: '*What are you eating?*' '*Banana*'. (2) Respond to a command: '*Take the toothpaste to Daddy and go and get your bib*'. Nigel did this, saying to himself '*daddy . . . noddy . . . train*' (He has the nickname of 'Noddy' and his bib carried a picture of a train). (3) Respond to a statement: 'You went on a train yesterday'. Nigel indicated that he had understood the statement by repeating it and then went on '*train . . . byebye*'. (4) Respond to a response: Nigel '*gravel*': Response '*Yes, you had some gravel in your hand*'. Nigel '*ooh*' (it hurt). (5) Initiate a dialogue: Nigel '*What's that?*' Response '*that's butter*'. Nigel '*Butter*'.

At this stage, '*What's that?*' was his only means of demanding a purely linguistic response and initiating a dialogue. Although he could not yet assign communicative roles to others, he had started to accept the roles which they assigned to him. The ability to respond appropriately to Wh-questions is a particularly important development since it represents the first step in the informative use of a language, separate from its pragmatic role.

It is hard to overestimate the importance of dialogue for the mathetic use of language. Significantly, Nigel's first verbal formula for initiating a dialogue is a request for the name of an object. Clearly, he has appreciated the referential aspect of language.

Phase III

As we have noted, research using the syntactic and semantic approaches has concentrated almost entirely on Phase III: the acquisition of the adult linguistic system. This requires the development of two main areas of meaning. Firstly, the child must greatly expand the ideational component of his linguistic system in order to express his knowledge and experience. Bloom, Brown and Edwards have described this process. Secondly, he must develop the interpersonal component which governs the various forms an utterance may take, depending on its function within the social structure of communication: declarative, interrogative and imperative. These options within the mood system of his grammar provide efficient means for indicating and controlling the assignment and adoption of communicative roles.

In Phase II, Nigel had no system of mood except the distinction between pragmatic and mathetic function, realised by rising and falling tones, respectively. His demand for the name of an object [ædydà] *'What's that?'* was not a true question. It was uttered with a falling tone because it had mathetic function. It was also a stereotyped, non-productive, grammatical formula. When Nigel first used the, productive, Wh-interrogative form *Where + personal name*, this was spoken with either rising or falling tone and only later did this and all other Wh-interrogative forms take on a rising tone exclusively. This was presumably adopted because a question demands the response of an answer and therefore has pragmatic function.

Later, Nigel acquired the polar (yes/no) interrogative form, but this was not at first used for asking questions. Instead, it was used with informative function to communicate an experience not shared by the listener, thus, *'did you fall down'*—'I want you to know that I fell down, although you didn't see it'—contrasted with *'you fall down'*: 'I fell down as you saw'. Notice the incorrect pronouns which are common at this stage of development.

In contrast to Phase II, where almost all utterances have either pragmatic or mathetic functions, the great majority of utterances in adult speech have both ideational and interpersonal meaning. The first indication of a breakdown in the clear dichotomy between utterances with one or other of these functions is an increasing number of sentences comprising a mathetic and a pragmatic component in succession, such as *dada got scrambled egg, mummy got for you scrambled egg*: 'Daddy's got some scrambled egg, now get some for me'. Halliday reports that, during the course of Phase III, it became increasingly difficult to classify Nigel's utterances, when taken in their contexts, as either pragmatic or mathetic, this distinction being progressively rendered obsolete by the development of the mood system, which operates simultaneously with the ideational component in determining the form of utterances. As a result of this, the intonation system is liberated from marking the distinction between pragmatic and mathetic function so that it can now take on the expressive role that it has in adult speech.

Symbolic Capacity and Semiotic Function

According to Halliday, the ideational component of adult language develops out of the use of language to learn about the world. It must therefore crucially depend on the ability of the child to represent mentally what it has learnt. Edwards (1973) has presented a detailed argument that sensorimotor intelligence, together with some socially derived concepts of permission and possession, provides the conceptual framework underlying early language. But sensorimotor intelligence is not, by itself, a sufficient basis for language. As Piaget (1950) says, 'The use of signs, like that of symbols, involves an ability which is quite new with respect to sensorimotor intelligence and consists of representing one thing by another' (p. 126). The development, during Phase II, of the mathetic function, in which knowledge is acquired through language, necessarily goes beyond sensorimotor intelligence, in which knowledge is derived from physical actions upon the environment. The symbolic capacity of the child develops both in order to represent and retain the knowledge which has been acquired and also to operate upon and use that knowledge. One particularly crucial symbolic process for the use of language is evocative memory in which events from the past are partially or fairly completely reconstructed in the mind. Without this ability it would be impossible to refer to past events; that is, to show temporal displacement of reference. With the further development of the faculty of imagination, reference to future or even purely hypothetical events becomes possible.

Piaget (1951, 1970) has put forward a theory of semiotic or symbolic function which derives from the ideas of the linguist de Saussure. Piaget first distinguishes between *signifiers* and the *significants* which they represent. He then distinguishes three classes of *signifiers* as follows (1970, p. 716):

'(a) Indexes are signifiers that are not differentiated from their significants since they are part of them or a causal result, for example, for an infant, hearing a voice is an index of someone's presence. (b) Symbols are signifiers that are differentiated from their significants, but they retain a measure of similarity with them, for example, in a symbol game representing bread by a white stone or vegetables by grass. (c) Signs are signifiers that are also differentiated from their significants, but are conventional and thus more or less "arbitrary": the sign is always social, whereas the symbol can have a purely individual origin as in symbolic games or dreams.

'We shall thus call the semiotic function . . . the ability, acquired by the child in the course of his second year, to represent an object which is absent or an event which is not perceived by means of symbols or signs, that is signifiers differentiated from their significants. Thus the semiotic function includes, in addition to language, symbolic games, mental and graphic images (drawings) and deferred imitation, (beginning in the absence of its model) which appears nearly at the same time (except for drawing which appears slightly later), whereas indexes (including the "signals" involved in conditioning) already play a role during the first few weeks. The transition from indexes to symbols and signs . . . is definitely related to the process of imitation . . . (which) also becomes the source of the symbols and the instrument of communicative exchange which makes possible the acquisition of language.'

If we examine Halliday's and Carter's observations in the light of Piaget's semiotic theory, the need for a further subdivision within the category of symbols becomes apparent. The sounds and gestures produced by a child in Phase I are social in the sense that they have become conventionalised between the child and its caretakers but they are not social in the sense that the adult language, acquired in Phase III, is a social construct which the child must acquire from others and which exists independently of the child himself. The communicative acts of a child in Phase I are not wholly differentiated from their significants (recall Carter's reference to gestures which indicate their goals by attempting to accomplish them), hence they should be classed as symbols. But, to the extent that they are social, they have some claim to be regarded as signs. It seems desirable to recognise a class of 'proto signs', which exist only within limited social groups.

Cognitive Foundations

Our knowledge of the cognitive basis of the interpersonal component of language is very incomplete. Bates (1976) claims that ' . . . minimal gestural communication during which the child appears to expect or await an adult response will occur only when the cognitive basis for the use of tools and agent-instruments is established, at sensorimotor stage 5' (p. 37). Bates (1976, pp. 62–3) draws attention to three parallel developments during this stage: (1) The use of supports, tools and instruments in non-communicative sequences of behaviour, (2) The use of adults as agent-tools in obtaining objects, (3) The use of objects as a means to gain the attention of adults. Bates also predicts that ' . . . while illocutionary processes can take place after certain sensorimotor developments, locutionary processes for constructing and projecting propositions must await the sixth sensorimotor stage with the development of symbolic capacity'. (p. 37).

The precise relation between cognitive development and the emergence of communication in the child was explored in a brilliant, but unpublished, study in 1973 by Susan Sugarman, which has had a strong influence on all subsequent discussion. An account of this highly original work has now appeared (Sugarman-Bell, 1978). Sugarman's central thesis is that language grows out of earlier social interaction by the child and its caretakers involving ritualised games, the giving and taking of objects, and so on. She believes that both social and object-oriented behavioural schemes are necessary for communication. Initially, these two classes of behaviours occur separately but they gradually become merged into complex communicative acts involving both other persons and objects. Sugarman's minutely careful observations detail this process of merger between the ages of four and fourteen months, and confirm the claim of Bates that true communication depends on developments in stage 5 of sensorimotor intelligence, involving the invention of new means to familiar ends. The fascinating observation that social and object-directed behaviours are initially separate has since been confirmed by Trevarthen (1975, 1977). This strongly suggests that the development of social behaviour in infants is separate from that of sensorimotor intelligence and cannot be subsumed within it.

The Conversational Approach

Chomsky's linguistics are concerned with the structure of single sentences considered in isolation from any context. But, except in certain forms of meditation, human language is used in social settings involving conversation. By definition, conversation consists of social interaction between two or more individuals in which their successive communicative acts are (or at any rate should be) related to what has been said earlier. Hence there is 'cohesion' not only between successive sentences uttered by the same speaker but also between the utterances of successive speakers.

Recently, a number of linguists, most notably William Labov, Emanuel Schegloff, and Ruquiya Hasan and Michael Halliday, have set out to extend the scope of linguistics to include the structure of conversation, and the role of social setting in determining what is said and how it is expressed. Coulthard (1977) provides a good introduction to these developments. Ervin-Tripp and Mitchell-Kernan (1977, pp. 1–3) list five characteristics of this new paradigm for linguistics: (1) Natural language elicited in ordinary life situations is the preferable source of data, rather than the private introspections of linguists. (2) Sentences are not the highest level of analysis. The connections between sentences, which make them into a coherent text rather than a string of unrelated sentences, must be described. This problem has recently been taken up by English-speaking linguists and knowledge is still limited, though

Halliday and Hasan (1976) have made a notable contribution. (3) Social context is relevant to linguistic rules. The classic example is that of pronouns of address in French and many other languages. The rule governing the choice between *tu* and *vous* must make reference to the relative social positions of the speaker and the person addressed. (4) Variability is a component of linguistic rules. By no means all rules are hard and fast. For example, 'Who do you believe?' is very often reduced to 'Who'd you believe?' in everyday conversation, but this optional process of contraction is less likely to occur in more formal speech such as lectures or sermons. It is thus governed by a probabilistic or variable rule, which is sensitive to the social variable of formality of the situation. (5) Language has diverse functions which are not directly mapped onto any structural features of utterances. Halliday's (1973) claim that '. . . it is characteristic of young children's language that its internal form reflects rather directly the function that it is being used to serve' (p. 346) applies only to very young children. As they develop, children learn to do many new things with language, such as telling stories, playing games, and learning in school. Linguists and psycholinguists must now study how children use language to achieve these diverse ends.

Egocentrism or Dialogue?

However, we must first establish that pre-school age children do indeed have conversations. This may seem obvious until one recalls the doctrine of childhood 'egocentrism', attributed to Piaget. In *The Language and Thought of the Child*, originally published in 1923, Piaget describes a series of observational and experimental studies which led him to conclude that nearly half of the speech produced by children up to about six years of age is 'egocentric' and lacks any communicative intention, having the character of monologue rather than dialogue. This view is unfortunately hardened into the dogma that the speech of young children is 'egocentric' until the age of six years when it becomes 'socialised'. Even the excellent text of Slobin (1971) contains the potentially misleading sentence 'Egocentric speech, for Piaget, is eventually replaced by socialised speech, which takes account of the point of view of the listener and makes true dialogue possible.' (p. 117).

Contrary to the impression conveyed by such statements, there is now considerable evidence that very young children are capable of genuine conversational exchange, both with adults and with their peers. Elinor Keenan (1977) quotes examples such as the following recorded when her twin sons Toby and David, then aged two years ten months, together with their nanny, Jill, were making a picture (p. 134):

Toby: Put it Toby's room/
Jill: Toby's got a worm?
Toby: No/Put it Toby's room/

David: Room/   ⎫
Toby: Toby's room ⎬   simultaneously
Jill: Toby's room?   ⎭
Toby: Yeah/
David: (?)
Jill: Oh, Put it in Toby's room
Toby: Yeah/

In this example, Toby and David are able to co-operate in a dialogue to get Jill to do something for them. When Jill indicates that she has not understood what Toby said, he is able to correct her, using anaphoric negations to deny her previous statement and repeating himself. Later, when Jill indicates by repeating it, that she has understood his request, he confirms that she has understood it correctly by 'Yeah'. One might expect the speech of twins, who spend so much time in each other's company, to be more than usually egocentric. In line with this, Luria and Yudovich (1959) describe a pair of twins, who had been left alone for long periods and whose very limited speech was so personal and egocentric as to be incomprehensible to others. The evidence from the Keenan twins therefore points strongly to the need for a reassessment of currently common ideas on childhood egocentrism. Nonetheless, twins are atypical, so we should also examine the speech of unrelated children. This was done by Garvey and Hogan (1973) who studied eighteen pairs of children, aged from three-and-a-half to five years, during fifteen minute play sessions. The children were all drawn from the same school. Again, their conversations showed little or no sign of egocentrism, containing well-organised argumentation, as in the following exchange (p. 565):

A. If I grow up my voice will change and when you grow up your voice will change. My mom told me. Did your mommy tell you?
B. No, your mommy's wrong. My voice, I don't want to change. Oh well.
A. Oh well, well stay little right?
B. What?
A. We'll stay little.
B. No, I don't want to. I *want* my voice to change. I don't care if it changes.
A. I care.

Young children are also able to modify their speech style according to their audience. Shatz and Gelman (1973) found that children as young as four years simplify their speech when talking to two-year-olds. Thus they use fewer complex constructions and more attention-directing utterances when addressing the two-year-olds than in their speech to other four-year-olds or adults. Sachs and Devin (1976) report that, by four years of age, children are capable of simplifying their speech in response to a suggestion that they talk to their mother 'like a baby just learning how to talk'. The children also spoke to a baby doll in the same way that they would speak to a real baby. This suggests that their use of simplified speech to infants is a deliberate stylistic choice and not a reaction to incomprehension by the infants.

At even younger ages, children's speech varies according to the social status of their audience. Ervin-Tripp (1977) describes an unpublished study by Craig Lawson of the directives used by a two-year-old girl. When requesting something of her peers she almost always used direct imperative sentences, but with adults she used either statements of desire (*Mommy, I want milk*) or permission requests (*can I have some milk*). She even distinguished among the two-, three- and four-year-olds at her nursery school. While two-year-olds were given plain commands, three-year-olds received commands generally modified by *please* or *OK*, and four-year-olds were treated like adults, being given indirect requests in the form of questions (*Can have the pen, Nida please*). At home, she discriminated in politeness in favour of her father.

Quite clearly, children are capable of socialised speech from a very young age. Piaget's original observations were made over fifty years ago without the benefit of modern audio-visual recording techniques. Because of this he would not have been able to perform the kind of fine grain analysis done by Keenan, which has often demonstrated that utterances which superficially appear to be monologues are nothing of the kind. Piaget also employed complex tasks, such as his 'Three Mountains Problem' to demonstrate egocentrism. Even with adults, a difficult communication task can result in speech which is poorly adapted to the needs of the listener, such as when an uncomprehending foreigner has the same message repeated to him more loudly. Such failures cannot however be taken as evidence for any general inability to take part in dialogue.

Prerequisites for Conversation

It is instructive to try to draw up a list of the cognitive and behavioural prerequisites for conversation. My provisional list would include:

(1) *Intersubjectivity.* Infants have to recognise other humans as being rather special objects who will respond to their behaviour and initiate behaviour toward them. This intersubjectivity, or basic desire to interact and communicate, is the result of imprinting among animals. Where adequate intersubjectivity either fails to develop or is lost, such as in Harlow's socially-deprived rhesus monkeys or in severely autistic children, normal conversational behaviour will never develop.

(2) *Temporal co-ordination of activity.* The participants in a conversation must be able to organise their communicative behaviour in a sequence of turn-taking and not hinder or obstruct each other. No more than one person should normally talk at any one time, so there must be 'traffic signals' to control conversational entries and exits.

(3) *An adequate repertoire of communicative acts.* To participate success-fully in a dialogue, a child must have a mastery of a basic set of communicative

acts, such as that described by Halliday (1975). (3.1) *An adequate repertoire of non-verbal behaviour.* If someone asks you to 'Pass the salt' you must be able to do just that. Conversation serves primarily to co-ordinate and control joint activity. If one of the participants cannot do his part, then the others will be frustrated and the purpose of the conversation will be lost.

(4) *Co-ordinated attention to external objects.* If a child wants something, he must be able to direct his caretaker's attention to that object if he is to have any chance of being given it. The caretaker, in turn, must be able to direct the child's attention to objects of importance. Scaife and Bruner (1975) found that, by nine months of age, infants will turn their heads and follow the line of regard of a person facing them, while Murphy and Messer (1977) describe the subsequent development of their ability to direct their attention toward an object which is being pointed out to them. This is achieved by the age of fourteen months. Conversely, Collis and Schaffer (1975) and Collis (1977) have shown that mothers can and do follow the line of regard of their infants and name objects which the infants are looking at. Co-orientation of attention initially depends on the mother following her child but, after the first year, she gradually becomes able to direct the child.

Given these abilities, a pre-linguistic conversation, falling within Halliday's Phase I, is possible. For a genuinely linguistic conversation, the additional prerequisites include:

(5) *An adequate linguistic repertoire.* The child must possess sufficient resources of semantics, grammar, phonology and phonetics to enable him to understand and produce sentences. The research undertaken using the syntactic and semantic approaches was concerned almost exclusively with the nature and origins of the productive aspect of these abilities. So far, relatively little progress has been made in studying their receptive side, as manifested in the development of comprehension. (5.1) *Adequate knowledge of the world.* Semantic competence depends on adequate general knowledge of the world. Edwards (1973) has argued that sensorimotor intelligence provides the basic framework of this knowledge, while Barrett (1978) has started to explore the cognitive basis of naming. Children must also possess specific knowledge of the world, since many sentences cannot be directly interpreted from their immediate context but depend for their understanding on information about particular objects and events, shared by speaker and hearer.

(6) *Co-ordination of attention to mental representations.* Speakers must be able to make clear to their audience what they are talking about and be able to grasp topics introduced by others. Pointing and other gestures may be enough to establish reference to objects in the immediate vicinity, but they are obviously not adequate to refer to objects existing at some distant time and place and currently represented only in the minds of the speaker and, hopefully, the hearer. To achieve such 'displacement of reference' some system of symbols is required to name objects, properties, actions and events. Barrett (1978) reports on the development of object-naming, while Keenan

and Schieffelin (1976) describe the subsequent development of the ability to introduce, maintain or change the topic of a conversation. Egocentrism consists of an assumption that this prerequisite is fulfilled.

(7) *Textual competence.* It is necessary to have adequate means for building up complex sentences and for linking together successive sentences to form a coherent sequence. Slobin (1977) notes that 'pidgin languages', which have only the most rudimentary means of doing these things, are ponderous and hard to use without ambiguity. Thus, textual competence underlies clarity and economy of expression.

(8) *Sociolinguistic competence.* Fluent and idiomatic expression requires mastery of the different speech forms which are appropriate in different social contexts and sufficient understanding of social norms to know when to say what. The fluent foreigner is often betrayed as a non-native speaker by minor deficiencies in his use of the appropriate, context and topic-dependent speech style or 'register'.

An Innate Faculty for Communication?

Colwyn Trevarthen (1975, 1977) has claimed that at least the first two of our prerequisites for conversation are innate. His evidence comes from films of very young children interacting with their mothers which, he claims,

> '. . . show that infants are adapted, at least by three weeks after birth, to approach persons and objects as if they are quite different. The elaborateness of social responses and social expressions in the second and third month of life, before an infant has begun deliberate and controlled handling and mouthing of objects, indicates that intersubjectivity is fitted into development from the start as a determining influence. Human social intelligence is the result of development of an innate human mode of psychological function that requires transactions with other persons' (1975, pp. 78–9).

He describes a variety of social behaviours, including hand waving and mouth movements, made by the infants in closely rhythmically co-ordinated 'conversations' with their mothers. Because of its resemblance to animated conversation in adults, Trevarthen calls such behaviour 'proto-speech'. Its real importance may well be not so much as a rehearsal of things to come but as a very effective stimulus for gaining attention, and the opportunity for social learning, from adults. Right from the start, mother and child show clear turn-taking in their 'conversations'. The subsequent development of the vocal and other means of controlling this are described by Schaffer *et al.* (1977).

Conversation as the Source of Language

MacNamara (1972), in an exploration of the implications of the semantic approach for the strategies which infants must employ to acquire language, argued that '. . . infants learn their language by first determining independent of language, the meaning which a speaker intends to convey to them, and by then working out the relationship between the meaning and their language. To put it another way, the infant uses meaning as a clue to language, rather than language as a clue to meaning.' (p. 1). Essentially, the same idea is spelt out, within the terms of the conversational approach, by Bruner (1975) who claims that ' . . . the child comes to recognise the grammatical rules for forming and comprehending sentences by virtue of their correspondence to the conceptual framework that is constructed for the regulation of joint action and joint attention.' Bruner (1975) regards joint action and attention by mother and child as the crucial foundation for language development, saying.

'The claim is that the child is grasping initially the requirements of joint action at a pre-linguistic level, learning to differentiate these into components, learning to recognise the function of utterances placed into these socially ordered structures, until finally he comes to substitute elements of a standard lexicon in place of the non-standard ones. The process, is of course, made possible by the presence of an interpreting adult who operates not so much as a corrector or reinforcer but rather as a provider, an expander and an idealizer of utterances while interacting with the child.' (p. 17).

In statements like these, Bruner is arguing that the mastery of the first four prerequisites for conversation in our list are a necessary foundation for the acquisition of language proper. They are built up through joint activities by the mother and her pre-linguistic child starting, if Trevarthan is correct, in the first few days of life.

Ninio and Bruner (1978) chart the development of naming through a longitudinal study of picture-book reading by a mother and her child, starting when it was eight months old. The labelling of objects depicted in the book is taught through a ritualised dialogue. Throughout the ten months of the study the mother relied upon four basic types of utterances: Attentional vocatives (*look*), used before the child had started to attend to the picture on which his mother had focused; Queries (*What's that?*) used when the referent of that had been established; Labels (*It's an X*) said when she was fairly confident which picture the child was attending to; and Feedback (*Yes* or *No*) in response to the child's utterance. The change came in the response required from the child before the mother would give a Feedback response. Up to fourteen months of age the child was unable to produce labels and a vocal response which was not a word would elicit a response of *Yes, its an X*. After the child had mastered labelling such a response would result in a query of *What's that* and only the uttering of a name would lead to Feedback of *Yes* or *No*. The mother appeared to be engaged in a systematic long-term programme of tuition in which she built up her child's knowledge of the names and properties of objects. Brown and Hanlon (1970) report that in the next stage of development, when children are capable of making statements, parental approval is dependent upon the truth of their utterances rather than their grammaticality. Although we cannot be certain how typical such behaviour is, it is clear that some parents at least do teach their children how to speak.

Observations made over the last six years have shown that adults employ a specialised, highly distinctive, manner of speech when addressing young children. The characteristics of this speech 'register', now called 'baby talk' or 'motherese' are currently under intensive study (see Snow and Ferguson (1977) for representative examples of this research). At a first approximation, we may say that it is a style of speech which is grammatical, slow, repetitive, restricted in vocabulary, exaggerated in intonation and higher in pitch than normal speech. It may also include simplifications in sound structure. All of these characteristics seem likely to assist children in cracking the linguistic code.

These observations constitute direct evidence against Chomsky's claim that children have to decipher language from disorganised and ungrammatical outpourings by their unhelpful parents. The accumulating evidence strongly suggests that parents speak to their children in a manner highly conducive to language learning. Maternal, and to a somewhat lesser extent paternal, speech style appears to be very closely attuned, in both form and content, to the capacities of the child and changes with the development of the child's linguistic abilities (see Moerk (1974), Seitz and Stewart (1975), Snow (1977) for maternal speech, Rebelsky and Hanks (1971) for paternal speech). As we noted earlier, children as young as four years simplify their speech when talking to two-year-olds.

Even nursery rhymes may serve a tutorial function, since many of them contain a high proportion of irregular verbs[1] which must be individually learned. Campbell and Anderson (1976) examined nursery rhymes of the 'Hickory, dickory, dock' type, taken from a variety of languages, and found that they shared many common features which could only be appreciated on the basis of knowledge of subtle properties of the sound system of their language. Burling (1970) reports that nursery rhymes show many similarities of form, irrespective of the language. Such evidence suggests a teaching role for the verbal play initiated by adults, since it is largely they who teach such rhymes to their children. Weir's (1962) observations of the monologues of her son Anthony, mentioned earlier, suggest that children themselves may explore the properties of their language through play. Cazden (1974) presents detailed argument that such play helps to develop 'metalinguistic' awareness of the properties of language itself.

The conversational approach to language acquisition has reinstated the verbal environment. This had been undervalued both by the syntactic approach, with its adherence to the innatism of Chomsky, and by the semantic approach, with its cognitive foundation in the sensorimotor intelligence of Piaget, which is acquired by acting rather than listening.

The indispensibility of appropriate input for effective language development is dramatically demonstrated by the case of Genie, described by Curtiss (1977). Perhaps the nearest case to an authentic wolf child ever systematically studied, she was rescued at the age of thirteen after at least ten years of near total isolation by her psychotic father. During this time she received almost no conversational experience and, at the time of her discovery, she was almost totally mute. Her subsequent development, though highly impressive after such dreadful mistreatment, is still far from complete even after seven years of rehabilitation.

Lessons from the Past, Directions for the Future

It is a pleasure to report on a success story in psychological research and it is also instructive to try to understand the reasons for such achievements. In this case, the source of success is clear: developmental psycholinguistics has been guided by good theories. Some of them, particularly certain of Chomsky's claims, have been wrong but they have been little the worse for that. A theory is adequate if it organises current knowledge, it is good if it leads to advances in knowledge. Here the successive theoretical emphases have drawn the attention of researchers to previously unexplored aspects of children's behaviour, but they have not led people to ignore what had been learnt before. For once the growth of knowledge has been cumulative and psycholinguists have not split into waring factions of semanticists, functionalists and so on (which is more than can be said of the linguists in recent years). The moral for psychologists is clear. In the words of Karmiloff-Smith and Inhelder (1975) 'If you want to get ahead, get a theory'.

The second significant characteristic of this research is that it is firmly based upon naturalistic observation. Good experiments have certainly been done but, at every stage, the main thrust has come from the nursery rather than the laboratory. The recent developments in sound and visual recording have increased enormously the amount and range of information that can be obtained by observation and it is only on the basis of the minute analysis of behaviour made possible by recording that researchers can hope for any success with the methods of 'rich interpretation' which underlie the semantic, functional and conversational approaches. However, the more information that is potentially available, the more selectively it must be examined, which brings us back to the importance of theories since they determine what aspects of behaviour will receive attention as well as what interpretations are placed upon observational and other data.

The conversational approach to language development poses two sets of problems. Firstly, we must attempt to describe the development of children's conversational abilities. Here we are not as well served by linguistic theories as were researchers using the syntactic, semantic or even functional approaches. As we noted earlier, serious linguistic study of the structure of conversation is a recent development. Secondly, adopting the conversational approach forces us to face the fact that first language learning is strictly by the Berlitz method of total all-day exposure to an unknown tongue. Language exists for conversation and is begotten in conversation. In conventional second-language teaching the pupil first learns some vocabulary, then tackles the rules of syntax needed to produce sentences, and finally he is given conversational practice in order to learn which sentences to use and how to combine them to achieve fluent communication. For the infant learning its first language, this order is almost reversed, as MacNamara (1972) pointed out. First the child and its caretakers learn to converse by pre-linguistic means. Next, some vocabulary is mastered and finally, the child works out the syntax, apparently with little direct tutoring from its parents. We now face the problem of discovering how pre-linguistic children discern their caretakers' communicative intentions and how they use this understanding to crack the linguistic code.

Much more research is needed to unravel the social roots of communication. The psychological theories which are currently available may not be sufficient for our needs. Piaget gave us the permanent object but we have yet to plot the development of the 'permanent person'. Trevarthen (1975, 1977) and Sugarman-Bell (1978) both claim that separate object- and person-directed behaviours can be distinguished in very young children. What is now required is a comprehensive account of the development of person-directed behaviour and social cognition. Fortunately, developmental psychologists are now alert to these problems, as can be seen from the proceedings of the conferences at Stirling (Markova, 1978) and Loch Lomond (Schaffer, 1977).

We have argued that the adoption of a succession of new approaches to the study of language development has not invalidated the previous research. This chapter is not a chronicle of false starts. Nor is it an account of definitive solutions to problems since we still have much to learn about the origins of syntax and semantics. Within the domain of semantics we will surely see a continuation of the 'Piaget program': the use of Piaget's theories as a blueprint for language acquisition. Edwards (1973) and Sugarman-Bell (1978) have made exceptionally fruitful use of his concepts of sensorimotor intelligence to account for the early stages of development, while Cromer (1971) has used his notion of 'decentration' to explain the development, at around four to six years of age, of the language of time. But Piaget has explored the origins of many other kinds of knowledge, including spatial and logical concepts, processes of seriation and comparison, and concepts of probability and causality. Each of these conceptual domains has related sematic domains of highly structured and interdependent words. Unravelling and explaining the course of development of these intellectual and linguistic structures through the whole of childhood is a central task for future research. It raises the perennial question of the relation between language and thought. Piaget has always emphasised the primacy of thought and only discussed language in the most general terms, but developments in linguistic semantics (see Lyons (1977) for an excellent survey) are now giving us the conceptual tools to explore this problem in detail. While sensorimotor intelligence arises from interaction with the physical environment, later intellectual development must depend on interaction with the verbal environment, both inside school and elsewhere. An understanding of how this occurs would have profound implications for psychology and education.

In a brilliant paper published in 1973, Slobin outlined the central task for the syntactic approach: the specification of the strategies by which children acquire syntax. Research will continue on this problem and on the questions of why syntax develops at all. We have argued, in this chapter, that young children can express many of the fundamental semantic structures of their language using sentences of only two or three words in length. At present, we have little idea what propels them to go on and acquire the elaborate syntactic structures of adult speech.

Notes

1. I am grateful to Jim McGivney for this observation. Consider, for example:
   Jack and Jill *went* up the hill
   To fetch a pail of water.
   Jack *fell* down and *broke* his crown
   And Jill *came* tumbling after.

Bibliography and Suggestions for Further Reading

Dale, P. S. (1976). *Language Development*, 2nd edn, Holt, Rinehart and Winston. The best introductory textbook. The first seven chapters provide a clear account of research using the syntactic and semantic approaches. The remaining four chapters cover development of the sound system and its relation to reading; the relations between language, thinking, memory and the control of behaviour; dialect differences; and measurement of language development

Brown, R. W. (1973). *A First Language: The Early Stages*, Penguin. A very thorough and careful account of the research of Brown and his associates, and of Braine, Ervin-Tripp and Miller, and Bloom. The theoretical standpoint is 'early semantic period', probably around 1970. An analysis in terms of Case Grammar is given, and the relevance of Piaget's theories is noted but the links between semantic theory and cognition are not worked out in detail

Lenneberg, E. H. and Lenneberg, E. E. (eds.) (1975). *Foundations of Language Development: A Multidisciplinary Approach. Vols. I and II*, Academic/Unesco Press. The first volume contains nineteen chapters covering the biological foundations of language, and language development. The second volume contains twenty-three chapters, divided into four sections: aphasiology (the study of language disorders); deafness and blindness; language in the clinic; reading and writing. Taken together, these two volumes provide an exceptionally wide range of material, including many topics missing from other textbooks

Ferguson, C. A. and Slobin, D. I. (eds.) (1973). *Studies of Child Language Development*, Holt, Rinehart and Winston. The best collection of readings. As can be seen from the references to this chapter, it contains many of the classic papers.

Bar-Adon, A. and Leopold, W. F. (eds.) (1971). *Child Language: A Book of Readings*, Prentice Hall. Many interesting excerpts from older work, some of them unfortunately far too short. Several important papers from the syntactic and semantic approaches

Schiefelbusch, R. L. and Lloyd, L. L. (eds.) (1974). *Language Perspectives— Acquisition, Retardation and Intervention*, The Macmillan Press. A book derived from a conference. The first four sections cover speech perception in infants; development of the conceptual foundations of language; the development of comprehension; and the relation between comprehension and production. The rest of the book is devoted to remedial problems. The first section, discussing recent claims that infants are innately tuned to detect speech sounds, is particularly useful since it includes both sides of the argument

Morehead, P. M. and Morehead, A. E. (eds.) (1976). *Normal and Deficient Child Language*, University Park Press. A selection of reprinted papers, together with some original chapters. The contributions of Bowerman and Cromer are especially recommended

Ervin-Tripp, S. and Mitchell-Kernan, C. (eds.) (1977). *Child Discourse*, Academic Press. An interesting selection of chapters by various authors illustrating the new wave of research into conversation

This chapter has not discussed the mechanisms by which language is learned. The research we have described was concerned with the 'what' of language acquisition, but psycholinguists are now going on to discuss the 'how'. Two of the best discussions of the cognitive strategies underlying the development of grammar are given by:

Slobin, D. I. (1973). Cognitive prerequisites for the development of grammar. In Ferguson and Slobin (see above)

Cromer, R. F. (1977). Developmental strategies for language. In Hamilton, V. and Vernon, M. D. (eds.) (1977). *The Development of Cognitive Processes*, Academic Press

The cognitive bases of language are also discussed by Richard Cromer in his chapter in D. and E. Morehead (above) and in:

Cromer, R. F. (1974). The development of language and cognition: The cognition hypothesis. In Foss, B. (ed.) *New Perspectives in Child Development*, Penguin, pp. 184–252

We have omitted any discussion of the development of the sound system of language. This was probably the central concern in most of the early research, but was pushed to the sidelines by the new developments in syntax and semantics. No single unified treatment is available. Two recent works which contain much interesting material are:

Ingram, D. (1976). *Phonological Disability in Children*, Edward Arnold

Smith, N. V. (1973). *The Acquisition of Phonology*, Cambridge University Press

Both of these works require some technical knowledge of phonetics and phonology.

References

Antilla, R. (1976). Child language, abduction and the acquisition of linguistic theory by linguists. In *Baby Talk and Infant Speech*. (eds. W. Von Raffler-Engel, and Y. Lebrun). Amsterdam, Swets and Zeitlinger. pp. 24–37

Bar-Adon, A. and Leopold, W. F. (eds.) (1971). *Child Language: A Book of Readings*, Englewood Cliffs, Prentice Hall

Barrett, M. D. (1978). Ostensive definition and overextension in child language. *Journal of Child Language*, 5, 205–19

Baron, N. S. (1974). Functional motivation for age-grading in linguistic innovation. In *Historical Linguistics I* (eds. J. M. Anderson and C. Jones), Amsterdam, North Holland, pp. 33–63

Bates, E. (1976). *Language and Context: The Acquisition of Pragmatics*. New York, Academic Press

Bloom, L. (1970). *Language Development: Form and Function in Emerging Grammars* New York, Academic Press

Bloom, L. (1971). Why not pivot grammar? *Journal of Speech and Hearing Disorders*, 36, 40–50. (Reprinted in Ferguson and Slobin, 1973)

Bloom, L. (1973). *One Word at a Time: The Use of Single Word Utterances Before Syntax*, The Hague, Mouton

Bloom, L., Lightbown, P. and Hood, L. (1975). Structure and variation in child language. *Monographs of the Society for Research in Child Development*, 40 (serial no. 160)

Braine, M. D. S. (1963). The ontogeny of English phrase structure: the first phase. *Language*, 39, 1–13. (Reprinted in Bar-Adon and Leopold, 1971 and in Ferguson and Slobin, 1973)

Brown, R. (1970). The first sentences of child and chimpanzee. In *Psycholinguistics: Selected Papers of Roger Brown*. New York, The Free Press, pp. 208–31. (Reprinted in Ferguson and Slobin, 1973)

Brown, R. (1973). *A First Language: The Early Stages*. Harmondsworth, Penguin

Brown, R. and Bellugi, U. (1964). Three processes in the child's acquisition of syntax. *Harvard Educational Review*, 34, 133–51. (Reprinted in Bar-Adon and Leopold, 1971, in Brown, 1970, and in Ferguson and Slobin, 1973)

Brown, R. and Hanlon, C. (1970); Derivational complexity and order of acquisition in child speech. In Hayes, J. R. (ed). *Cognition and the Development of Language*. New York, John Wiley and Sons, pp. 11–53. (Reprinted in Brown, 1970)

Brown, R. W. and Fraser, C. (1963). The acquisition of syntax. In Coper, C. N. and Musgrave, B. (eds), *Verbal Behaviour and Learning*, New York, McGraw-Hill, pp. 158–97

Bruner, J. S. (1975). The ontogenesis of speech acts. *Journal of Child Language*, 2, 1–19

Burling, R. (1970). *Man's Many Voices: Language in its Cultural Context*. New York, Holt, Rhinehart and Winston

Campbell, M. A. and Anderson, L. (1976). Hocus-pocus nursery rhymes. *Papers from 12th Regional Meeting of the Chicago Linguistic Society*, pp. 72–95

Carter, A. L. (1974). The development of communication in the sensorimotor period: A case study. Unpublished doctoral dissertation, University of California at Berkeley

Carter, A. L. (1975). The transformation of sensorimotor morphemes into words: a case study of the development of "more" and "mine". *Journal of Child Language*, 2, 233–50

Cazden, C. (1974). Play with language and metalinguistic awareness: One dimension of language experience. *Urban Review*, **7**, 23–39

Chomsky, C. S. (1969). *The Acquisition of Syntax in Children from 5 to 10*. Cambridge, Mass., M.I.T. Press

Chomsky, N. A. (1957). *Syntactic Structures*, The Hague, Mouton

Chomsky, N. A. (1965). *Aspects of the Theory of Syntax*. Cambridge Mass., M.I.T. Press

Chomsky, N. A. (1971). Language and the Mind. In *Child Language: A Book of Readings*, pp. 425–33, (ed. A. Bar-Adon and W. F. Leopold). Englewood Cliffs, Prentice Hall.

Collis, G. M. and Schaffer, H. R. (1975). Synchronisation of visual attention in mother-infant pairs. *Journal of Child Psychology and Psychiatry*, **16**, 315–20

Collis, G. M. (1977). Visual co-orientation and maternal speech. In *Studies in Mother-Infant Interaction* (ed. Schaffer, H. R.), London, Academic Press, pp. 355–75

Coulthard, M. (1977). *An Introduction to Discourse Analysis*. London, Longman

Cromer, R. F. (1971). The development of the ability to decenter in time. *British Journal of Psychology*, **62**, 353–65

Curtiss, S. (1977). *Genie: A Psycholinguistic Study of a Modern-Day "Wild Child"*. New York, Academic Press

de Villiers, J. G. and de Villiers, P. A. (1974). Competence and performance in child language: Are children really competent to judge? *Journal of Child Language*, **1**, 11–22

de Villiers, J. G. and Flusberg, H. B. T. (1975). Some facts one simply cannot deny. *Journal of Child Language*, **2**, 279–86

Dore, J. (1974). A pragmatic description of early language development. *Journal of Psycholinguistic Research*, **4**, 423–30

Dore, J. (1975). Holophrases, speech acts, and language universals. *Journal of Child Language*, **2**, 21–39

Ervin-Tripp, S. and Mitchell-Kernan, C. (eds) (1977). *Child Discourse*. New York, Academic Press

Ervin-Tripp, S. (1977). Introduction. In *Child Discourse* (ed. S. Ervin-Tripp and C. Mitchell-Kernan), pp. 1–23, New York, Academic Press

Edwards, D. (1973). Sensory-motor intelligence and semantic relations in early child grammar. *Cognition*, **2**, 395–434

Edwards, D. (1978). The sources of children's early meanings. In *The Social Context of Language* (ed. I. Markova), Chichester, John Wiley and Sons, pp. 67–85

Ferguson, C. A. and Slobin, D. I. (eds) (1973). *Studies of Child Language Development*, New York, Holt, Rinehart and Winston

Fillmore, C. J. (1968). The case for case. In *Universals in Linguistic Theory* (eds E. Bach and R. T. Harms), New York, Holt, Rinehart and Winston, pp. 1–90

Flavell, J. H. (1963). *The Developmental Psychology of Jean Piaget*. Princeton, Van Nostrand Reinhold

Garvey, C. and Hogan, R. (1973). Social speech and social interaction: egocentrism revisited. *Child Development*, **44**, 562–8

Gleitman, L. R., Gleitman, H. and Shipley, E. F. (1972). The emergence of the child as grammarian. *Cognition*, **1**, 137–64

Goldin-Meadow, S. and Feldman, H. (1977). The development of language-like communication without a language model. *Science*, **197**, 401–3

Goldin-Meadow, S., Seligman, M. E. P. and Gelman, R. (1976). Language in the two-year old. *Cognition*, **4**, 184–202

Greenfield, P. M. and Smith, J. H. (1976). *The Structure of Communication in Early Language Development*. New York, Academic Press

Halliday, M. A. K. (1970). Language structure and language function. In *New*

Horizons in Linguistics (ed. J. Lyons), Harmondsworth, Penguin, pp. 140–65

Halliday, M. A. K. (1973). *Explorations in the Functions of Language.* London, Edward Arnold

Halliday, M. A. K. (1975a). Learning how to mean. In Lenneberg, E. E. (eds), *Foundations of Language Development*, Vol. I, New York and Paris, Academic/Unesco Press, pp. 240–65

Halliday, M. A. K. (1975b). *Learning How to Mean.* London, Edward Arnold

Halliday, M. A. K. and Hasan, R. (1976). *Cohesion in English.* London, Longman

Hockett, C. (1950). Age-grading and linguistic continuity, *Language*, **26**, 449–57

Howe, C. J. (1976). The meaning of two-word utterances in the speech of young children. *Journal of Child Language*, **3**, 29–47

Karmiloff-Smith, A. and Inhelder, B. (1975). "If you want to get ahead, get a theory". *Cognition*, **3**, 195–212

Keenan, E. O. and Schieffin, B. (1976). Topic as a discourse notion: a study of topic in the conversation of children and adults. In *Subject and Topic* (ed. C. Li), New York, Academic Press, pp. 335–84

Keenan, E. O. (1977). Making it last: repetition in children's discourse. In *Child Discourse* (eds S. Ervin-Tripp and C. Mitchell-Kernan), New York, Academic Press, pp. 125–38

Klima, E. S. and Bellugi, U. (1966). Syntactic regularities in the speech of children. In *Psycholinguistics Papers* (eds J. Lyons and R. J. Wales), Edinburgh, Edinburgh U.P., pp. 183–213. (Reprinted in Bar-Adon and Leopold, 1971 and Ferguson and Slobin, 1973)

Klima, E. S. and Bellugi, U. (1972). The signs of language in child and chimpanzee. In *Communication and Effect: A Comparative Approach*, (eds T. Alloway, L. Kramer and R. Pliner), New York, Academic Press, pp. 67–96

Leopold, W. F. (1939–49). *Speech Development of a Bilingual Child* (4 Vols). Evanston, Northwestern University Press

Limber, J. (1973). The genesis of complex sentences. In *Cognitive Development and the Acquisition of Language* (ed. T. E. Moore), New York, Academic Press, pp. 169–85

Luria, A. R. and Yudovich, F. I. (1956). *Speech and the Development of Mental Processes in the Child*, Harmondsworth, Penguin

Lyons, J. (1977). *Semantics* (2 vols). Cambridge, Cambridge University Press

Lyons, J. (in press). Deixis and anaphora. In *The Development of Conversation and Discourse* (ed. T. Myers), Edinburgh, Edinburgh University Press

McCarthy, D. (1954). Language development in children. In *Manual of Child Psychology* (ed. L. Carmichael), New York, Wiley, pp. 452–630

MacNamara, J. (1972). Cognitive basis of language learning in infants. *Psychological Review*, **79**, 1–13

McNeill, D. (1966). Developmental psycholinguistics. In *The Genesis of Language: A Psycholinguistic Approach*, (eds F. Smith and G. A. Miller), Cambridge, Mass, M.I.T. Press, pp. 15–84

Markova, I. (1978). *The Social Context of Language*, Chichester, Wiley

Mesangkay, Z. S., McCluskey, K. A., McIntyre, C. W., Sims-Knight, J., Vaugh, B. E. and Flavell, J. H. (1974). The early development of inferences about the visual percepts of others. *Child Development*, **45**, 357–66

Moerk, E. (1974). Changes in verbal mother-child interactions with increasing language skills of the child. *Journal of Psycholinguistic Research*, **3**, 101–16

Murphy, C. H. and Messer, D. J. (1977). Mothers, infants and pointing: a study of a gesture. In *Studies in Mother-Infant Interaction* (ed. H. R. Schaffer), London, Academic Press, pp. 325–54

Nelson, K. (1973). Structure and strategy in learning to talk. *Monographs of the*

Society for Research in Child Development, **38** (Serial No. 149)

Nelson, K. (1974). Concept, word and sentence: interrelations in acquisition and development. *Psychological Review*, **81**, 267–85

Nelson, K. (1975). The nominal shift in semantic-syntactic development. *Cognitive Psychology*, **7**, 461–79

Nelson, K. (1976). Some attributes of adjectives used by children. *Cognition*, **4**, 13–30

Ninio, A. and Bruner, J. S. (1978). The achievement and antecedents of labelling. *Journal of Child Language*, **5**, 1–15

Petretic, P. A. and Tweney, R. D. (1977). Does comprehension precede production? The development of children's responses to telegraphic sentences of varying grammatical complexity. *Journal of Child Language*, **4**, 201–9

Piaget, J. (1950). *The Psychology of Intelligence*, London, Routledge and Kegan Paul

Piaget, J. (1951). *Plays, Dreams and Imitation in Childhood*, London, Routledge and Kegan Paul

Piaget, J. (1953). *The Origin of Intelligence in the Child*, London, Routledge and Kegan Paul

Piaget, J. (1954). *The Construction of Reality in the Child*, London, Routledge and Kegan Paul

Piaget, J. (1970). Piaget's theory. In *Carmichael's Manual of Child Psychology*, Vol. I (ed. P. Mussen), New York, John Wiley and Sons, pp. 103–32

Ramer, A. L. H. (1976). Syntactic styles in emerging language. *Journal of Child Language*, **3**, 49–62

Rebelsky, F. and Hanks, C. (1971). Father's verbal interaction with infants in the first three months of life. *Child Development*, **42**, 63–8

Sachs, J. and Devin, J. (1976). Young children's use of age-appropriate speech styles in social interaction and role-playing. *Journal of Child Language*, **3**, 81–98

Sachs, J. and Truswell, L. (1978). Comprehension of two-word instructions by children in the one-word stage. *Journal of Child Language*, **5**, 17–24

Scaife, M. and Bruner, J. S. (1975). The capacity for joint visual attention in the infant. *Nature*, **253**, 265–6

Schaffer, H. R. (ed) (1977). *Studies in Mother-Infant Interaction*. London. Academic Press

Schaffer, H. R., Collis, G. M. and Parsons, G. (1977). Vocal interchange and visual regard in verbal and pre-verbal children. In *Studies in Mother-Infant Interaction* (ed. Schaffer, H. R.) London, Academic Press, pp. 291–324

Schlesinger, I. M. (1971). Production of utterances and language acquisition. In *The Ontogenesis of Grammar*. (ed. D. I. Slobin) New York, Academic Press, pp. 63–101

Schlesinger, I. M. (1974). Relational concepts underlying language. In Schiefelbusch, R. L. and Lloyd, L. L. (eds): *Language Perspective – Acquisition, Retardation and Intervention*. London and Basingstoke: Macmillan

Schlesinger, I. M. (1975). Grammatical development – the first steps. In Lenneberg, E. H. and Lenneberg, E. (eds) *Foundations of Language Development: A Multidisciplinary Approach, Vol. I*. New York and Paris: Academic/Unesco Press. 203–22

Seitz, S. and Stewart, C. (1975). Imitations and expansion: Some developmental aspects of mother-child communication. *Developmental Psychology*, **11**, 763–8

Shatz, M. and Gelman, R. (1973). The development of communications skills: Modifications in the speech of young children as a function of listener. *Monographs of the Society for Research in Child Development*, **38** (Serial No. 152)

Shipley, E. F., Gleitman, C. S., and Smith, L. R. (1969). A study of the acquisition of language. *Language*, **45**, 332–42

Skinner, B. F. (1957). *Verbal Behaviour*. London, Methuen

Slobin, D. I. (1966). The acquisition of Russian as a native language. In Smith, F. and Miller, G. A. (eds): *The Genesis of Language: A Psycholinguistic Approach.* Cambridge, Mass. M. I. T. Press. pp. 129–48

Slobin, D. I. (1970). Universals of grammatical development in children. In Flores D'Arcais, G. B. and Levelt, W. J. M. (eds): *Advances in Psycholinguistics,* Amsterdam: North Holland, pp. 174–84

Slobin, D. I. (1971). *Psycholinguistics.* Glenview, Ill., Scott, Foresman

Slobin, D. I. (1972). Seven questions about language development. In Dodwell, P. C. (ed): *New Horizons in Psychology* Vol. 2, pp. 197–215

Slobin, D. I. (1973). Cognitive prerequisites for the development of grammar. In Ferguson and Slobin, 1973. pp. 175–208

Slobin, D. I. (1977). Language change in childhood and in history. In Macnamara, J. (ed): *Language Learning and Thought.* New York: Academic Press

Snow, C. E. (1977). The development of conversation between mothers and babies. *Journal of Child Language,* **4,** 1–22

Snow, C. E. and Ferguson, C. A. (eds) (1977). *Talking to Children.* Cambridge: C.U.P

Sugarman-Bell, S. (1978). Some organizational aspects of pre-verbal communication. In Markova, I. (ed) *The Social Context of Language.* Chichester: John Wiley and Son, pp. 49–66

Traugott, E. C. (1974). Explorations in linguistics: Language change, language acquisition and the genesis of spatio-temporal terms. In Anderson, J. M. and Jones, C. (eds) *Historical Linguistics I.* Amsterdam: North Holland pp. 263–314

Trevarthen, C. (1975). Early attempts at speech. In Lewin, R. (ed). *Child Alive.* London: Temple Smith pp. 62–80

Trevarthen, C. (1977). Descriptive analysis of infant-communicative behaviour. In Schaffer, 1977. pp. 227–70

Wason, P. C. and Johnson-Laird, P. N. (1972). *Psychology of Reasoning: Structure and Content.* London: Batsford

Weir, R. (1962). *Language in the Crib.* The Hague: Mouton

Weisenburger, J. L. (1976). A choice of words: two-year-old speech from a situational point of view. *Journal of Child Language,* **3,** 275–81

Wieman, L. A. (1976). Stress patterns in early child language. *Journal of Child Language,* **3,** 283–6

Wode, H. (1977). Four early stages in the development of L.I. negation. *Journal of Child Language,* **4,** 87–102

7 The Nature of Educational Competence

J. G. WALLACE
(School of Education, Deakin University, Victoria, Australia)

Introduction

The 'raison d'etre' of this chapter is to consider the actual and possible contribution of developmental psychology to the resolution of educational issues and, in particular, the problem of divining the nature of educational competence. As this represents the theme for a tome rather than a chapter a well-defined and delimited structure is required to render it manageable. The approach adopted will involve a consideration of two lines of research concerned with 'competence'. It will be argued that the current situation in both indicates the desirability of the same research strategy in developmental psychology if progress is to be made towards the understanding of educational competence. The reasons that this strategy has not been characteristic of developmental psychological research to date will be discussed and the chapter will conclude with a consideration of aspects of ongoing research which suggest trends towards its adoption.

It will become evident in the discussion of the two lines of research which follows that the term 'education' is being used in its broadest sense. This involves viewing it as synonymous with learning. The child interacts with his environment and as a result the structured experience in memory which represents his model of the world and himself undergoes change. In the formal setting of an educational system an explicit attempt is made to control environmental interaction in order to produce specific structural changes which are regarded as desirable. Viewed from this perspective 'educational competence' comprises the ability to construct and revise a world model on the basis of experience of the environment and to employ it as a means of achieving and maintaining effective environmental interaction.

Linguistics, Social Anthropology and Competence

The first line of research to be considered has its disciplinary roots in linguistics and social anthropology, but is concerned with issues of considerable significance to psychology. The focus of the work is on cross-cultural and inter-subcultural comparisons of cognition. Its point of departure is the deficit hypothesis which maintains that variations between cultural and subcultural groups in intellectual performance arise from differences in their underlying level of competence. These differences are attributed to the presence or absence of cultural or subcultural features which facilitate or inhibit the development of competence. The features which have attracted the greatest attention are those that are regarded as being responsible for the relatively poor academic performance and test scores of children from socially disadvantaged groups. They include a lack of adequate parental attention and, above all, a deficit in the symbolic and linguistic environment of the child.

The deficit hypothesis has proved to be highly controversial but no attempt will be made here to rehearse the arguments. Cole and Bruner (1971) provide a succinct review of a body of data and theory which 'casts doubt on the conclusion that a deficit exists in minority group children, and even raises doubts as to whether any nonsuperficial *differences* exist among different cultural groups'. For our present purpose the most important aspect of this work is the emergence of an alternative account of the relationship between competence and performance. It is argued by Labov (1970) and others that the data in support of the deficit hypothesis have been obtained by experimental methods which are incapable of identifying distinctions in underlying competence. This has obscured the fact that so-called culturally deprived groups have the same underlying competence as those in the mainstream of the dominant culture. Observed differences in performance are due to variations in the situations and contexts in which the competence is expressed. Given the appropriate situation and context, members of culturally deprived groups are enabled to reveal their competence in successful performance.

Acceptance of Labov's argument fundamentally alters the objectives of the study of the competence–performance relationship. The main aim is no longer to use a sample of performance as a means of ranking individuals and groups on the basis of an underlying level of competence that is assumed to hold good across all situations. There are two major objectives. A range of test situations must be sought which enables equally successful performance to be demonstrated by individuals or groups being compared. In addition, it is necessary to explore the range and nature of the situations in which individuals or groups reveal equal performance.

It should be pointed out parenthetically at this point that reassessment of the competence–performance relationship has not been confined to a linguistics–social anthropological background. Study of the effects of situational variations on performance has led to the adoption of a modified theoretical approach to competence by some psychologists. Flavell and Wohlwill (1969), for example, proposed a modified theory as a result of a consideration of the inconsistent performance data obtained in experimental studies prompted by Piaget's account of intellectual development.

Their point of departure is illustrated by means of a comparison of the performance of three hypothetical subjects on a range of tasks involving transitive inferences of the type $X > Y$ and $Y > Z$ logically implies $X > Z$. Child A (age four) fails to exhibit anything resembling transitive inference on any of the tasks even with the help of brief training or prompting. Child B (age eight) gives clear evidence of transitive inference on some of the tasks but not on others. Training produces success on some of the tasks previously failed but no improvement in performance on the more complex tasks. Child C (age 14) applies the transitivity rule correctly, without any training, in almost all of the problems presented to him. Child A is viewed as differing from both B and C in that there is no evidence that a transitivity rule is, as yet, part of his cognitive competence whereas it must be included in the competence descriptions of B and C. The difference between B and C, in contrast, is explained in terms of another aspect of competence namely the processes by which the subject transforms the task data into suitable coded form and accesses and utilises the functional equivalent of the transitivity equation. Child B has the transitivity rule in his competence repertoire but is unable to access and use it in all of the situations where it is appropriate. Child C does not exhibit such limitations on the transfer and generalisation of the transitivity rule. In short, there is an evident difference in competence between B and C but it is not the same kind of competence difference as that which distinguishes A and B.

Flavell and Wohlwill have based a general model for the analysis of the formation of stages in intellectual development on this distinction between aspects of competence. For our present purpose the most interesting feature of it is that fluctuations in performance level due to situational variations are presented as necessary consequences of the nature of competence. The child's performance in a cognitive task is determined by the rules, structures or 'mental operations' embodied in the task and by the actual mechanisms required for processing the input and the output. These situational features are built into a model which specifies three parameters that, it is asserted, jointly determine a child's performance. The first is the probability that a given operation has become fully established and is a functional aspect of the competence of a particular child. The second parameter is an attribute of the task situation. It represents the likelihood for any given situation that the necessary operation, if functional in the child, will in fact be called into play and its end product translated into the desired output. The value of this parameter is determined by a large number of factors related to task difficulty. These comprise, for example, the amount of irrelevant information from which the relevant information has to be abstracted and the size of the information load placed on the child in dealing with the problem. The third parameter reflects the aspect of the child's competence concerned with processing of input and output and indicates the extent to which his development has reached a point at which his ability to abstract, code and process information is commensurate with the demands of the specific task situation. The degree of success achieved in performance is attributed to the result of an interaction between these two aspects of the child's competence and the demands of the specific situation.

The broadening of the conception of competence illustrated in the work of Flavell and Wohlwill and in the arguments arising from the linguistics–social anthropological approach poses many theoretical and empirical problems which will require a significantly enriched approach for their resolution. In identifying the problems and seeking the necessary enrichment we will continue to follow proposals that have emerged from a linguistics–social anthropological background. Cole and Scribner (1974) criticise cross-cultural studies aimed at determining whether some particular group described by anthropologists 'has' or 'has more' or 'has less' of cognitive capacities, such as 'abstract thought', 'perceptual analysis' or 'logical structure', considered to be characteristic of normal psychological functioning in industrialised Western societies. These are not unitary entities but vary in their nature with differences in the situations that give rise to their operation. Cole and Scribner argue that in cognition we are dealing with processes, not with properties. Understanding of cultural variations in cognitive capacities is attained when it is possible to specify the operations or processes which they comprise in given situations and how these processes and situations differ from one population to another. In the cross-cultural context this entails asking questions about how particular groups go about cognitive tasks such as interpreting pictorial material, learning a discrimination problem and classifying geometric material.

There are three main facets of the account of the relationship between competence and performance which emerges from this line of argument. In a given situation a child's level of performance is determined by the availability of a functional system appropriate to the demands of the task. The nature of the functional systems which form part of the child's competence repertoire is, in turn, determined by his previous situational experience. Differences across cultures and subcultures in situational experience arise from differing environmental demands. As a consequence, the functional systems acquired by their members vary.

In addition to differences in the repertoire of functional systems, cultures and subcultures vary in the nature of the environmental or situational conditions which activate systems that are functionally equivalent. Two subcultures, for example, involve environmental demands which require the construction of a functional system representing the same general principle or rule. If the situational experience provided by the subcultures is widely different, the functional systems acquired by their members will be equivalent in terms of the general rule but vary significantly in the nature of the situational conditions that activate them. It is this aspect which highlights the importance of investigating competence in an appropriate context. It is not only necessary to establish whether a particular competence is exhibited in performance in a range of situations but, also, to determine that the significance of the selected situations is in terms of the environmental demands made by the culture of the person being studied. Atypical situations may lead to an underestimate of competence by failing to satisfy the activation conditions of existing functional systems.

The third facet concerns a similarity rather than difference in competence across cultures and subcultures. A major implication of the linguistics–social anthropological approach is that cross-cultural differences are unlikely to be found in basic component cognitive processes. There is no evidence that any cultural group wholly lacks basic processes such as abstraction, inferential reasoning or categorisation. These are required if interaction with environmental situations and demands is to result in the construction of appropriate functional systems. It is, also, reasonable to assume that the range of processes which constitute the building blocks for functional systems is relatively constant across cultures although the nature of the functional systems varies.

What pointers to desirable directions in developmental psychological research can be derived from the linguistics–social anthropological approach to educational competence? The paramount point is the emphasis on process. If cross-cultural and inter-subcultural differences in cognition are to be understood, it is essential that accounts in process terms of both situational or task demands and functional systems should be available. This is necessary for illumination of the interaction between situation and functional systems that determines the nature of performance. Understanding of the construction of functional systems, also, requires an account of the basic processes which bring this about. These requirements can only be met if psychological research provides a valid theory of the development of cognitive processes that occur in real time when a child from a specific cultural or subcultural background interacts with a specific environmental situation.

We will return to the evident enormity of this objective for developmental psychological research later in the discussion. Up to this point we have considered educational competence entirely from a social–cultural perspective. The second of the two lines of research to be reviewed emphasises the individual rather than social–cultural aspects of competence.

The Problem of Adaptation

Few in our contemporary society would dispute children's right to differential education provided that the differences or variations are aimed at allowing each child to reach the limit of his educability. This near unanimity gives way to bitter controversy as soon as the question of the nature of the determinants of educability is raised (Kamin, 1974). As a result, it can be argued that the most significant contribution towards the elucidation of educability which developmental psychology could offer would be the resolution of the nature–nurture or heredity–environment issue. The type of resolution envisaged would involve demonstrably valid quantification of the relative contributions of heredity and environment to determining educability.

At the conclusion of a recent review of the heredity–environment evidence, Vernon (1976) suggests that abstracting heredity and environment as separate, unitary agents may blind us to the complexities of psychological growth. Certain groups differ in their gene pools and, thus, in their potentialities for development along different lines, but this tells us nothing about the mental characteristics of the individual group members.

'If we could overcome such irrational thinking, we might be more successful in modifying social and educational environments to suit individuals with differing patterns of abilities, instead of imposing a single system which inevitably condemns large numbers of children to fail.' (Vernon, 1976, p. 42)

A similarly trenchant criticism of simplistic approaches to the heredity–environment issue is offered by Cronbach and Snow (1969). They maintain that arguing in terms of a unidimensional ranking of individuals on the basis of measurements of general intelligence or g which is applicable across all situations, or a unidimensional ranking of environments on the basis of their suitability for all individuals is equally inappropriate. Only when the focus of attention shifts to the interaction between specific individuals and specific environments is the problem of adapting conditions to permit the attainment of the limits of educability being confronted in its full complexity.

What is involved in viewing differential education in interactive terms? As indicated above, education in its broadest sense is synonymous with the learning which underlies the initial construction and subsequent modification of the child's model of the world and himself as a result of interaction with the environment. An educational system provides a formal setting in which the child's environmental interaction is controlled in an attempt to produce specific changes in his structured experience which are regarded as desirable by society. If differential education is to take account of the interaction between specific individuals and specific environments, both the structural changes or objectives and the environmental controls or treatments must be positively adapted to differences between individuals. This is a tall order and, as Cronbach (1967) points out, formal educational systems have largely ignored this challenge. Few attempts at positive adaptation are made and the inconvenience arising from variations between individuals is minimised by resorting to a variety of organisational expedients.

Positive adaptation entails the selection of both goals and treatments appropriate to the current condition of each child. In psychological terms implementation of this prescription requires the capability to analyse the demands which attaining specific educational objectives makes upon cognitive processes and to assess the aptitude of individual children expected to attain the objectives. Following Cronbach and Snow (1977), 'aptitude' in this context is defined as 'the complex of prior cognitive characteristics that accounts for an individual's end state after a particular educational treatment'. The nature of the treatment accorded to an individual learner should be determined by a comparison of the results of the analysis of cognitive demand and assessment of aptitude.

If this approach to adaptation to individual differences is to be fully implemented, psychologists must provide educationists with a valid theory of the development of cognitive processes. The statement of the theory in process terms is essential, since the adaptation of goals and treatments hinges on the availability of a step by step account of the processes which occur in real time when a child interacts with an environmental situation. Neither a theory presenting an account of the structure underlying cognition nor one confined to relationships between directly observable situations and performance offers such an account.

Two facets of the requisite process theory can be distinguished. As indicated above, the substantive outcome of education is change in the world model stored in the child's long term memory (LTM). Such modification involves two broad categories of processes. The first are of general applicability since they are responsible for monitoring the sequence of interaction with the environment and deciding when and how the world model should be modified in the light of this experience. The second are much more specific and represent processes added to LTM as a result of interaction with particular environmental situations. They constitute the vast majority of the processes stored in LTM.

Both of these aspects of the child's process repertoire must be incorporated in a theory of cognitive development if education is to be adapted to individual differences. If the appropriateness of a specific objective for a child is to be determined an explicit account is required of the processes underlying the performance defining the objective. A decision should be reached by comparing it with an account of the processes incorporated in the section of the child's LTM model relevant to the current objective. Similarly, in adapting the treatment, the features which characterise the child's modification processes must be determined and due allowance made in designing the experience that he is to undergo. The pedagogical implications of any interaction between these features and the specific processes linked to the objective must, also, be considered in designing the treatment.

At this point the reader may feel that a simplistic view of the heredity–environment issue has simply been replaced with a simplistic prescription for the adaptation of education to individual differences that grossly under-estimates the complexity of human cognition and the intractable problems which must be overcome if a valid theory is to be constructed. The remainder of this discussion will, hopefully, dispel this opinion.

We have reviewed two lines of research which exemplify approaches to the study of educational competence emphasising social and individual aspects respectively. It has been argued that the current situation in both supports the adoption of the same research strategy in developmental psychology. This places the major emphasis on the analysis of cognition in process terms with a view to the production of a valid theory of cognitive development, which would permit step by step accounts of the processes involved in meeting the demands of specific environmental situations or educational objectives, in the operation of functional systems or educational treatments and in the construction of the child's world model on the basis of interaction with the environment. The type of strategy advocated has not been characteristic of developmental psychological research to date. In the next section we will consider some of the reasons underlying this state of affairs and indicate features of the current situation which suggest that a change in emphasis is underway.

Psychometrics, Experimental Psychology and Process Theory

The psychological literature amply documents the difficulty of producing valid theories of delimited aspects of development and, thus, emphasises the enormity of setting an aim as grandiose as the construction of a compre-hensive theory of cognitive development expressed in process terms.

The lack of significant progress over the years is certainly indicative of the extreme difficulty of the problems posed by the study of the development of cognitive processes. It may, however, give rise to an unnecessarily pessimistic prognosis since until comparatively recently the dominant trends in psy-chological study were not conducive to success. In support of this assertion, the main trends will be briefly reviewed to assess the degree of concern accorded to cognitive developmental theory in general and the analysis of cognitive processes in particular.

Cronbach (1957) highlighted the distinction between psychometrics, the study of individual differences, and experimental psychology, the search for the basic laws governing all human and animal functioning. Their separation has over the years perpetuated directions in research within both traditions which have minimised their contribution to the production of a process theory of the development of cognition. The concern of psychometrists with individual differences has been in the context of prediction. The search for successful predictive instruments has customarily led to an emphasis on the content of performance rather than the processes underlying it. Evidence of this is to be found in the practice of naming group factors derived by factor analytic techniques, such as v, k and n, after the nature of the tests for which they have high loadings. Psychometrists have traditionally been interested in the course of intellectual development but their concern with performance content and successful prediction is responsible for the absence of the unifying theory of cognition underpinning test construction criticised by Hearnshaw (1972). At present an increasing interest in the processes underlying performance can be discerned among psychometrists. A specific example is provided by the revival of the use of introspective reports in attempts to elucidate the basis of the loading pattern derived for a test by factor analysis (Elshout, 1974). The genesis of this trend can be traced through Eysenck's (1967) paper on intelligence assessment, Guilford's (1967) inclusion of basis psychological processes in the framework for his scheme of ability factors and Bunderson's (1965; Dunham and Bunderson, 1969) studies of the changing relationship between cognitive processes at different points in the performance of concept attainment problems. A particularly interesting recent example in the context of this discussion is the work of Hunt and his collaborators who, admittedly, are not psychometrists but cognitive psychologists (Hunt *et al.*, 1973, 1975). Their interest in psychometric issues represents welcome interaction across the Cronbach 'divide'. The point of departure for their studies is concern on both scientific and social philosophical grounds with the dubious procedure of basing decisions on mental measurement without a theory of how the measure works. Cognitive power ought to be measured by use of an instrument whose design is based on our understanding of the cognitive process.

From this general concern Hunt addresses the specific question of whether the subtests of a contemporary intelligence test differentiate between individuals who also differ in ways which a cognitive psychologist finds theoretically interesting. Of particular interest would be the finding that psychometric tests require one sort of ability and cognitive psychological tasks require another, but the same individuals who possess or lack one set of abilities possess or lack the other. This hypothesis has been tested in a series of experiments. The results indicate that university students who score high on a test of verbal ability do unusually well on a variety of information processing tasks. They display a superior ability to make the type of rapid conversion from a physical representation to a conceptual meaning involved in recognising a particular visual pattern as a word or letter. The high verbal, also, exhibit superior ability to retain in short term memory (STM) information about the order in which stimuli are presented and to manipulate data in STM in the manner required by scanning and simple computational tasks. Hunt argues that high verbal subjects know more about the linguistic aspects of their culture because they are more rapid in carrying out information processing tasks, rather than the reverse. Their superior information processing ability enables them to abstract and fix more information in LTM as a result of exposure to a linguistic environment.

Most interestingly for our present purpose Hunt relates his findings to the adaptation of educational treatments to individual differences.

'A test of current information processing ability should be useful in determining the manner in which information should be presented to a specific person, in order to maximise the probability of the information's being retained. We believe that the aptitude treatment interactions much sought after by educators are more likely to be found if "aptitude" is defined by the parameters of the information processing process than if it is defined by one's relative standing in a population'.

Although not offered in a developmental context Hunt's presentation of a process-based approach to matching treatments to individuals suggests that a valuable contribution to the production of a process-based theory of cognitive development may yet emerge from a concern with psychometrics.

Some support for this view can be derived from present trends in the psychometric work on aptitude–treatment interaction to which Hunt referred. This is of considerable relevance to our main concern since it is aimed at devising methods of positively adapting treatments to take account of individual differences. Measurements of individual difference are only useful in making decisions about the appropriate educational treatment for individuals if they can be shown to interact with treatment. If two groups, selected so that they reflect the same range of performance on an aptitude measure, are assigned to different educational treatments and the performance of each group subsequently plotted on a graph with achievement on one axis and aptitude on another then a significant interaction effect is called ordinal when the lines for the two groups do not cross. This indicates that one educational treatment produces greater achievement in subjects from all aptitude levels and, as a consequence, the outcome provides no information on which differential treatment decisions can be taken. A disordinal interaction occurs when the lines for the two groups do cross, and this is interpreted as evidence of aptitude–treatment interaction. Subjects high on the aptitude measure perform better, for example, after the first treatment than after the second, while those low on the aptitude measure perform better after the second treatment than after the first. When aptitude–treatment interaction occurs a basis is provided for the differential assignment of subjects to educational treatments to maximise learning.

Generally accepted aptitude constructs have not proved to be a productive way of measuring those individual differences that interact with different educational treatments. There is an impressive degree of unanimity about the reasons for the generally negative results of attempts to obtain disordinal interactions between measures of individual differences in ability and educational treatments. Bracht (1970), Glaser and Resnick (1972) Cronbach

(1975) and Cronbach and Snow (1977) agree that the aptitude constructs used are not a productive way of measuring individual differences which interact with different educational methods because these measures stem from a psychometric, selection-oriented tradition that does not relate to the processes underlying performance. Both educational treatments and aptitudes should be characterised in terms of specific processes; in the words of Glaser and Resnick (1972) 'successful attempts to adapt instruction to individual differences will depend upon a line of research on process variables in instruction and performance that is only now beginning to emerge'. The proliferation of such process-based research will undoubtedly produce an increasing interest among psychometrists in cognitive theory, and, as an inevitable result, cognitive development theory.

An overview of experimental psychology reveals that the goals adopted in the mainstream of both empirical and theoretical work have, until comparatively recently, diminished its potential contribution to the construction of a process theory of cognitive development. The nomothetic approach with its emphasis on the search for general laws discouraged interest in individual differences. Since the generality of the laws was assumed to run across both ontogenetic and phylogenetic divisions, the difficulties involved in conducting experiments with humans, and young humans in particular, could be legitimately avoided. Concern with theory was fitful and theory construction tended to be confined to narrow, compartmentalised aspects of behaviour. Consistent with these trends the focus of the vast bulk of research was on performance rather than the processes underlying it.

As in the case of psychometrics, trends can be discerned in more recent work in experimental psychology which give grounds for optimism that it, too, may contribute to the understanding of the processes underlying cognitive development. The study of cognition in humans which has been a consistent feature of British and Continental experimental psychology is enjoying something of a worldwide boom. Most importantly for our purpose, the focus is on the information processing involved in such aspects of cognition as attention, perception, conceptualisation and memory. The prominence of information-processing analysis emerges very strikingly from a swift pass through the abstracts of the papers presented at the International Congress of Psychology in Paris in July 1976.

A greater concern with individual differences can be detected in the theoretical discussions and empirical research of some experimentalists (Underwood, 1975). An indication of this trend, as Glaser and Resnick (1972) point out, is the application of the process constructs of contemporary theories of learning to the conceptualisation of individual difference variables advocated by Melton (1967). A clearcut empirical example of this approach is the work of Rohwer (1971) on individual differences in the process of mental elaboration in paired associate learning.

Concurrently with displaying greater concern for the study of cognitive processes and individual differences experimental psychologists are according much greater significance to developmental issues. This may be attributable, in part, to disillusion with the search for laws transcending phylogenetic and ontogenetic boundaries (Hinde and Stevenson-Hinde, 1973). The stimulation provided by the work of Jean Piaget has, also, played a significant part.

Although allusion to Piaget as an experimental psychologist will produce raised eyebrows in certain quarters, he and his collaborators certainly fall on this side of Cronbach's dichotomy. Despite its status as a landmark in developmental psychology, Piaget's theory does not meet the specifications of a process theory of cognitive development. As Wohlwill (1966) has pointed out, for all its formal elaboration and complexity, it is basically a structural analysis of children's performance on cognitive tasks at different levels of development. Being couched in structural rather than process terms it offers an account of the logical structures which, it is alleged, underlie performance, but not of the process that determines the step-by-step temporal unfolding of mental processes and resulting behaviour when a child is confronted with a problem such as a conservation task. As a result, it cannot be demonstrated that the structures comprising the theory are sufficient to account for performance. The tenuous nature of the relationship between structure and performance is illustrated in Flavell's (1963) observation that the logical groupings which form the core of Piaget's description of the level of concrete operations were not wholly derived from observations of children's thinking. Grouping IV, co-univocal multiplication of classes, and Grouping VIII, co-univocal multiplication of relations, were invented because they describe logically possible cognitive structures and were not empirically derived from experimental evidence.

In comparison with the structural analysis of children's cognitive performance at different levels of development Piaget's treatment of the transition problem, the nature of the processes by which these changes take place, is much less complete. The accounts of equilibrium in terms of the complementary processes of assimilation and accommodation resemble Piaget's accounts of the developmental stages in being abstract and divorced from the actual step-by-step performance of the reorganisation process in relation to specific content. The single exception is a description of the emergence of conservation of continuous quantity (Piaget, 1957, 1960). This deals only with the classic experimental situation using clay, however, and is not directly concerned with the processes determining performance since it is based on a sequence of four strategies defined in terms of variations in the probabilities of response to two dimensions of the situation.

Two main reasons for this relative emphasis on structure rather than process have been outlined by Cellérier (1972). The first is Piaget's preoccupation with epistemology. Structures are excellent building-blocks in 'the reconstruction of the Kantian *a priori* categories of knowledge as developmental necessities'. The second factor is the adoption in his main work on groupings of a type of mathematical formalisation which is 'at least twice removed, in its degree of abstraction, from the actual actions and situations with which the child or the adult deals' (p. 117).

This critical discussion has been based on the classic account of Piaget's theory which has proved so seminal in research on cognitive development. There are, however, indications that changes in the viewpoint of the Genevan group are carrying their work in directions more relevant to process analysis. Cellérier (1972) attributes to Piaget an increased concern with process and outlines the consequences of this alteration of emphasis for his general theory of development:

> 'This type of analysis gives rise to a picture of cognitive development as a parallel evolution of cognitive categories, each composed of a neat "filiation" of progressively stronger structures. It has been recently complicated by the discovery that many different schemes and concepts may be applied by the child to the same problem, also that this seems to be a general rule and that the different cognitive categories seem to evolve at slightly different rates. The net result is that lateral interactions . . . appear at the decomposition and recombination level. These interactions (Piaget describes them as reciprocal assimilations between schemes, resulting in new coordinations) take place between elements that are heterogeneous in two ways: they originate from different categories and their degrees of completion are not necessarily the same. Thus, Piaget's picture of development now incorporates vertical relations (intra-category filiations), horizontal ones (inter-category lateral interactions) and oblique ones (interactions between elements of different "operatory levels").'

This marked shift in theoretical viewpoint is closely linked with series of learning experiments conducted by Inhelder and her collaborators (Inhelder, 1972; Inhelder *et al.*, 1974), and aimed at observing 'not the coordination process, but a close series of snapshots of its effects: how the schemes are decomposed, what are the successive recombinations that are generated and tried out, what are the guiding constraints their generation is subjected to' (Cellérier, 1972). Further confirmation of an increasing emphasis on process is provided in Piaget's (1974) report on the development of children's awareness of how they succeed in carrying out a variety of sensorimotor tasks, and in the account of his continuing and planned research presented to the International Congress of Psychology in Paris (Piaget, 1976).

The increased concern with process in Piaget's current view of developmental states is, according to Cellérier (1972), paralleled in a recent revision of the equilibration model. This resembles Pascual-Leone's (1975) account of the emergence of truly novel behaviour in being based on the idea that a child's functioning in a problem environment is determined by a process that produces new rules and concepts by decomposing and recombining those which he already possesses. The new combinations are evaluated on the basis of their effects on the external problem environment and the outcome gives rise to a new recombination sequence. A cyclic chaining of external observations and internal combinations is thus established. By generating the extension of certain rules, new properties of the environment can be discovered and these new properties serve to invent new rules that can then be used to discover new properties. The cycle stops when nothing new is generated, under a given definition of the problem environment. Although this revised version of equilibration is a better starting point for process analysis than earlier accounts, it is still a considerable distance from providing a step-by-step account of the operation of the reorganisation process.

In summary, this brief but wide ranging review has identified the broad trends which have minimised the contribution of psychometrists and experimental psychologists to the construction of a comprehensive theory of cognitive development expressed in process terms. It has, also, pinpointed features which provide grounds for optimism that these impediments are being removed. In particular, there is an increased interest in theory construction and in the study of cognition, individual differences and developmental issues. Above all there is a widespread movement to the employment of process analysis.

Definition of a Tractable Problem

In spite of the optimistic trends in current research it would be wildly unrealistic to select as an objective the construction of a process theory of cognitive development sufficiently comprehensive to include all aspects of educational competence covered in the discussion of the two lines of research. In seeking manageable aims the optimal strategy entails retaining as many of the fundamental problems as possible in the field of concern while reducing the complexity of the undertaking as much as possible. The key problem posed by both the social and individual approaches to educational competence is the nature of the interaction between environmental situations and individual competence which determines performance. For complete understanding, it is necessary to provide a detailed account of this interaction across a wide range of cultural and subcultural backgrounds. As Bruner (1972) has pointed out, pedagogical theory must relate to the specific political, economic and social setting of the educational process. It is possible, however, to narrow the field of concern by excluding cultural and subcultural variations while retaining the core of the problem. There can be no illumination of the nature of educational competence until it is possible to provide an account in process terms of the demands posed by an environmental situation or task and of the procedures responsible for the initial construction and subsequent modification of the child's world model in LTM.

This restriction of concern to the key issue goes some way towards the definition of a tractable problem. The construction of a theory of cognitive development sufficiently comprehensive to enable the representation in process terms of any relevant section, and, thus, potentially all, of a child's model of his world and himself is, however, still a tall order. A more realistic immediate objective for psychological research would be to focus on specific aspects of the LTM model such as those which provide the basis for the fundamental linguistic and mathematical skills that enjoy universal prominence in lists of educational priorities. This objective is consistent with a general strategy of emphasising the study of 'cold' as opposed to 'hot' cognition which would for the present ignore the complexities of the representation of the self and affectively highly charged areas of the LTM model. Adoption of this strategy does not imply a denial of the profound effect of these aspects on the functioning of cognition as a whole. It is entirely motivated by the necessity to simplify the problem to permit an empirical attack. This further restriction of the area of concern in no way diminishes the aspects of the processes concerned in the modification of the LTM model which must be considered.

Before considering continuing psychological research relevant to this revised objective comment on its suitability will be offered from two viewpoints. The first is particularly apposite since it represents the views of an instructional psychologist on the nature of an appropriate distribution of effort within psychological research relevant to the adaptation of instruction to individual differences. Resnick (1976) argues that the type of information processing analysis being advocated in this chapter is much too time consuming to be applied to a large number of content areas in order to facilitate adaptation. It should be reserved for the analysis of generalised skills such as learning to learn abilities. In the terms of this discussion Resnick's prescription would involve confining information processing analysis to study of the generally applicable processes which modify the LTM world model as a result of environmental interaction and eschewing analysis of aspects of the model relevant to specific tasks.

The type of analysis which Resnick advocates as a basis for the adaptation of aspects relevant to specific tasks is rational process analysis. This has its genesis in Gagné's (1970) conception of learning hierarchies. In his view there are eight types of learning which can be arranged in a hierarchy such that each type requires as a prerequisite all other types in lower levels of the hierarchy. The notion of a learning hierarchy has provided the basis for a method of tackling the problem of determining the optimal sequence of presentation of material in a curriculum and the adaptation of instructional goals to individual differences. As Resnick points out, hierarchies for instruction are generated by posing for any particular task under consideration the question:

'What kind of capability would an individual have to possess to be able to perform this task successfully?' When prerequisite capabilities are identified these are, in turn, viewed as tasks and the same question is applied to each of them. This method involves an implicit type of process analysis since responding to the question which generates the hierarchy involves some consideration of the processing steps taken by an individual performing the task. Gagné makes no attempt to introduce an explicit process analysis.

Rational task or process analysis, as the name implies, is a development of Gagné's approach which involves explicit consideration of the processes underlying task performance. Resnick (1976) defines it as an attempt to specify the processes involved in highly efficient performance of a given task. It gives rise to a detailed description of an idealised performance with a minimum number of processing steps. With the processes hypothesised to be involved in particular task performances explicitly stated it is possible to decide on a probable hierarchical ordering of the tasks.

Figure 7.1, derived from Resnick (1976), provides an example of the results of employing rational process analysis in designing an early mathematics curriculum. The top box indicates the task being analysed, in this case counting a set of moveable objects. The entry above the line describes the presented stimulus and the entry below the line the expected response. The second line in Figure 7.1 depicts a sequence of processing steps hypothesised to underlie task performance and the lower portion of the diagram presents capabilities regarded as either prerequisites for performance of the target task or helpful in learning it.

In this form rational task analysis has much in common with information processing analysis since it involves a description of task performance in terms of a sequence of processing steps in real time. It, also, involves reference to the demands made by specific tasks on general perceptual and memory processes. The divergence from information-processing analysis lies in the incomplete nature of the account of the processing sequence and the absence of attempts to establish its validity as a description of how children actually perform the task. Success in producing attainment of the required instructional objectives is considered sufficient evidence of the validity of a hierarchy derived by rational task analysis.

With this explication of rational task analysis it becomes clear why Resnick advocates its use in the aspect of adaptation relevant to specific tasks. If the achievement of instructional objectives is the main criterion, rational task analysis in many cases is a perfectly adequate approach and makes relatively modest claims on time and effort. There may, however, be very complex tasks which defy idealised analysis, or analyses that fail to produce the desired instructional objective. There is, also, no understanding of the processes underlying the instructional successes achieved. For further progress on these fronts recourse must be had to a more elaborate information processing analysis.

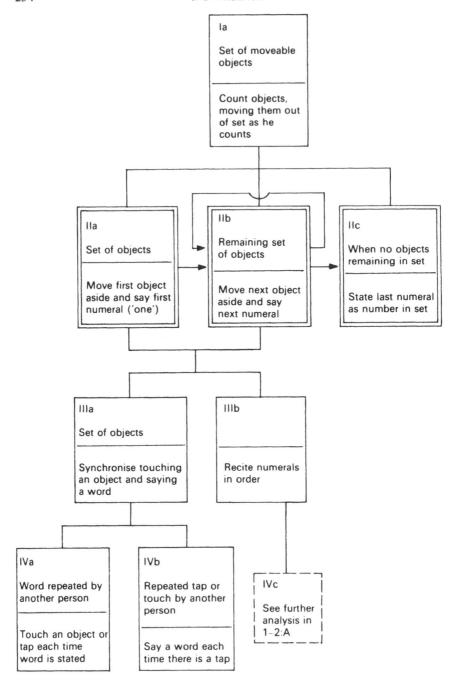

Figure 7.1   Analysis of objective 1–2:B (from Resnick, 1976)

The priorities dictated by the needs of instructional psychology do not coincide with the requirements of developmental psychology. If the immediate concern is the applied objective of devising optimal instructional sequences to produce specific target types of performance today, such practical short-term goals cannot be reconciled with a protracted wait for the appearance of a comprehensive process theory of cognitive development. On the other hand, a developmental psychologist focusing on the task of providing a complete solution to the problem of adaptation, rather than an immediate practical *modus vivendi*, would disagree with several features of Resnick's prescription. Confining information processing analysis to the study of generalised skills and applying rational task analysis to the specific content areas involves a distinction which is entirely artificial. Any information processing analysis of generalised skills including the generally applicable processes which modify the LTM world model must, of necessity, spill over into a consideration of the nature of the LTM representations of specific content areas constructed by the modification processes. The accounts of sequences of processing steps that form part of rational task analyses remain entirely isolated. No attempt is made to render them mutually consistent by basing them on a unifying process theory. Finally, an assessment of instructional effectiveness is not a satisfactory substitute for establishing the validity of a processing sequence as a description of how children actually perform a task.

From a developmental psychological viewpoint a solution to the problem of adaptation would have three components. The basic feature would be a valid account of the structure of the human information processing system (IPS). This would provide the foundation for an account of the representation in LTM of specific aspects of the world and of the processes which modify LTM representations as a result of interaction with the environment. If such a solution could be achieved in the long term it would produce an optimal situation for the requirements of instructional psychology. A valid sequence of processing steps would be available for each specific task and a process account of generalised skills both couched in terms of the same IPS.

A recent comment by Cronbach (1975) on the nature of realistic objectives for psychological research is of relevance to this description of the nature of a solution to the adaptation problem. In expressing unease with the intellectual style of psychological research he maintains that enduring systematic theories about man in society are not likely to be achieved. A general statement can be highly accurate only if it specifies interactive effects that it takes a large amount of data to pin down. In the case of devising individualised instructional treatments, persistent work in many contexts may give rise to an actuarial generalisation of some power but this will rarely be a basis for direct control at the individual level. The generalisation gives no guarantee of the success of the treatment with a particular individual because it ignores additional variables. Instead of prescribing a fixed treatment on the basis of a generalisation from prior experience with other persons or in other locales short-run empiricism should dominate. Responses to the treatment should be monitored and adjustments made accordingly.

This profoundly pessimistic view of the likelihood of abstracting generalisations about human functioning that hold good across individuals and across time to any significant degree is largely founded on the results of the type of psychometric studies of aptitude–treatment interaction described above. The adoption of process as a focus rather than the dimensions customarily tapped by psychometric tests may reduce the need for recourse to short-run empiricism. As progress is made in determining the basic structure of the IPS and the nature of the processes which modify the world model, a relatively stable basis for generalisation should be established since, although no exceptions to change on an evolutionary time scale, the main features should for practical purposes provide a quasi-constant common background onto which individual differences can be mapped.

Problem definition has already proved to be a protracted process and we will prolong it no further. The remainder of the chapter will be devoted to a consideration of continuing research relevant to the construction of the type of process theory of cognitive development required to provide accounts of the demands made by tasks, the structure of the IPS, the specific aspects of the LTM world model underpinning the 'cold' cognitive functions delineated above and the general processes responsible for modification of the model and, thus, underlying transition in development. As some of the relevant research lies outside the avowedly developmental area the discussion which follows will range across the field of cognitive psychology as a whole.

The Structure of the Information Processing System

Memory makes possible the construction by the child of the representations of his world and of himself which are essential for effective interaction with the environment. Comprehension is assisted if memory is regarded as being composed of a number of related stores or buffers. There is, however, current controversy as to whether there are a number of stores or only a single memory with several distinct functions in its mode of operation. The development of the latter viewpoint can be seen in the writings of Craik and Lockhart (1972) and Craik and Jacoby (1975) who attribute the phenomena of short-term retention to the functioning of perceptual analysis. Rather than regarding primary or short-term memory (STM) as a structure or store in which items are placed, they regard this type of memory as the activation of some part of the perceptual analysing system by the processes of conscious attention.

A possible configuration for the structure of memory is presented in Figure 7.2. This is broadly consistent with the views of psychologists currently

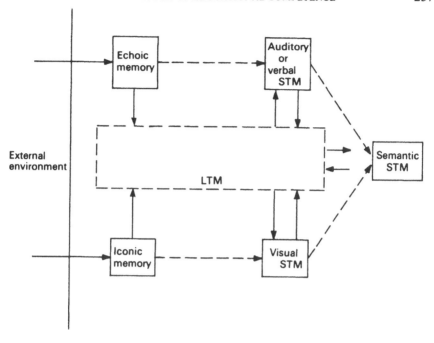

Figure 7.2 A possible configuration for the structure of memory

supporting the multiple-store concept (Klahr and Wallace, 1976). The structure comprises five short-term stores and a long-term memory (LTM). Two of the short-term stores, iconic memory (IM) and visual short-term memory (VSTM), are concerned with visual information derived from stimulation of the eyes. Auditory information registered by the ears is stored sequentially in echoic memory (EM) and auditory short-term memory (ASTM). Semantic short-term memory (SSTM) receives information from both the visual and auditory channels. Storage capacity would be useless without processes to insert information and transfer it from buffer to buffer. These processes are themselves located in LTM. The sensory stores, SSTM and LTM, will be briefly considered in turn. The functions assigned to the short-term stores will be illustrated by considering the processing that ensues when stimulation from the external environment impinges on the sense organs. The present discussion will be confined to visual and auditory stimulation.

If the stimulation is visual, it gives rise to a representation in iconic memory. This is an unselective form of memory for everything that strikes the visual sense organs. Information is stored in it in a very primitive and sensory form of representation which immediately begins to decay and vanishes in about half a second. During this time interval the contents of IM are processed by visual encoding processes capable of making crude distinctions such as that between a figure and its surrounding ground. These processes select parts of the representation for further processing and preserve them by transferring them to VSTM.

VSTM is a buffer of a limited capacity. There is also some evidence that information represented in it tends to decay with time (Murdock, 1960; Broadbent, 1970). The processes which work on its contents give rise to 'perceptual recognition'. This takes place when the encoded information is transferred to SSTM. The information placed in SSTM by these processes is in a form which satisfies the demands of the LTM processes that correspond to meaningful recognition of stimulation from the environment.

Auditory stimulation from the environment produces a similar sequence of activity in the auditory processing chain. As in the case of vision, auditory stimulation produces a representation in an unselective memory store which is called echoic memory (EM). Information stored in EM is, also, immediately subject to decay. This is a more protracted process, however, than in the case of IM; estimates of its duration range from one to two seconds. During this period the sensory representation of auditory events undergoes analysis by the processes whose function is to transfer segments of such input to ASTM. ASTM is a store of limited but possibly greater capacity than VSTM. As indicated above, information stored in SSTM must be included in a form recognisable by LTM. Accordingly, the processes that govern the transfer from auditory to SSTM must be capable of accepting auditory input and converting it to semantic form.

In the interest of clarity, this account has been presented in terms of two distinct storage and processing chains entirely devoted to coping with incoming information. This is, of course, an oversimplification, since the operations of the system involve a two-way flow of information along the processing chains, and also a considerable amount of interaction between them. The two-way flow of information in the visual chain is exemplified in the control exercised by the contents of SSTM over the encoding processes operating on VSTM. This control determines the features which are attended to and the level of detail at which they are processed. A two-way flow of information is also essential to the functioning of the auditory chain. The processes operating on the contents of ASTM require information on the current semantic context in SSTM to enable them to function. Interaction between the functioning of the auditory and visual chains is, also, the rule rather than the exception. Such interaction is, for example, essential for the functioning of the reading process.

The development of the functioning of the sensory stores has been discussed elsewhere (Klahr, 1976; Klahr and Wallace, 1976; Wallace, 1978). Only a few comments based on Klahr (1976) will be offered here. It is consistently found that children are from 50 to 200 ms slower than adults in tasks where they are to respond as rapidly as possible to a visual or auditory signal. Physiological explanations, such as the time to transmit information through the nervous system, can be ruled out: children's nerves are shorter than adults', and their conduction rate is about the same (Elliott, 1970). However, children are also more affected by 'non-processing' variables, such as practice, motivation, incentive, and attentiveness, and experimental attempts to control these factors often produce marked improvements in children's performance. A recent review of this area (Wickens, 1979) concludes that since no such study has yet produced performance in children equal in speed to that of adults, it is reasonable to assume that there is some central processing limitation which renders children slower than adults. However, such a central deficit, if indeed it does exist, is small, relative to the gross differences in cognitive capacities of children and adults on complex tasks such as learning concepts, inducing sequential patterns and solving algebra word problems and numerical puzzles.

The study of perceptual development in infancy is one of the most lively areas in contemporary developmental psychology and the functioning and relationships of the sensory encoding channels are involved in some of the more controversial issues (Cohen and Salapatek, 1975). An example is provided by the development of object constancy, the appreciation that the identity of an object remains constant across changes in its position and in the observer's point of view. Controversy surrounds the nature of the processes underlying the achievement of constancy and the age at which it is attained. For Piaget (1954) co-ordination of touch and vision in the infant's contact with the object is essential and this is not attained until about nine months. More recent research (Bower, 1974; Butterworth, 1976) suggests that the infant may achieve at least a form of object constancy through the processing of visual information alone and that this may appear as early as three months of age.

As indicated above 'perceptual recognition' takes place when encoded information is transferred to SSTM. The information placed in SSTM by these processes is in a form which satisfies the demands of the LTM processes that correspond to meaningful recognition of stimulation from the environment. This process involves complex discrimination based on representations in LTM of environmental attributes and their values. Information transferred to SSTM becomes part of the individual's current knowledge state and is available as input to the processes which underlie human problem solving. Information represented in SSTM is not subject to decay with time, but the amount of information which it can hold is limited. The alternative views on the question of capacity have recently been discussed by Broadbent (1975) in a paper devoted to the question of the number which sets limits to processing. In preference to a uniform seven or five with an extra two in the case of memory span, he argues that the underlying number is three. Incoming events, outgoing actions, and transfers of information from one process to another are handled in terms of a module of three and the traditional seven arises from the particular opportunity provided in the memory span task for the retrieval of information from different forms of processing.

For the developmental psychologist the crucial question is whether the capacity of SSTM increases as a function of maturation. Two examples of theorising based on affirmative answers to this question are provided by the Piagetian literature. McLaughlin (1963) speculated on the relationship between the number of properties storable and the possibility of operating at each of Piaget's levels. More recently Pascual-Leone (1975) has assigned an important role to maturation in the construction of a neo-Piagetian theory of cognitive development. The Piagetian conception of a scheme is adopted as the basic unit of analysis and defined as an ordered pair of active components. The first one is a 'releasing component' or set of conditions which are activated by external or internal input, while the second is an 'effective component' which provides the basis for the execution of internal or external actions. Any given input activates a set of schemes which is termed the 'field of activation'. Not all of these schemes are applied and actually contribute to producing the child's actions. Only those which are dominant in 'activation weight' determine the response, while the weaker schemes are inhibited.

The activation weight of schemes is decided by the operations of independent neurophysiological processes called 'scheme boosters'. The developmental importance of maturation is represented in a scheme booster, the 'M' operator. 'M' is a central working memory in which task-relevant schemes can be placed in order to boost their activation weight. The number of different schemes which 'M' can boost simultaneously increases with age. Pascual-Leone (1975) presents an account of the growth of the capacity of 'M' in terms of chronological age and of Piaget's sub-stages. Each transition from substage to substage corresponds to a unit increase in 'M'.

A more widely accepted view is that the capacity of SSTM does not increase with age and comprises a constant number of 'chunks'. Klahr (1976) adopts this viewpoint in discussing the differences between children and adults in short-term memory performance. A chunk is a recognisable, familiar unit of information and since the complexity of such units varies greatly a fixed SSTM capacity for chunks does not imply a fixed capacity for total information held in SSTM. Children's effective SSTM span is less than that of adults due to the relative poverty of their LTM world model which inhibits the encoding of groups of elements as single chunks. They are, also, handicapped by failure to use the rehearsal strategies that enable adults to prevent important chunks of information from being dislodged from SSTM and by their lack of adequate strategies for the allocation of the fixed fund of attention (Simon, 1972) which determines the information transferred from the sensory buffers to SSTM and subsequently the elements incorporated in LTM. The prevalence of unresolved issues extends to LTM. The structure and organisation of LTM are far from being understood, but many of the representations which have been proposed share common features. Objects, values, attributes and relations are represented in terms of a complex graph or associational network which is hierarchically organised. This structure comprises the individual's knowledge of the world obtained by abstracting regularities detected through past environmental interaction and generalised to provide a basis for future interaction. Acceptance of this broad view does not mark an end to controversy since, for example, there is a lively debate on the relative merits of competing theories of the retrieval of information from a hierarchical network (Johnson-Laird, 1975). For our present purpose, however, we will confine discussion to the more fundamental structural issues raised by proposals for additions to or departures from a hierarchical model of LTM.

From a developmental perspective the most significant addition is an episodic memory which Tulving (1972) suggested 'receives and stores information about temporally dated episodes or events, and temporal-spatial relations among these events' (p. 385). This adds a temporally organised record of specific events and episodes to the hierarchically organised LTM network, an addition which appears essential if modifications to the individual's world model are to be made on the basis of the detection of regularities in environmental interaction. The proposal of the existence of an episodic memory has gathered a considerable amount of support, although there is disagreement on the extent to which it constitutes a system independent of the rest of LTM (Craik and Jacoby, 1975).

The suggestion of the existence of a temporally organised record of specific events and episodes is closely linked to proposals for much more radical departures from the hierarchical model of LTM. In contrast to the view that most information is stored in a hierarchically organised LTM, Schank (1975a) argues that any sequence of new information forms an episode in memory and any piece of information within an episode can only be accessed by referencing the episode in which it occurs. In a manner similar to Minsky's (1975) concept of a 'frame' this renders experiential groupings the core of LTM organisation. Contexts supercede subset–superset relations in determining associations. Once a context is entered, a person is more likely to think of another item in that context than an item from a different context that might be classed in the same superset. Some of the difficulties involved in attempting to reconcile the opposed views by incorporating frames within a hierarchically organised network have been outlined by Winograd (1975).

Study of the general structure of LTM from a developmental viewpoint is as yet a relatively uncolonised area. A single example will be briefly described to illustrate the type of outcome which emerges when an attempt is made to base an account of development on the currently open-ended state of research on LTM. Klahr and Wallace (1976) have presented an information processing theory of the developmental states underlying pre-operational and concrete operational performance on five Piagetian tasks. The theory is based on a view of the IPS which reflects the main trends in research outlined above.

Processing is postulated to occur in a sequence of phases consistent with the system of memory stores depicted in Figure 7.2. Routines in LTM control information transfer between the processing phases.

The representation of knowledge in LTM takes the form of production systems (Newell and Simon, 1972). A production is a rule which consists of a condition and an associated action. The condition tests the current knowledge state of the system as defined by the contents of the STM stores. If a condition is satisfied, then its actions are executed, changing the state of knowledge. A collection of productions which serve a specific function is called a production system.

Since all knowledge in the system is represented by productions and production systems it is all potentially active and, consequently, there are no inert data structures. Objects are represented by tokens corresponding to the productions which are consistently evoked when the objects are presented to the system. In addition they have descriptive symbols attached to them corresponding to information about their properties such as colour or size. These values are in turn represented by the same kind of production-system structure, and this homogeneity is continued in the representation of high-level generalisations such as attribute names like shape. Further details of this representation cannot be provided here, but they are functionally similar to many current network representations of highly associative memories (Anderson and Bower, 1973; Norman et al., 1975).

The sheer magnitude of the proposed collection of productions requires a plausible structure for LTM. The structure proposed has implications for the temporal sequence in which productions are tested. As Figure 7.3 indicates, LTM is divided into three tiers, and within each tier there are multiple levels. The tiers are searched in sequence, starting with tier 1. Within each tier, each level is also tested sequentially. In a given level, however, the search for true productions takes place in parallel. Finally, once a production system is activated, search is again sequential.

Each tier contains productions which serve different functions and arise from different aspects of development. Tier 1 contains the results of specific experience encountered by the system. Tier 2 contains a repertoire of general problem solving strategies and procedures, such as means ends analysis. Finally tier 3 contains the productions that underlie the self-modification capacity of the system and, thus, cognitive development.

In discussing episodic memory above it was pointed out that such an aspect of LTM appears to be essential if development is to take place. The system must have some means of monitoring its own activity if appropriate new productions are to be constructed and added to LTM. The particular mechanism adopted is a 'time line' containing a sequential record of the system's activity. Any regularities occurring in the system's interaction with the environment are represented in the time line. Self modification takes place through the detection of this regularity and the subsequent addition to LTM

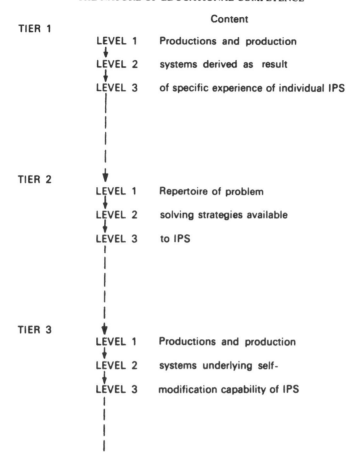

Figure 7.3   Structure of long-term memory (LTM)

of productions which will capitalise upon it. The nature of the self modification processes will be discussed below. In the present context it will only be pointed out that the new sequences are organised in sub-systems bearing a broad resemblance to the 'frame' type of experiential grouping. The sub-systems correspond to particular recurring contexts and control of behaviour shifts from sub-system to sub-system with movement from situation to situation.

Representation of Specific Content Areas

In attempting to define a tractable problem it was suggested that a realistic immediate objective for psychological research would be to focus on the specific aspects of the child's world model in LTM which provide the basis for 'cold' cognitive functions such as fundamental linguistic and mathematical skills. The otherwise daunting task of reviewing continuing research in this area is rendered manageable by the twin restrictions that it must be relevant to the construction of a theory of cognition expressed in process terms and, also, take account of the developmental dimension. The latter criterion rules out the vast majority of process-based studies of linguistic skills conducted from either a cognitive psychological or artificial intelligence orientation. The position is reversed in the area of mathematical skills where developmental studies are legion, but adoption of a process-based viewpoint is rare.

In a recent review of cognitive developmental research Wallace (1976) highlighted a current trend towards an emphasis on process rather than structure in the study of developmental states. This is exemplified in the marked shift in the theoretical viewpoint of Piaget and the Genevan group already described above. Significant though this Genevan shift of emphasis may be, the most explicitly process-based studies of the development of mathematical and linguistic skills are being conducted elsewhere. In the mathematical area a number of studies have arisen from attempts to apply the methodology of information processing analysis devised by Newell and Simon (1972) to cognitive development. The basic paradigm initially involves posing the question 'What routines for processing information would a child need in order to perform this task?' The ultimate objective is the construction of a computer program which is a completely explicit, demonstrably sufficient theory of the processes involved in task performance. Using this approach, Baylor and Gascon (1974) and Young (1976a) have produced programs which are theories of the developmental states or specific aspects of LTM underlying the performance of individual children on seriation tasks. A different strategy has been adopted by Klahr and Wallace (1970, 1972, 1973, 1976) who focus on normative rather than individual performance and seek to construct programs which are state theories covering an increasingly broad range of tasks. To date, this approach has produced a program representing a theory of the processes underlying performance in quantification, class inclusion, conservation and transitivity tasks.

Although the vast majority of studies of linguistic skills fail to satisfy both the process and developmental criteria there are indications that the situation is changing rapidly. Two examples of the trend are the continuing studies of children's comprehension and memory (Paris, 1975) and the interest in developmental issues which characterises some of the current artificial intelligence work on natural language (Schank, 1975b). In terms of the account of the structure of the IPS offered above the most directly relevant studies are concerned with the construction of semantic networks which constitute models of the representation of specific items of knowledge. These networks are characterised as directed graph structures and in their fully explicit form are expressed as computer programs. Although the bulk of this work is concerned with semantic memory in adults, there are indications of an increasing interest in the developmental dimension. Norman *et al.* (1975) outline successive states of the network structures which may underlie a child's acquisition of language. On a more specific level Gentner (1975) has analysed the network structures underlying the verbs 'give, take, buy, sell, spend-money, trade', derived an order of acquisition for them and predicted an order of developmental acquisition of the verbs on this basis which was confirmed by experimental data subsequently obtained.

The potential relevance of Gentner's work to the type of adaptation of education to individual differences with which we are concerned is obvious. An explicit attempt to demonstrate the educational importance of the results of process analysis aimed at producing representations of specific LTM content areas has been made by Greeno (1975). The aspect of the educational process on which he focuses is analysis of the demands which attaining specific educational objectives makes upon cognitive processes. These demands are characterised as cognitive objectives which are developed by analysing the psychological processes sufficient to produce the behaviours indicating acquisition of the knowledge intended as the outcome of learning. As illustrations of cognitive objectives Greeno has constructed descriptions of the states underlying successful performance on a range of tasks involving quantitative concepts. The tasks comprise fractional numbers as taught to nine-year-olds, Euclidean geometry for thirteen-year-olds and auditory psychophysics as presented to eighteen-year-old undergraduates. The state descriptions represent a degree of methodological integration since both production systems and semantic networks have been employed in their construction. Greeno's continuing work on educational objectives is in line with the general approach to adaptation being advocated in this paper. So, too, are his prescriptions for future research since he supports task analyses more strongly embedded in general psychological theory and stresses the need for a relatively complete process analysis of specific content areas. The examples quoted, fractions, geometry or psychophysics, are subsections of the area of mathematical skills.

Self-Modification Processes

It will be recalled that the third requirement for the construction of the type of process theory of cognitive development required for the illumination of competence is an account of the general processes responsible for modification of the child's LTM world model in the light of environmental interaction. Restriction of the area of concern to the 'cold' cognitive functions of mathematical and linguistic skills in no way affects these processes since they underlie the construction of all aspects of the LTM model.

As in the case of representations of specific content areas, the type of theory of self-modification required must present a step by step account of the real time sequence of processes involved. The same trend towards an emphasis on process is marked in the study of developmental states and the transition rule governing the movement from state to state in development (Wallace 1976). The adoption of a process-based approach has not yet produced a step by step account of the self-modification processes underlying transition in cognitive development. It is in the area of artificial intelligence rather than developmental psychology that examples of the requisite type of process account of self-modification are to be found, although even there they are far from thick on the ground. Of particular interest is the work of Waterman (1974) who has constructed a number of production systems which are capable of self-modification on the basis of feedback on errors. Through the common use of production systems as a form of representation these studies are likely to exert a considerable influence on at least one strand of process-based developmental psychology.

The strand in question is based on the information processing approach outlined above. It has not yet given rise to a sufficient theory of transition in cognitive development expressed in the form of a running computer program although this is its most important current objective. Young (1976b) is focusing on two kinds of processes which his earlier work on seriation suggests may be involved in transition. These are anticipation, the moving forward in time of a mental operation, and the internalisation of regularities in the effect of the child's own actions on the physical environment. Simulation of these processes requires modelling at a finer level of detail than the production system representations of seriation. Young is currently engaged in assessing the relative merits of production systems and three alternative formalisms as means of attaining this objective.

The internalisation of regularities revealed in the child's interaction with his environment is, also, central to the approach to the study of transition adopted by Klahr and Wallace (1976). As indicated in the discussion of the structure of the IPS, development is regarded as taking place in a system innately endowed with self-modification productions. The general principle governing their operation is a least-effort or processing-economy principle. The system has such a limited capacity workspace, and such a huge LTM, that there is a high premium on making the symbols being processed as information laden as possible and on avoiding any unnecessary processing. The former objective is achieved by detection via the time line of regularities in the system's interaction with the environment and the consequent addition to the LTM world model of a new composite process representing the consistent sequence. The appearance of such developmental landmarks as object constancy and the ability to quantify are attributed to the result of a succession of such cycles of aggregation of information.

The goal of avoiding unnecessary processing gives rise to two features of the functioning of the self-modification productions. The addition to LTM of representations of consistent sequences paves the way for the elimination of redundant processing by monitoring the extent to which interactive effectiveness would be impaired by the omission of a section of the sequence. Conservation of quantity emerges in this fashion. Consistent sequences are used to predict the effect of transformations on the relationship between the initial and resultant collections. The relationship is simply read off the sequence without carrying out quantifications after the transformation. The predictions are verified by quantitative comparison with the initial collection. Success in this prediction phase results in confirmation that quantification of the collection after the transformation and the subsequent quantitative comparison constitute unnecessary processing and may be eliminated.

It was pointed out above that new sequences added to LTM are organised in sub-systems resembling the 'frame' type of experiential grouping. Since elimination of redundant processing represents an important step forward in achieving processing economy the more widely shortened sequences are applied the greater the. gain in efficiency. The range of applicability of a shortened sequence is initially confined to the sub-system in which it was generated and subsequently attempts are made to generalise its application to other sub-systems. In the case of quantification, for example, the consistent sequences representing small cardinal numbers function as a sub-system. The subjective evidence of the continued existence of this sub-system in adults is the experience of apparently immediate awareness of the number of objects in collections of up to five elements. The process underlying this immediate apprehension of quantity is called subitising to distinguish it from counting and the process of estimation employed in quantifying continuous material or large collections of discontinuous elements. Klahr and Wallace (1976) maintain that conservation rules are initially derived from the subitising consistent sequences and that their subsequent application to the operations of counting and estimation provides an example of the generalisation of rules from the sub-system in which they were derived to other sub-systems in the pursuit of processing economy.

Although the detection and elimination of redundant processing makes a substantial contribution to the achievement of economy, it is clearly preferable if unnecessary processing is not included in the child's repertoire to begin with. There are indications from studies dealing with a variety of age levels between birth and seven years that processes concerned with achieving this objective may be part of the child's innate endowment. These processes can be regarded as functioning in accordance with the general principle that in interaction the environment should be coped with in as large or global units as possible consistent with the preservation of effectiveness. Breaking up or analysing the environment into smaller or more finely grained units should only be resorted to when negative feedback from the environment indicates that it is necessary.

Some examples of this self-modification principle, Klahr and Wallace

(1976) argue, are provided by developmental events in the four to seven years age range. When confronted with three red and two blue squares arranged in a row and asked to 'count the squares', many four-year-olds proceed to count only the red or the blue squares. Most five and six-year-olds have no problem with the counting task, but if they are asked 'are there more reds or more squares?' proceed to base their reply on an erroneous comparison of the number of red squares and the number of blue squares. This is, of course, the classic Piagetian class inclusion task. Seven-year-olds are typically successful on both tasks. A common pattern can be discerned underlying this developmental sequence. In both tasks the children who fail carry out the quantification adequately but interpret the instructions in terms of global objects rather than the values of particular dimensions characterising objects. They are not counting occurrences of the values 'red' and 'square' but of 'red *and* square' and 'square *and* blue' objects. In each case the move from a global orientation to operating on the basis of separate dimensions is a consequence of negative environmental feedback.

In this section we have reviewed current research relevant to the construction of the type of process theory of cognitive development necessary to provide accounts of the demands made by tasks, the structure of the IPS, the specific aspects of the LTM world model underpinning fundamental linguistic and mathematical skills and the general processes responsible for modification of the model and transition in development. If progress towards the understanding of educational competence is to be made experimental studies are required which possess some or all of the attributes identified in our definition of a tractable problem. The ideal study would involve process analysis of the demands of a task. The task in question would call upon basic mathematical-logical processes and entail producing profiles of individual children in terms of the processes which comprise the current state of the specific aspect of their LTM world model relevant to the task situation. Key features of the study would be derived from a process theory of the operations governing modifications of the world model in LTM as a result of experience of interacting with the environment. Finally, it would directly address the problem of the nature of educational competence since the process analysis of task demand and the status of individuals would be employed as a basis for designing experience intended to facilitate acquisition of the processes required for successful task performance.

Current trends in empirical research provide grounds for guarded optimism that approaches possessing many of the features of this recommended strategy are increasing in popularity. An account of a representative selection of the relevant studies is presented by Glaser (1977). They include investigations of basic linguistic (Resnick and Beck, 1976) and mathematical skills (Woods *et al.*, 1975) and studies concerned with the general nature of educational competence (Schadler and Pellegrine, 1974; Resnick and Glaser, 1976).

Conclusion

Two lines of research concerned with competence have been reviewed and the necessity of the construction of a process theory of cognitive development identified if the nature of educational competence is to be understood. Although current trends in psychology in general, and developmental psychology in particular, appear to be comparatively favourable to such an outcome it is hardly a short-term aim. With a view to selecting a realistic objective for current research the focus of concern was narrowed to the provision of an account in process terms of the interactive demands made by an environmental situation and of the procedures responsible for the initial construction and subsequent modification of the child's world model in LTM. It was, also, proposed that emphasising work on specific aspects of the LTM model such as those underlying basic linguistic and mathematical skills would be a prudent tactic. The production of a process theory of the development of the fundamental linguistic and mathematical skills constitutes a more realistic, if still daunting goal. Progress towards its attainment appears to be most probable with a continuation and increase in the current cross-pollination between research in artificial intelligence, cognitive psychology and developmental psychology.

References

Anderson, J. R. and Bower, G. H. (1973). *Human Associative Memory*, Wiley, New York

Baylor, G. W. and Gascon, J. (1974). *Cog. Psychol.*, **6**, 1–40

Bower, T. G. R. (1974). *Development in Infancy*, W. H. Freeman, San Francisco

Bracht, G. H. (1970). *Rev. educ. Res.*, **40**, 627–45

Broadbent, D. E. (1970). *Proc. Royal Soc. London*, Series B, **175**, 333–50

Broadbent, D. E. (1975). In *Studies in Long Term Memory* (ed. A. Kennedy and A. Wilkes), Wiley, London

Bruner, J. S. (1972). *The Relevance of Education*, London, George Allen and Unwin

Bunderson, V. C. (1965). Transfer of Mental Abilities at Different Stages of Practice in the Solution of Concept Problems. Ph. D. Dissertation, Princeton University, N. J.

Butterworth, G. (1976). In *Piaget, Psychology and Education* (ed. V. P. Varma and Williams), Hodder & Stoughton, London

Cellérier, G. (1972). In *Information Processing in Children* (ed. S. Farnham-Diggory), Academic Press, New York

Cohen, L. B. and Salapatek, P. (eds.) (1975). *Infant Perception: From Sensation to Cognition:* Vol. 1 and 2, Academic Press, New York

Cole, M. and Bruner, J. S. (1971). *Am. Psychol.*, **26**, 867–76

Cole, M. and Scribner, S. (1974). *Culture and Thought*, Wiley, New York

Craik, F. I. M. and Lockhart, R. S. (1972). *J. verb. L. verb. Beh.*, **11**, 671–84

Craik, F. I. M. and Jacoby, L. L. (1975). In *Cognitive Theory*, Vol. 1 (ed. F. Restle *et al.*), Lawrence Erlbaum Associates, Hillsdale, New Jersey

Cronbach, L. J. (1957). *Am. Psychol.*, **12**, 671–84

Cronbach, L. J. (1967). In *Learning and Individual Differences* (ed. R. M. Gangé), Merrill, Columbus, Ohio

Cronbach, L. J. (1975). *Am. Psychol.*, **30**, 671–84

Cronbach, L. J. and Snow, R. E. (1969). *Individual Differences in Learning Ability as a Function of Instructional Variables*. Final Rep. Sch. Educ., Stanford Univ. Contract xo. OEC 4-6-061269-1217 US Off. Educ

Cronbach, L. T. and Snow, R. E. (1977). *Aptitudes and Instructional Methods*, Irvington, New York

Dunham, J. L. and Bunderson, V. C. (1969). *J. educ. Psychol.*, **60**, 121–5

Elliott, R. (1970). *J. exp. Child Psychol.*, **9**, 86–104

Elshout, J. J. (1974). Referenced in N. H. Frijda (1975). In *Studies in Long Term Memory*, (ed. A. Kennedy and A. Wilkes) Wiley, London

Eysenck, H. J. (1967). *Br. J. educ. Psychol.*, **37**, 81–98

Flavell, J. H. (1963). *The Developmental Psychology of Jean Piaget*, Van Nostrand, New York

Flavell, J. H. and Wohlwill, J. F. (1969). In *Studies in Cognitive Development*, (ed. D. Elkind and J. H. Flavell) Oxford University Press, New York

Gagné, R. M. (1970). *The Conditions of Learning*, 2nd ed., Holt, Rinehart and Winston, New York

Gentner, D. (1975). In *Explorations in Cognition*, (ed. D. A. Norman, D. E. Rumelhart and L. N. R. Group) W. H. Freeman, San Francisco

Glaser, R. (1977). *Adaptive Education: Individual Diversity and Learning*, Holt, Rinehart and Winston, New York

Glaser, R. and Resnick, L. B. (1972). *Ann. Rev. Psychol.*, **23**, 207–76

Greeno, J. G. (1975). In *Cognition and Instruction*, (ed. D. Klahr) Lawrence Erlbaum Associates, Hillsdale, New Jersy

Guilford, J. P. (1967). *The Nature of Human Intelligence*, McGraw-Hill, New York

Hearnshaw, L. S. (1972). In *Advances in Educational Psychology* 1, (ed. W. D. Wall and V. P. Varma) University of London Press, London

Hinde, R. A. and Stevenson-Hinde, J. (eds.) (1973). *Constraints on Learning*, Academic Press, New York

Hunt, E. G., Frost, N. and Lunneborg, C. L. (1973). In *Advances in Learning and Motivation*. Vol. 7, (ed. G. Bower) Academic Press, New York

Hunt, E. G., Lunneborg, C. L. and Lewis, J. (1975). *Cog. Psychol.*, **7**, 194–227

Inhelder, B. (1972). In S. Farnham-Diggory (ed.) *Information Processing in Children* Academic Press, New York

Inhelder, B., Sinclair, H. and Bovet, M. (1974). *Learning and the Development of Cognition*, Routledge, London

Johnson-Laird, P. N. (1975). In *Studies in Long Term Memory*, (ed. A. Kennedy and A. Wilkes) Wiley, London

Kamin, L. J. (1974). *The Science and Politics of I. Q.*, Lawrence Erlbaum Associates, Hillsdale, New Jersey

Klahr, D. (1976). In *International Encyclopedia of Neurology, Psychiatry, Psychoanalysis and Psychology* (ed. B. B. Wolman).

Klahr, D. and Wallace, J. G. (1970). *Cog. Psychol.*, **1**, 350–87

Klahr, D. and Wallace, J. G. (1972). In *Information Processing in Children*, (ed. S. Farnham-Diggory) Academic Press, New York

Klahr, D. and Wallace, J. G. (1973). *Cog Psychol.*, **4**, 301–27

Klahr, D. and Wallace, J. G. (1976). *Cognitive Development: an Information–Processing View*, Lawrence Erlbaum Associates, Hillsdale, New Jersey

Laboy, W. (1970). In *Language and Poverty*. (ed. F. Williams) Markham Press, Chicago

McLaughlin, G. H. (1963). *Br. J. educ. Psychol.*, **33**, 61–7.
Melton, A. W. (1967). In *Learning and Individual Differences*, (ed. R. M. Gagné) Merrill, Columbus, Ohio
Minsky, M. (1975). In *The Psychology of Computer Vision*, (ed. P. Winston) McGraw-Hill, New York
Murdock, B. B. Jr. (1960). *J. exp. Psychol.*, **60**, 222–34
Newell, A. and Simon, H. A. (1972). *Human Problem Solving*, Prentice-Hall, New York
Norman, D. A., Rumelhart, D. E. and Group, L. N. R. (1975). *Explorations In Cognition* Freeman, San Francisco
Paris, S. G. (1975). In *Cognitive Theory*, Vol. 1, (ed. F. Restle *et al.*) Lawrence Erlbaum Associates, Hillsdale, New Jersey
Pascual -Leone, J. (1975). *Constructive cognition and substance conservation: towards adequate structural models of the human subject.* Toronto: York University, pre-publication draft.
Piaget, J. (1954), *The Construction of Reality in the Child*, Basic Books, New York
Piaget, J. (1957). In *Logique et Equilibre. Etudes d' Epistémologie Génétique*, Vol. 2, pp. 27–113. (ed. L. Apostel, B. Mandelbrot and J. Piaget)
Piaget, J. (1960). In *Discussions on Child Development*, IV, (ed. J. M. Tanner and B. Inhelder) Tavistock, London
Piaget, J. (1974). *La Prise de Conscience*, Presses Universitaires de France, Paris
Piaget, J. (1976). *"Lee Réel, le possible et le nécessaire (recherches en cours)"*. Paper delivered at XXIst International Congress of Psychology, Paris
Resnick, L. B. (1976). In *Cognition and Instruction*, (ed. D. Klahr) Lawrence Erlbaum Associates, Hillsdale, New Jersey
Resnick, L. B. and Beck, I. L. (1976). In *Aspects of Reading Acquisition*, (ed. J. T. Guthrie) Johns Hopkins University Press, Baltimore
Resnick, L. B. and Glaser, R. (1976). In *The Nature of Intelligence*, (ed. L. B. Resnick) Lawrence Erlbaum Associates, Hillsdale, New Jersey
Rohwer, W. D. Jr. (1971). *Rev. educ. Res.*, **41.** 191–210
Schadler, M. and Pellegrino, J. W. (1974). *Maximizing performance in a problem solving task.* Unpublished manuscript, Learning Research and Development Centre, University of Pittsburgh
Schank, R. C. (1975a). In *Representation and Understanding*, (ed. D. G. Bobrow and A. Collins) Academic Press, New York
Schank, R. C. (1975b). *Conceptual Information Processing.* North-Holland, Amsterdam
Simon, H. A. (1972). In *Information Processing in Children*, (ed. S. Farnham-Diggory) Academic Press, New York
Smedslund, J. (1964). *Monogr. Soc. Res. child Dev.*, Serial No. 93
Tulving, E. (1972). In *Organization of Memory*, (ed. E. Tulving and W. Donaldson) Academic Press, New York
Underwood, B. J. (1975). *Am. Psychol.*, **30**, 128–34
Vernon, P. E. (1976). In *Piaget, Psychology and Education*, (ed. V. P. Varma and P. Williams) Hodder & Stoughton, London
Wallace, J. G. (1972). *Stages and Transition in Conceptual Development: an Experimental Study*, National Foundation for Educational Research, Slough, England
Wallace, J. G. (1976). In *Piaget, Psychology and Education*, (ed. V. P. Varma and P. Williams) Hodder and Stoughton, London
Wallace, J. G. (1978). In *The Education of the Young Child*, (ed, Fontana, D.). London, Open Books

Waterman, D. A. (1974). *Adaptive Production Systems*, C. I. P. Working Paper 285, Carnegie-Mellon University. Department of Psychology, Pittsburgh

Wickens, C. D. (1979). *Psychol. Bull.*, in press

Winograd, T. (1975). In *Representation and Understanding*, (ed. D. G. Bobrow and A. Collins) Academic Press, New York

Wohlwill, J. F. (1966). *Amer J. ment. Def. Monogr. Supply*, **70**, 57–83

Wohlwill, J. F. (1968). *Child Dev.*, **39**, 449–65

Woods, S. S., Resnick, L. B. and Groen G. J. (1975). *J. educ. Psychol.*, **67**, 17–21

Young, R. M. (1976a). *Seriation by Children: An Artificial Intelligence Analysis of a Piagetian Task*, Basel, Birkhaüser

Young, R. M. (1976b). *Modelling Cognitive Development*, D. A. I. Research Report 17, University of Edinburgh, Department of Artificial Intelligence, Edinburgh

8 The Significance of Sex Differences in Developmental Psychology

JOHN ARCHER* and BARBARA LLOYD†

(* *School of Psychology, Preston Polytechnic, Preston, Lancs., England and* † *School of Social Sciences, University of Sussex, Falmer, Brighton, Sussex, England*)

The Scientific Study of Sex Differences

The division of the human species into male and female is such a basic fact that it has rarely required explanation. One need not search far, however, to find accounts of the differences between the sexes. St Thomas described the female as but a male *manqué*, biologically, intellectually and, of course, spiritually less than the male. Today we may dismiss medieval scholasticism for not being scientific but what have we learned from the scientific study of the sexes? The scientific study of the sexes has a brief history. Biologists only began to understand the contribution of both egg and sperm in reproduction towards the end of the nineteenth century when the microscope came into general use.

The great biological discoveries of the nineteenth century preceded the scientific study of human behaviour. The date arbitrarily chosen to mark the founding of Experimental Psychology is 1879 when Wundt established his laboratory at Leipzig. At about the same time, precise and detailed observation of human development was undertaken by eminent scientists and recorded in the 'baby biographies' which these fathers published (Darwin, 1877; Preyer, 1888). Awareness of the brief history of developmental psychology and a limited account of scientific investigations of children's behaviour may help us appreciate the current state of knowledge concerning the development of sex differences.

A full account of the achievements of developmental psychology is beyond the scope of this chapter, but it is useful to remember that in the early days psychologists fought resolutely to establish their independence from philosophy. The study of child psychology was solidly empirical, often in an atheoretical manner. Catalogues were made of behaviours which could be readily measured and these included reaction times, memory span and speed of problem solving. Chronological age was used as a mark against which to describe these measurable differences in performance.

As the field of psychology grew, specialisms became sub-disciplines with clear identities. For example, perception and psychometrics were the terms introduced to describe and to differentiate studies of the organism's reaction to immediate stimulation from investigations of individual differences in intellectual abilities. Other separate areas of psychology now include neuropsychology, personality, educational, social and clinical psychology.

Age and sex differences can be studied within any of the sub-disciplines in psychology. Of course, not all investigators approach their problems from a developmental perspective, noting changes with age; and sex differences are sometimes deliberately ignored. In the construction of intelligence tests those items which favour one sex are eliminated. Another common strategy is to study a phenomenon in individuals of one sex only. But when sex differences are observed the explanations offered to account for them reflect the theoretical development within the sub-discipline. Explanations of sex differences are thus of varying depth and complexity.

Developmental accounts of sex differences reflect the history of psychology. While the empirical approach to behaviour yielded useful normative data, it offered few explanations to account for the changes in behaviour which were observed to occur with age. The ambitious theories of Piaget and Freud which gained prominence in the 1930s did not attempt to explain the empirical findings of earlier workers. Piaget was uninterested in individual differences apart from those which occurred as a function of age, while the Freudian model explained sex differences as part of a complex theory of personality development. The influence of behaviourism was reflected in a search for antecedent conditions or stimuli for the consequent responses. By and large, little attempt was made to explain sex differences beyond suggesting different histories of reinforcement.

In the latter half of this century psychologists have once more begun to look inside the organism in seeking explanations of behaviour. The verbal learning studies which explored a variety of situational factors affecting the learning of sets of three-letter nonsense syllables (e.g., Underwood and Schulz, 1960) are rivalled by natural language studies. These attempt to illuminate the structure of memory (cf. Collins and Quillian, 1969) or the processes of sentence comprehension (Bransford et al., 1972). The change of approach can be described as a growing concern with process, be it of personality formation, intellectual functioning or perceptual inference. And this current interest in process promises a more complete understanding of observed differences whether in comparisons by age, sex, culture or even across species.

The concern with process and explanation is reflected in the structure of our chapter. In the first part we describe the scientific study of psychological sex differences. Particular attention is given to the developmental histories of the four firmly established differences: those in verbal, mathematical and spatial abilities and also in aggression. The second and longest part, presents analyses of biological, psychological and situational explanations for these differences and then considers the implications of these accounts for the changes in the pattern of sex differences which occur over a life-time. In the final part of the chapter we look at the social implications of biological and cultural explanations and argue that a full understanding of human sex differences requires an appreciation of many interacting factors.

Psychological Sex Differences

In their book, *The Psychology of Sex Differences*, Maccoby and Jacklin (1975) attempted to produce as detailed, extensive and accurate a review as possible of the large literature on psychological sex differences. They claimed to have included all the studies on a particular topic, including those reporting no sex differences and those which included both male and female subjects but did not include separate data for the two sexes in the published report. Maccoby and Jaklin's aim was to deduce which widely-held beliefs about sex differences were supported by the evidence.

The conclusions were summarised under three main headings. The first referred to 'unfounded beliefs about sex differences', differences which had been claimed in the lay and scientific literature, but which were not supported by the studies Maccoby and Jacklin reviewed. This category included supposed differences in sociability, self-esteem, analytic cognitive style and achievement motivation. The second heading referred to sex differences that were fairly well established by the review of the evidence. These consisted of aggression and three types of ability, verbal, spatial and mathematical. The third heading referred to 'open questions', where the evidence was too sparse or too contradictory for Maccoby and Jacklin to offer an opinion one way or the other as to the 'reality' of the supposed sex difference. This group included tactile sensitivity, fear and anxiety, general activity during infancy and childhood, competitiveness, dominance, compliance and nurturance.

Maccoby and Jacklin's review identified only four attributes for which there was clear-cut evidence of a sex difference. In assessing the significance of their conclusions it is important to consider how they were reached. The reviewers considered, for each type of psychological measure, the number of studies reporting particular findings, but with little reference to the quality of the data base (see criticism by Block, 1976). In addition, Maccoby and Jacklin's criteria for accepting a sex difference as established were stringent and rather inflexible: the evidence had to provide a clear-cut answer in terms of numbers of studies finding a difference in a consistent direction.

Maccoby and Jacklin's 'open questions' category contained some features for which there was limited evidence for the existence of sex differences. One instance referred to a well-established difference (activity level during childhood), but one which Maccoby and Jacklin concluded was subject to situational variation (note that in this instance, Block (1976) claimed there were errors of omission which would have led to a more definite positive conclusion). In another case, 'compliance', there was good evidence for some form of sex difference, but this term implied one which was far wider than the evidence justified: girls were more compliant to the directions of adults than were boys, but they were not more compliant than boys to the directions of age-mates. For a further group of characteristics, fear, timidity and anxiety, it was difficult to tell whether the instances of reported sex differences referred to a basic characteristic such as fearfulness, or whether women were simply more ready to admit to such feelings than were men.

The three summary headings described above do not cover all the psychological measures reviewed in Maccoby and Jacklin's book. There is, for example, scant reference in their concluding section to possible sensory and perceptual differences, although evidence for such differences was mentioned in earlier sections of the book (see also McGuinness, 1976a, b; McGuinness and Lewis, 1976).

If we consider these possible sex differences omitted from the summary discussion, in addition to those 'open questions' for which there is reasonable evidence for some form of sex difference, a fairly extensive list of possible sex differences can be compiled. Thus, the identification of four rather certain sex differences is by no means the only, or major, conclusion to be derived from Maccoby and Jacklin's review. Rather, their book is noteworthy for its negative conclusions and for pointing out areas of uncertainty. To assess the significance of this cautious or 'minimalist' approach to the sex difference evidence, we should consider their work in the context of previous reviews of the psychological evidence on sex differences. These have produced more extensive and definite lists. For example, the list drawn up by Anastasi (1958) included three atrributes on which Maccoby and Jacklin reported no sex differences, memory, social orientation and achievement motivation. Anastasi's review also identified the four well-established differences described by Maccoby and Jacklin, and some others which they consider 'open questions' (e.g. 'emotional stability').

Gerai and Scheinfeld (1968) published an extensive review of psychological sex differences. Again, they produced a longer list of differences than those identified by Maccoby and Jacklin. Moreover, the names given to the psychological characteristics in which sex differences were found tended to be of a more general nature than the terms used by Maccoby and Jacklin. The principal differences between these two sets of conclusions can be used to highlight the contrasting attitudes of the reviewers to the subject.

When considering perceptual sex differences, Garai and Scheinfeld concluded that females showed greater tactile sensitivity and pain sensitivity. On neither of these measures did Maccoby and Jacklin reach a definite conclusion: tactile sensitivity appeared in the 'open questions' category, and pain was mentioned only briefly early in the book (no conclusions were drawn, owing to the difficulty in distinguishing between sensitivity to, and tolerance of, pain).

Garai and Scheinfeld, like Maccoby and Jacklin, identified sex differences in verbal, spatial and mathematical abilities. But the earlier writers described the spatial ability difference as one of 'cognitive style', whereas Maccoby and Jacklin referred to the more restricted characteristic of 'visual-spatial ability' (see Sherman, 1967; Maccoby and Jacklin, 1975; McGuinness, 1976a, for further discussion of this distinction). Essentially, Maccoby and Jacklin concluded that the sex difference was of a different, more test-specific, nature than was claimed by Garai and Scheinfeld (and others: e.g., Witkin *et al.*, 1962). This general point applies also to other attributes. Garai and Scheinfeld have placed more emphasis on the certainty of their conclusions and on the extensiveness of the psychological variables involved than have Maccoby and Jacklin. For example, Garai and Scheinfeld attach added importance to the greater female manual dexterity, by claiming that 'It has led to their (i.e. women's) assignment to assembly-line work and similar operations' (see discussion on 'psychological reductionism', later in this chapter).

Garai and Scheinfeld also placed more emphasis on the extent of the sex difference in memory, claiming simply that females show better memory than males. Maccoby and Jacklin offered a more qualified conclusion, claiming that girls may have some advantage over boys on tasks involving verbal content in memory (presumably because of their all-round greater verbal ability), but that 'it cannot be said that either sex has a superior memory capacity . . . when a variety of content is considered'.

Maccoby and Jacklin's more cautious approach makes their conclusions the more reliable ones, but it may also mean that for some characteristics they risked discounting a 'real' sex difference when the evidence was relatively inconclusive. The more extensive list produced by Garai and Scheinfeld also illustrates the point that common ideas about sex role stereotypes, and the types of psychological characteristics that these are associated with, influence the extent of the sex differences identified by different psychologists (see Archer, 1977). Thus, when we consider that previous reviews have tended to err on the side of too wide generalisations from the test measures and perhaps have been too readily influenced by popular beliefs about sex differences, Maccoby and Jacklin's caution in reaching conclusions and generalisations can be better appreciated, and can be seen as reflecting the need for reappraisal of the conclusions drawn by previous reviewers.

More recently, Fairweather (1976) has reviewed sex differences in cognition, and has concluded that the evidence indicates even fewer clear-cut differences than Maccoby and Jacklin described, claiming that their evidence for verbal ability was based on a small number of studies with inconsistent findings.

In view of the discrepancies between the conclusions of different reviewers, it is difficult to draw up a categorical list of the nature and extent of human psychological sex differences. There would appear to be some agreement over the sex difference in aggression and in spatial, mathematical and verbal abilities (with the exception of Fairweather's reservations over the latter). It also seems clear from Maccoby and Jacklin's review that sex differences which have been claimed by other reviewers for certain attributes, such as sociability, achievement motivation, analytical cognitive style, self-esteem, problem-solving, and memory, are not supported by more careful and critical examination of the evidence. In general a sex difference on a particular task (e.g. a verbal memory task or a visual-spatial analytical task) has been uncritically described by a general term, often one conforming to previously held beliefs about sex differences. There are also measures on which there is evidence—of varying degrees of certainty—of a sex difference but which has not been clearly identified by Maccoby and Jacklin owing either to their cautiousness (e.g. their 'open question' category), or to their omission from the summary discussion of some characteristics mentioned in the review (e.g. manual dexterity), or because the original studies were not reviewed or included in the tables (see Block, 1976, for an account of some of these omissions).

In a recent discussion of perceptual and cognitive sex differences, McGuinness (1976a) has concluded that females show greater sensitivity to changes in volume, i.e. have a greater appreciation of intensity changes, and that this forms the basis of a sex difference in musical ability. McGuinness (1976a,b) also concluded that in the visual modality men show greater acuity than women (Garai and Scheinfeld came to a similar conclusion) but that this only applies to daytime (photopic) vision. In the dark, McGuinness concluded that women showed greater visual sensitivity.

Developmental Profiles of Four Psychological Sex Differences

Introduction

In discussing developmental change, we restrict our examination to the four main sex differences identified with greatest certainty by Maccoby and Jacklin: verbal, mathematical and spatial abilities, and aggression. We realise that differences in other areas may be of considerable importance in development, but the evidence for these four attributes is the most extensive and amenable to analysis, though not without its problems.

Maccoby and Jacklin note that it is difficult to map developmental changes in sex differences and suggest two sources of ambiguity. First the evidence is uneven since infants in the first two or three days of life, nursery school children and University students are over-represented in the published research. Secondly, a method which is totally adequate for measuring an attribute in a four-year-old may be quite inappropriate for assessing the same variable in an adult. With these warnings in mind we summarize the developmental histories of verbal, mathematical and spatial skills and of aggression.

Verbal Ability

The generally accepted view of mature female superiority in verbal abilities was supported in the studies examined by Maccoby and Jacklin but their conclusions challenged the opinion that this advantage appears early in life and is maintained throughout development. Their examination of the research evidence showed that by adolescence, however, females exhibit a clear verbal superiority, not only on measures such as spelling, punctuation and fluency, but also on more complex tasks such as comprehension of difficult written texts, understanding of verbally expressed logical relations and even on tests of verbal creativity.

The developmental profile which emerged from analysis of the recent evidence is puzzling. Studies undertaken in the 1930s and 1940s and quoted in McCarthy's (1954) major review showed a variety of small differences indicating that girls babble first, produce their initial words earlier, articulate more clearly and use longer sentences. Although these differences were small they consistently favoured females. Maccoby's own summary presented in 1966 offered a similar picture and she stated that the female advantage was maintained throughout the preschool years and into the early primary school period. Although the female vocabulary superiority had disappeared by the beginning of formal education girls learned to read sooner and with fewer problems. Boys caught up in reading skills by the age of ten, but the female advantage in spelling, grammar and fluency persisted throughout the school years.

Recent developmental research on language has taken a different direction and rather than studying standard linguistic achievements in large groups of children attention has focused on individual language acquisition. Generally samples have been small and there has been little concern with representativeness. Of the twenty studies of children under three years of age reported by Maccoby and Jacklin thirteen found no differences in verbal behaviour or abilities. However, the seven differences which were reported all favoured females. These were greater vocal responsiveness to the mother's vocalisation but not in overall production at three months (Lewis and Freedle, 1972), more vocalization to mother in free play at six months (Lewis, 1969), more talk to play-mates and more play noises at 2 to 4 years (Smith and Connolly, 1972), more talking to mothers at 2.5 years (Halverson and Waldrop, 1970) and also at 2.5 years, teachers' rating of better speech development in girls (Bell *et al.*, 1971). In terms of tested abilities few studies yielded significant differences, but Moore (1967) reported a higher speech quotient for girls at 18 months though not at six months or 3 years while Clarke-Stewart (1973) found a female superiority in comprehension and vocabulary at 17 months. Although these studies consistently favour females, differences are highly specific: viewed overall they are in the minority and they generally fail to present a clear picture of female precocity. Maccoby and Jacklin consider that boys catch girls up in verbal development by 3 years.

Equivocal evidence is furnished by the extensive array of recent studies on children 3 to 10 years examined by Maccoby and Jacklin. In only four studies out of ten were significant differences reported and of these two favoured boys and two girls. Boys of 3 to 5 years were shown to verbalise more in play with other boys (Mueller, 1972) and at 4 to 5 years to verbalise more in competitive but not in co-operative games (Szal, 1972). Girls on the other hand made more appropriate verbalisations while watching a film at 4 to 5 and 7 to 8 years (Coates and Hartrup, 1969) and at 9 to 10 years requested more information and evaluation from mothers (Greenglass, 1971).

Tests of verbal abilities produced inconclusive patterns of differences. The most consistent sex differences were reported among children from disadvantaged families. In two extensive studies, one on the East Coast and the other on the West Coast of the United States, preschool girls were found to be ahead on a large number though not on all measures of linguistic ability (Shipman, 1971; Stanford Research Institute, 1972). Maccoby and Jacklin suggested that girls may maintain their slight advantage longer in underprivileged families due to the general susceptibility of boys to hazards. Thus, under normal conditions boys reach the same level of verbal skills as girls by 3 years, but where nutrition, health and other factors are poor, boys require more time to achieve verbal competence equal to that of girls.

Although the general picture is one of little sex differentiation in verbal skills between the ages of 3 and 11 years we should note Brimer's study (1969) of English children. He tested over 8000 boys and girls between the ages of 5 and 11 years; while there were no significant differences at 5 years, at all other age levels he found a consistent male superiority on vocabulary tests. These results run counter to those reported from the United States where a consistent female superiority has been found, but only with children from disadvantaged families. In one such study a female superiority on a number of verbal tests was reported for 5 to 8 years by the Stanford Research Institute.

A female superiority in verbal abilities becomes clearer after the age of 10 or 11 years. Even then, measures which test general knowledge as well as verbal skills may produce confusing results. Despite these methodological hazards the consensus which emerges is one of a female superiority by adolescence on a range of verbal tasks. The developmental sequence is not clear, although the evidence which is available suggests that verbal abilities are susceptible to environmental acceleration and retardation and that developmental sex differences in verbal skills must be examined in context taking into account cultural variables as well as the traditional dimensions of age and sex.

Empirical evidence beyond the age of 21 when individuals are usually no longer in full-time education and available for research is exceedingly limited as it is for other abilities (see the following sections). Tests of gifted adults at 29 and 41 years and of their spouses produced a male superiority on verbal tasks which probably involved a major reasoning component (Bayley and Oden, 1955). In a study of individuals at 64 and 84 years a female advantage was shown on a verbal reasoning task and on vocabulary at 84 (Blum *et al.*, 1972). But it is worth noting that even in the well researched age range of 18 to 21 years the results though consistently favouring females are not overwhelming.

Mathematical Ability

The development of sex differences in mathematical ability is straightforward and by adolescence males generally show a superiority. The magnitude of the difference in levels of performance between the sexes is, however, affected by the social context. In addition there are assessment problems associated with the presentation of mathematical problems in a verbal form or in a visual spatial format.

Mathematical ability is initially assessed at 3 years of age by counting tasks or problems such as the Piagetian conservation of number. In the latter the child usually counts a small number of objects arranged in a line. Although no objects are added or removed the position of the items is altered so that the line appears longer or shorter. The young child is often deceived by the visual display and fails to realise that the number of objects has remained the same. In 1966 Maccoby suggested that girls learned to count before boys, but the recent evidence reviewed by Maccoby and Jacklin leads to the conclusion that there are no sex differences in mathematical ability in the preschool period or in the early primary school years.

Research with children from disadvantaged families again provides an exception. Girls aged 3–4 years were found to excel on counting tasks (Shipman, 1971) and 5 and 7-year-old girls performed better on quantitative problems (Stanford Research Institute, 1972). These studies were carried out with large samples and are probably reliable; nonetheless they are exceptional and suggest yet again the greater male suceptibility to adverse conditions. In the years between 9 and 13 the evidence on mathematical ability consistently favours boys.

Comparisons of the performance of adolescents on tests of mathematical ability show a consistent male superiority, but the magnitude of the difference in levels of performance is variable and often not very great. Indeed, Maccoby and Jacklin concluded that the studies they reviewed failed to provide sufficient evidence to enable prediction of the size of the male superiority in any particular sample. The data they review include reports of performance only to the age of 21. At present there is no evidence available about differences in performance in later life, again reflecting the lack of research on older subjects commented upon in the following section on spatial ability.

The source of the male superiority in mathematical tasks has not been adequately explained. The appealingly simple hypothesis that the boys achieve higher levels of performance on tests due to their greater interest in the subject as reflected in further training has not found empirical support. An analysis of the test performance of 17-year-olds who had had the same number of courses in mathematics still revealed a male superiority (Flanagan *et al.*, 1961).

Studies showing that mathematical ability is not a unitary factor but is probably multi-dimensional may offer a fruitful line for future research. There is evidence, for example, that mathematical ability in males involves a spatial component which has not been found in the factor analysis of female performance. Going a step further it seems that problems in mathematics can be solved by following different strategies. Maccoby and Jacklin's suggestion that analysis of mathematical styles be undertaken to help in understanding sex differences in mathematical ability seems valid. It may well lead back, however, to further consideration of differences in spatial ability.

Spatial Ability

Spatial ability has been measured in adults as a factorial trait in intelligence tests, and by specific tests such as the embedded figure test (EFT) and rod and frame test (RFT). Both the EFT and RFT measure the ability to separate part of the visual field from its background. The EFT involves separating a simple figure embedded in the distracting background of a complex figure, and has been widely used, particularly by Witkin and his colleagues (Witkin *et al.*, 1962; Witkin, 1967). Modified versions have also been constructed for use with young children. The RFT involves matching a rod to the true vertical in the face of a distracting background, and performance on this test is highly correlated with that on the EFT. Men frequently obtain higher scores than women on both the EFT and RFT. The precise stage of development at which the male superiority appears is uncertain; different studies have reported different ages. Maccoby and Jacklin (1975) reviewed data which indicated that there were no consistent sex differences in children aged 3 to 5. Studies by Coates (Coates, 1974) using a preschool version of the EFT found that between the ages of 3 and 5, girls performed better than boys (i.e. the reverse of the adult difference) and that the female advantage narrowed thereafter and disappeared by the age of 6. Other studies (Maccoby and Jacklin, 1975, p. 95) have not found this early female superiority.

Maccoby and Jacklin's review showed that from the age of 8 to young adulthood the finding of a sex difference was inconsistent from one study to another, but that where it occurred males performed better than females. Sherman (1967) also concluded that there are only slight differences in young children, and that these differences become greater with age and experience.

Studies carried out on adults have generally shown a male superiority on the EFT and RFT and similar spatial tests such as the Block Design, which involves the replication of a pattern using blocks. The majority of investigators have studied young people, mostly in the 17–25 age range. Two studies (Green, 1955; Schwartz and Karp, 1967) have found a male superiority in samples of ages 17–40 and 30–39, but there was no evidence on possible changes with age within these samples. In two studies on older subjects, one involving ages 58–82, and the other on 64 and 84 year olds, no sex differences were found for the EFT, RFT and Block Design tests. On the basis of these two studies it seems that the male superiority may not be maintained after middle age but further studies are required before any definite conclusions can be reached.

Aggression

In contrast to the specific abilities discussed in the previous sections, 'aggression' is an abstraction used to refer to a number of loosely-related measures. These include, in children, observations of fighting and other aggressive acts (in play and classroom situations), destructive responses to a toy, ratings of aggression provided by teachers, peers or parents, and the measurements of aggressive responses to a confederate or peer in an experimental situation. The last of these is used mainly on older children and adolescents. A measure of aggression towards peers has been derived from young adults' willingness to administer 'shocks' to a confederate in a simulated learning task. Self-appraisal ratings and questionnaire studies (e.g. the various Hostility scales) have also been commonly used for measuring aggression in adults.

Irrespective of the measure used, most studies of the two sexes have found greater male aggressiveness, occurring from a very early age onwards: this sex difference has been reported in free-play situations at ages of 2–3 and 2–4 years (Maccoby and Jacklin, 1975).

The ages studied in the research on sex differences in aggression reflect the availability of children, adolescents and young adults for study. As a result we again cannot provide a complete developmental profile from the psychological literature. From sources, such as violent crime statistics (*Social Trends*, 1974) and cross-cultural surveys (Rosenblatt and Cunningham 1976) it is apparent, however, that the sex difference in aggression continues a long way through the life span. The extent to which it is maintained into old age is not known.

Explanations

Anastasi (1958) pointed out that the bulk of the available data on sex differences are descriptive, and that we know very little about their developmental origins. Twenty years later, we still know comparatively little, but a variety of theoretical explanations have been suggested. These can be divided usefully into the following three types: first, biological theories, in which the sex differences are viewed as being a direct result of physiological differences between the sexes; secondly, psychological explanations, in which early experience is seen as the major determinant of the adult sex difference; and,thirdly, situational explanations (also referred to as cultural relativism) in which the sex difference is seen as being a direct result of the prevailing social conditions.

Biological Explanations

At first sight, it may seem that a bewildering variety of biologically-based explanations have been offered to account for psychological sex differences. They can, however, be usefully classified into four categories: first, genetic explanations, secondly those involving sex hormones, thirdly those involving brain development and finally a recent account in terms of rates of development or maturation. This classification does not divide the explanations into mutually exclusive categories since genetic differences (the first type) would have to operate through a developmental process (e.g. hormones, growth or brain development).

Genetic Explanations

The chromosomal difference between men and women resides in their sex chromosomes, XY in the male and XX in the female. The X chromosome is fairly large, carrying several known structural genes and paired only in the female, whereas the Y chromosome is comparatively small and carries very little genetic material. One consequence of this difference is that recessive genes on the X chromosome are more likely to be expressed in the male since it is 'unguarded', whereas in the female another gene of the same type would be required on the second X chromosome for expression of recessive genes. Thus, certain types of physical disorders such as haemophilia and colour blindness are more common in men than in women because they are controlled by recessive genes on the X chromosome. These are termed sex-linked characters.

On the behavioural side, it has been suggested that a gene influencing spatial ability is also a sex-linked recessive, and that this can provide a genetic explanation for the sex difference in spatial ability. Stafford (1961) made this suggestion on the basis of the correlations between the spatial ability scores of parents and both children. Other studies have confirmed Stafford's findings (see Maccoby and Jacklin, 1975, pp. 120-2), and they have been widely quoted as having established the existence of this sex-linked mode of inheritence for spatial ability (e.g. Kolakowski and Malina, 1974; Jensen, 1975). The evidence is, however, much weaker than is usually claimed, since there is only an approximate correspondence between the theoretical prediction and the reported correlations. One dissenting note is that of Garron (1970), who pointed out that Stafford's hypothesis would predict high spatial ability in patients with Turner's syndrome (i.e. only one X chromosome) since basically the same argument would apply as in the case of normal males. Predictions deriving from a sex-linked inheritance mechanism are fulfilled for other known sex-linked recessive conditions, such as colour blindness, but not for spatial ability. In fact, Turner's syndrome patients show marked deficiency in spatial ability.

In contrast to sex-linked characteristics, carried on the X chromosomes, the influence of the Y chromosome is largely restricted to starting gonadal development, since it is thought to possess few structural genes (Glucksmann, 1974). Nevertheless, Selmanoff *et al.* (1975) have suggested that, in mice, variations in aggression may be controlled by genetic variations on the Y chromosome. They base this hypothesis on comparisons of the level of aggression in two strains of mice and their F_1 hybrids, and they attempt to link their results to claims that human males with two Y chromosomes (XYY males) are more common amongst violent criminals. There are two large conceptual leaps in this argument: first, from mouse aggression to human aggression, and secondly from abnormal males (XYY) to normal males (XY). Other researchers and writers on this subject have been cautious in ascribing a higher incidence of aggression to the human XYY genotype. It has been shown that the incidence of XYY males is rather more common in criminal institutions than in the newborn population, but the reason for this does not appear to be that XYY males are more aggressive than normal XY males (Meyer-Bahlberg, 1974).

A third type of genetic explanation has been suggested, to account for sex differences in I.Q. distribution and in academic and artistic achievement. This explanation links these behavioural differences to physical sex differences. Throughout life, the human male is more vulnerable to a variety of disorders and environmental influences. Ounsted and Taylor (1972) attributed this to the male Y chromosome producing development which is slower in males than in females with the consequence that more genetic information is expressed in males. Thus, it is suggested that both more disadvantageous and more beneficial traits will occur in males. Hutt (1972a) has extended this theory to explain the different distribution of I.Q. scores between the sexes, thus accounting for proportionately more men with very high and very low scores (Hutt, 1972a, p.89).

There are, however, fundamental difficulties with the Y chromosome hypothesis. Trivers (1972) listed three reasons why the higher mortality of males cannot be accounted for by their having an 'unguarded' X chromosome. Two of the three objections apply equally well to any hypothesis linking sex differences in mortality with chromosomal differences, including Ounsted and Taylor's. Trivers' first objection is a crucial one: he pointed out that males show greater mortality than females even in species where both sexes have XX chromosomes (homogametic), e.g. in fish, and in species where the female is XY (heterogametic) e.g. in birds and insects. Secondly, data for castrated male humans and for castrated domestic cats show that these live much longer than normal males do. Hence the mechanism for producing the differential mortality must depend on a process controlled by the male gonad rather than the sex chromosomes, which remain the same before and after castration. It, therefore, seems likely that higher male than female mortality and susceptibility to disease is a function of the metabolic effects of androgen rather than a direct result of the influence of the Y chromosome in development.

Thus the chromosomal explanation for the different I.Q. distributions of the sexes suggested by Hutt is based on a hypothesis inconsistent with comparative evidence from other groups of animals.

Hormone Theories

Animal studies have shown that sex hormones can influence not only physical characteristics but also behaviour (Rogers, 1976; Messent, 1976). There are two stages in the life history of a mammal when sex hormone secretion is important: first, prenatally (or shortly after birth in some species), after which time circulating levels of sex hormones decline practically to zero (Knorr *et al.*, 1974); and secondly, from the time of puberty onwards.

The possible influence of prenatal and pubertal hormonal secretions on behaviour has been widely studied in rodents and in some other animal groups. Principally as a result of these studies, a number of theories have been advanced to explain human sex differences in terms of different hormonal actions on the brains of the two sexes. The theories of Dawson (1972), Broverman *et al.* (1968) and Andrew (1972) refer to human cognitive abilities, and that of Gray (1971) to fear and aggression. All have been discussed extensively elsewhere (Archer, 1971, 1975, 1976a), and detailed arguments have been presented against each one. One psychological characteristic for which there is most consensus for a biological explanation is aggression; studies of many different species of birds and mammals show a clear facilitating effect of the male hormone (Archer, 1976b). Yet when the evidence from studies of human males is examined, there are no conclusive data that such a relationship exists in man (see Archer, 1977).

Brain Lateralisation

Another influential biologically-based theory for explaining sex differences in cognitive abilities has been the lateralisation hypothesis. The two halves of the cerebral cortex control different types of abilities, the dominant (left) hemisphere being concerned with verbal ability and the right hemisphere being concerned with spatial ability. Buffery and Gray (1972) suggested that verbal ability is more completely lateralised (and hence more effective) in females because of the more advanced development of the brain of the female at the time of language acquisition. It is also suggested that an indirect consequence of the less complete lateralisation of language in the male is that spatial ability becomes more widely distributed in both hemispheres of the male, which leads to more effective spatial reasoning.

Fairweather (1976) has provided a thorough review of the evidence on sex differences in brain lateralisation, and concluded that it indicates the reverse of Buffery and Gray's predictions, i.e. there is evidence for clearer and earlier lateralisation in boys than in girls (see also Witelson, 1976). Thus girls show less evidence of hemispheric difference, which according to Buffery and Gray's argument should lead them to more bilateral representation of spatial ability and hence to greater spatial skill. As an explanation for adult sex differences in cognitive abilities, Witelson (1976) suggested that the earlier and greater lateralisation for spatial tasks in boys may be a cause of their higher spatial ability, i.e. exactly the opposite to Buffery and Gray's argument. There are two main objections to this alternative lateralisation hypothesis: first, the discrepancy between the age at which the sex difference in spatial ability is clearly evident (from about 10 years onwards) and the age at which lateralisation sex differences are recorded (much earlier, at 6 years, according to Witelson, 1976, and at a younger age according to studies reviewed by Fairweather, 1976). Secondly, a related point is the lack of correspondence for other abilities between localisation in the dominant hemisphere, and male or female superiority (Maccoby and Jacklin, 1975; McGuinness, 1976a).

In conclusion, while there is evidence (though not conclusive or unanimous evidence: see Fairweather, 1976) of earlier lateralisation for spatial ability in girls, this finding does not provide a causal explanation for the adult cognitive sex differences.

Maturational Rates

Another explanation of sex differences in hemispheric lateralisation has recently been put forward by Waber (1977) who suggests that maturational rate, regardless of sex, must be considered since it influences the development of higher cortical functions which determine differences in verbal and spatial abilities. Waber compared the performance of 10–16-year-olds on three verbal and three spatial measures, as well as on a lateralisation test based upon syllable recognition when different sounds were fed to the right and left ear.

Although Waber hypothesised that early maturers, regardless of sex, would perform better on verbal than on spatial tasks, while the reverse would hold for late maturers, only the spatial superiority of later maturers was confirmed.

The appearance of greater hemispheric lateralisation in late maturers was restricted to older adolescents of both sexes and was explained in terms of a behavioural disruption influenced by the growth spurt at puberty.

An innovation in Waber's proposals is the suggestion that the continuous variable, maturation rate, replace the dichotomous dimension sex, with values only of male and female. Although maturation varies with sex, the variables are not perfectly correlated and males are to be found among early maturers just as there are females among late maturers. Nevertheless, girls generally mature faster than boys, on average reaching puberty two years earlier, and on average have less spatial ability than boys, but the sex difference in spatial ability only alerts one to the problem and a useful explanation cannot be found by noting only the simple sex differences. General growth processes appear to play a determining role too.

Psychological Explanations

Three different psychological explanations of sex differences can be readily identified. These are the approaches from psycho-analysis, social learning theory, and Witkin's theory of psychological differentiation. Although many issues separate these formulations they share a common concern with development.

Psycho-analytic

Among Freud's major contributions to our understanding of human behaviour was his recognition of the role of early experience. Within the psycho-analytic tradition theorists differ in their interpretations of the events of infancy and early childhood but they agree on the importance of these experiences in shaping adult character and personality. Social learning theorists may offer quite different accounts of the early socialisation processes which result in sex-typed behaviour, but they too have an intellectual debt to Freud for bringing attention to this period in human development.

Freud's own views on the development of sex differences changed over the years though he was always concerned to describe emotion or affect and would have sought to account for differences in aggression and have been much less interested in providing an explanation for differences in cognitive capacities. In his early writings on sexuality (cf. *Three Essays on the Theory of Sexuality*, 1905) Freud not only extended the use of the concept of sexuality to include pleasure-seeking from birth onwards but he proposed that until puberty individuals were psychologically bisexual. Later Freud argued that as early as 5 years and with the resolution of the Oedipal Complex boys and girls were psychologically differentiated; identification with the same-sex parent resolved the romantic triangle and allowed the child to incorporate the standards and behaviour of the same-sex parent.

Juliet Mitchell (1974) suggests that Freud's awareness of the ambiguities in the conventional terms 'masculinity' and 'femininity' which fuse and confuse three levels of meaning appropriate to biological, sociological and psychological concerns led Freud to seek clarification by arguing for an initial bisexuality. The strategy allowed him to avoid defining the terms. However, by the mid 1920s the problems inherent in this resolution were apparent to Freud and he urged psycho-analytic researchers to seek understanding of sex differences in early infancy (Freud, 1925).

The oedipal conflict and its resolution is central to the psycho-analytic explanation of sex differences. The boy's desire for his mother is threatened by competition with his father and fear of castration. The resolution of this painful dilemma is seen in the boy's identification with his father and through this process his renunciation of his sexual impulses towards his mother and incorporation of the rules of his society as personified in his father. For the girl resolution through same sex identification is not as simple. Originally Freud argued that the girl held her mother responsible for her lack of a penis and desired her father and a baby to assuage her envy of the male. Nonetheless, the girl was expected to identify with her mother to the extent of acquiring a female sex role. Freud believed that the resolution of the dilemma was less clear for females and left them ambiguously differentiated and with less strongly structured moral rule systems or superegos. Thus, according to psycho-analytic theory the emotional dynamics of family life and sexual desire in a broad sense give rise to important psychological sex differences.

Social Learning Theory

In a major review of the social learning approach to sex differences Mischel (1970) focused on the socialisation of sex differences in social behaviour although he noted that there are many other observable differences, including, of course, sexual activity. Many of these could be explained, at least in part, by hormonal conditions, brain functions, and other factors, as well as by early learning. Included in his domain are not only those acts which are differentially rewarded and punished when performed by males and females, that is sex-typed behaviour, but also the stereotypes by which individuals in a particular society describe and categorise the behaviour which they hold to be specifically appropriate for a man or woman.

Among the personality traits which differentiate the sexes aggression and dependence have received considerable attention although only for aggression is there a sufficient body of evidence to draw sound conclusions. Kagan and Moss (1964) have ascribed the difficulty in tracing the developmental course of dependence in boys and aggression in girls to the differential acceptance of these traits in the very young and in mature males and females. Thus girls who were observed to be more aggressive in preschool play may appear more like their female peers in adulthood. Similarly for boys, dependence may be tolerated in the young but not at maturity.

It is easy to fall into the trap of assuming that social learning theorists are concerned only with those sex-typed behaviours which have immediate consequences for the actor, but Mischel discusses at length the process of vicarious or observational learning and its function in sex-typing. Unlike the unique and complex process of identification which is assumed to result in the resolution of the oedipal conflict yielding sex-typed behaviour and superego, social learning theorists believe that the principles which describe the acquisition and performance of sex-typed behaviours are the same as those which explain the learning of any behaviour. Questions such as: Are observers more likely to imitate the behaviour of a model they see being rewarded or punished? might be raised in any context but the study which shows that it is successful models whose behaviour is more often modelled (Bandura *et al.*, 1963) is particularly important in a discussion of sex differences. In our own society, for example, children are much more likely to see successful engineers, architects and physicists who are male. Here then is a possible explanation for sex differences in career choice which may have as much force as explanations based on the recognised sex differences in spatial and mathematical skills.

Whether learning is by reinforcement or by observation recent discussion has highlighted an important distinction between the acquisition of sex-typed responses and the performance of appropriate behaviour. Indeed, Maccoby and Jacklin suggest that before the age of 10 years children may acquire knowledge of responses appropriate to both sexes and that it may only be in terms of actual performance that behaviour is sex-typed. Although this distinction is difficult to pursue in empirical research, it suggests that the socialisation of overt behaviour in sex appropriate directions may be achieved more easily than the training of attention upon which observational learning depends. The socialisation of sex differences is, undoubtedly, a long learning experience.

Psychological Differentiation

Witkin's theory of psychological differentiation, with its claim that an individual's cognitive style can be described in terms of greater or lesser dependence upon the field in which stimuli are embedded, has raised many questions about sex differences. Although Witkin would include all aspects of psychological functioning in his account of differentiation, empirical studies have focused on perceptual tasks. We noted earlier that there has been considerable controversy about the interpretation of sex differences in spatial tests such as the embedded figures test (EFT). The essential question is whether the sex differences reflect differences in analytic ability (or 'differentiation') as Witkin claims, or whether the task specifically measures differential spatial abilities. The uniqueness of the former, also called 'perceptual disembedding', is maintained in a recent review of Witkin's theory from a cross-cultural perspective (Witkin and Berry, 1975) and it is alleged that disembedding skill is factorially distinguishable from spatial ability. Opinions differ sharply on this issue.

Aspects of the socialisation process important in differentiation theory are those practices which would lead a child to develop an autonomous identity and thus an articulated or field independent cognitive style. These include training for independence, learning how to handle impulses, especially aggression, and the development of behavioural constraints either through conformity or internalisation (Witkin, 1967).

Cross-cultural evidence (Barry *et al.*, 1957) suggests that socialisation practices may vary with subsistence economy such that hunter-gatherer societies place greater pressure on independence training for both sexes, while in sedentary agricultural societies, with greater emphasis on responsibility training, girls receive more severe socialisation. In the cross-cultural context, societal factors as well as eco-cultural dimensions and socialisation are important in explaining sex differences. Witkin and Berry give little attention to the influence of biological variables in explaining the pattern of sex differences in cognitive style.

Situational Explanations

The view that sex differences cannot be adequately explained in terms of biological or individual psychological processes but are a function of the wider social system has been expounded passionately by advocates of the Women's Movement. It is also a fundamental assumption of sociological analysis.

Unlike the feminist movement at the turn of the century, which sought equality in the political realm, the contemporary Women's Movement is concerned directly with marriage and sexuality (Dixon, 1972). Inequality in the family is explained by economic analysis and not by resort to biology. The family is considered a crucial instrument of male oppression. Work within the home and childcare are demanded of women but are valued less by society than male labour in the marketplace, since the latter produces wealth or capital. The charge of male domination arises not only from sex-typed family role assignment, but male supremacy and exploitative capitalism are held to ensure that women are the last to be hired and the first to go in hard times, that they are paid less because they are deemed less able and that their domestic work awaits them when their paid labour is complete. Beyond the exploitation of the family and the work-a-day world it is agreed that women are exploited biologically, treated as sexual objects and deprived of control of their own biological functions.

Evidence for the pervasiveness of social inequality comes from accounts of women's consciousness-raising groups. Gornic (1971) asserts that when women get together and discuss problems of presumably individual existence it rapidly becomes apparent that despite difference of age, class and even race there is a common struggle with inequality and male domination. This evidence strengthens their argument that society produces sex differences.

Obviously the Women's Movement draws theoretical insights from Marxism and in particular from Engel's analysis of the family. Using modern ethnographic data, Sacks (1974), an anthropologist, has re-evaluated Engel's theory, that the patriarchial, male-dominated family and class society arose with the advent of private property. The cross-cultural evidence led her to agree that there is greater sexual equality in non-class societies but to doubt that male property ownership provided the essential impetus to inequality in class societies. Rather, she argued that the separation of domestic and public life was supported by an ideology of sex differences which allowed the ruling classes to exploit male labour and left men, in return, masters in the home. For women to gain the status of adult members of society the division between the economic spheres of family and society would have to be resolved. Only then would it be reasonable to seek to identify sex differences unmarked by social inequality.

A much more cautious analysis of the role of society and culture in individual development is provided by the sociologist, Chinoy (1961). In seeking to explain the relationship between society and the individual and of culture and personality he asserts that neither society nor culture are dependent upon particular individuals and that both persist beyond the life-span of single human beings. In addition, he argues that human beings only survive and grow to maturity within a social setting. Feral children are intriguing but rare and both accounts of their early years, as well as explanations of their ability to acquire ordinary human skills in later life are controversial.

Stated most conservatively the sociological explanation of sex differences asserts that the close and continuing dependence of the human infant on his social milieu implies that many aspects of his behaviour could be explained without reference to unique psychological traits. Thus we can predict that in the USSR one is likely to have one's appendix removed by a female surgeon while in the UK or USA the surgeon would most likely be male. The explanation of this difference lies not with the physical stamina, manual dexterity or intellectual capacities of men and women but in the social systems of East and West. Explanations of this nature do not tell us why a particular Russian woman or American man becomes a surgeon but do illustrate the range of phenomena which the sociological perspective can illumine in a discussion of sex differences.

Discussion: The Developmental Approach

All the explanations we have considered take as their reference point the sex differences found in young adults and then seek causal factors operating at some time in the person's life-history. Biological explanations invoke intrinsic properties of the individual, genetic, hormonal, neural or maturational. Socialisation theorists view the developmental history of the child as being of primary importance. Cultural relativists point to a wider environmental influence exerted through social and cultural factors present throughout life.

None of these three types of explanation can be said to provide a complete representation of all the processes which result in an adult sex difference. In each case, an attempt has been made to isolate particular factors, regarded as being of special importance. The choice of a particular source of influence as being especially important usually reflects a polarisation of emphasis at one or other extreme of the nature–nurture dichotomy. Writers such as Hutt (1972a), Gray (1971) and Tiger (1970), place great emphasis on biology, whereas others, such as Mischel (1966) and Witkin (1967), place major emphasis on environmental influences. This debate involves no basically new issues, since it is one that has recurred in different forms throughout the history of psychology.

Lehrman (1970) has argued that such disputes between proponents of innate or learnt determinants of behaviour pose semantic and conceptual problems, and are thus not settled by any new empirical evidence. This point is important when viewing the conflicting interpretations of research on psychological sex differences: very often, one-sided perspectives are brought to bear on a particular issue, so that the debate is not so much about the validity or otherwise of research findings, but about the overall interpretation, conceptualisation and significance of the findings. Just as this sort of debate has in the past been influenced by the ideological beliefs of the protagonists (Crook, 1970), so too has the present debate on sex differences (Archer, 1977). Those who would seek to preserve traditional sex roles have used biological findings to argue against the desirability of change (Hutt, 1972a and b; Goldberg, 1972; Tiger, 1970), whereas those who advocate change have argued against the relevance of biological considerations (e.g., Millett, 1971). Other writers, including ourselves, have suggested an interactionist approach which takes account of both biological and social influences in the development of sex differences (Archer and Lloyd, 1975). We have argued that a more complex representation, which takes account of both biological and social factors more adequately, represents the developmental influence contributing to sex differences. This 'interactonist' approach depends upon the constant interaction between biological and environmental factors throughout development: it is a two-way process rather than the inborn expression of the child's nature and the effect of socialisation on the child.

The interactionist approach is clearly a developmental one. This is not the case for all the explanations which we have reviewed. They can readily be divided into those which are developmental, and those which are not. The developmental views include, of course, all the socialisation explanations, but also some of the biological theories: Hutt (1975) has argued that although there are pre-existing biological bases producing sex differences, development nevertheless has an important role to play, but this is restricted to amplifying or reducing the pre-existing basic difference. Some other biological theories are, in contrast, non-developmental, e.g. those involving genetic differences generally make no reference to the way in which the genetic influence might operate during development. Hormonal explanations likewise imply a difference which is dependent on a static or even a readily-reversible biological process. Thus the influence of testosterone on human attentional processes, important for the theories of Broverman *et al.* (1968) and Andrew (1972), is demonstrated by an experiment carried out by Klaiber *et al.* (1971). They infused testosterone into male volunteers and measured differences in performance on a mental arithmetic test. Such a short-lived effect stands in direct contrast to the longer-term influence of socialisation variables. Similarly, the brain lateralisation hypothesis of Buffery and Gray (1972) suggests that the adult sex difference is the result of a process occurring at one time only in developmental history.

We can thus make a distinction between 'developmental' and 'non-developmental' theories. All the developmental theories we have discussed so far have in common that they take adult sex differences as a fixed reference point. But they account for their developmental trajectory in different ways. An alternative type of developmental theory could take adult sex differences not as an end-point in themselves but as part of a continuing process of change from birth to old age. In this context, 'development' refers not to the usual period of birth to maturity, but to the period of birth to senescence. Such a perspective is clearly not one which has hitherto been adopted in discussions of psychological sex differences: most of the published studies of adults' are of young adults, with information on middle or old aged samples almost completely lacking (see section on Developmental profiles).

The advantages of adopting an approach which encompasses the whole life-process are not only that this is a more complete view but also that it is more value-free. By this we mean that it is less influenced by the everyday view of childhood as 'growing-up' and by the higher prestige attached to young as opposed to older adults in our society.

Such a perspective would also lead to changes of emphasis for the study of sex differences. Any discussion of biological influences could be widened to include not only prenatal and pubertal developmental, but also the various reproductive phases of the adult female, such as the menstrual cycle, childbirth, lactation and the menopause. These topics are not generally discussed in terms of their contribution to 'sex differences' but as part of 'the psychology of women' (Bardwick, 1971; Sherman, 1971). There are other physical sex differences which assume importance during the later years of life, but not during young adulthood, and these include the greater male susceptibility to disease at older ages. This difference has social consequences, including the greater incidence of bereavement for women than for men during middle and old age (Parkes, 1975): this difference is one of major importance when considering sex differences in affective processes and psychopathology at older ages (Mayo, 1976).

Occurring in parallel with, and in interaction with, the biological sex differences of adulthood are the very different social worlds occupied by adult men and women: for women, the earlier part of life typically involves housework and looking after children, followed in many cases by readjustment to the loss of the maternal role during middle-age (see Bart, 1971). For men, there are typically fewer role changes, and the point of readjustment is usually delayed until retirement (Bromley, 1974).

Viewing development as a process occurring throughout life raises the possibility of discontinuous developmental profiles. Thus a sex difference occurring early in development would not necessarily have the same cause as a difference favouring the same sex found at a later age. An example is the sex difference in verbal ability at different ages; a slight female advantage was reported during the first 3 years of life but no consistent differences were found again until about 10 or 11, after which a clear female superiority was apparent. Maccoby and Jacklin offered different accounts of these differences in verbal ability. They suggest that the earlier, short-lived one may reflect the differential susceptibility to childhood disorders in the two sexes, whereas the later sex difference is more long-lasting and may have a separate origin.

Similarly, we believe that any attempt to find a developmental explanation for the sex differences in characteristics such as aggression and anxiety would benefit from considering the possibility that different, and largely unrelated, causal factors might operate at different ages, to produce what is superficially a sex difference in the same direction. Thus, any sex differences in anxiety and depression (Mayo, 1976) might, in young adulthood, result from factors associated with the socialisation for different sex roles, whereas in a middle-aged sample they might be the result of adjustment to a changed social role in women (Bart, 1971).

These examples also raise the question of sex differences during old age. By adopting a life-history approach, and viewing sex differences as possibly discontinuous over time, any differences found in older aged people would not necessarily be viewed as mere extensions of sex differences occurring earlier in life, but as a result of processes specifically associated with middle and old age. Social influences such as the impact of retirement, psychological processes such as bereavement and reactions to other forms of loss (Parkes, 1975), biological changes such as the menopause and ageing itself, will all create new sex differences of a quite different nature from those found earlier in life.

We would, therefore, argue that a 'developmental life-history approach', incorporating all age groups would enable the study of sex differences to be extended from the current preoccupation with childhood and young adulthood. It would also raise the possibility of discontinuities in the development of sex differences at different ages.

Social Implications of Psychological Sex Differences

Introduction

Evidence of behavioural differences between the sexes is, as we have shown, interpreted as indicating differences in psychological processing. These inferred differences in intra-psychic functioning are influenced by biological, social and cultural factors, as well as by the individual's particular life-history. They are, therefore, of theoretical interest not only to psychologists but also to biologists and sociologists who seek to understand them in terms of their own particular academic disciplines. Difficulties arise when scholars operating within the confines of a single discipline attempt to offer what they presume to be complete explanations of these multidimensional phenomena.

To illustrate the dangers of such oversimplification, we have constructed two diagrams (Figures 8.1 and 8.2) depicting the reasoning involved in two restricted explanatory models of sex differences. The first (Figure 8.1) we refer to as the situational view or cultural relativism. Briefly, cultural relativism seeks to account for behavioural differences between the sexes in terms of social processes involving different social roles and expectations. These social processes include sex-typed occupational recruitment and domestic responsibility, socialisation for different sex roles (involving education both

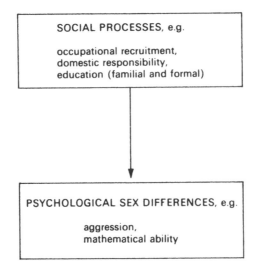

Figure 8.1   Diagrammatic representation of cultural relativist explanation of psychological sex differences

familial and formal), and differences in economic and political participation within society at large. The cultural relativist view is concerned with the broad cultural forces operating in a society which can account for why in our society, for example, men become doctors and women become nurses. The question of individual differences, and hence individual decision-making, is not pursued.

The cultural relativist view has also been adopted to provide a very general explanation for sex differences in abilities and temperament. Thus the finding that boys are more aggressive than girls, and that they excel in spatial and mathematical skills is seen as reflecting the cultural conditioning associated with different adult social roles and expectations. That such cultural forces provide multiple inputs into the environment which influences individual psychological development is undeniable (and forms the basis of the socialisation explanations described earlier). But to view psychological development solely in terms of the child absorbing cultural and political ideologies and stereotypes (a view adopted, for example, by Ingleby, 1974), is to neglect certain important aspects of development. In particular, it neglects the subtle and interactive nature of development, from which arises a realisation that the detailed study of individual development can reveal subtle influences on behaviour that a theory couched in terms of broad sociological forces cannot encompass. To appreciate such influences, a detailed investigation of the interaction of the infant or child with its adult social world is necessary: such studies require a psychological or individually-oriented (rather than a sociological or society-oriented) level of analysis (see, for example, studies reviewed by Schaffer, 1971).

In contrast to the situational or cultural relativist view, which concentrates on the sociological level of analysis to the exclusion of the psychological or individual level, the viewpoint we identify as psychological reductionism (Figure 8.2) concentrates too exclusively on the psychological level and neglects the explanatory power of social processes. Briefly, psychological reductionism (which is discussed in some detail below) refers to explanations of social processes, such as occupational recruitment, in terms of psychological phenomena: e.g. sex differences in specific abilities are cited as explanations for differences in occupational recruitment between the sexes (e.g. Garai and Scheinfeld, 1968).

Both cultural relativism and psychological reductionism are limited in that they seek to relate a specific and restricted level of analysis to more complex phenomena which involve additional factors best considered by a different level of analysis. Thus, when cultural relativist explanations are extended to sex differences in development or adulthood, both individual development and adult individual differences are neglected; similarly, when psychological explanations are extended to social processes the influence of broadly-conceived social forces is neglected.

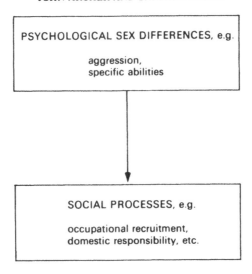

Figure 8.2   Diagrammatic representation of psychological reductionist explanations of social
processes

Psychological Reductionism

In the previous section, we introduced the term 'psychological reductionism' to describe the belief that sex differences in social processes (such
as occupational recruitment, domestic responsibility, education and political
participation) depended directly on the different psychological disposition of
the sexes. In this section, we consider in more detail some examples of this
type of reasoning.

The first example concerns the relationship between academic, professional
and artistic achievement, and the pattern of I.Q. scores found in the two sexes.
Hutt (1972a, p. 90) noted that there were higher proportions of men at the
extremes of the I.Q. distribution, and that this finding could explain both the
higher numbers of men than women in institutions for the mentally defective
and predominance of men in the higher levels of intellectual and creative
attainment. However, other reviews of psychological sex differences, e.g.
Anastasi (1958), point out that much of the evidence for the greater male
variability is suspect for methodological reasons, principally because of the
difficulty in finding large samples of men and women with equivalent
backgrounds. Anastasi also argued that the detection of 'feeblemindedness'
(i.e. low I.Q.) amongst girls and women (and consequently their admission to
institutions) was less likely than for boys and men, who could not so easily be
shielded in a domestic situation. Similarly, she claimed that the excess of men
with high achievement may reflect inequalities of opportunity rather than any
underlying I.Q. differences between the sexes. In seeking to explain the

phenomena in terms of differences in intellectual ability, Hutt under-rates the importance of social factors: many other writers regard the social consequences of the position of women as the major reason for the underrepresentation of women in creative occupations. Simone de Beauvoir (1972), for example, summed up the limitations placed upon creativity in women by their situation thus:

'Art and thought have their living springs in action. To be situated at the margin of the world is not a position favourable for one who aims at creating anew'.

Anastasi (1958) offered three related reasons why more men than women have achieved eminence: first, the existence of sex stereotyped roles (e.g. the notion that a woman's place is in the home), secondly that educational opportunities are unequal, and thirdly that many occupations (particularly many professions) are closed to women, or have been until very recently. We can illustrate the second of these, the disadvantage of women in education, by referring to some of the available educational statistics.

In the UK the male population is shown to be consistently better qualified than the female population in terms of the numbers obtaining a degree or equivalent, or A-level passes or O-level passes (*Social Trends*, 1974). These inequalities have, however, narrowed greatly over the last 10 years.

Considering inequalities in the various professions, data on the numbers of women in particular professions do show an overwhelming male bias, far larger than could be explained by the supposed greater numbers of men at the higher end of the I.Q. distribution: e.g. in 1972 the percentage of women who were university professors was 1.7, for solicitors the figure is 5.2, and for architects 5.8.

It seems reasonable to conclude that a number of interrelated social and educational factors can account for the relatively poor record of female intellectual achievement. The differential distribution of I.Q. scores, a psychological phenomenon, suggested by Hutt to account for the social phenomenon of differential achievement is of such slight magnitude (and could itself merely be a result of social factors) that it does not provide a plausible explanation of the sex differences in achievement.

It is, nevertheless, interesting to consider the reasoning employed in this type of explanation: I.Q. scores are taken as the basic phenomenon, which subsequently are regarded as determining the social process. In this argument, intelligence is regarded as a stable and basic property of the individual, from which scholastic and occupational achievement follows without the intervention of other social processes. A more accurate account of what really occurs would involve a more complex representation which enabled both psychological phenomena (development of intelligence) and social events (e.g. influences from school and parents in relation to sex role stereotypes, and occupational recruitment) to occur simultaneously.

The assumptions underlying 'psychological reductionism' are, therefore, as follows: first, that the psychological process is relatively fixed; secondly, that the influence is one-way, psychological event determining social event (an assumption which precluded consideration of possible influences in the reserve direction); thirdly, that other phenomena (e.g. tradition and beliefs about the sex roles of men and women) do not provide adequate explanations for the social events.

These particular assumptions can be illustrated by considering additional examples from the psychological literature on sex differences. Garai and Scheinfeld (1968), claimed that psychological sex differences 'foreshadow the different occupational goals of men and women'. Both they, and Broverman et al. (1968), have argued that women perform better than men on rapid repetitive tasks requiring delicate manual skills and frequent shifts of attention, including many of those required for clerical occupations (termed 'clerical skills' by Garai and Scheinfeld, 1968). Garai and Scheinfeld argued that the combination of greater clerical and verbal abilities in women equipped them better than men for both clerical occupations and for the rapid repetitive work of the assembly-line. They also argued that greater female verbal ability results in women aspiring to join professions involving fine arts and languages, and that because men show greater visual-analytical and mathematical skills, they therefore seek to enter the scientific professions.

These arguments involve the assumptions outlined above, that psychological sex differences are fixed entities, exerting a one-way influence on social processes. Thus it is claimed that sex-typical ability fits people for certain types of occupations, so that they choose one of these in order to use more successfully the skills associated with their particular sex.

A similar form of determinism is apparent in Garai and Scheinfeld's comments on the educational implications of sex differences, as when they note that the educational system fails to take account of sex differences in abilities, interests, personality traits and motivation. Again, the implication is that these psychological attributes are fixed and occur prior to the social events they are supposed to explain (rather than as parallel interacting phenomena), and that the social phenomena have no influence on the psychological phenomena or other social events.

'Psychological reductionism'—the belief that social processes can be reduced to psychological events—is taken one stage further in certain biologically-based accounts of psychological sex differences: here the psychological events are said to be determined by biological processes involving genetic, hormonal or neural activities (Figure 8.2).

The argument implies not only that social processes can be explained in terms of a static psychological construct such as I.Q. or a specific ability (as above) but also that the psychological construct is a direct result of some biological influence. The addition of a biological dimension thus underlies the implication that the sex difference constitutes a stable intrinsic property of the individual. The social process can then be regarded as resulting from an even more rigidly fixed individual process than is the case with psychological reductionism. The earlier section dealing with biological explanations gives some examples of the types of biological processes that have been used in these explanations (see also Archer and Lloyd, 1975; Archer, 1971, 1976a, 1977).

Evolutionary Determinism

In the remainder of this section, we intend to concentrate on one particular variation of the biological reductionist argument, 'evolutionary determinism'. This type of explanation seeks to explain differences in social roles between the sexes in terms of their correspondence to evolutionary adaptations. Thus Hutt (1972a, b) claimed that many supposed psychological characteristics of human females—such as 'stability' and 'conformity'—can be explained as evolutionary adaptations for the maternal role. Similarly, Tiger (1970) viewed the present-day female role as an adaptation for domesticity and child-rearing, and the male role as an adaptation for hunting in all-male groups (for which, he argued, there are modern substitutes).

The main factual objections to such explanations are that they incorporate modern sex role stereotypes into their view of the life of evolving hominids, who were, as far as we know, hunter-gatherers (Pfeiffer, 1969; Pilbeam, 1972). In modern hunter-gatherer societies, the female is neither sedentary nor economically a non-contributor (Slocum, 1975; Draper, 1975).

A more conceptual question raised by this type of explanation concerns the nature of the determining influence. In the biological reductionist explanations described above, the determining influence is a within-individual biological process, such as a genetic influence on development, or an interaction between a sex hormone and the brain. Evolutionary determinism involves an ultimate influence residing in the evolutionary ancestry of the species. This has to be transformed into a series of genetically-controlled events which will produce the 'adaptive' feature in adult members of that species. One view of this process, implicit in the writings on sex differences of Goldberg (1970), Tiger (1970) and Gray and Buffery (1971), is that the adult feature is fairly precisely coded in the genetic material: 'specified in the gene pool', as Buffery and Gray wrote, or 'biologically programmed', as Tiger put it. The case for such rigid genetic determinism is difficult to maintain in the face of cross-cultural and clinical evidence of the flexibility of human sex roles (Archer, 1976a).

In view of such obvious objections to rigid genetic determinism, more subtle ways in which 'evolutionary adaptations' could determine present-day sex roles have been suggested. Hutt (1972a, b), e.g., suggested that to depart from evolutionary adaptative sex roles is 'undesirable' (i.e. not necessarily impossible, but would lead to harmful consequences). There are several objections to such a view. First it is difficult to decide from present-day evidence what are the evolutionary adaptive behavioural features of the human species. Second, even if we could decide what these are, they would be unlikely to be appropriate for present-day conditions (since the environment of modern man is so different from that of evolving man). A third difficulty arises out of the second one and relates to the notion of a feature being 'undesirable': this implies that something deleterious will result if the evolutionary feature is not followed under present-day conditions. This conclusion does not necessarily follow. Writing on child-rearing practices, Blurton-Jones (1972) claimed that 'The presence of adaptations to one type of rearing need not imply that things will go wrong with subsequent development if the rearing practice is changed'. All it does imply is that the child will be ill-adapted to the environment in which the behaviour evolved (the second point raised above). Thus the argument that we have basic biological adaptations and that to try to change these will necessarily produce undesirable features, is not a sound one in view of the difficulties in deciding what types of evolutionary adaptations our ancestors developed, and the dissimilarity between the environments of early hominids and modern man. These difficulties apply to all arguments of this type, whether they refer to sex roles (Hutt, 1972a, b) or to some other feature such as the long-term consequences of mother–infant separation (Bowlby, 1970).

The supposed implications of this type of reasoning can be illustrated by considering Tiger and Shepher's (1975) account of the Israeli kibbutz in which they attribute the failure to achieve sexual equality to the existence of evolutionary determined biological constraints.

According to Tiger and Shepher (1975), in the early kibbutzim over half the women worked in production yet today there is a sharp sexual division of labour and older members of the kibbutz are usually among the most anxious to fulfill their occupational commitments in sex-appropriate jobs. This polarisation of the sexes is also seen in political decision making with few women occupying positions of authority. Despite an explicit ideological commitment to equality of the sexes, women are reported to opt for a sexually stereotyped social organisation and it is argued that women are responsible for the rise of the family to its importance as the basic unit of social structure. Along with the expanding function of the family there appears to be a high and growing rate both of birth and marriage as well as a declining divorce rate. In sum Tiger and Shepher assert that the modern women of the kibbutz have challenged their own equalitarian socialisation and the values of their community in order to be more fully involved in private, maternal activities.

Tiger and Shepher's explanation, like that of Hutt referred to above, rests not on genetic determinism (cf. Tiger, 1970) but on the supposition that departure from evolutionary adaptive sex roles will be harmful to physical and psychological development. Thus, they write: 'The ethological argument, then, is not that the genetic process is omnipotent but that biologically necessary social interactions are basic to both emotional and physical health.' (Tiger and Shepher, 1975, p. 273). Note that this so-called ethological argument is in direct contrast to the quoted comment of Blurton-Jones, himself an ethologist.

Thus Tiger and Shepher argue that whilst the founders of the kibbutzim sought to build societies based upon an ideology of sexual equality, they failed to take account of biologically determined female motivation to care for their own young. In this regard, it may be noteworthy that these alleged egalitarian planners never envisaged a society in which the primary responsibility for child-care fell to men. Once children were born to members of the kibbutz it was assumed that females would care for them. Thus the experiment was not as radical as Tiger and Shepher would have us believe. Neither, as we have discussed, was their 'ethological argument' as sound as they claimed.

The Role of Culture in Human Sex Differences

We have discussed, and rejected as inadequate and restricted, two theoretical models which either see sex differences as the result of social forces or social differentiation as a reflection of sex differences. In this final section, we discuss the role of culture in human sex differences. The sense in which cultural relativist and socialisation theories relate culture to observed sex differences is that of culture creating a sex difference. We reject this view as a total explanation, though it provides a partial description of the developmental process. The developmental processes is best described as an interaction between biological and environmental influences in their wider sense, including not only broad cultural influences but also physical and social inputs.

We also identify a second way in which culture influences sex differences, that of creating meaning, of interpreting the outcome of the biological and social interaction. This process is one which occurs in conjunction with the interaction of social and biological influences in development. Thus the particular social and cultural environment in which development occurs assigns values and creates meaning: on the cultural level, the significance of a sex difference resides not so much in the difference *per se* (as it would be viewed by a psychologist) but in what culture attributes to it. A general example of this process is given in the discussion of sex differences in occupational recruitment by Kipnis (1976). She described how the status of bank clerks in the USA and doctors in the USSR declined as these roles changed from predominantly male to predominantly female occupations.

In a more general sense, 'sex differences' (at the individual biological or psychological level) may be invented, enhanced or neglected by culture. The evidence for the former in terms of sex role stereotypes (e.g. Bem, 1974) and restrictions on woman's entry into many occupations is well known. Cultural enhancement of sexually dimorphic physical features can be seen in men and women's fashions, with for example shoulder padding in men's jackets, and the large variety of ways in which different parts of the female form have been emphasised. Enhancement of behavioural features includes cultural elaboration of male aggression, so that occupations involving physical violence or the risk of physical violence (e.g. boxing, wrestling, the armed forces, the police force) are predominantly male ones. Finally, there are some examples of cultural neglect of a sex difference. It is not common knowledge that sex differences in sensory thresholds and musical ability have been reliably recorded in our own society (McGuinness, 1973, 1976a, b; McGuinness and Lewis, 1976). Perhaps we are less aware of these because our culture has not elaborated the male–female theme in this domain (e.g. there is no predominantly female interest in music which parallels the measured sex difference).

In conclusion, we suggest that a purely psychological analysis of sex differences is inadequate in so far as it ignores culture. Culture takes as its object the behaviour of its men and women, the product of the social environment (including cultural influences) and biological influences, interacting with one another throughout development, and from a selection of these differences creates meaning and significance.

References

Anastasi, A. (1958). *Differential Psychology*, Macmillan, New York.

Andrew, R. J. (1972). Recognition processes and behavior with special reference to effects of testosterone on persistence. In *Advances in the Study of Behaviour*, Vol. 4 (ed. D. S. Lehrman, R. A. Hinde and E. Shaw), Academic Press, New York and London

Archer, J. (1971). Sex differences in emotional behaviour: a reply to Gray and Buffery. *Acta Psychologica*, **35**, 415–429

Archer, J. (1975). Rodent sex differences in emotional and related behavior. *Behavioral Biology*, **14**, 451–479

Archer, J. (1976a). Biological explanations of psychological sex differences. In *Exploring Sex Differences* (ed. B. B. Lloyd and J. Archer), Academic Press, London and New York

Archer, J. (1976b). The organisation of aggression and fear in vertebrates. In *Perspectives in Ethology*, Vol. 2 (ed. P. P. G. Bateson and P. Klopfer), Plenum Press, New York

Archer, J. (1977). Biological explanations of sex role stereotypes: conceptual, social and semantic issues. In *The Sex Role System: Psychological and Sociological Perspectives* (ed. J. Chetwynd and O. Hartnett), Routledge and Kegan Paul, London

Archer, J. and Lloyd, B. B. (1975). Sex differences: biological and social interactions. In *Child Alive* (ed. R. Lewin), Temple Smith, London

Bandura, A., Ross, D. and Ross, S. A. (1963). A comparative test of the status envy, social power and secondary reinforcement theories of identificatory learning. *Journal of Abnormal and Social Psychology*, **13**, 173–199

Bardwick, J. M. (1971). *Psychology of Women: A Study of Bio-cultural Conflicts*, Harper and Row, New York

Barry, H., Bacon, M. K. and Child, I. L. (1957). A cross-cultural survey of some sex differences in socialization. *Journal of Abnormal and Social Psychology*, **55**, 327–332

Bart, P. B. (1971). Depression in middle-aged women. In *Woman in Sexist Society* (ed. V. Gornick and B. K. Moran), Basic Books, New York

Bayley, N. and Oden, M. (1955). The maintenance of intellectual ability in gifted adults. *Journal of Gerontology*, **19**, 91–107

Bell, R. Q., Weler, G. M. and Waldrop, M. F. (1971). Newborn and preschoolers: organization in behaviour and relations between periods. *Monographs of the Society for Research in Child Development*, **36**, no. 142

Bem, S. L. (1974). The measurement of psychological androgyny. *Journal of Consulting and Clinical Psychology*, **42**, 155–162

Block, J. H. (1976). Debatable conclusions about sex differences. *Contemporary Psychology*, **21**, 517–522

Blum, J. E., Fosshage, J. L. and Jarvik, L. F. (1972). Intellectual changes and sex differences in octogenarians: a twenty-year longitudinal study of aging. *Developmental Psychology*, **7**, 178–187

Blurton-Jones, N. (1972). Comparative aspects of mother-child contact. In *Ethological Studies of Child Behaviour* (ed. N. Blurton-Jones), Cambridge University Press, London

Bowlby, J. (1970). *Attachment*, Penguin, Harmondsworth

Bransford, J. D., Barclay, J. R. and Franks, J. J. (1972). Sentence memory: a constructive vs interpretive approach. *Cognitive Psychology*, **3**, 193–209

Brimer, M. A. (1969). Sex differences in listening comprehension. *Journal of Research and Development in Education*, **3**, 72–79

Bromley, D. B. (1974). *The Psychology of Human Ageing*, Penguin, Harmondsworth

Broverman, D. M., Klaiber, E. L., Kobayashi, Y. and Vogel, W. (1968). Roles of activation and inhibition in sex differences in cognitive abilities. *Psychological Review*, **75**, 23–50

Buffery, A. W. H. and Gray, J. A. (1972). Sex differences in the development of spatial and linguistic skills. In *Gender Differences, Their Ontogeny and Significance* (ed. C. Ounsted and D. C. Taylor), Churchill, London

Chinoy, E. (1961). *Society: an Introduction to Sociology*, Random House, New York

Clarke-Stewart, K. A. (1973). Interactions between mothers and their young children: characteristics and consequences. *Monographs of Society for Research in Child Development*, **38**, no. 153

Coates, B. and Hartrup, W. W. (1969). Age and verbalization in observational learning. *Developmental Psychology*, **1**, 556–62

Coates, S. (1974). Sex differences in field independence among preschool children. In *Sex Differences in Behavior* (ed. R. C. Friedman, R. M. Richart and R. L. Vande Wiele), Wiley, New York

Collins, A. M. and Quillian, M. R. (1969). Retrieval time from semantic memory, *Journal of Verbal Learning and Verbal Behavior*, **8**, 240–247

Crook, J. H. (1970). Introduction – social behaviour and ethology. In *Social Behaviour in Birds and Mammals*, Academic Press, London and New York

Darwin, C. (1877). A biographical sketch of an infant. *Mind*, **2**, 28–294

Dawson, J. L. M. (1972). Effects of sex hormones on cognitive style in rats and men. *Behavior Genetics*, **2**, 21–42

De Beauvoir, S. (1972). *The Second Sex*, Penguin, Harmondsworth

Dixon, M. (1972). The rise of women's liberation. In *Female Liberation* (ed. Roberta Salper), Knopf, New York. Reprinted in *Readings on the Psychology of Women* (ed. J. M. Bardwick), Harper and Row, 1972, New York, Evanston, San Francisco and London

Draper, P. (1975). !Kung women: contrasts in sexual egalitarianism in foraging and sedentary contexts. In *Toward an Anthropology of Women* (ed. R. Reiter), Monthly Review Press, New York and London

Fairweather, H. (1976). Sex differences in cognition. *Cognition*, **4**, 231–280

Flanagan, J. C., Dailey, J. T., Shaycoft, M. F., Gorham, W. A., Orr, D. B., Goldberg, I. and Neyman, C. A. (1961). Counsellor's technical manual for interpreting test scores (Project Talent), Palo Alto, California. (Listed in Maccoby and Jacklin)

Freud, S. (1905). *Three Essays on the Theory of Sexuality*, Standard Edition, vol. VII

Freud, S. (1925). *Some Psychical Consequences of the Anatomical Distinction Between the Sexes*, Standard Edition, Vol. XIX

Garai, J. E. and Scheinfeld, A. (1968). Sex differences in mental and behavioral traits. *Genetic Psychology Monographs*, **77**, 169–299

Garron, D. C. (1970). Sex-linked, recessive inheritance of spatial and numerical abilities, and Turner's syndrome. *Psychological Review*, **77**, 147–152

Glucksmann, A. (1974). Sexual dimorphism in mammals. *Biological Reviews*, **49**, 423–475

Goldberg, S. (1972). *The Inevitability of Patriarchy*, Morrow, New York

Gornick, V. (1971). Consciousness and raising. *New York Times Magazine*, Jan. 10, 1971. Reprinted in *Readings on the Psychology of Women* (ed. J. M. Bardwick), Harper and Row, 1972, New York, Evanston, San Francisco and London

Gray, J. A. (1971). Sex differences in emotional behaviour in mammals including Man: endocrine bases. *Acta Psychologica*, **35**, 29–46

Gray, J. A. and Buffery, A. W. H. (1971). Sex differences in emotional and cognitive behaviour in mammals including man: adaptive and neural bases. *Acta Psychologica*, **35**, 89–111

Green, A. (1955). The relation of dancing experience and personality to perception. *Psychological Monographs*, **69**, 399

Greenglass, E. R. (1971). A cross-cultural study of the child's communication with his mother. *Developmental Psychology*, **5**, 494–499

Halverson, C. F. and Waldrop, M. F. (1970). Maternal behavior toward own and other preschool children: the problem of 'ownness'. *Child Development*, **41**, 839–845

Hutt, C. (1972a). *Males and Females*, Penguin, Harmondsworth

Hutt, C. (1972b). Sex differences in human development. *Human Development*, **15**, 153–170

Hutt, C. (1975). Sex differences: biology and behaviour. In *Child Alive* (ed. R. Lewin), Temple Smith, London

Ingleby, D. (1974). The psychology of child psychology. In *The Integration of a Child into a Social World* (ed. M. P. M. Richards), Cambridge University Press, London

Jensen, A. R. (1975). A theoretical note on sex linkage and race differences in spatial visualization ability. *Behavior Genetics*, **5**, 151–164

Kagan, J. and Moss, H. A. (1964). *Birth to Maturity: a Study in Psychological Development*, Wiley, New York ·

Kipnis, D. M. (1976). Intelligence, occupational status, and achievement motivation. In *Exploring Sex Differences* (ed. B. B. Lloyd and J. Archer), Academic Press, London and New York

Klaiber, E. L., Broverman, D. M., Vogel, W., Abraham, G. E. and Cone, F. L. (1971). Effects of infused testosterone on mental performances and serum LH. *Journal of Clinical Endocrinology*, **32**, 341–349

Knorr, D., Bidlingmaier, F., Butenandt, O., Fendel, H. and Ehrt-Wehle, R. (1974). Plasma testosterone in male puberty. I. Physiology of plasma testosterone. *Acta Endocrinologica*, **75**, 181–194

Kolakowski, D. and Malina, R. M. (1974). Spatial ability, throwing accuracy and man's hunting heritage. *Nature*, **251**, 410–412

Lehrman, D. S. (1970). Semantic and conceptual issues in the nature–nurture problem. In *Development and Evolution of Behavior* (ed. L. R. Aronson, E. Tobach, D. S. Lehrman and J. S. Rosenblatt), Freeman, San Francisco

Lewis, M. (1969). Infants' responses to facial stimuli during the first year of life. *Developmental Psychology*, **1**, 75–86

Lewis, M. and Freedle, R. (1972). Mother-infant dyad: the cradle of meaning. Paper presented at a Symposium on Language and Thought: Communication and Affect, Erindale College, University of Toronto, March, 1972. (Listed in Maccoby and Jacklin)

Maccoby, E. E. (1966). Sex differences in intellectual functioning. In *The Development of Sex Differences* (ed. E. E. Maccoby), Stanford University Press, Stanford

Maccoby, E. E. and Jacklin, C. N. (1975). *The Psychology of Sex Differences*, Oxford University Press, London

McCarthy, D. (1954). Language development in children. In *Manual of Child Psychology* (ed. L. Carmichael), Wiley, New York

McGuinness, D. (1973). Hearing: individual differences in perceiving. *Perception*, **1**, 465–473

McGuinness, D. (1976a). Sex differences in the organization of perception and cognition. In *Exploring Sex Differences* (ed. B. B. Lloyd and J. Archer), Academic Press, London and New York

McGuinness, D. (1976b). Away from a unisex psychology: individual differences in visual, sensory and perceptual processes. *Perception*, **5**, 279–294

McGuinness, D. and Lewis, I. (1976). Sex differences in visual persistence: experiments on the Ganzfeld and afterimages. *Perception*, **5**, 295–301

Mayo, P. (1976). Sex differences and psychopathology. In *Exploring Sex Differences* (ed. B. B. Lloyd and J. Archer), Academic Press, London and New York

Messent, P. R. (1976). Female hormones and behaviour. In *Exploring Sex Differences* (ed. B. B. Lloyd and J. Archer), Academic Press, London and New York

Meyer-Bahlburg, H. F. L. (1974). Aggression, androgens and the XYY syndrome. In *Sex Differences in Behavior* (ed. R. C. Friedman, R. M. Richart and R. L. Vande Wiele), Wiley, New York

Millett, K. (1971). *Sexual Politics*, Hart Davis, London

Mischel, W. (1966). A social-learning view of sex differences in behavior. In *The Development of Sex Differences* (ed. E. E. Maccoby), Tavistock, London

Mischel, W. (1970). Sex typing and socialization. In *Camichael's Manual of Child Psychology* (ed. P. H. Mussen), Wiley, New York

Mitchell, J. (1974). *Psycho-analysis and Feminism*, Penguin, Harmondsworth

Moore, T. (1967). Language and intelligence: a longitudinal study of the first eight years. *Human Development*, **10**, 88–106

Mueller, E. (1972). The maintenance of verbal exchanges between young children. *Child Development*, **43**, 930–938

Ounsted, C. and Taylor, D. C. (1972). The Y-chromosome message: a point of view. In *Gender Differences: Their Ontogeny and Significance* (ed. C. Ounsted and D. C. Taylor), Churchill, London

Parkes, C. M. (1975). *Bereavement: Studies of Grief in Adult Life*, Penguin, Harmondsworth

Pfeiffer, J. E. (1969). *The Emergence of Man*, Nelson, London

Pilbeam, D. (1972). *The Ascent of Man*, Macmillan, New York

Preyer, W. (1888). *Die Seele des Kindes*, T. Grieben, Leipzig

Rogers, L. (1976). Male hormones and behaviour. In *Exploring Sex Differences* (ed. B. B. Lloyd and J. Archer), Academic P:ess, London and New York

Rosenblatt, P. C. and Cunningham, M. R. (1976). Sex differences in cross-cultural perspective. In *Exploring Sex Differences* (ed. B. B. Lloyd and J. Archer), Academic Press, London and New York

Sacks, K. (1974). Engels revisited: Women, the organization of production, and private property. In *Women, Culture and Society* (ed. M. Z. Rosaldo and L. Lamphere), Stanford University Press, Stanford

Schaffer, H. R. (1971). *The Growth of Sociability*, Penguin, Harmondsworth

Schwartz, D. W. and Karp, S. A. (1967). Field dependence in a geriatric population. *Perceptual and Motor Skills*, **24**, 495–504

Selmanoff, M. K., Jumonviule, J. E., Maxson, S. C. and Ginsburg, B. E. (1975). Evidence for a Y chromosomal contribution to an aggressive phenotype in inbred mice. *Nature*, **253**, 529–530

Sherman, J. A. (1967). Problems of sex differences in space perception and aspects of intellectual functioning. *Psychological Review*, **74**, 290–299

Sherman, J. A. (1971). *On the Psychology of Women*, Thomas, Springfield, Illinois

Shipman, V. C. (1971). Disadvantaged children and their first school experiences. Educational Testing Service Head Start Longitudinal Study. (Listed in Maccoby and Jacklin)

Slocum, S. (1975). Woman the gatherer: male bias in anthropology. In *Toward an Anthropology of Women* (ed. R. Reiter), Monthly Review Press, New York and London

Smith, P. K. and Connolly, K. (1972). Patterns of play and social interaction in pre-school children. In *Ethological Studies of Child Behaviour* (ed. N. B. Jones), Cambridge University Press, London

Social Trends (1974). H. M. Stationery Office, London

Stafford, R. E. (1961). Sex differences in spatial visualization as evidence of sex-linked inheritance. *Perceptual and Motor Skills*, **13**, 428

Stanford Research Institute (1972). Follow-through pupil tests, parent interviews, and teacher questionnaires, Appendix C. (Listed in Maccoby and Jacklin)

Szal, J. A. (1972). Sex differences in the co-operative and competitive behaviors of nursery school children. University of Stanford, M.A. (Listed in Maccoby and Jacklin)

Tiger, L. (1970). The possible biological origins of sexual discrimination. *Impact of Science on Society*, **20**, 29–45

Tiger, L. and Shepher, J. (1975). *Women in the Kibbutz*, Harcourt, New York and London

Trivers, R. L. (1972). Parental investment and sexual selection. In *Sexual Selection and the Descent of Man* (ed. B. Campbell), Aldine, Chicago

Underwood, B. J. and Schulz, R. W. (1960). *Meaningfulness and Verbal Learning*, Lippincott, Chicago

Waber, D. P. (1977). Sex differences in mental abilities, hemispheric lateralization, and rate of physical growth at adolescence. *Developmental Psychology*, **13**, 29–38

Witelson, S. F. (1976). Sex and the single hemisphere: specialization of the right hemisphere for spatial processing. *Science*, **193**, 425–427

Witkin, H. A. (1967). A cognitive-style approach to cross-cultural research. *International Journal of Psychology*, **2**, 233–250

Witkin, H. A. and Berry, J. W. (1975). Psychological differentiation in cross-cultural perspective. *Journal of Cross-Cultural Psychology*, **6**, 4–87

Witkin, H. A., Dyk, R. B., Faterson, H., Goodenough, D. R. and Karp, S. A. (1962).

Psychological Differentiation, Wiley, New York

Witkin, H. A., Goodenough, D. R. and Karp, S. A. (1967). Stability of cognitive style from childhood to young adulthood. *Journal of Personality and Social Psychology*, **7**, 291–300

9 Universality and Plasticity, Ontogeny and Phylogeny: The Resonance between Culture and Cognitive Development

NEIL WARREN

(*School of African and Asian Studies, University of Sussex, Falmer Brighton, Sussex, England*)

Lévi-Strauss once prophesied that marked cultural differences will sometime in the twenty-first century disappear in favour of a single humanity. As the world shrinks and the planetary culture begins to take shape, it is already much more difficult than it was for our grandfathers to identify any cultures which we might dare to call 'primitive'. We still accept that there are cultural differences; but not necessarily that those cultural variations result from, or even result in, psychological differences of a fundamental kind. Cultural differences may, however, be—I would say obviously are to some extent—an overlay on psychological universals.

To speak of psychological universals is of course not to imply that all people are the same to a nicety. People vary; and *vive la différence*! If we hold that they are really all the same, we have in mind some fundamental, generative sense of universality: they are variations on a common theme or common set of principles. In non-Western or traditional cultures people also vary individually one from another, although this may often be obscured in ethnographic accounts. Thus in consideration of universals we think of the fundamental ways in which people may be the same, the themes on which all are variations. An old expression for this is 'the psychic unity of mankind'. An English folk saying has it that 'human nature doesn't change'.

It is the same psychological processes which will be universal, and so it is comprehension of these processes which can specify the limiting cultural conditions for both similarities and differences. There is in fact a new emphasis today on psychological universals (Cole and Scribner, 1974; Rosch, 1975, 1977; Dasen, 1977a; Gay, Lloyd and Bruner, in press); and it begins to seem as if we are all more alike in certain fundamental respects than an earlier generation of social scientists, stressing man's plasticity, thought (not to speak of those who have from time to time linked surface differences with race). Part of this new look consists in pointing out the extent of commonality required between investigator and subjects for a cross-cultural study to be conducted at all. This observation will apply even to those studies which take the commonality for granted and seek to emphasise cultural differences in their reports. It may be that you need an awful lot of commonality to pin down a difference, between individuals or between cultures. The paradox here is only apparent; but conceptual and methodological muddle has to be avoided with care.

Let me give an example: the investigation of colour perception. The assumption of commonality long obscured difference: even the common form of human colour blindness was not identified until the very end of the eighteenth century. (Most pet-lovers to this day assume that their cats and dogs see the world in colour, which is almost certainly not true.) Then, however, the belief in differences obscured commonality: reports began to filter back to the West during the nineteenth century that various 'primitives' lacked many colour names, and the view was readily formed that such people had defective colour vision. This assumption was eventually scotched by some of the earliest cross-cultural research in psychology. In the twentieth century a more complex position (often identified with the linguist Whorf) was taken up: the colour sense is everywhere the same but the continuous colour spectrum is variously and arbitrarily categorised by the colour terms of different languages. This thesis juxtaposed sensory commonality and linguistic-cum-cognitive diversity, but has in turn been dismissed by a spate of recent research brilliantly initiated by Berlin and Kay (1969): there now appear to be eleven universal foci of perceptual salience within the colour solid, these are named by basic colour terms in certain sequence, and cultures differ in how many their languages have named, from two to eleven. But within this universality there do now seem to be certain sensory differences in colour vision, reflecting the extent of retinal pigmentation, which acts as a kind of filter (Bornstein, 1973). This is where we are now, only a fool would wish to conclude that the story is finished.

Berlin and Kay (1969), in beginning their research on colour terms, noted the ease with which they and others had been able to learn the colour vocabulary of other cultures, in spite of the host of reports of cultural differences in colour terminology. Berlin has also had to revise an initial assumption (Berlin et al., 1966) that folk taxonomies of botanical and zoological classification would vary greatly from each other and from Western taxonomies (Berlin, 1972; Berlin et al., 1973). Rosch (1977), who has made remarkable psychological contributions to the cross-cultural study of colour categories and to a general theory of human categorisation, observes:

'The facts about a new culture which are most likely to be observed and noted by a naive observer are the ways in which the strange culture differs from the familiar. Thus, we do not find reports of other cultures which tell us that the people chew their food, or that they smile, or that it was possible to learn their words for familiar objects or for colours. All such facts are taken for granted and . . . tend to be overlooked' (p. 4)

And Cole and Scribner (1974), in conclusion of their survey of culture and cognition, point to the small likelihood of finding cultural differences in basic component cognitive processes. It is this basic commonality which enables differences to be sought, and stressed and probably, in many cases, over-stressed.

Child Development

The point applies equally well to child development, whose commonalities are taken for granted or under-stressed. There is some indication from baby-test data, for instance, that African infants develop a little more rapidly in certain—mostly locomotor—respects over the first year and a half than the Western babies who comprised the standardisation samples for these tests (see Warren, 1972, 1973). This may also be so for non-Western or 'pre-industrial' infants in general (Werner, 1972). Or rather a certain precocity may be a feature of infants in less 'modern' environments, as suggested, for instance, by African difference by social level (Warren, 1972) or by the early precocity of Moroccan-Jewish infants in Israel in comparison with European-Jewish babies (Smilansky et al., 1976). Bovet, Dasen and others (summarised by Dasen, 1977a) have approached this same issue in the Piagetian manner, studying the sensorimotor development of African village infants in the Ivory Coast, and also find certain specific advances over Parisian norms, though not an overall precocity. The matter has been further and well elucidated by Super (1976) in Kenya: he studied both infant development over time and infant care stimulation in several cultural groups, and his complicated results indicate the role of both biological and cultural influences in promoting African development in certain motor elements of behaviour. Because the groups which manifest infant precocity seem also to be those whose intelligence test performance falls below average in later years, some authors (e.g. Jensen, 1969, 1973; Eysenck, 1971) have used the earlier African findings to draw large theoretical inferences in support of contentions about racial differences in intelligence. I believe their arguments to be extremely tendentious, given our profound ignorance of the causal relations between infant and adult performances. The long-term developmental import of small, specific and inconsistent differences in infant growth rates is certainly unknown, and may plausibly be nil. Throughout the above work, moreover, (possibly excepting Dasen (1977a)) infant commonalities have been under-emphasised almost as if the investigators were wearing blinkers.

Whatever differences there may be rest on a remarkable and usually unacknowledged base of commonality. The same elements of infant development emerge wherever studies are conducted. To take an example relevant to the above precocity issue, Warren and Parkin (1974) found few differences between African and European newborns: these differences were small, not clinically obvious, and did not indicate the congenital precocity of either group. Much more striking was the fact that exactly the same set of 45 responses and reflexes was observed in both groups. Only two reflexes were difficult to elicit in either group. Konner (1972) also noted that the reflex repertoire of Bushman newborns (possibly a distinct race) corresponds precisely with their European counterparts.

Similarly for behaviour later in infancy. Dasen (1977a) rightly considers that the most important conclusion from African sensorimotor studies may be obscured by attention to cultural differences in developmental rate:

'It is, in fact, that the qualitative characteristics of sensorimotor development are quite similar or even identical in French and African infants, in spite of vast differences in their cultural environment. Not only are the structural properties of the sub-stages, and therefore their order of appearance, identical in both groups, but even the actions and schemes, and the way these are slowly built up into more complex action-patterns which eventually enable the infant to solve rather difficult problems, seem to be identical' (p. 165).

Dasen provides a remarkable example. Around twelve months of age, when given a plastic tube and a chain of paper clips, virtually every infant, African or European, looks for some way of making the chain pass through the tube. The African village baby has never seen such things before, and yet he combines them exactly as Parisian infants do: he makes the same errors, and follows the same sequence of progressively adaptive solutions. He also, as it happens, can do this at a slightly earlier age, on the average; there again is the small quantitative difference in rate resting on a huge and impressive commonality. Many other examples could be given. The sub-stage 4B of object permanence, when babies search for an object behind a first screen even though they have seen it moved so as to be behind a second screen, is exactly duplicated by African children (again, a little earlier). It may well be that our received conceptions of scientific method give the wrong bias, for cross-cultural and for developmental problems: we are taught to respect quantitative over qualitative approaches, and that is clearly mistaken here; and our research designs and statistics are sensitised to differences and often ignore commonalities (cf. Meehl, 1967). In fact, in the classical experimental designs which have so greatly influenced the statistical thinking of psychologists, commonality is deliberately controlled so as not to be the focus of statistical or rational judgement.

The topic of language affords similar observations. Of course people of different cultures both think and speak of different things to some extent; this is part of what we mean by distinguishing cultures at all. It is also part of the reason why communication between cultures and translation between languages are sometimes difficult. Undoubtedly, some languages lack terms that others have, such as for certain abstract generics or for particular refinements of detail. And frequently the apparently 'same' terms, used for rough translation across languages, will differ in what they precisely include and exclude and in their structural oppositions. But again, to stress the differences could obscure the commonalities. The phenomenon of universality in the focal categories of colour names was noted above. Other studies have documented striking generalities across language-families and cultures in the use of physical terms such as 'warm' or 'hard' as metaphors for psychological attributes (Asch, 1958), in the affective connotations of colour terms (D'Andrade and Egan, 1974) and in the connotative structure of a large range of adjectival dimensions (Osgood, 1962; Osgood et al., 1975). Visual-verbal synaesthesia (Osgood, 1960)—cross-language correspondence between words and abstract schematic pictures—is another example. Phonetic symbolism—a correspondence between the sound of a word and its meaning, other than in onomatopeia—is another curious but documented cross-language phenomenon, first studied fifty years ago by Sapir and more recently by Brown (1958), Brown et al. (1955), Ertel (1969) and Klank et al. (1971). And on the question of semantic diversity, Hockett (1954) concluded from a study of Chinese and English that languages differ not so much in what can be said but in what it is easy or difficult to say.

A large range of purely linguistic universals has been noted (Greenberg, 1966), and Miller (1970) has suggested that these reflect universal psychological processes. Rosch's (1977) theory of human categorisation, drawing in part on Garner's (1974) information-theoretic insight that the real world (as distinct from the experimentally created world of most psychological studies of categorisation) is made up of subsets of occurrences rather than total sets of all possibilities, shows how perceptual and semantic categories may offer themselves for naming. Chomsky's theory of syntax, on the other hand, pointed to the 'innate ideas' of the human organism: Chomsky's (1968) well-known contention was that a universal deep structure of language and a correspondingly universal mental competence underlie all language acquisition. Chomsky initially had little cross-cultural evidence on language acquisition to draw on; and his actual theory of syntax is now one among alternative theories whose semantic and psychological component is differently deployed (e.g. Fillmore, 1968; Anderson, 1971; Halliday, 1975). But each theory appears to suggest universality in language acquisition, and as the relevant cross-cultural evidence accumulates, empirical indications of a universal sequence of language acquisition emerge, both for grammar and syntax and for communicative competence (Slobin, 1970, 1971; Ferguson and

Slobin, 1973; Bowerman, 1973; Sanches and Blount, 1975). These indications are the more compelling because they include such unrelated languages as Finnish, Samoan, African Nilotic, Mexican Indian, American English (black and white) and Japanese. The studies, as well as current general theories, also point to the dependence of language acquisition on the prior establishment of cognitive-semantic principles or heuristics, which again would be universal. It seems possible that, eventually, investigations of language development—especially semantics and communicative competence—will contribute as much to the cross-cultural study of cognitive development as will conventional psychological approaches to cognition. These are as yet very early days, and the study of language development is one of the liveliest in social science. I shall further suggest below that there is more yet of value for the cross-cultural psychologist to comprehend by the consideration and study of an obviously unnatural aspect of language development: that of literacy and its cognitive requirements and consequences. Literacy clearly entails a cultural difference which is in some way superimposed on the commonalities of oral language acquisition.

Piaget has paid curiously little attention to language development, although he insists that language has no special causal role as an external shaper or transformer of the child's basic cognitive processes, rather the contrary. One of his followers, Sinclair de Zwaart (1967), has done research in explication of this position. Piaget's cognitive theory, whatever its ultimate merits as such, is clearly compatible with latter-day findings implicating the prior necessity of a set of cognitive-semantic principles for the acquisition of language. Indeed, a number of commentators (MacNamara, 1972; Edwards, 1973; Bates, 1976) have used Piaget's theory to articulate cogent accounts of child language learning. Piaget clearly posits universals of ontogeny; not, as some seem to think, by reference to heredity but as the necessary epigenetic outcome of the sequential interaction between an intact and maturing human organism and the successive environments he is able to construe. I have mentioned sensorimotor development above; but the bulk of cross-cultural Piagetian work is on conservation, and thus the supposed transition to concrete operations. Formal operations are much more problematic, and have scarcely been studied cross-culturally in any direct way.

Given that Piaget's is a stage theory, one may properly ask whether the same qualitative sequence of development appears in all cultures. It was noted above that the Parisian (and Genevan) detail and sequence of sensorimotor sub-stages was found to be precisely paralleled in a study of infants in the Ivory Coast. Cross-cultural Piagetian studies of infant development are actually still as scarce as studies of formal operations; and longitudinal studies following the same children over many years in non-Western cultures are also virtually non-existent. However the sensorimotor parallels observed are so remarkably exact, even with objects totally unfamiliar to African babies, as to inspire confidence in a necessarily tentative conclusion that the same broad sequence is followed everywhere as far as the transition to fully operational thought. But for this transition—or at any rate for the much-studied conservation concepts which are supposed to be symptomatic of the transition—the picture is so confused that it would hardly be profitable to take space here to analyse it in detail. The reader is referred to Dasen (1972, 1973, 1977a,b). Suffice it to say here that the Genevan sequence (*décalage*) of conservation concepts—such as quantity→weight→volume—appears to vary cross-culturally, but the variation is not obviously systematic. Non-Western children who go to school, however, do seem to come closer to the Genevan pattern of *décalage*. Further, there are a few puzzling instances of apparent 'regression' in development or of 'pseudo-conservation'. It also seems possible, on the face of it, that some individuals in some cultures do not complete the Piagetian sequence of development at all (I shall take up this matter in the next section of this paper). This cross-cultural research is obviously of great importance in the long run; and in that long run not only will longitudinal studies have to be conducted but also the more immediately feasible task of analysing the sequence of conservation concepts for each child individually (which has often not been done) will have to be addressed. Piaget's general theory attempts no real explanation of *décalages*, and thus is not especially perturbed by these cross-cultural findings. Piaget himself (1977) finds them of great interest; and holds to the logical impossibility of a general theory of *décalages*. At the same time he is at pains to point out (1) that cross-cultural replications of the broadly conceived developmental stages would seem to rule out a thorough-going environmentalist account of child learning, and (2) that the *décalage* differences are difficult to explain by a theory of innate preformation. Thus one would be left with his own type of theory: of self-organisation and epigenesis. It remains, however, for present purposes, that with the acquisition of conservation and the move to operational thinking we can no longer discern neat cross-cultural parallels in ontogeny.

A glance at the cross-cultural application of intelligence tests may also be worthwhile in this context. In line with my earlier insistence that one requires a great deal of commonality to find a difference, it is necessary to acknowledge that the very fact that psychological tests can be used at all in non-Western cultures is itself a huge endorsement of the commonality of those processes—cognitive, perceptual and linguistic—that are required in taking the tests. Standardised psychometric tests of intelligence and ability are currently in almost total disrepute among cross-cultural researchers. In the past, out-rageous conclusions have been drawn from the facile administration of intelligence tests to non-Western groups. Cross-cultural psychometricians are, these days, much more careful (e.g. Irvine, 1969; Vernon, 1969); but they are also scarce outside the 'applied' field of educational and occupational selection in third-world countries. Even so, one occasionally sees findings which reinforce the point I have been emphasising above, of a remarkable but unremarked commonality across cultures. Moreigne and Senecal (1962) and Massé (1969) tested Senegalese children aged three to six with a slightly modified version of the Stanford-Binet (Terman-Merrill) test. I.Q. values were below the American average, as one might reasonably expect for various reasons, including the purely methodological. But the correlations of I.Q. from year to year compare nicely in size with American Terman-Merrill data for these ages and show the entirely usual trend of an increasing correlation with age and a decreasing one as the interval between testings is lengthened. Thus, measured intelligence in Senegal shows the same stability over this age range as in the United States. Further, there is a slight superiority of girls over boys at this early age which is precisely replicated in the Senegalese sample. I suggest that these commonalities, which are independent of mean level of intelligence quotient, are far more substantial than putative differences in mean level across cultures.

Universality and Difference

I hope I have been making clear that the issue is only very superficially one of commonality versus difference: it is ultimately one of commonality and difference. Differences are discernible only against a ground of commonality; they are likely to be variations on a common theme; and they must ultimately be predictable or intelligible by means of a general and universal set of theoretical principles. To quote Rosch (1977) again:

'In so far as psychology is to be a science whose statements are of some interest and some beauty, it must attempt to formulate principles of the mental and behavioural functions of humans which are general and universal. That is not to say that theory must focus only on the ways in which humans are the same; rather, the universality of theory comes from its ability to encompass and predict differences as well as universals in human thought and behaviour' (p. 1).

To return briefly to the elegant example of colour, cultures *differ* in the number of basic terms they have available for naming the *universal* eleven colour foci, which can be scaled into a single *common* sequence. Such, at any rate, is our understanding at the time of writing.

There is an old Western idea of a Primitive Mentality or Savage Mind, which supposedly holds that the thought and consciousness of 'primitives' is essentially different from our own (we seem virtually to be condemned by our very consideration of the issue to reside in the non-primitive camp, whether we like it or not, though see Price-Williams (1975) for a fine new twist to this). The notion of a Primitive Mentality is repeatedly repudiated in these egalitarian and culturally relativist times; but it dies an astonishingly hard death. In fact it keeps arising in muted form, even, as we shall see, from premises of universality, and is clearly not to be put to rest by fiat.

Although the general idea is certainly much older, the first scholarly characterisation and analysis of Primitive Mentality was by Lucien Lévy-Bruhl, a philosopher—sociologist who compiled several volumes (1910, 1922, 1927, 1931, 1935) on the matter in the first decades of this century. Lévy-Bruhl, of course, did not set foot outside Europe, and like other contemporary analysts of primitive culture—Frazer, Durkheim, Freud—worked from the reports of others. His contentions were taken seriously and criticised by Durkheim, by Malinowski, and by Evans-Pritchard, and to some extent he responded to their criticisms. Evans-Pritchard in particular, despite his criticisms, was sympathetic to and stimulated by Lévy-Bruhl; and one may reasonably view his major works (Evans-Pritchard, 1937, 1956) as responses to questions posed by Lévy-Bruhl. Recent years have seen a definite revival of scholarly interest in the writings of Lévy-Bruhl and in the concept of Primitive Mentality: for example, articles by Horton (1967, 1973a, 1973b), the volume *Modes of Thought* edited by Horton and Finnegan (1973), Skorupski (1976), and a number of recent articles on Primitive Mentality in the journal *Man*. Rodney Needham (Evans-Pritchard's successor in the Oxford chair), as one of a panel of intelligentsia requested by the *Times Literary Supplement* to nominate for their Christmas 1976 issue the most unjustly neglected books of the century, gave one of Lévy-Bruhl's books as his choice.

Lévy-Bruhl referred Primitive Mentality to primitive culture (*représentations collectives*), not to primitive neurology. He firmly rejected earlier suggestions that primitive thought is a rudimentary or perfunctory version of that of educated Westerners. He emphasised that, for primitives, emotion is inextricably fused with perception and thought, thus entailing a 'mystical' view of reality: persons and things, spirits and objects 'participate' one in another to the point of virtual identity. 'Participation' takes precedence over logical contradictions, for a thing may be itself and at once something else; this aspect Lévy-Bruhl termed 'pre-logical' mentality. A person 'participates' in his world, and all objects in that world are imbued with a personal or spiritual quality. Lévy-Bruhl's conception did not lend itself to easy explication in the first place, and inevitably loses cogency in summary form: it is best understood from its constant repetition, development and exemplification in his own works.

Despite his unfortunate use of the term 'pre-logical', Lévy-Bruhl viewed Primitive Mentality as completely discontinuous with and opposed to 'modern' thought. Durkheim (1913) accepted Lévy-Bruhl's characterisation of Primitive Mentality, but insisted rather on an evolutionary continuity between the primitive and the modern (cf. the analysis and comparison of Lévy-Bruhl and Durkheim by Horton, 1973b). The American anthropologist Boas (1911, 1935) is also sometimes cited today as having put Lévy-Bruhl in his place. True, Boas successfully demolished the 'race' concept as an explanation of cultural differences; but this was by no means Lévy-Bruhl's thesis in any case. And true, Boas was at pains to argue, in part from his own first-hand experience of American Indians, that minds are everywhere fundamentally the same, only their contents differ by culture. However, Webb (1977) has looked again at Boas' writings, and finds certain equivocations: for example, Boas says that man everywhere is rational, but elsewhere that there are different criteria for rationality; and in another place that Western man has developed his rationality beyond that of primitive man.

Even Lévy-Bruhl himself eventually equivocated. He became sensitive to criticism from those who had conducted fieldwork and attested that primitive man is most of the time intelligibly using his commonsense, not engaged in mystical participation. In his last book (Lévy-Bruhl, 1938) and in his posthumously published notebooks (Lévy-Bruhl, 1949), Lévy-Bruhl withdrew his term 'pre-logical' and accepted that primitives use ordinary commonsense and only at times veer on to the mystical plane. Some have judged that he retracted his earlier position, and certainly he modified it. It is as if both Lévy-Bruhl and Boas were drawn to equivocate somewhat between the two sides of the same coin of commonality and difference because they could not take it as a single coin.

Influential recent discussions of this same issue, most of which set out with some charity so as not readily to raise *us* above *them*, come to draw a distinction nonetheless. Of course, if some distinction were not drawn, there would be no issue to discuss; and most writers are at pains also to stress the adequacy of 'primitive thought and the primitiveness of much Western thought. Let me mention, however, some of the distinctions only. Lévi-Strauss (1966) finds primitive thought restricted to tangible attributes in categorisation and to the form of creative thinking he calls *bricolage*. Horton (1967) finds traditional cultures 'closed' in the sense that they have developed awareness of alternatives to their basic beliefs. Gellner (1973) lists four distinguishing features of the Savage Mind. Hallpike (1976) we shall come to later.

Approaches from developmental psychology splay this issue along two dimensions, those of age and culture. And again difference is thought to arise out of universality: now, it is the developmental sequence which is universal, as emphasised earlier; but the rate and extent of developmental progression which may differ by culture, to be taken up here. Werner (1940) characterised both children's and primitives' thinking as lacking abstract and differentiated modes of thought. The Russian psychologist Luria was involved in a research expedition to remote villages in Soviet Central Asia in 1931–2, some details and conclusions of which have recently been published in English (Luria, 1971, 1976). Luria's account purports to show how new forms of work organisation and short literacy courses transformed the consciousness of the villagers to a higher level of mentality, including a move from the concrete and situational to more abstract, analytic and generalising thought processes.

Both Werner and Luria refer to Lévy-Bruhl, and their accounts of the less developed forms of consciousness contain such strong echoes of his account of Primitive Mentality as to seem to be influenced by it. More recent cross-cultural studies have led their prime mover, Bruner (Bruner *et al.*, 1966; Greenfield and Bruner, 1969) to conclude that cognitive development in some cultures may be adequate for concrete tasks but not for matters involving abstract conception:

'... some environments "push" cognitive growth better, earlier and longer than others. What does not seem to happen is that different cultures produce completely divergent and unrelated modes of thought .... (Our biological) heritage makes it possible for man to reach a form of intellectual maturity that is capable of elaborating a highly technical society. Less demanding societies—less demanding intellectually—do not produce so much symbolic embedding and elaboration of first ways of looking and thinking' (Greenfield and Bruner, 1969, p. 654)

There is thus something of a consensus: we are abstract, they concrete thinkers; and this because we have been carried further along a common developmental course. The hubris of this stance is of course too much for many to bear; and it is firmly opposed, most notably by Cole (e.g. Cole and Scribner, 1974). Even Bruner may be thought to have tempered the position cited above (see Cole and Bruner, 1971). But Piaget can be counted as within the consensus: he has suggested more than once that in some cultures adult thinking may not proceed beyond the level of concrete operations (Inhelder and Piaget, 1958; Piaget, 1966, 1971). In referring above to cross-cultural Piagetian research, I attended only to the striking commonality of qualitative and sequential aspects. It was necessary to do so because commonality is so often obsured, and because it is in any case the primary feature. It is time now to turn to the issues of developmental rate and the completion of the sequence.

In doing so I shall again not dredge the literature: one necessarily relies on Dasen's (1972, 1973, 1977a,b) surveys. It is clear that non-Western infants do not seem to lag in development behind Western infants: they may do so, perhaps, if they are severely malnourished, but otherwise there are some indications of even an early precocity, as mentioned earlier. The real interest, however, is as usual in the acquisition of conservation and the transition to fully operational thinking. Early views of cross-cultural comparisons in conservation were greatly influenced by Price-Williams' (1961) study of Tiv children in Nigeria. Price-Williams found unschooled Tiv children achieving the conservation concepts at something like the Genevan ages; and a very few other studies have reported similar findings. It is now clear, however, that these few studies are exceptions. It can be seen from Dasen's tabulations that non-Western samples typically show a marked 'lag' in the development of conservation. Whatever this may mean, the fact of it is now inescapable.

The interpretation of the observed lag is the subject of controversy. This is not primarily a controversy about Piaget's theory, which in its pure form has no concern with developmental rate or with the age at which developmental milestones are found. Piaget himself (1966) has accepted a certain lag as consistent with his theory; but this particular article of Piaget's— unfortunately the only one in which he has addressed himself directly to the cross-cultural issues—sorts oddly with his other theoretical writing. It can be argued that systematic variation in developmental rate by culture bears at least indirectly on a central aspect of Piaget's theoretical model: cultural differences may imply more environmental influence on development than a conception of biological epigenesis can allow. If so, a basic revision of Piaget's theory would be in order; and Piaget (1966) can be read as making room for such a revision. Piaget (1977), however, returns to an emphasis on the qualitative generality of cognitive development as a particular case of biological epigenesis, with leeway for fluctuations which depend on environmental differences. This theoretical problem will obviously not be an easy one to resolve. It has recently been further complicated by Kamara and Easley's (1977) detailed methodological critique of cross-cultural studies of conservation.

Slowness of development would actually have little practical importance if the sequence were eventually completed. But this may not be the case for all cultures. We actually do not know from good evidence whether all or most people in the West come to employ fully formal operational thought. Piaget (1972) appears to think they do, but has increased the upper age of attainment from 15 to 20. Even with the extension, it would not be very surprising were Piaget's view to turn out to be over-optimistic. The cross-cultural issue, however, has arisen even over the lower stage of concrete operations. A fair number of non-Western samples—some including adolescents and adults— do not approach 100 per cent success in conservation tasks or other supposed indices of concrete operations. The most striking examples seem to be from aboriginal Australian and Papua New Guinean cultures. This ought to mean, in Piagetian terms, that operational thinking has not been fully attained by many members of certain cultures; and Piaget's suggestions that adult thinking in some cultures may be restricted to concrete operations therefore begin to seem plausible, given that the findings themselves are acceptable. Not even Piaget had supposed that there are cultures based on less than operational intelligence.

Cole and Scribner (1974), however, consider the findings unacceptable in themselves. Curiously, this is not because of the methodological deficiencies of the studies, certain of which are open to criticism if invidiously so. Rather, Cole and Scribner (1974) are flatly unable to believe the findings: 'Can we imagine an adult who would pour water from a small bucket into a larger one and believe that the amount of water has been decreased by this act? In desert communities where water is a treasured commodity, everyone can be expected to conform to certain laws of conservation' (pp. 151–2). This rationalist construction of what must be the case is a little odd within a book which continually points to the necessity to prefer empirical evidence to such rationalist construction. One is reminded that when Piaget's research first became widely known there were those who could not believe that children below a certain age are unable to conserve. Dasen (1977a) points out that De Lemos (1969) describes a practical situation in which adult aboriginal women in central Australia were given the choice between one measure of sugar poured into a tall and narrow container and two measures poured into a larger one: two-thirds of the women chose the measure with less sugar but a higher level. It does not seem to me obvious beyond all doubt that the logical ability to conserve is necessary for survival. A certain practical ability to judge quantity probably is, for adults; and as Cole and Scribner among others have shown, this ability seems to be extremely well developed in some non-Western people, given familiar substances and containers. One may in principle be a good judge of quantity without a sedimented logic of the conservation of quantity. Or, to put it the other way round, the most highly educated and logically minded Westerner may easily be a very poor judge of quantity.

There are other possibilities. One is that the people in question fully understand the logic of conservation in other situations, but cannot display it on the Piagetian task, which asks of them something awkward and unfamiliar. This seems not implausible, but it makes a mare's nest of the cross-cultural findings. More than that, it calls into question the whole relation of Piagetian evidence to Piagetian theory. Given that Western developmental research has of late been tending to similar conclusions, this may not be a bad thing; but it does set the Piagetian enterprise, on whose ground the research became conceivable in the first place, into a peculiar and uncertain position. The immediate problem here is that manifest conservation responses on the Genevan tasks may not after all be especially symptomatic of concrete operational thought. Heron (1974) has even proposed 'a *clear separation* of conservation from other cognitive behaviours'; Dasen (1977a) has argued that a grasp of the logic of conservation is a cognitive competence which can be studied only through a particular performance, and the particularities of performance are likely to be partly culture-bound. Heron and Simonsson (1969) have coined the expression 'cognitive ambience' to refer to cultural differences in the *Lebenswelt* of the child: they mean by this the mundane and implicit assumptions of the culture (which in fact constitute 'culture') about what is and is not important in life. It is Heron and Simonsson's impression that Zambian culture brings little precision to questions of quantity or identity. Aboriginal Australian and Papua New Guinean cultures, from which most of the reports of adult non-conservers emanate, may give even less precision to such issues. For instance, Dasen (1974) mentions that the

Australian languages of his subjects lacked a system of abstract number terms. This is also generally the case for Papua New Guinean languages, which use body-part mnemonics for any number beyond a few if counting is thought necessary. The languages of the New Guinea Highlands also lack comparatives: in them, one cannot literally say that something is 'bigger' or 'more'.

There are two problems with this kind of argument, both major. One is that psychologists, at least, have no articulated way of characterising 'culture'. We are reliant on Heron and Simonsson's impressions, or on very tentative inferences from linguistic facts. There is something odd—ironic, even—about the way psychologists take and analyse precise measurements from cognitive tasks and then seek to explain these measurements by recourse to a casual and impressionistic notion of 'culture'. It is not only Piagetian research that suffers in this way: for instance, Berry's (1976) studies of ecology, culture and cognition manifest the same disparity. And not only cross-cultural research, much of the Western study of 'cultural deprivation' in 'disadvantaged' children has the same feature: precise measurement and statistical analysis of data from cognitive tasks, tendentious impressions of 'culture'. Cole (Cole *et al.*, 1971; Cole, 1975) is to be admired for his efforts to develop an 'ethnography of cognition' for the detailed study of practical reason. His example has yet to be widely followed, however. And it remains unclear to me how Cole's ethnography, important and useful though it obviously must be in practice, is to be theoretically articulated with the results of more controlled studies of cognitive processes.

The second problem concerns us more directly here. It is that cultural differences in 'cognitive ambience' and the like may just as plausibly be argued to affect the development of competence as to affect performance. Heron (1974), Cole and Bruner (1971), and latterly Dasen (1977a) seem to have decided that it is performance differences that are to be explained by reference to cultural background. If, however, there are ontogenetic stages, each representing a different level and type of competence, then precisely the same arguments concerning the effect of culture may always be proposed with respect to cognitive competence. Take the example of the lack of numerical and comparative reference in Australian and New Guinean languages, mentioned above; and suppose that members of these cultures, prior to Westernisation, do not habitually engage in counting or in comparisons. True, the Piagetian tasks (performance) will be awkward and perhaps unsuitable for them. But it also seems very reasonable to suppose that they will not as children develop the cognitive competence for conservation as readily as Western schoolchildren. Conservation of number normally appears first in the Genevan *décalage*, and an intuitive grasp of quantity and of identity and difference is presupposed by all the conservation concepts. Conservation of number may also be discovered and validated by counting (the other conservation concepts can be checked by ordinary experience only if, paradoxically, one is already a conserver); but of course, not if one is not used to counting and comparison and can scarcely talk about them. So that the Australian and New Guinean child in his traditional culture may not benefit from the head start that number conservation gives to concrete operations. Westerners, including Piaget, may simply take for granted their cultural practices of counting and comparison, as Heron and Simonsson (1969) and Heron (1974) imply; the fact that they comprise part of our 'cognitive ambience' may well hasten the operational development of our own children but blind us to the effect of cultural differences in such mundane practices on the development of cognitive competence. I do not see how this argument can be restricted to performance alone. And since the above arguments are concerned with the transition to the lower level of operational thought, it still seems to be an open possibility that in some traditional cultures adults operate only at the concrete level.

Nor is it so very far-fetched to believe that *all* cultures were at the concrete level at best not so long ago in human history—two or three thousand years, at most, anywhere. The cultural evolution of the relevant institutions of human 'civilisations' is, in these terms, very recent. What is meant by 'Westernisation' or 'modernisation' is also a form of cultural evolution; and though the independent variables are much too gross for comfort, we have some indications of the effects on cognitive development, as summarised by Dasen (1972). European contact and the consequent acculturation improves operational development, or at least the relevant performance on con-servation tasks. So does urbanisation. Schooling of the Western type appears to make a striking difference in some cases but not in others, a curiosity to which I shall return later. These 'modernising' variables are generally compounded together in any case, and are difficult to isolate one from another. They also cry out for 'unpacking', so that we may know what they actually mean in terms of the organisation of children's knowledge and experience. I shall accordingly concentrate attention below on one variable, that of literacy, which is coming to be of major interest to developmental and cross-cultural researchers.

Before passing on, let me glance again at developmental studies using standardised tests in non-Western cultures, suspect though they may be. These also show a 'lag'. As age is built into their metrics, however, the lag takes the form of a systematically increasing psychometric deficit with age from early childhood onwards. The Senegalese study mentioned above to illustrate commonality (Moreigne and Senegal, 1962; Massé, 1969), for instance, is just like the Piagetian studies in that taken in another perspective it illustrates difference: mean Senegalese I.Q. was 95 at age 3, 93 at age 4, 88 at age 5, 87 at age 6. In this field there is actually a painstaking longitudinal study (Holtzman et al., 1975) which compares large numbers of children in Mexico City and Austin, Texas, over twelve grades of schooling. Within very complex findings a trend emerges: in the early grades there were similar levels of cognitive ability in the two groups, but with increasing age the Mexican children—schooled, literate and urban in this case—steadily fell behind.

Primitive Mentality, Ontogeny and Literacy

The first article by an anthropologist which takes Piaget and developmental psychology seriously in consideration of the issue of Primitive Mentality is Hallpike's (1976) 'Is there a Primitive Mentality?'. Hallpike chastises his fellow anthropologists—in my view, quite rightly—for their neglect of developmental psychology. (Social anthropology, at least in Britain, has long been hostile to any but commonsense versions of psychological approaches and explanations.) However, as is liable to happen to those who enthusiastically draw on disciplines other than their own, Hallpike to some extent falls foul of theoretical differences among psychologists. I believe he over-states the causal role granted to the social environment by Piaget's theory of ontogeny; but as we have seen, it is on just this point that Piaget's theory may require revision, in the direction favourable to Hallpike's interpretation. He also seems unaware that the differences between Piaget's and Bruner's approaches to cognitive development (which he treats as more or less reinforcing each other) have been and remain a matter of sharp controversy: in particular, Piaget does not grant a major causal role in cognitive growth to language and literacy; Bruner of course does; and so does Hallpike.[1]

Hallpike wishes to explain cultural differences in mentality with reference to developmental differences. He holds that 'primitive' thought and the thinking of members of 'modern' societies reflect the different developmental levels at which cognitive growth may stabilise in a culture; this point is consonant both with Piaget's position and that of Bruner in the 1960s. He further identifies formal schooling and particularly literacy as a crucial influence on cognitive growth, which takes him into some good company, as we shall see, but, strictly speaking, cuts him off from orthodox Piagetians. Hallpike (1976) finds it astonishing:

'that anthropologists, and for that matter philosophers, trying to explain the difference between European and primitive thought, have not considered the obvious point that people who go to school for a number of years and acquire literacy and numeracy, are likely to think in rather different ways from those who have never had this experience' (p. 263)

Can it really be so simple? Are the great debates over Primitive Mentality, which have so often been finessed by anthropologists as concerning 'religion' rather than 'thought', to be resolved in as straightforward a manner as Hallpike suggests? Certainly the question needs to be asked.

I have already mentioned several psychologists whose views and findings sort well with Hallpike's position. The research expedition to Soviet Uzbekistan recently reported by Luria (1971, 1976) was planned in association with Vygotsky, who was too ill to make the journey and died not long afterwards. The Soviet school of cognitive psychology, stemming originally from Parlov, has always maintained that human psychological activity is transformed by processes of verbal mediation; and Vygotsky (1961) emphasised that the acquisition of literacy effects a further transformation. Although they do not enable us to sort out the precise effects of literacy itself, it is good that, long after Vygotsky's death, we have Luria's extensive documentation of the changes in consciousness—and in *self*-consciousness—that appeared to result from collectivisation and crash courses in literacy in those remote Asian villages. It is also worth noting, in anticipation of an argument to be developed later, that the changes are characterised as 'developmental' both in the individual-ontogenetic and in the cultural-historical sense, each partaking of the other.

In our own time, Bruner (1966) and Scribner and Cole (1973) have honoured the Soviet psychologists in arguing that literacy and formal schooling are among the important cultural forces that can produce a sharp difference in cognitive growth. Scribner and Cole observe that the unschooled take each problem singly and afresh, and do not transfer a rule for solution; the schooled, on the other hand, seek a general rule which is transferable from one problem to another. The schooled become prepared to use language to describe the principles of what they are doing; the unschooled may say no more than 'my sense told me'. In formal education, language is almost exclusively the means of communication, and what is being taught, rather than who is doing the teaching, becomes paramount. Schooling, as Bruner emphasises, is 'learning out of context' and is also 'deutero-learning', i.e. learning to learn. Concepts are learned 'downwards' at school, so that one goes from superordinates to particular instances. Informal learning is usually quite different, starting (and sometimes finishing) with concrete particulars.

The evidence for these distinctions is, as Scribner and Cole emphasise, not as extensive as one would prefer; but their case is a persuasive one. These authors believe that most current suppositions rather romantically over-estimate the continuity between formal and informal education; and in stressing that school experience largely runs counter to everyday life experience they embrace a thesis of discontinuity. Their bias is suitably corrective, and is no doubt appropriate for a traditionally non-literate culture such as the Kpelle of Liberia, among whom Cole and Scribner have conducted much of their research. It is strikingly appropriate for cultures such as are found in the New Guinea Highlands, not far from the Stone Age, where cultural continuities which may have lasted for thousands of years are suddenly broken when the first generation of children turn up nervously at the new primary school. Scribner and Cole's generalisations may need to be tempered, however, to allow for variation in culture as well as variation in the schooling of individuals. It will be recalled that there is actually an oddity concerning the effects of schooling on operational development: schooling makes a marked difference in some cultures but not in others. In resolution of this anomaly, it makes some sense to suppose that schooling makes a difference when it is a major source of cultural stimulation of a novel, 'modern' kind for a basically non-literate culture. Otherwise, as in Hong Kong (Goodnow, 1962, Goodnow and Bethon, 1966), schooling is not necessarily a primary lever of cognitive growth. If correct, this supposition will also apply to Western societies (cf. Mermelstein and Shulman, 1967, who found no real effects of lack of schooling in the US): thus the 'deschooling' of society (Illich, 1971) can seem plausible to some, Western culture having been brought—probably in large part by the institution of universal schooling, not so long ago—to a general level of stimulation of its young which ironically lessens the direct differential effect of formal schooling on cognitive growth.

To turn round on literacy and inspect its workings is—for us literates—an element of the reflexive movement of 'modernism' by which mentality discovers and examines its own media. Bertrand Russell once said that until he was in his forties he had taken language as entirely transparent, a medium only. Russell was to live on not only through the heyday of linguistic philosophy but into the time of Marshall McLuhan's fame. Now that literacy has ceased to be to social scientists as water to the fish, we have seen a recent quickening of interest in its study. Hallpike's professed astonishment that anthropologists have not seen the importance of literacy is that of one who states the obvious when the obvious has only just become visible, under our very noses.

The obvious is more readily visible by contrast, in this case with 'nonliteracy'. It is therefore understandable that within social science it is an anthropologist, Goody, who has done most to stimulate interest in literacy (Goody and Watt, 1963; Goody, 1968, 1977). Even Goody seems to have been helped to see the obvious by long acquaintance with cultures of Northern Ghana over a period during which formal schooling and literacy were gradually being introduced. Goody is careful not to endorse any simple dichotomy between wild and domesticated minds: 'modern man', he points out, is emerging every day in contemporary Africa, seemingly without a total transformation of thought. Yet at the same time, Goody will not fall into that empty form of cultural relativism which holds that the thinking of all societies is essentially the same. He concentrates on 'the mechanics of communicative acts', in the context of cultural evolution. The media of communication—literate and numerate techniques—partly transform the content of messages and even mentality itself. We are reminded that the first great civilisation of the world had, in the ancient Greek alphabet, the first comprehensibly phonetic and easily learnable system for the transcription of speech. The idea of 'history', stemming from a sense of the past dependent on annals and records, probably arose in classical Greece; as certainly did the idea of 'logic' as an impersonal mode of reason.

Goody's evolutionary perspective leads him to emphasise the variety and detail of the changes brought about by literacy: historically, there cannot have been any sudden transformation, either of cultures or of mentalities. Lévy-Bruhl, however, was also a cultural evolutionist who did not, as it happens, concern himself with the processes of evolutionary change. If Goody were to draw only the analytical distinction, he would be (and from time to time is) found speaking of different mentalities. Lévy-Bruhl's thesis in fact finds new ground in Goody and Watt's (1963) account:

> ' . . . there may . . . exist general differences between literate and non-literate societies somewhat along the lines suggested by Lévy-Bruhl. One reason for their existence . . . may be . . . that writing establishes a different kind of relationship between the word and its referent, a relationship that is more general and more abstract, and less closely connected with the particularities of person, place and time, than obtains in oral communication' (p. 331).

To this characterisation, Goody (1977) adds further emphases, among them that of 'following a formula'. Although he develops the idea of 'formula' beyond that of Ong, Goody's quotation from Ong deserves repetition: 'Lengthy verbal performances in oral cultures are never analytic but formulaic. Until writing, most of the kind of thoughts we are used to thinking today simply could not be thought' (Ong, 1971, p. 2).

Similar ideas are pervasive in recent discussions. A literate society stresses telling out of context rather than showing in context, so that learning becomes an art in itself (Bruner, 1965). Reading and writing foster context-independent speech and thought; and linguistic contexts can be manipulated, transmuted and juxtaposed far more readily than real ones (Greenfield and Bruner, 1966). The utterances of an oral language are one symbolising step removed from concrete reality; the texts and the speech of a written language are likely to be two steps removed, and that greater independence of distance makes for generalisation and abstraction (Greenfield, 1972). Greenfield also takes the consequences of the difference between oral and written language/ speech to characterise social class differences in the USA in maternal teaching styles (Hess and Shipman, 1965) and in linguistic codes as characterised by Bernstein (1961). Olson (1975) extends the argument, utterance is to text as commonsense is to theoretical knowledge:

> ' . . . writing turns utterances as descriptions into propositions with implications. Sentences may be treated in either way; and while our children treat them as descriptions of events, our adults treat them as logical propositions. This jump is fundamental to development in a

literature culture but it is achieved, I suggest, primarily through the reflection on statements made possible by writing systems' (p. 369).

Cogent though the arguments may be, these matters are not easy to study in systematic fashion. For one thing, the very large majority in a Western society—above a certain age—is literate, and the few illiterates may be atypical in many other ways also. Many non-Western countries, however, contain as yet a high proportion who are not literate; and it therefore falls to cross-cultural psychology to tease out the cognitive consequences of literacy. The problem there is that usually literacy is compounded with other influences: urbanisation, modernisation and whatever effects formal education may have on children over and above teaching literacy. It is therefore difficult precisely to single out the cognitive effects of literacy from those of the modernising imbroglio which renders literates different from illiterates in a range of correlated respects.

Nonetheless, the professional concern with research design which psychologists bring to anthropological studies is already producing some refinements. Cross-culturally, Cole and Scribner have led the way. Extensive earlier research among the Kpelle of Liberia reported by Cole *et al.* (1971) found that the really large qualitative differences in performance on cognitive tasks resulted from literacy and Western-style education; in contrast, between younger and older non-literate Kpelle there were only small and negligible quantitative differences. A further Kpelle study by Scribner found various effects of schooling on classification and the explication of criteria for classification: in particular (and this is borne out by other studies), schooling seems to promote the search for a principle or rule, the awareness of possible alternative principles and the ability to explain one's own mental operations. Well aware that schooling provides more than literacy, and that psychological changes can occur without schooling, Cole and Scribner have more recently turned their attention to another Liberian tribe, the Vai, among whom literacy for one script is not compounded with other features of acculturation.

Vai is a Mande language spoken in northeast Liberia, and the Vai people rank among the few societies in the history of the world to have developed their own script. Vai culture is now multiliterate, for the international written languages of Arabic and English have found their way to Vai country. Vai literacy is not taught in schools, rather being learned from a friend or relative; so that one encounters here the truly rare phenomenon of literacy without education. We may speak of 'unschooled literates'. Scribner and Cole (1977) are at pains to point out, however, that literacy in Vai, whose most common use is in letter-writing, is not profound. In fact, Scribner and Cole found no marked differences between unschooled Vai literates and complete non-literates on logical and classificatory tasks. However, Vai literates were better than both non-literates and Arabic literates in explaining, out of context, a simple board game to another person. This kind of thing, i.e. communication of detail and sequence in an orderly manner without reliance on mutual perception, has frequently been observed to be painfully difficult for non-literates (e.g. Cole *et al.*, 1971); more difficult, in fact that educated moderns can easily credit. Vai literates tended to give a general characterisation of the game before going into rules of play and other details. Vai literates were also better than non-literates in verbal learning, though here Arabic literates (who do no more than learn the Koran by rote) were superior. These are only preliminary findings, pending the eventual full report (see also Scribner and Cole, 1978). One also wonders how Vai non-literates, partaking of a somewhat literate culture of long standing, may compare with historically non-literate tribes nearby.

Olson (1975; 1977) has approached the design problem in another way. Although considering the consequences of literacy in a somewhat broad cross-cultural and historical fashion, Olson has chosen to study the differences between Western—in this case, Canadian—children and adults in the drawing of implications from sentences. It is likely that the experiments can be transposed fruitfully to another cultural context in which literacy can be varied independently of age. The general conclusion of Olson's studies is that young children do not calculate the logical implications of propositions as many adults do, but rather take sentences as potential descriptions of events about which they have knowledge and expectations. When these modes conflict, children get their inferences wrong, or so it appears to adults. If it is the influence of literacy rather than ontogenetic change which transforms the analysis of implications, Olson expects non-literate adults to resemble Canadian children in their understanding of sentences, and he points to Kpelle evidence from Cole *et al.* (1971) which conforms to his expectations. Neither Cole and Scribner nor Olson, therefore, take cognitive epigenesis *per se* as the basis for differences in mentality, and thus are somewhat at variance with Piaget and Piagetians and with any epigenetic stage theory of development. Of the anthropologists, Goody barely considers child development, and uses the term 'developmental' to refer to cultural evolution. Hallpike (1976) both draws on Piagetian epigenesis and grants a critical causal role to literacy and schooling, but may not realise what a theoretical mix he has generated. None of these writers conceives of cultural development and individual ontogeny as analytically separate but in dialectical relation one to the other.

Culture as Institutionalised Operativity

It was suggested earlier that literacy and schooling may have different consequences for cognitive development in different cultures; but also that the cultural differences in question depend in large part on literacy and schooling. In case this seems madly paradoxical, let me stress that there is a twofold level of analysis involved: cultural difference, change or evolution on the one hand, and individual change or development on the other. A traditional oral culture is one whose children may be cognitively transformed by schooling, in comparison with the remaining unschooled children and adults. When, however, schooling is universally institutionalised and literacy widespread within a society, not only does speech in general tend towards the less context-dependent and more abstract forms of a written language, but the other social and technological changes of 'modernisation' tend to occur at the same time. Modernisation, whatever its prime movers and channels of diffusion, is an evolution of social, cultural, economic, psychological and linguistic dimensions all rolled into one immense transformation. Schooling is a critical change agent for a traditional society not only because of its cognitive consequences but because it breaks the cultural continuity between the generations, perhaps for the first time ever. Illiteracy and lack of schooling for an individual in a modern society will obviously have important social consequences for that person—he is, after all, a 'deviant'—but may no longer restrict his cognitive development in any fundamental way. For the modern world he lives in is itself a 'school' for this thought; operativity has been institutionalised in the external environment. I mean here something like, but more extensive yet than, the insistence of Inkeles and Smith (1974) that in the third-world process of 'becoming modern' the urban factory is a kind of 'school' for modernity. And perhaps something approaching the more profound semiological argument of Derrida (1976), who points out that 'writing' has a larger sense than that of the written word alone. Derrida would have us think of it as the entire intervention of human culture into nature, the human 'inscriptions' on the world which are our ways of life. To retain the Piagetian evocation, I shall speak of 'institutionalised operativity'.

As, in writing this, I look out from my window, virtually everything I can see has the mark of man's thought and intentions upon it. Not only the people themselves who come and go, and the occasional vehicle; also the buildings, road, and paths. The grass and flowers have been planted and tended, the trees have been planted or left in the landscape. Even the weeds may be taken as a sign of inefficient gardening or cuts in university expenditure. In this particular view, only the sky and its clouds, perhaps, will escape my interpretive hermeneutic of man's doings. For the most part, this hermeneutic operation is an easy mundane activity, sedimented in my perceptions and cognitions; but I can also push the mundane constructions further, by conscious reflection and by extending my knowledge of, say, architecture, engineering, horticulture and landscape design. An awareness of the rules of the local social contract also enlarges my vision: this car is illegally parked; that hump in the road is to slow down the vehicles, the man in the blue jacket is a porter.[2]

Institutionalised operativity confronts children in any man-made environment, *par excellence* in a modern city. The principles—and errors—in the thought, intentions and work of man are there to be inferred, written in the invitational mood in the concrete reality itself. They are also there to be asked and talked about, or the attention of children may be drawn to them by the explicit speech of literate adults. A modern environment is both complex and diverse, and will present contrasts and conflicts of understanding so as to provoke thought and explanation. 'Society', too,—social and economic organisation—is in part the work of man; and 'pluralisation' within it (cf. Berger *et al.*, 1974) offers similar contrasts as invitations to thought. Eventually, even the media of understanding themselves become objects of knowledge in a peculiarly Kantian but unphilosophical manner: perception, language, culture, thought itself. It is the scrutiny of literacy and mentality, after all, which has brought us to this point in our argument. The process is reflexive and dialectical, and may never end. Riegel (1973) considers that it extends beyond formal operations, developmentally.

It is necessary to think both of cultural development and child development, separately but in relation one to the other. Suppose, for instance, that one is obsessed only with individual ontogeny. One may note the common lag and the occasional arrest in cognitive development observed in non-literate cultures, and conclude that primitive children are first of all identical with Western children but that primitive adults may be no more developed intellectually than older Western children. It would be a seductive conclusion from that standpoint, but it would be a mistake. Few social scientists now make that mistake, though it used to be common. The current mistake seems to be a reaction against the hubris of that first mistake. It involves various degrees of derogation of the cross-cultural findings on cognitive development: either the findings are explained away as 'performance', leaving 'competence' unplumbed; or the findings are simply not believed; or the dimension of individual development is simply dropped from consideration. We now seem to have the odd situation in which cognitive psychologist Cole seems not to grant child development any meaningful systematicity, while anthropologist Hallpike rests his argument centrally on developmental psychology.

I have stressed the cultural level of institutionalised operativity in an attempt to put the comparison into proper perspective. Hallpike (1976) has part of the answer when, sticking to Piagetian concepts, he says that in primitive societies 'cognitive skills appropriate to the pre-operatory and concrete operations stages are selected for development to a very high degree of expertise' (p. 260). The complementary features of the cultural environments of those societies will be that their artefacts and techniques—the way they 'inscribe' culture on nature—will offer little or no built-in invitation to more complex or formal modes of thought. One may thus understand how a culture and the cognitive development of its members may 'stabilise' at certain levels, for the equilibrium involves each partaking of the other. The equilibrium, short of enslavement or colonisation, will not be easily broken. The refinement of skills based on concrete thought may easily surpass anything that Western children and Western adults are ordinarily capable of. This is unfortunately obscured by cross-cultural research, including all that in the Piagetian vein, which does no more than examine the supposedly critical indicators of developmental level. And it is of course doubly obscured by the cross-cultural use of standardised intelligence tests.

The most beautiful example is Trukese navigation (Gladwin, 1964, 1970). Truk is a small island in the Pacific. Gladwin and Sarason (1953) had commented on the strikingly concrete level of the thinking of the Trukese. Gladwin (1964) describes Trukese thought as a sort of *bricolage*, as relying on 'the cumulative product of the adding together of a great number of discrete bits of data, summed together in accordance with predetermined parameters, to arrive at a desired conclusion'. Gladwin is also of the opinion that the Trukese would perform poorly on even an appropriate intelligence test; and observed that they could not master the principles required to locate a fault in an internal combustion engine which they could take apart and reassemble almost blindfold.

The Trukese, however, are very great navigators. They voyage in small canoes over astonishing distances of open ocean, without instruments and without sight of land. Their destinations are tiny islands, invisible from the ocean surface unless one is very close, and so easily missed unless navigation by dead reckoning is perfectly accurate. Navigation is by stars and wind direction and wave pattern, on a dark and starless night, by the sound of the waves and the feel of the boat. The navigator can accomplish feats of steering involving long and complex tacking which on Western theoretical grounds are possible only with advanced navigational equipment, nowadays electronic. But the Trukese does it in his head, in an automatic routine. He survives, with no need to tell the tale.

As Gladwin describes the navigation, it combines the information of a large number of discrete observations, each concrete and factual. The navigator always knows where he is in relation to every island and reef within the limits of his total ocean world. Each move seems to be successively determined on an ad hoc basis. The Trukese cannot give a verbal account of all that he is doing, although he can always point to where his destination will be. The European navigator can typically give a logical account of what he is doing. But strip him of his technical aids, put him in the Trukese situation, and he would almost certainly perish. Put the Trukese in another ocean, and he too would probably perish. His knowledge is profound but contingent, and the contingencies would presumably differ.

Allow the European his techniques and instruments, however, and he could do the job. He uses deductive principles which are highly abstract and will thus serve him anywhere. This is not to say, nonetheless, that the European navigator himself necessarily has those abstract principles firmly sedimented in his own head. It is likely, in this case, that he understands them to some extent through his navigational training and by his experience of their use.

But he need not, as, more obviously, car drivers and computer users need not understand how their machines work. He too could be a concrete thinker vis-à-vis navigation, and vastly inferior as such to the Trukese. For formal operativity is built into his techniques and instruments, and he need only know how to use them, properly but mechanically. The literate and scientific culture which lies behind him has taken care of the formal thought: somebody has had to understand fully those abstract principles and their implementation in planning and monitoring navigation. This is institutionalised operativity.

Piaget (1971, pp. 116–117) criticises Lévi-Strauss for his assumption, in *The Savage Mind*, that the apparent 'logic' of social and cultural institutions in a given society gauges the logical level of its members' thought. Kinship systems and language structures, however complex, are the products of socio-cultural (and sometimes biological) evolution, over very long periods of time, not of the creative thought of individuals. They depend on institutions, and the sociological point is that their power surpasses the resources of individuals:

' . . . . . the real problem is to make out how the ensemble of these collective instruments is utilised in the every day reasoning of each individual. It may very well be that these instruments are of a level visibly superior to that of Western logic—Lévi-Strauss reminds us that there are plenty of natives who can "calculate" the implicit relations of a kinship system exactly. But the kinship systems are finished systems, already regulated, and of limited scope. What we want to know about is individual inventions' (Piaget, 1971, p. 117).

Beginnings have now been made, as if in accord with part of Piaget's advice, in studying the development in non-Western children of an understanding of kinship systems (Levine and Price-Williams, 1974; Price-Williams *et al.*, 1977; Greenfield and Childs, 1977) and of dreams (Shweder and Levine, 1976). A remarkable (if poorly documented) study by Kohlberg (1969) may approximate the extreme case in which culture not only arrests but may dissipate or even reverse the ontogenetic course of development. Kohlberg investigated the dream concept among the Atayal, a Formosan aboriginal people. He found that the dream concept develops in Atayal children exactly as in Genevan children studied by Piaget. That is, the child first of all conceives of dreams as real and coming from outside himself, but by middle childhood he has come to think of dreams as unreal and internally generated. However, he is subsequently introduced to the fundamental lore of the society: this is a 'dream culture', taking dreams as of great significance and viewing them as real and externally generated. Thus the child, in preparing to be an Atayal adult, has to learn what he has 'grown out of'. It seems possible that his conceptions of reality and causality are perturbed by this cultural learning, and Kohlberg reports that conservation responses become uncertain as Atayal are initiated into the dream culture. The report of this research is very sketchy, which is most unfortunate. For it relates not only to my present concern to distinguish the order of cultural institutions from the developmental level of individual cognition, but it could also provide a rare and dramatic test of the aspect of Piagetian theory which we have already found problematic, that of the role of cultural 'learning' as opposed to individual 'development'.

Schweder and Levine (1976) present more detail in their study of dream concepts of Hausa children in Northern Nigeria. They take issue with Kohlberg's cognitive-developmental account of invariant sequence in the child's understanding of the dream concept. Their evidence shows alternative sequences by which Hausa children change their comprehension of dream-events. This is logically impossible according to Kohlberg's theory, by which a single sequence is logically entailed. Schweder and Levine therefore take theoretical issue with Kohlberg's—and, implicitly, Piaget's—stress on 'logic' in the temporal sequencing of development. They argue that the 'rationality' involved is not that of logic: children 'change their minds' according to the 'good reasons' for application of one form of understanding rather than another and according to the 'good reasons' for recognising particular evidence as relevant. It is the content and meaning of perception and thought which is important, not its supposed 'logic'. In support of their argument, Schweder and Levine draw on Wason and Johnson-Laird's (1972) work: these authors showed how ready their British subjects are to leave the logical requirements of intellectual tasks behind, and concluded that the rationality of everyday reasoning cannot be satisfactorily characterised by logic. Toulmin's (1971, 1972) account of 'rationality' similarly moves away from logic and formal coherence to the criteria for relevance, contexts and forms of understanding.

The point of Piaget's comments on Lévi-Strauss, quoted above, should not be restricted to primitive or traditional cultures. Western society too has evolved its ensemble of collective instruments and creations, forms of institutionalised operativity. Do they gauge the logical level of its members' thought? The suspicion is plausible that most of the thought of individuals in modern society, most of the time, is not particularly abstract or principled or logical. As with the example of modern navigation, this can be so even if a certain human enterprise incorporates formal principles into its totality by means of the techniques utilised. Other examples are hybrid: one may skilfully drive a car with no understanding of the principles of the internal combustion engine. But still, what kind of thinking is involved in negotiating one's way within a mass of traffic? Is it not far more like Trukese navigational thought than the formal operations of the scientific intellect? Perhaps we should look in wonder on our own car-driving skills, as did George Kelly (1955): 'the orderly, extremely complex, and precise weaving of traffic is really an amazing example of people predicting each other's behaviour through subsuming each other's perception of a situation' (p. 95). Kelly refers to only part of the cognitive achievement; but clearly such a collective endeavour is mostly an integration of individual calibrations, and whatever it is, it does not appear to be formalised thought.

Are we, then, more like the Trukese than we had assumed, in ways and domains that we tend to take for granted? Is this another equivalent of water to the fish? I am inclined to believe so. Only in this case it is not just the mundane character of our thinking which conceals from us its obvious quality. It is also the positivist stance of our century, which seems to have tempted everyone from Lévy-Bruhl to Piaget to characterise the highest level of thinking as very like the formal, logical model of scientific rationality. For one thing, 'scientific rationality' may not conform in practice to its latter-day formal model, as Polanyi (1958) and Feyerabend (1975) have argued. But for another, it is simply inappropriate to apply formal thought and abstract principles to many human enterprises which, nonetheless, may be approached with fine and orderly judgement. Two readily visible examples which come to mind are legal reasoning and the sensibilities of good comedians. Legal thinking, which combines the evaluative and the factual, the application of rules and of commonsense, all with a certain order and according to their appropriateness (cf. Levi, 1949; Dibble, 1973) is so impressive that it has been proposed as an alternative model of scientific enquiry (Levine, 1974). But it is not easily recognisable as formal thought. Nor is the genius of a comedian, which I despair of being able to characterise adequately. Both these forms of human judgement and sensibility, however, are admirable and high-level uses of essentially cognitive rather than affective or motivational faculties.

I do not mean to imply that the lawyer and the comedian, any more than the navigators of Truk and the Murngin (those Australians who operate the most impossibly complex kinship system), represent the highest forms of human thought and knowledge. I mean only to dethrone the ideal model of formal scientific or mathematical thought. I believe it is no accident that Piaget is so interested in logic and in mathematics and seems to consider them the ultimate flower of intellectual and biological evolution: for his theory has it that children are, as it were, steadily moving towards this end-product. It is not an utter mistake; for there is such thought, and the capacity for it develops. But it is a mistake of narrow emphasis; for there are other forms of rationality, which must also develop, and could also be emphasised, both by psychological theory and by cultural practices. Piaget's narrowness of emphasis is, for him, a curiously positivist one. He is on the face of it anything but a positivist as a scientist and theoretician himself: Piaget, less than most thinkers, would transform epistemology into philosophy of science, as positivism does. However, it is as if he is a positivist of the second order; it is the Piagetian child who is supposed to equilibrate towards the positivism of formal operations. Piaget once said that the child is first a Humean and becomes, with operativity, a Kantian; one might add that the Piagetian adolescent is supposed to go on to qualify for the Vienna Circle. What Piaget does not seem to allow is that he should become a Hegelian, or engage in the kind of thought peculiar to law, poetry, scholarship or cooking.

The mistake could easily be a general one, an error of practical reason, and if so, it is a mistake peculiar to modern Western culture. It is that of trying to apply formal principles to domains for which they are inappropriate or ill worked out. The obvious example is the practical rationality of human affairs and politics. The human sciences being what they are, when it comes to dealing with people and managing social relations modern Western thought is probably comparable with that of Trukese navigation: at its very best, a refined *bricolage* of discrete adhocisms, critically dependent on interpretation and on the deployment of criteria for recognition and for relevance. This applies whether we are speaking of saints or of great villains. After all, very few psychologists, who employ formal theoretical principles in the course of their research, are fool enough to try to apply those principles in any thoroughgoing manner to their daily lives outside the research context. They know it cannot be done. Those psychological theories which are found useful in daily life are significantly the very ones which will not pass the test of formal scientific status. Freudian thinking is the best example here: to describe Freudian theory as a refined *bricolage* of concepts and parameters, each of whose applicability and appropriateness has to be decided anew and with sensitivity in each case, is not necessarily derogation, in the light of what I have already said.

Modern society, therefore—which is frequently called 'scientific' or 'technological'—is not modern because it successfully applies formal thought to human affairs. It contains some unsuccessful attempts to do so, but they are of little importance in characterising modern culture. At first sight, the institution of 'bureaucracy' might seem to be a formal approach to human affairs and bureaucracy truly does differentiate modern society from others. On second thoughts, however, bureaucracy does not incorporate formal thinking as Western navigation does. Its 'formality' is of another kind, that of 'impersonality'. Its rules are low-level 'if–then' rules with no explanatory status. And its whole purpose, if successful, is to transcend human frailty, to deny leeway to the acknowledged incompetence of most human thought and judgement. Bureaucrats need not have much grasp of the principles of bureaucratic organisation.

Nonetheless, they are there to be grasped, and somebody has had to grasp them. And the same goes for the properly formal scientific principles applied in navigation, engineering, agriculture or medicine. This is what truly differentiates modern culture. The abstract principles have been understood and formulated in literate form, others have tested, accepted and refined them, others yet have implemented and maintained them in institutionalised operativity. Given literacy, individual inventions are unlikely to be lost, as they would probably be in a nonliterate culture; although of course most principles will be rejected as wrong, for formal thought is no ultimate guarantee of validity or utility. In modern society, formal thought is a vocation to a noticeable minority. The principles are taught to children, and some of it sticks. And the man-made environment in all its extensive aspects is both concrete fact and semiotic invitation to the principles of its creation and functioning.

In this way modern society lifts itself by its own bootstraps. The process is epigenetic and evolutionary, involving both the cognitive evolution of the child and the historical evolution of the culture. The same process over time must also occur in traditional and primitive cultures; for it is an illusion that these are static. Number systems, comparatives, colour terminology, knowledge of biological paternity and of witchcraft: these presumably develop in the same twofold way. Modern culture has sedimented more general and abstract principles in certain domains, which is more important. Modern culture retains, comprises, and uses far more knowledge and principles than any single child or adult can possibly learn: that is probably the most important difference, at root a sociological one, between modern and non-modern societies. It is not that ontogeny recapitulates phylogeny; it may appear so in some cases, but in general that seductive error has long been exposed. It is rather that individual ontogeny and cultural phylogeny each stimulate and partake of the other. The institutionalised operativity of the cultural *Lebenswelt* both enhances and is enhanced by the level and refinement of the cognitive repertoires of individuals. This complex conception of the dynamic interdependence of the changing individual and a changing society is extensively discussed and illustrated by Riegel (1975, 1976).

Epigenetic evolution, of course, is not necessarily 'progress'; or, at any rate, it is so only by the tautological yardstick of its own developmental progression. An example comes from the study of word associations; this began early in experimental psychology, and systematic changes in word association norms of American adults are analysed by Jenkins and Russell (1960) for 1910–1952, and for children, 1916–1963, by Koff (1965). In brief summary, the historical change in word associations over this period was in the direction of 'maturity', maturity being objectively defined by age differences in the earliest studies. The conclusion that Americans have grown more mature in their thinking is tempered, however, by further inspection of the kinds of associations involved. This 'maturity' contained more automatic, stereotyped responses and fewer associations based on logical connections. Progress indeed!

Concluding Remarks

This survey and discussion have been an interim stocktaking. That of course must always be the case; for science and scholarship flow on submerging those who pronounce on their contemporary state. Physicists are unlikely ever again to err as they did in the nineteenth century by considering physics to be virtually a finished enterprise, little more than a mopping-up job. Psychologists and social scientists are only too well aware that their reach exceeds their grasp; and with this topic, culture and cognitive development, one can even feel that the ground is moving under one's feet. The fields I have spanned above are all moving fast. Cross-cultural work is expanding exponentially. So is the study of cognition and language in child development; and the impact of psycholinguistic and sociolinguistic approaches on the cross-cultural field is due to be felt. Literacy is being studied as I write, and present efforts are just beginnings. Conceptions of primitive and modern mentalities are no longer altogether shunned as ethnocentric. The idea of 'culture' is perhaps coming to be articulated in a way that makes sense for psychologists; and the tricky problem of relating individual development and cultural-historical change or evolution is being addressed.

Research to date suggests a remarkable correspondence across cultures in cognitive development in infancy and early childhood. From middle childhood on, variations become manifest in three important respects. First, qualitative similarities across cultures are no longer so clear-cut. Second, non-Western children appear frequently to lag behind Western children in so far as the same qualitative sequence of development can be observed. Third, there is reason to believe that literacy and formal schooling may powerfully affect the development of children's thought. I would add that if literacy and schooling turn out to be as important as certain psychologists (Cole, Scribner, Olson) and anthropologists (Goody, Hallpike) persuasively hold them to be, Piaget's basically epigenetic conception of cognitive growth will have to be modified. I have also suggested, however, that literacy, schooling and the other trappings of modernity do not operate simply as the 'independent variables' beloved of psychologists reared on experimental designs. Individual ontogeny and cultural change are to some extent in dialectical relation each with the other, and a culture may include forms of institutionalised operativity whose effects mimic and therefore render partially dispensible the direct impact of schooling and literacy on the cognition of the individual child and adult.

All in all, it appears likely that cognitive development can potentially be much the same in all cultures, both in its processes and its products. To conclude thus, however, one must allow that there are probably elaborate forms of 'rationality' which are not captured by Piaget's concept of 'formal operations' or by his logicism in general. If there are inherent biological differences which correlate with cultural differences, such as in colour vision or in African infant motor precocity, they operate to a tiny or negligible extent in influencing the course of cognitive growth. Cultural differences, for example in schooling and in the institutionalisation of operativity in the man-made world, are obviously the important influences. With 'modernisation' (however desirable or undesirable it may be), cognitive development in all cultures is likely eventually to follow much the same course at much the same rate. Lévi-Strauss' vision of a single world culture will then be well on the way to fulfilment. If people react to the prospect of homogenisation, as I suspect they will, by increasingly setting up communities and subcultures deliberately to foster chosen cultural and personal ideals, there may then be great variation in what people know and how they behave, but much less variation in the process of knowing and the development of that process. Cultivated variations in the forms of rationality, however, such as those described in fictional form in Hesse's *Glass Bead Game*, will be of great importance to those involved. Like the difference between one unique individual and another, they will seem to make all the difference.

Notes

1. Since writing the above strictures on Hallpike's (1976) article, I have been able to read the manuscript of a forthcoming book by Hallpike, entitled *The Foundations of Primitive Thought*. It is clear from the book that Hallpike is much more sensitive to the problems I mention here than I allowed from a reading of his article. It must also be accepted that Hallpike can hardly use Piagetian theory to argue his thesis and simultaneously sort out problems in Piagetian theory. That would be too much to ask, as the one task is difficult enough. The book also brings a wealth of detail to the argument of Hallpike's case which was not—and no doubt could not—be presented in the article.
2. Cf the following passage from Karl Marx's *Economic and Philosophic Manuscripts* of 1844:
   'The eye has become a *human* eye when its *object* has become a *human*, social object, created by man and destined for him. The senses have therefore become directly *theoreticians* in practice . . . the thing itself is an *objective human* relation to itself and to man, and vice versa.'

   An earlier version of part of the argument developed in this chapter appears in Oates, J. (1978) (ed.). Cultural variation and commonality in cognitive development, in *Early Cognitive Development*, Croom Helm in association with the Open University.

References

Anderson, J. (1971). *The Grammar of Case*, London and New York, Cambridge University Press

Asch, S. E. (1958). The metaphor: a psychological inquiry. In *Person Perception and Interpersonal Behaviour* (ed. R. Tagiuri and L. Petrullo), Stanford, California, Stanford University Press

Bates, E. (1976). *Language and Context: the Acquisition of Pragmatics*, London and New York, Academic Press

Berger, P. L., Berger, B. and Kellner, H. (1974). *The Homeless Mind*. Harmondsworth, Penguin

Berlin, B. (1972). Speculations on the growth of ethnobotanical nomenclature. *Language in Society*, **I**, 51–86

Berlin, B., Breedlove, D. E. and Raven, P. H. (1966). Folk taxonomies and biological classification. *Science*, **154**, 273–275

Berlin, B., Breedlove, D. E. and Raven, P. H. (1973). General principles of classification and nomenclature in folk biology. *American Anthropologist*, **75**, 214–242

Berlin, B. and Kay, P. (1969). *Basic Colour Terms: Their Universality and Evolution*. Berkeley: University of California Press

Bernstein, B. B. (1961). Social structure, language and learning. *Educational Research*, **3**, 163–176

Berry, J. W. (1976). *Human Ecology and Cognitive Style: Comparative Studies in Cultural and Psychological Adaptation*, New York: Wiley

Boas, F. (1911, revised edition 1935) *The Mind of Primitive Man*, London, Macmillan

Bornstein, M. H. (1973). Colour vision and colour naming: a psycho-physiological hypothesis of cultural difference. *Psychological Bulletin*, **80**, 257–285

Bowerman, M. (1973). *Early Syntactic Development: A Cross-Linguistic Study with Special Reference to Finnish*. London and New York, Cambridge University Press

Brown, R. (1958). *Words and Things*. New York, The Free Press

Brown, R., Black, A. H. and Horowitz, A. E. (1955). Phonetic symbolism in natural language. *Journal of Abnormal and Social Psychology*, **50**, 388–393

Bruner, J. S. (1965). The growth of mind. *American Psychologist*, **20**, 1007–1017

Bruner, J. S., Olver, R. and Greenfield, P. M. (eds.) (1966). *Studies in Cognitive Growth*, New York, Wiley

Bruner, J. S. (1966). On cognitive growth 2. In Bruner *et al.* (1966)

Chomsky, N. (1968). *Language and Mind*, New York, Harcourt

Cole, M. (1975). Towards an ethnography of cognition. In *Cross-cultural Perspectives on Learning*. (ed. R. Brislin, S. Bochner and W. J. Lonner) New York and London, Wiley

Cole, M. and Bruner, J. S. (1971). Cultural differences and inferences about psychological processes. *American Psychologist*, **26**, 867–876

Cole, M., Gay, J. H., Glick, J. A. and Sharp, D. (1971). *The Cultural Context of Learning and Thinking*, London, Methuen

Cole, M. and Scribner, S. (1974). *Culture and Thought: a Psychological Introduction*. New York and London, Wiley

D'Andrade, R. G. and Egan, M. (1974). The colours of emotion. *American Ethnologist*, **1**

Dasen, P. R. (1972). Cross-cultural Piagetian research: a summary. *Journal of Cross-Cultural Psychology*, **3**, 23–39

Dasen, P. R. (1973). *Canadian Psychologist*, **14**, 149–166

Dasen, P. R. (1974). The influence of ecology, culture and European contact on cognitive development in Australian aborigines. In *Culture and Cognition* (ed. J. W. Berry and P. R. Dasen) London, Methuen

Dasen, P. R. (1977a). Are cognitive processes universal? A contribution to cross-cultural Piagetian psychology. In *Studies in Cross-Cultural Psychology*, Vol. I. (ed. N. Warren) London and New York, Academic Press

Dasen, P. R. (1977b). Introduction. In *Piagetian Psychology: Cross-Cultural*

Contributions. (ed. P. R. Dasen) New York, Gardner Press

De Lemos, M. M. (1969). The development of conservation in Aborginal children. *Int. J. Psych.*, **4**, 255–269

Derrida, J. (1976). *Of Grammatology.* Baltimore and London, Johns Hopkins University Press

Dibble, V. K. (1973). What is and what ought to be: a comparison of certain characteristics of the ideological and legal styles of thought. *American Journal of Sociology*, **79**, 511–549

Durkheim, E. (1913). Review of Lévy-Bruhl. *Année Sociologique*, **12** (1909–1912, published 1913), 33–37

Edwards, D. (1973). Sensory-motor intelligence and semantic relations in early child grammar. *Cognition*, **2**, 395–434

Evans-Pritchard, E. E. (1937). *Witchcraft, Oracles and Magic Among the Azande*, Oxford, Clarendon Press

Evans-Pritchard, E. E. (1956). *Nuer Religion.* Oxford, Clarendon Press

Eysenck, H. J. (1971). *Race, Intelligence and Education*, London, Temple Smith

Ferguson, C. A. and Slobin, D. I. (eds.) (1973). *Studies of Child Language Development*, New York, Holt

Feyerabend, P. (1975). *Against Method.* London, New Left Books

Fillmore, C. J. (1968). The case for case. In *Universals in Linguistic Theory.* (ed. E. Bach and R. T. Harms) New York, Holt

Garner, W. R. (1974). *The Processing of Information and Structure.* New York, Halsted

Gay, J., Lloyd, B. B. and Bruner, J. S. (eds.) (In press) *Psychological Universals in Africa*

Gellner, E. (1973). The savage and the modern mind. In *Modes of Thought.* (ed. R. Horton and R. Finnegan) London, Faber

Gladwin, T. (1964). Culture and logical process. In *Explorations in Cultural Anthropology* (ed. W. H. Goodenough), New York, McGraw-Hill, pp. 167–177

Gladwin, T. (1970). *East is a Big Bird*, Cambridge, Mass., Harvard University Press

Gladwin, T. and Sarason, S. B. (1953). *Truk: Man in Paradise*, New York, Wenner-Gren Foundation

Glick, J. A. (1975). Cognitive development in cross-cultural perspective. In *Review of Child Development Research*, Vol. 4. (ed. E. M. Hetherington *et al.*) Chicago, University of Chicago Press

Goodnow, J. J. (1962). A test of milieu effects with some of Piaget's tasks. *Psychological Monographs*, **76** (36), Whole no. 555

Goodnow, J. J. (1969). Cultural variations in cognitive skills. In *Cross-Cultural Studies*, (ed. D. R. Price-Williams) Harmondsworth, Penguin. (Also in *Cognitive Studies*, vol. 1)

Goodnow, J. J. and Bethon, G. (1966). Piaget's tasks: the effects of schooling and intelligence. *Child Development*, **37**, 573–582

Goody, J. (ed.) (1968). *Literacy in Traditional Societies.* Cambridge, Cambridge University Press

Goody, J. (1977). *The Domestication of the Savage Mind.* London, Cambridge University Press

Goody, J. and Watt, I. (1963). The consequences of literacy. *Comparative Studies in Society and History*, **5**, 304–345

Greenberg, J. (1966). *Universals of Language.* 2nd edition. Cambridge, Mass., M.I.T. Press

Greenfield, P. M. (1972). Oral or written language. *Language and Speech*, **15**, 169–178

Greenfield, P. M. and Bruner, J. S. (1966). Culture and cognitive growth. *International Journal of Psychology*, **1**, 89–107

Greenfield, P. M. and Bruner, J. S. (1969). Culture and cognitive growth. In *Handbook of Socialisation Theory and Research*. (ed. D. A. Goslin) New York, Rand McNally

Greenfield, P. M. and Childs, C. (1977). Understanding sibling concepts: a developmental study of kin terms in Zinacantan. In *Piagetian Psychology: Cross-Cultural Contributions*. (ed. P. R. Dasen) New York, Gardner Press

Halliday, M. A. K. (1975). *Learning How to Mean: Explorations in the Development of Language*, London, Arnold

Hallpike, C. R. (1976). Is there a primitive mentality? *Man*, **11**, 253–270

Heron, A. (1974). Cultural determinants of concrete operational behaviour. In *Readings in Cross-Cultural Psychology*. (ed. J. L. M. Dawson and W. J. Lonner) Hong Kong University Press

Heron, A., and Simonsson, M. (1969). Weight conservation in Zambian children: a non-verbal approach. *International Journal of Psychology*, **4**, 281–292

Hess, R. D. and Shipman, V. (1965). Early experience and the socialisation of cognitive modes in children. *Child Development*, **36**, 869–886

Hockett, C. (1954). Chinese vs. English: an exploration of the Whorfian theses. In *Language in Culture*. (ed. H. Hoijer) University of Chicago Press

Holtzman, W. H., Diaz-Guerrero, R. and Swartz, J. D. (1975). *Personality Development in Two Cultures: a Cross-Cultural Longitudinal Study of School Children in Mexico and the US*, Mexico, University of Texas Press

Horton, R. (1967). African traditional thought and Western science. Part I: *Africa*, **37**, 50–71; Part II, **37**, 155–187

Horton, R. (1973a) Lévy-Bruhl among the scientists. *Second Order*, **2**, 1

Horton, R. (1973b). Lévy-Bruhl, Durkheim and the scientific revolution. In Horton, R. and Finnegan, R., 1973, pp. 249–305

Horton, R. and Finnegan, R. (1973). *Modes of Thought*, London, Faber and Faber

Illich, I. D. (1971). *Deschooling Society*. London, Calder and Boyars

Inhelder, B. and Piaget, J. (1958). *The Growth of Logical Thinking From Childhood to Adolescence*, London, Routledge and Kegan Paul.

Inkoles, A. and Smith, D. H. (1974). *Becoming Modern: Individual Change in Six Developing Countries*, London, Heinemann

Irvine, S. H. (1969). Factor analysis of African abilities and attainments: constructs across cultures. *Psychological Bulletin*, **71**, 20–32

Jenkins, J. and Russell, W. A. (1960). Systematic changes in word association norms: 1910–1952. *J. of Abnormal and Social Psychology*, **60**, 293–304

Jensen, A. R. (1969). How much can we boost IQ and scholastic achievement? *Harvard Educational Review*, **39**, 1–123

Jensen, A. R. (1973). *Educability and Group Differences*, London, Methuen

Kamara, A. I. and Easley, J. A. (1977). Is the rate of cognitive development uniform across cultures? – a methodological critique with new evidence from Themne children. In *Piagetian Psychology: Cross-Cultural Contributions* (ed. P. R. Dasen), New York, Gardner Press

Klank, L. J. K., Huang, Y. H. and Johnson, R. C. (1971). Determinants of phonetic symbolism. *Journal of Verbal Learning and Verbal Behaviour*, **10**, 140–148

Kelly, G. A. (1955). *The Psychology of Personal Constructs*. New York, Norton

Koff, R. H. (1965). Systematic changes in children's word association norms, 1916–63. *Child Development*, **36**, 299–305

Kohlberg, L. (1969). Stage and sequence: the cognitive-developmental approach to socialisation. In *Handbook of Socialisation Theory and Research*. (ed. D. A. Goslin) New York, Rand McNally

Konner, M. J. (1972). Aspects of the developmental ethology of a foraging people. In *Ethological Studies of Child Behaviour*. (ed. N. G. Blurton-Jones) London, Cambridge University Press

Levi, E. H. (1949). *An Introduction to Legal Reasoning*. Chicago, University of Chicago Press

Levine, M. (1974). Scientific method and the adversary model: some preliminary thoughts. *American Psychologist*, **29**, 661–677

Levine, R. A. and Price-Williams, D. R. (1974). Children's kinship concepts: cognitive development and early experience among the Hausa. *Ethnology*, **13**, 25–44

Lévi-Strauss, C. (1966). *The Savage Mind*. London, Weidenfeld and Nicholson

Lévy-Bruhl, L. (1910). *Les Fonctions Mentales dans les Sociétés Inférieures*. Paris, Alean

Lévy-Bruhl, L. (1922). *La Mentalité Primitive*. Paris, Alean

Lévy-Bruhl, L. (1927). *L'Âme Primitive*. Paris, Alean

Lévy-Bruhl, L. (1931). *Le Surnatural et la Nature dans la Mentalité Primitive*. Paris, Alean

Lévy-Bruhl, L. (1935). *La Mythologie Primitive*. Paris, Alean

Lévy-Bruhl, L. (1938). *L'Expérience Mystique et les Symboles chez les Primitifs*. Paris, Alean

Lévy-Bruhl, L. (1949). *Les Carnets de Lucien Lévy-Bruhl*. Paris, Presses Universitaires de France

Luria, A. R. (1971). Towards the problem of the historical nature of psychological processes. *International Journal of Psychology*, **6**, 259–272

Luria, A. R. (1976). *Cognitive Development*. Cambridge Mass., Harvard University Press

Luria, A. R. and Vygotsky, L. S. (1930). *Essays in the History of Behaviour* (untranslated from the Russian; mentioned in M. Cole's introduction to Luria (1976))

MacNamara, J. (1972). Cognitive basis of language learning in infants. *Psychological Review*, **79**, 1–13

Massé, G. (1969). *Croissance et Développement de l'Enfant en Dakar*. Paris, Centre Internationale de l'Enfance

Meehl, P. L. (1967). Theory-testing in psychology and physics: a methodological paradox. *Philosophy of Science*, **34**, 103–115

Mermelstein, E. and Shulman, L. S. (1967). Lack of formal schooling and the acquisition of conservation. *Child Development*, **38**, 39–52

Miller, G. A. (1970). Linguistic communication as a biological process. Herbert Spencer lecture, Oxford University, November 13, 1970. Cited by Cole and Scribner (1974)

Moreigne, F. and Senecal, J. (1962). Résultats d'un groupe d'enfants africains au Terman-Merrill. *Revue de Psychologie Appliquée*, **12**, 15–32

Olson, D. R. (1975). The language of experience: on natural language and formal education. *Bulletin of the British Psychological Society*, **28**, 363–373

Olson, D. R. (1977). From utterance to text: the bias of language in speech and writing. *Harvard Educational Review*, **47**, 257–281

Ong, W. J. (1971). *Rhetoric, Romance and Technology*, Ithaca, New York, Cornell University Press

Osgood, C. E. (1960). The cross-cultural generality of visual-verbal synaesthetic tendencies. *Behavioural Science*, **5**, 146–169

Osgood, C. E. (1962). Studies on the generality of affective meaning systems. *American Psychologist*, **17**, 10–28

Osgood, C. E., May, W. H. and Miron, M. S. (1975). *Cross-Cultural Universals of Affective Meaning*, University of Illinois Press

Polanyi, M. (1958). *Personal Knowledge: Towards a Post-Critical Philosophy*, London, Routledge

Price-Williams, D. R. (1961). A study concerning concepts of conservation of quantities among primitive children. *Acta Psychologica*, **18**, 297–305

Price-Williams, D. R. (1975). Primitive mentality – civilised style. In *Cross-Cultural Perspectives on Learning*. (ed. R. Brislin, S. Bochner and W. Lonner) Sage Publications

Price-Williams, D. R. (1976). Cross-cultural differences in cognitive development. In *The Development of Cognitive Processes*. (ed. V. Hamilton and M. D. Vernon) London and New York, Academic Press

Price-Williams, D. R., Hammond, O. W., Edgerton, C. and Walker, M. (1977). Kinship concepts among rural Hawaiian children. In *Piagetian Psychology: Cross-cultural Contribution*. (ed. P. R. Dasen) New York, Gardner Press

Piaget, J. (1966). Nécessité et signification des recherches comparatives en psychologie génétique. *International Journal of Psychology*, **1**, 3–13

Piaget, J. (1971). *Structuralism*. London, Routledge and Kegan Paul

Piaget, J. (1972). Intellectual evolution from adolescence to adulthood. *Human Development*, **15**, 1–12

Piaget, J. (1977). Préface. In *Piagetian Psychology: Cross-cultural Contributions*. (ed. P. R. Dasen) New York, Gardner Press

Riegel, K. F. (1973). Dialectic operations: the final period of cognitive development. *Human Development*, **16**, 346–370

Riegel, K. F. (1975). *The Development of Dialectical Operations*. Basel, S. Karger

Riegel, K. F. (1976). *The Psychology of Development and History*. New York, Plenum Press

Rosch, E. (1975). Universals and cultural specifics in human categorisation. In *Cross-cultural Perspectives on Learning*. (ed. R. Brislin, S. Bochner and W. Lonner) New York, Halsted Press

Rosch, E. (1977). Human categorisation. In *Studies in Cross-cultural Psychology*, Vol. 1 (ed. N. Warren), London and New York, Academic Press

Sanches, M. and Blount, B. G. (eds.) (1975). *Sociocultural Dimensions of Language Use*, London and New York, Academic Press

Scribner, S. and Cole, M. (1973). Cognitive consequences of formal and informal education. *Science*, **182**, 553–559

Scribner, S. and Cole, M. (1977). Unpackaging literacy. Paper presented to the National Institute of Education Conference on Writing, June 1977

Scribner, S. and Cole, M. (1978). Literacy without schooling: testing for intellectual effects. *Harvard Educational Review*, **48**, 448–461

Shweder, R. A. and Levine, R. A. (1976). Dream concepts of Hausa children. In *Socialisation as Cultural Communication*. (ed. T. Schwartz) Berkeley, University of California Press

Sinclair de Zwaart, H. (1967). *Acquisition du Langage et Développement de la Pensée*. Paris, Dunod

Skorupski, J. (1976). *Symbol and Theory: a Philosophical Study of Theories of Religion in Social Anthropology*. London, Cambridge University Press

Slobin, D. I. (1970). Universals of grammatical development in children. In *Advances in Psycholinguistics* (ed. G. B. Flores D'Arcais and W. M. Levelt) Amsterdam

Slobin, D. I. (1971). *Psycholinguistics*. Glenview, Illinois, Scott Foresman

Smilansky, S., Shephatia, L. and Frenkel, E. (1976). *Mental Development of Infants from Two Ethnic Groups*. Research report no. 195, Henrietta Szold Institute, Jerusalem, Israel

Super, C. (1976). Environmental effects on motor development: the case of 'African infant precocity'. *Developmental Medicine and Child Neurology*, **18**, 561–567

Toulmin, S. (1971). From logical systems to conceptual populations. In *Boston Studies in the Philosophy of Science* (eds. Buck, R. C. and Cohen, R. S.). Vol. VIII, Dordrecht, Reidel, 552–564

Toulmin, S. (1972). *Human Understanding*, Vol. 1. Princeton University Press

Vernon, P. E. (1969). *Intelligence and Cultural Environment*. London, Methuen

Vygotsky, L. S. (1962). *Thought and Language*. Cambridge, Mass., M.I.T. Press

Warren, N. (1972). African infant precocity. *Psychological Bulletin*. **78**, 353–367

Warren, N. (1973). African infancy in psychological perspective. Invited paper for the Burg Wartenstein symposium on *Cultural and Social Influences on Infancy and Early Childhood*

Warren, N., and Parkin, J. M. (1974). A neurological and behavioural comparison of African and European newborns in Uganda. *Child Development*, **45**, 966–971

Wason, P. C. and Johnson-Laird, P. N. (1972). *Psychology of Reasoning: Structure and Content*. London, Batsford; Cambridge, Mass., Harvard University Press

Webb, A. (1977). The psychic unity of mankind. B.A. Honours Dissertation, University of Sussex

Werner, E. (1972). Infants around the world: Cross-cultural studies of psychomotor development from birth to two years. *Journal of Cross-cultural Psychology*, **3**, 111–134

Werner, H. (1940). *The Comparative Psychology of Mental Development*. New York, Follett

10 Society's Cradle: An Anthropological Perspective on the Socialisation of Cognition

BILLIE JEAN ISBELL and LAURIS McKEE
(Department of Anthropology, Cornell University, McGraw Hall, Ithaca, New York, USA)

Introduction

As a species, we have universal capacities for perceiving the world, and cognitively structuring what we perceive. Nonetheless, the stimuli available to perception and the cultural values which give meaning to the objects and events perceived determine that cognitive skills may covary in some manner with the meaningful stimuli available to perception.

Most researchers who have studied cognition in non-Western cultures have come to realise that certain kinds of experiences (such as the training imposed by formal Western education) elicit and rehearse different skills which have different instrumental functions. Cole asserts that it is more useful to view education as the way in which 'societies organize children's experience to fit the demands of their adult lives in specific rather than in general terms' (Cole, 1978, p. 58). Cole's orientation, and the broad definition of 'education' that it allows, points the way to a profitable change in the emphasis in the study of the socialisation of cognition. Anthropologists and psychologists are turning to the environment of the child to determine the mechanisms by which ecological factors contribute to the development of different cognitive skills and what the adaptive functions of these might be.

We are encouraged, both by this new approach to cross-cultural studies and by the theory of perception and cognition recently proffered by Ulric Neisser (1976) to present what is essentially an exercise in heuristics. We have constructed a model of infant caretaker interaction in order to focus upon the perceptual and cognitive trends such interaction possibly could generate.

We begin with an examination of the Western, ethnocentric definitions of cognition and discuss the consequences these have had on cross-cultural research. We argue that language-centred definitions of cognition have not only biased the design of cross-cultural research, but have resulted in ethnocentric interpretations of the findings. We then present a case study of the effects of an extremely limited environment and what it offered to the perception of a developing child who was imprisoned within it. The point of the case study is not to explore a pathological context of cognitive development, but rather to adduce evidence that the perceptual skills and cognitive schemata which Genie did develop were closely tied to the kinds of stimuli available to her. As a result, some schemata developed to a remarkable degree, whereas the necessary stimuli for language development, for example, were not present. The schemata this child developed, we suggest, were specific to the available perceptual information in her environment.

We turn from the limited environment of Genie to the richer but still controlled and limited environment of the infant. We offer a cultural model for the investigation of the effect of child-care customs and the perceptual opportunities they afford infants, positing that during the period of infancy the stimuli presented to the infant are restricted, relative to the richness of the stimulus environment available to the mobile child. We speculate that information about the proximity of the caretaker is selectively sought for, or in Neisser's terms, anticipated. Moreover, we suggest that the development of early perceptual selections and cognitive trends may be related to whether the information is transmitted primarily through the medium of tactile or vocal messages. Specifically we propose that in many non-Western cultures, tactile communication between infants and caretakers is a dominant mode which has consequences for later cognitive development. We are especially interested in the intermodal processing of non-verbal stimuli and the anticipatory schemata that may become dominant in early life in non-literate cultures. We are guided throughout our discussion, by what we view as the ineluctable relationship between perception, cognition and reality.

Towards a View of Cognition as Interaction

Anthropologists and psychologists share a common interest in discovering the link between social experiences and cognition (Cole and Scribner, 1975). Both disciplines, until very recently, generally have defined cognition as a language-related phenomenon. For most psychologists cognition is the 'process by which man acquires, transforms and uses information about the world' (Cole and Scribner, 1974, p. 2). The majority of the cross-cultural research that has attempted to study these processes has either studied language directly, or has utilised test situations in which language is necessary to infer the operation of other cognitive skills.[1]

Within North American anthropology, language has been assumed to play a central role as a determining factor in cognition. This has led to the development of 'cognitive anthropology' and the sub-fields of ethnoscience and ethnosemantics, which are concerned primarily with folk classifications.

Sturtevant (1964, p. 100), a leader in the field of ethnosemantics, maintains that a culture amounts to the sum of a given society's folk classifications: its particular ways of classifying its material and social universe. The usual method has been to investigate a society's classificatory system through its language. The end results are usually culture-specific taxonomies, which, until recently, have been assumed to divide up the world with a kind of formal precision that reflects the collective cognition of the society.[2]

Comparing the perspectives in cross-cultural research of the two disciplines, Cole and Scribner (1974) note that cognitive psychology focuses upon the *process*, within the perceiver, by which information about the world is acquired and transformed. Neisser (1976) has called this perspective, 'the glorification of the perceiver'—without the orderly processing of phenomena by the perceiver, it is believed that the world would be a meaningless chaos. Cognitive anthropologists, on the other hand, see cognition reflected in the systematic classification of the objects of perception—the ordered content of folk categories. Cognitive psychology, until the 1970s, was concerned with the states of the messenger, whereas, cognitive anthropology was concerned with the states of the messages (Maclay, 1973). The sharing of a language-centred, or logocentric definition of cognition, provided the basis for early collaboration between the two fields. Consider the derivation of logocentric—*logos*, from the Greek, meaning 'word', 'reason', 'speech', 'thought' and 'account', as distinct from cognition—*cognoscere*, from the Latin meaning 'to become acquainted with'—to perceive directly with the mind of the senses. While everyone realises that one perceives the world through all of the senses, the Western philosophical tradition has developed a view that the word (*logos*), is the manifestation of reason, thought and intelligence. Cognitive anthropologists have been mainly concerned with how words (classificatory systems) are culturally organised. Cognitive psychologists, by contrast, have focused upon the organiser.[3]

Perception and cognition 'are usually not just operations in the head but transactions with the world. These transactions do not merely *in*form the perceiver, they also *trans*form him. Each of us is created by the cognitive acts in which he engages' (Neisser, 1976, p. 11). We propose that these transactions with the world can be viewed as three interacting spheres: (1) the biological bases of human perception; (2) the phenomena the environment presents to the individual at different stages of development as the objects of perception; and finally, (3) the cultural selections that result in the increasing development of some cognitive skills, at the expense of others. These skills can be thought of as cultural cognitive endpoints. The processes to be investigated, then, are the dynamic interactions of these three spheres, and the resulting cognitive strategies employed by the developing child at any given stage of growth. Such a proposal demands longitudinal, interdisciplinary research directed toward the study of how individuals develop within a particular physical and social environment.

Our argument is a simple one. Human beings universally share the same basic cognitive capacities (Cole and Scribner, 1974), but nonetheless, environmental pressures and cultural selection will result in the adaptive development of specific cognitive skills, depending upon the environmental and cultural demands which confront the developing child. We propose that one source of the selection of special sets of cognitive skills is found in the culturally determined structure which mediates communication between babies and caretakers.

Neisser (1976, p. 54) defines a cognitive schema as 'that portion of the entire perceptual cycle which is internal to the perceiver, modifiable by experience, and somehow specific to what is being perceived'. He describes schemata as being similar to a computer-programming language or format, which specifies that information must be of a certain sort if it is to be interpreted. Simultaneously, a schema functions as a plan for finding out about objects and events in the world. The plan is a means to obtain more information, which in turn expands the format (the specifications of acceptable information). This cyclic process is such that the information that fills in the format in one interaction becomes a part of the format in the next. The schema is not only the plan but also the executor of the plan (Neisser 1976, p. 54). To use the vocabulary of Cole and Scribner (1975), we see that a schema is *both* process *and* content. The perceptual content (or objects of perception) increases the specifications of acceptable information for future interactive events. Content, then, becomes an integral part of the plan or process for attending to the specific information picked up previously. One can see that in such a model the distinction between process and content becomes less interesting than a model of cognition as dynamic interaction. 'Perceiving is often most effective during motion: we localise sounds with maximum accuracy if we move our heads while we listen, and feel the shapes of objects especially well if we explore them actively with our hands' (Neisser, 1976, p. 107). The cross-cultural study of cognition, taken as the interaction of processes and contents, or the schemata which develop as a child becomes acquainted with the world, should begin by carefully documenting the types of information that are communicated to infants in different cultures as well as the means of information transmission. We propose that the cultural selection of certain modes of communication (non-verbal ones, for example) would prepare a child to accept those kinds of information, which in turn engender the development of non-verbal cognitive skills. In addition, such cultures would place high value on such skills and perhaps subscribe to a theory of intelligence that differs somewhat from our own.

It would be enlightening to know whether social success, smartness and the skills associated with economic (or with expressive, artistic specialities) are considered related in any given culture (see Nerlove and Snipper, in press; Wober, 1974; Dube, 1977; and Berry, 1974). Moreover, how do adults decide which child is to become an artisan, a priest, a dancer, a shaman, a weaver, a potter, or an agriculturalist? Who should attend the newly established school?[4] Upon what types of interactive information are these selections made? We are arguing for basic ethnographic research on the socialisation of cognition. We suggest that in order to document the forms and types of non-verbal communication between children and their environment, it would be helpful to suspend our logocentric view of cognition in order to be able to perceive the roles played by the perceptual schemata that, in some environments, may have been culturally selected for over-verbality. Perhaps for horticulturalists or hunter–gatherers, perception of minute differences in the environment may be critical.[5] Acting upon such information may be vital. But explaining why certain actions were taken may be superfluous.

In order to set the scene for an exposition of non-verbal communication and its relation to the development of cognitive schemata, it perhaps would be helpful to discuss briefly the development of one of the burgeoning areas of interdisciplinary research that began with a strong logocentric definition of cognition. We will briefly trace the changes in assumptions that have occurred between 1950 and 1970 in the field of psycholinguistics, which we believe have culminated in challenging *logos*, the word, as the core of cognition.

Psycholinguistics: an Exercise in Logocentrism

An excellent exposition of the shift in assumptions and methodologies concerning cognition has been provided by Maclay (1973) in an overview of the historical development of psycholinguistics, a field that has had two decades of collaborative research. The first decade (the 1950s) is characterised by Maclay as a period of extremely good relations between structural linguistics and behaviourist psychology. The two disciplines shared a common commitment to an operationalist philosophy which emphasised the use of observable data. Linguists concentrated on the description of languages as organised systems of a relatively small number of discrete categories. Psychologists, on the other hand, relied on statistical description of data in terms of probabilities or frequencies. Linguists derived their data from natural language, while psychologists derived theirs from experimental situations. Structural linguistics, the approach most often used by anthropologists in the study of American languages, concentrated on the states of the messages, whereas psychologists using behaviourist models, focused on the state of the communicators. This clearcut division of labour obscured the possible conflicts between the two fields. Many anthropological linguists viewed cognition as a culture-specific phenomenon determined by language (i.e., the Whorfian hypothesis). Behaviourist psychologists, in contrast, relied on explanations based on drives, habits, conditioning and reinforcement.

Maclay (1973) claims that by 1960 the vigorous but rather chaotic activities of psycholinguists were ripe for a new paradigm. The efforts to substantiate the argument that language imposes a world view on culture and cognition proved inconclusive (Carroll and Casagrande, 1958; Maclay, 1974). One of the major problems unresolved by this period of research was the fact that any speaker (and hearer) of a natural language had the ability to generate novel utterances. Furthermore, the attempts of psychologists to describe grammaticality in terms of drives, habit strength, reinforcement, or by imitative learning, seemed inadequate (see Maclay, 1973, pp. 573–574 and Saporta, 1961, p. 5).

Maclay designates the decade of the 1960s as 'The Linguistic Period', and he asserts that it was the impact of Chomsky's distinction between competence and performance which destroyed both the original collaboration between anthropologists and psychologists which had been based on operational methods and the division of labour between them. In *Syntactic Structures* Chomsky (1957) argued that formal deductive analysis was required to construct adequate grammars of natural language. His argument that linguistic theories must somehow account for the knowledge, or competence, of a speaker, directed linguists toward the state of the communicator, and away from the states of the messages. Linguistics was declared a subfield of psychology. The proposal of a deep structure, coupled with the model of a Language Acquisition Device (LAD), provided psycholinguists with a clear paradigm for research. Moreover, learning a language became equated with learning the rules for producing syntactically well-formed utterances. In spite of Chomsky's warnings to the contrary (Chomsky, 1961), psycholinguists adopted generative–transformational theory, a formal deductive model of language, as a psychologically real model of the language-acquiring child. The new paradigm led to experimental efforts to demonstrate the direct relationship between the syntactic complexity of sentences and the perception and production of speech (Miller, 1962; Miller and Isard, 1963). The notion was that the greater the number of derivational rules needed to generate a sentence from a deep structure (presumed competence), the more complex the psychological processes were that enabled a speaker to process, understand and retain the sentence. Fodor and Garrett (1966), in a review of the research to date, concluded that there was no direct relationship between the grammatical complexity in deriving a sentence and the psychological complexity in understanding it. The new paradigm of the 'Linguistic Period' proved inadequate for linguists and psychologists attempting to demonstrate the relationship between cognition and language through experimental, operationalist approaches. Nevertheless, a new dialogue had begun.

The psychological reality of transformational grammar came under even stronger attacks after 1970, the period in psycholinguistics designated by Maclay (1973) as the Cognitive Period. The significance of this change in focus is that researchers began to debate the nature of cognitive capacities that result in language production. On the one hand, a strong innate hypothesis (McNeill, 1966) was proposed that argued for the existence of syntactic knowledge as a capacity intrinsic in human beings' ability to learn language. On the other hand, many investigators questioned such a strong position, and proposals concerning innate, or intrinsic cognitive capacities ranged from McNeill's argument, discussed above, to a direct attack on the 'centrality of grammar' by Bever (1970), who asserted that the syntactic structures, considered universal and innate by transformational linguists and psycholinguists, are based upon general mechanisms of perception, learning and cognition. Bever concluded that there is not a universal grammar as such, but rather psycholinguists had been examining a linguistic reflection of general cognitive structures. The major question for research, according to Bever, is to understand how the general structures of perception, learning and cognition become integrated in human communicative behaviour.

The major impact of Bever's article was to encourage many investigators who had begun to question the centrality of grammar, and the competence–performance distinction,[6] to propose that an interactive model of the developing individual within a socio-cultural environment is fundamental for a theory of cognition. A final consequence of this shift was that many psycholinguists re-evaluated the various arguments concerning innate structures, or intrinsic cognitive capacities, which then led to the formulation of hypotheses attempting to separate the biological from the cultural bases of human communicative behaviour. As the division of labour between linguists and psychologists broke down and as formal deductive approaches replaced behaviourist-operational ones, linguists and psychologists became at ease with speculations, models and theories about what goes on 'inside someone's head' as cognitive prerequisites for language. This development led to three major avenues of research: (1) the search for cognitive and language universals, (2) the performance of natural language within a social context and (3) a concern for methods and theories to investigate the biological bases of languages and cognition.[7] The recent research in these three areas points toward the efficacy of constructing a model of cognition as a means of 'becoming acquainted with the world'.

The challenge is to construct a theoretical model of cognition that takes into account the interaction of a perceiving individual with a cultural and physical environment. Cross-cultural cognitive psychologists confronted with cultural and physical environments foreign to their own experience, are abandoning their tendency 'to glorify the perceiver, who is said to process, transform, recode, assimilate, or generally give shape to what would otherwise be a meaningless chaos' (Neisser, 1976, p. 9). Linguists and anthropologists are formulating theories that challenge the notion that language, or grammar, is the major determining factor in cognition. Anthropologists are considering what the biological and environmental influences may be on the cognitive processes of the members of a given society, rather than defining a culture as a sum total of a society's classifications as ethnoscience has done in the past. Space has only permitted us to highlight the major trends, but as an illustrative exercise, let us consider a logocentric investigation of a child deprived of *logos*.

Genie. A Child Without Words

Genie is a woman, who, in 1970 at the age of almost 14, began the process of becoming human through socialisation (Curtiss, 1977;[8] Curtiss *et al.*, 1974). Before that time she had existed in one of the most bizarre groups that has ever masqueraded as a human family. She had been tied naked to a potty chair, and harnessed so that she could only move her hands, fingers, feet and toes. At night she was placed in a sleeping bag that had been sewn in such a way so that she could not move her arms and legs. Her father had fashioned both the harness and the sleeping bag himself. During the night, Genie was placed, in her already confining sleeping bag, in an infant's crib with wire mesh on the sides and a wire mesh cover. Thus she spent her days and nights for thirteen years in a bare room harnessed to a potty chair with her cage of a crib to look at, along with the sparse items she was reportedly given from time to time: empty cottage cheese cartons, empty thread spools, and the like (Curtiss, 1977, p. 6). In addition, Genie was given two plastic raincoats to play with occasionally, one yellow and one clear.[9] She could also see a bit of the sky out of one window of her room and a bit of the wall of the building next door out of the other window. The windows were covered except for a couple of inches at the top. Her father kept a large piece of wood in the corner of Genie's room with which to beat her when she made any sound. Her room was a dirty salmon colour with one door, the two windows and a wall of closets. A bare light bulb completed Genie's visual array.

In terms of auditory stimuli, it appears that Genie did not hear any language outside her door. Her father would not tolerate any noise at all, which meant that all verbal interaction in the rest of the house was carried out in low whispers. There were no television or radio sets in the house. The bedroom adjacent to Genie's was vacant. The sounds she heard predominantly were the sounds from the adjacent bathroom. She may have heard traffic or other environmental noises on occasion, but her room was in the back of the house and very little street noise reached her.

Her mother claims that she managed to spend a few moments with the child each day during Genie's initial confinement, but Genie's mother found it very hard to maintain this contact as she was rapidly losing her eyesight. It is unclear how much Genie's mother spoke to her through the years. But, Genie's father never spoke to her, instead he growled, snapped and barked like a wild dog. He let his nails grow long and scratched her. As Genie's mother became incapable of feeding her, due to increasing blindness, Genie's only sibling, an older brother, took over the task of feeding her three times a day. The boy had been taught to interact with Genie like a wild dog by his father, who also demanded that no one stayed too long in the captive girl's room. Therefore, the mother reports that Genie was fed hurriedly, by stuffing her mouth full of baby food, or other soft foods. Genie did not know how to chew; she had to wait until her saliva broke down the food. So complete was her socialisation for silence that she could not sob or cry. The only sound she could emit was a faint whimper. The auditory stimuli afforded by her environment were even more restricted than the visual and tactile stimuli: language and the correlated movements of the tongue and lips had been suppressed to such a degree that Genie could not even chew or swallow properly.

When Genie was discovered and hospitalised in 1970, she was suffering from malnutrition, weighed only 59. pounds and stood only 54 inches tall, which is about the stature of a six-year-old. She had become nearsighted: her range of focused vision wàs 10 feet, exactly the distance from the door of her room to the potty chair. She could not stand erect, could not straighten her arms or legs, could not run, hop, jump, nor climb. She could walk only by shuffling her feet and swaying from side to side. Curtiss (1977, p. 9) concludes the above description by stating that: 'Genie was unsocialized, primitive, hardly human'. However, she was alert and curious about her new surroundings and she was extremely hungry for human contact. She quickly formed attachments for certain members of the hospital staff, she gained weight, grew taller and rapidly showed signs of sexual maturation. Her continuing cognitive development is carefully documented by the data from a large battery of verbal and non-verbal tests administered during the period between 1971 and 1975.

Two of the most remarkable facets of Genie's case are that: (a) she survived at all; and (b) she changed physically, biologically, socially and cognitively far beyond the prognosis of the experts who worked with her. We would like to speculate that she survived and developed because her first year of life appears to have been relatively normal. In addition, there are no indications that she was retarded, slow or deficient during that time. This evidence comes from the paediatrician who saw her four times during her first eleven months of life (Curtiss, 1977, p. 4). Up until that time, Genie's development was well within the normal range for infants. The doctor noticed a congenital dislocation of the hip which was treated with a pillow splint between four and one-half and eleven months of age. At three months of age she had good head control, at five months she was observed to be alert and to engage in hand-to-mouth movements. Her physical growth continued to range within the 50th percentile until her last visit at eleven months of age, at which time, it was noted that her weight had dropped dramatically to below the 16th percentile. Nevertheless, the doctor recorded that Genie could sit alone, she was alert and had normal primary dentition. Genie was taken to the doctor only once again. At fourteen months of age she developed pneumonitis and was taken to a different paediatrician who stated that she showed signs of retardation but, because she had such a high fever, he could not be sure. Genie's father used this statement as justification to begin her thirteen years of confinement.

Genie's mother claims that Genie was not a cuddly baby, and that she did not coo or babble a lot. Her reports concerning early language are inconsistent: she claims that Genie had begun to talk and then stopped and, conversely, she claims that Genie never talked at all. Whichever story is true, it is certain that Genie began her silent, harnessed, confinement at about 20 to 24 months of age. Her mother states that occasionally Genie was allowed to play in a playpen or on the back steps when she was small. All of these excursions into the outside world stopped once her father confined her to her potty chair and cage.

For Curtiss and her associates there were two major research questions to be addressed (Curtiss, 1977, p. 10): (1) What lay beneath the silent surface of Genie's behaviour? Did she possess linguistic competence that must be activated into performance, a passive knowledge that had been suppressed? Or (2) Was Genie a pubescent adolescent over thirteen and a half years old who did not understand or speak? If the latter were true, had she passed what Lenneberg (1967) termed the critical period for the development of human language? Lenneberg's critical age hypothesis can be interpreted two ways: '(1) a strong version: a human being cannot acquire a first language naturally (by "mere exposure") after puberty, and (2) a weak version: *normal* language acquisition cannot occur naturally beyond the critical period' (Curtiss, 1977, p. 208). Four years of intensive instruction and testing support the weaker version of Lenneberg's hypothesis. Genie did not speak or understand initially, rather she attempted to communicate through gestures, and she was very adept at attributing meaning to people's facial expressions, hand and body gestures. As of 1975, Genie's comprehension and production continue to be abnormally disparate. Genie has not developed normal language. As Curtiss (1977) remarks:

'It is possible that even normal adults as well as children call upon this "incomplete" or "gestalt" type of linguistic processing ability, making use of the entire context in which a sentence is spoken with all its redundancies and extralinguistic cues, for most of their everyday language processing.[10] To the extent that this is true, Genie in effect comprehends everyday English. A formal test, however, reveals the deficiencies in the grammar which in everyday usage are compensated for by nonlinguistic factors, and through such testing we find that Genie's comprehension of English is incomplete.' (p. 142)

The relationship between competence and performance is summarised as one in which Genie often manifests less linguistic ability than her underlying competence would allow. The term competence is used to refer to the highly abstract idealised model of grammar. Curtiss agrees with Chomsky's (1975, p. 141) suggestion that it is necessary to 'distinguish between the grammar and a system of information processing *perhaps not specific to language, and to account for actual behavior in terms* of the *interaction of these systems'* (cited in Curtiss, 1977, p. 203, emphasis ours).

We would like to suggest that it would be profitable to look at the 'system of information processing perhaps not specific to language' in order to account for Genie's behaviour now that Curtiss and her associates have determined that Genie cannot acquire normal language naturally (supporting Lenneberg's critical period hypothesis), and, moreover, that she does not appear to have a passive knowledge of English that is waiting for realisation. Genie's environment did not provide the stimuli necessary for language development, however, other kinds of information were available. We will turn to the evidence on Genie's nonverbal and nonsequential skills in order to understand the cognitive development of a child without words.

If Genie had been tested only on verbal, or sequential tasks, she would have been judged severely retarded. Not only could she not speak or understand speech when she was discovered, she was (and remains) slow at sequential motor tasks. However, there were no medically reported signs of retardation during her first year of life. Therefore, it is highly probable that her relationship with her physical and social environment changed dramatically during her second year of life, the period that marked the beginning of her confinement, which resulted in the development of extraordinary perceptual schemata. Nonverbal and nonsequential tests demonstrate that Genie is not retarded. Rather, she became highly skilled at certain cognitive tasks as she accommodated to a very peculiar environment in which only restricted types of information were available to her. Her continued interaction and perception of the objects and events available to her resulted in very different schemata of her 'real world' than that of a normal child. Curtiss (1977, p. 234) concludes that Genie is a 'right hemisphere thinker'. She apparently processes not only language, but many other perceptual phenomena with her right hemisphere, even though left hemispheric localisation would be normally expected due to the fact that she is right handed. She is what Bogen (1973) terms an appositional or gestalt thinker.[11] Many of her perceptual skills exceed the levels known for normal adults.

Even before Genie was tested for nonverbal cognitive skills, it was noticed that she possessed a remarkable ability to gestalt numbers one through seven.

'When asked to get five napkins, or when asked how many trays there were in a pile, for example, Genie responded immediately, without counting, and always correctly. She would simply reach into a drawer and pull out the number of items requested.

Genie responded faster than we could count. It was as if she had the tactile image of what three, four, five, or whatever, "felt" like, and the visual image of what one through seven looked like. (Her ability to gestalt numbers stopped at seven.)

In contrast, she did not know how to count in serial order, and it took over 2 years of work to get her to count at all successfully. This cognition of numbers (one through seven) reflected a more general well-developed gestalt perception ability as evidenced by her performance on tests specifically designed to tap this ability' (Curtiss, 1977, p. 222).

It is interesting to note that her ability to count sequentially is now somewhat surplanting her ability to gestalt numbers. However, her attempts to learn language have not diminished her other gestalt skills. In various gestalt tests (Street Gestalt, Harshman Figures, Thurstone Closure Speed Test, and the Mooney Faces Test), Genie's performance placed her well above the average adult range. All of these tests measure a subject's ability to perceive a seemingly disorganised or unrelated group of parts as a meaningful whole. For example, the widely used Mooney Face Test, considered the most reliable, requires the subject to identify whether or not black and white drawings are real faces or false faces. In Genie's case, all possible 70 pictures of the test were used: 50 silhouette-type drawings of real faces; including 20 'false' faces, and 10 questionable items that are often eliminated because few people are able to classify them. In order for a response to be considered correct, the subject must be able to identify facial features in the drawing. Genie scored 100 per cent on the real faces and 75 per cent on the false faces. Her errors were due to overinterpretation: faces that could have been masks or caricatures. Curtiss (1977, p. 224) concludes: 'Despite this fact, Genie's performance is, to my knowledge, the highest performance reported in the literature for either child or adult on this test.'

Another surprising skill that contrasts with the slowness with which she performs sequential tasks is the speed with which she gestalts numbers (i.e. faster than the researchers can count the items) and the speed with which she performs the Nebes (1971) Arc/circle Test which normally requires one-half hour to one hour to perform. The test requires a subject to match Plexiglass arches to one of three Plexiglass circles. The models are visually presented and labelled before the test is begun and then removed from view. The model circles can be touched at any time throughout the test, but only with one finger. The arches are never presented visually. Forty-five stimuli are presented and the test is divided into three parts separated by two two-minute breaks. Genie completed the test in thirteen minutes, including the required breaks. Her performance is among the best reported to date (Curtiss, 1977, p. 224–225).

It is perhaps possible to explain Genie's behaviour with an interactive model of cognition, in which we take three spheres of interaction into account: (1) the perceptual 'equipment' Genie began with as an infant; (2) the types of information the environment had to offer; and (3) the preferred modes of transmitting information to Genie through the aberrant selections made by her family. The interactions of these three spheres, in turn, resulted in the development of certain cognitive endpoints, perhaps at the expense of others. We assume that Genie was normal as an infant. We know the sparse contents of her physical environment which were presented to her primarily through visual and tactile perceptual modes due to the apparent absence of affective human contact and language as communication. Isolated in her one-room prison with her potty chair, cage, occasional plastic items and her own body as the only objects available to perception, Genie developed anti-cipatory schemata to interact with the restricted, unchanging stimuli around her in such a way that she was able to increase the perceptual information available through continued practice. The result was that Genie developed highly skilled tactile and visual schemata to perceive her environment in a gestalt manner. She became increasingly expert at picking up the limited information which was available to her, which accounts for the great disparity between her language (and other sequential) skills and her appositional (gestalt) skills.

Neisser (1976, p. 9) asserts that perception is where cognition and reality meet; and moreover, he argues that each of us is created by the cognitive acts in which we engage (1976, p. 11). Genie was transformed into a mute, but highly skilled appositional perceiver, whose neurological structures reflect the magnitude of the environmental pressures under which she developed.

We would like to suggest that this extreme case of social and physical deprivation has much to tell us about normal development of children in differing environments. We have argued that such an aberrant social and physical environment can produce cognitive endpoints that evidence skilled perceptual abilities which are quite disparate from those endpoints which are the goals of normative Western socialisation. Genie has taught us that perception and cognition are not entirely logocentric. Therefore, we would like to propose that nonverbal, nonsequential, appositional skills could develop in normal cultural environments where an extreme value on logocentrism is absent. It is perhaps possible that other cultures could select types of perceptual information as valued cognitive endpoints. For example, tactile, or visual information might serve as the bases for the development of nonverbal and nonsequential schemata. Differing environments exact differ-ing perceptual requirements, and the necessity to acquire information selectively about one's security and survival through the medium of a particular set of perceptions very possibly can encourage the formation of specific early cognitive trends. Therefore, we must pay heed to the real perceptual world of infants and young children who develop within different cultures and subcultures. Let us turn to the discussion of the possible effects of one aspect of reality upon the developing cognitive schemata of infants.

The Structure of Caretaker–Child Interaction and its Relationship to Cognitive Trends in Infancy

The initial obligation of a cultural group to its offspring is to ensure their survival by offering them security and nurturance in their infancy. The second obligation is to inculcate the appropriate cultural meaning of behaviours that will allow children to participate satisfactorily in the social life of the group. These considerations are major determinants of the kinds of communication which pass between infants and caretakers. In this section we propose a heuristic model of early communication which we hope will prove useful to investigate the links between the discharge of these obligations and the establishment of cultural differences in cognitive orientations beginning in infancy. First we will outline the model, and then we will discuss the implications such a model could have for the cross-cultural study of cognition and the relationship between cognitive orientations and early experience. Finally, we will raise questions about the relationships which may exist between culturally preferred styles of communicating with infants and the predominant styles of instruction a culture makes use of to educate their young people.

The major points of our argument are as follows. Each culture has a customary mode of infant caretaking which patterns the communications taking place between caretaker and infant. Conceivably, differences in cognitive orientations—in the development of anticipatory schemata—may arise from differences in the way these communications are structured. In turn, variations in structure arise from variations in caretaking patterns, which ensure that different sets of stimuli are presented to the infant's perception.

Although we think that in order properly to study communication and its relationship to cultural differences in the development of individual cognitive skills, it would be necessary to study all the pathways through which significant information is transmitted to infants and young children, such an investigation is too ambitious to be attempted here. We propose, therefore, to limit our inquiries and discussions to some of the earliest communications occurring in the life of infants. We will restrict our use of the term 'communication' to three aspects of patterned caretaker–child interaction, which are: (1) communication as a vehicle for the transmission and reception of messages about the proximity of a caretaker, (2) communications which inform the caretaker about the state of the infant,[12] and (3) communications which inform the infant of the cultural meaning of her/his own behaviour. This third type of communication takes place when caretakers consistently interpret and respond to their infant's vocalisations and actions in terms of the meanings they impute to these behaviours (cf. Trevarthen, 1974). Caretakers derive these meanings from cultural beliefs about the nature of infants, and what they require to maintain their physical and emotional well-being. We posit that the early development of specific perceptual skills (that is, skills related to the kind of information which is actively sought) may be linked to culturally standardised styles of transmitting information to infants, and that infants become linked to the meanings implicit in the social reality of their own culture by the slow crystallisation of intersubjectivity developed through caretakers' interpretations of their behaviour.[13] These meaningful messages which pass between infant and caretaker can be transmitted through either vocal or tactile channels and can be received through the mediation of any pertinent perceptual modality, i.e. any combination of auditory, olfactory, visual, tactile and (even) gustatory perceptions.[14]

To a great extent, the kinds of stimuli available to an infant in order to perceive whether or not a caretaker is close by depend on the standardised caretaking customs of a culture. These determine the kinds of messages about proximity that will occur. The structure of the caretaking situation (i.e. whether children are carried on the back, on the caretaker's side, or are distanced, and carried relatively little), is conducive to the development of cognitive anticipations for both the *messages* and the *media* by which they are transmitted (McLuhan, 1964; Wober, 1966, 1974).[15] Information pick-up by infants thus becomes increasingly skilled in relation to these media (e.g. whether perception is focused on the reception of tactile messages, or vocal messages, etc.). By continuously accommodating a particular type of information, the cognitive schemata increasingly become better prepared selectively to direct attention toward the pick-up of additional, similar information (Neisser, 1976).[16] In our discussion of communication, the term 'structure' refers to the differences in patterning of caretaker–child re- lationships, for each of the patterns we will describe structures the perceptions of the interactors. These structures take three basic forms (although there are many variations on each of these): (1) those in which the proximity of the caretaker is signalled to the infant primarily by tactile stimulation,[17] (2) those in which the infant is separated in space from the caretaker and must be assured that the caretaker is close by, primarily through auditory (and later, visual) stimulation,[18] and (3) those communications which are structured by a combined form of these two. We should mention that there is a fourth, artificial form of communication which 'deceives' the infant and enhances feelings of security by mimicking contact with a caretaker. Two examples of deceptive forms are proprioceptive stimulation due to swaddling (Brackbill, 1971, 1973)[19] and vestibular stimulation afforded by being rocked in a cradle or swung in a hammock (Ter Vrugt and Pederson, 1973; Korner and Grobstein, 1966; Korner and Thoman, 1972).

Although we do not equate proximity and security, we suggest that an infant's awareness of the presence of a protective other may be necessary to a basic sense of security, and is phylogenetically adaptive for the reasons proposed by Bowlby (1969),[20] as well as being a contemporary, culturally adaptive means for acquiring the basic social understandings and modes of intersubjective exchange which are specific to the infant's own culture (cf. Richards, 1974; Brazleton, 1977; Brazleton *et al.*, 1974).

The dialectical process of a developing intersubjectivity was observed by Trevarthen and his colleagues as a characteristic of the 'conversational' exchanges between five North American middle-class mothers and their infants (Trevarthen, 1974, pp. 230–235). This research indicates that affective exchange of communications between mother and infant has the adaptive function of integrating the child into the social group.[21] Trevarthen posits that babies are endowed with a 'growing innate social function' which forms the foundation of interpersonal communication (Trevarthen, 1974, p. 235). The mechanism he suggests is that as infants act (e.g. move their limbs, smile, grimace, vocalise, sneeze, blink their eyes, etc.) these actions are interpreted by caretakers as meaningful and acted upon accordingly. Trevarthen's work concentrates on face-to-face communicative interaction in which vocality and gaze exchange are the most salient features. It appears reasonable that the communicative form through which the social function is developed may potentially be resonant with any one of the three basic communicative forms mentioned above, each of which is uniquely organised by the socialisation practices of the culture into which a child is born. These forms provide both a physical and psychological framework in which the cognitive processes of the child encounter certain stimuli as more meaningful, more affectively charged, and more consistently presented to her/his sensory receptors than other stimuli.

The particular structure of a communicative form is culturally determined, and further, may be the product of adaptation by a group to its ecological environment.[22] Although all caretakers combine both tactile and vocal media to afford their infants information regarding the caretaker's proximity (e.g. infants everywhere are carried, caressed, spoken to, made noise at, held on the lap, etc.), still, cultural ideas concerning what is necessary to maintain the well-being of infants will determine whether tactile or vocal stimulation is selected as the dominant form of communicating. LeVine asserts that the child-rearing practices in traditional cultures are adaptive strategies which have evolved over generations. They persist because they act effectively to counter environmental hazards that jeopardise the health and well-being of infants and children. Some standardised child-rearing strategies are universal, while others are dictated by particular environmental constraints, but they are all encoded in customs and transmitted socially, through generations. The particular selective mechanism LeVine suggests works through mothers who transmit their own successful strategies of child-rearing to their (consequently) more numerous off-spring and to other women who accept their methods and advice (LeVine, 1977).[23] Thus, the child-rearing customs encountered by the neonate generally exist because they have been ecologically adaptive in the past. However, the evolved customs provide the cultural matrix for communication between infant and caretaker and ensure a regularity and consistency in the quality and content of mother–child interactions. The caretaking customs in the USA which are viewed as necessary to ensure the health and safety of infants frequently require that infants be 'distanced' from their parents' bodies for significant periods of time during the day. The relatively minimal time United States parents spend in physical contact with their infants has been noted by several investigators (Clay, 1966, after Montague, 1971; Lewis and Freedle, 1977; Ainsworth, 1977b). Infants generally are placed in cribs, playpens, infant-seats, or highchairs for many of their waking hours, and it is usually considered unhealthy and dangerous for infants to sleep in the same bed with their parents. Distancing leads to proportionately greater reliance on vocal signals than on kinesic signals by both infants and caretakers. Distancing also tends to establish a demand – response pattern in which infants often must take the initiative and 'inform their caretakers about state-fluctuations by emitting a variety of vocal signals (i.e. contented babbling, frets, or cries) which are monitored and responded to in terms of the meaning they have for the caretaker.

In contrast, in many traditional communities infants are maintained in virtually constant, close physical contact with caretakers (Konner, 1972, 1977; Marvin *et al.*, 1977; Tulkin, 1977; Ainsworth, 1967, 1977b; Goldberg, 1977) and have little need to rely on vocal distress signals.[24] In fact, in traditional communities in the northern Andes of South America, a baby's cry is perceived as an indication of illness, and as a result much effort is expended to maintain babies in a quiescent state by allowing them to nurse frequently, and by carrying them on the back for most of the day.[25] While on the caretaker's back, infants receive constant stimulation (e.g. tactile and/or proprioceptive and vestibular stimulation) due to contact with the caretaker's body and to experiencing the caretaker's movements. In this contact communication structure, the infant's first stirrings of distress or feelings of discomfort are perceived by the caretaker via the baby's movements[26] (McKee, 1979), which are interpreted and responded to by caretakers. Thus, by immediate response to perceived needs, caretakers are able to suppress effectively infant vocality. This suppression has been noted by a number of investigators in Latin American communities where infants are carried on the back (e.g. Brazleton, 1977; LeVine, 1977; Klein *et al.*, 1977). Within these cultures, in early infancy vocal communication is a secondary channel of message exchange between caretaker and child, and kinesic-tactile communication is the culturally sanctioned primary channel.

Brazleton reports on the message-carrying power of infant movements to elicit maternal response among a group of Maya Indians: 'The child-rearing emphasis is on subdued motor activity and on averting a demand–response pattern. When the infants' motor activity was elicited in our test situation, the lactating mothers' breasts leaked milk. In the United States culture, such a 'let-down' response follows a baby's cry' (Brazleton, 1977, p. 176). It should be pointed out, however, that in cultures in which infants are carried, once children begin to walk and are off the back for long periods of time during the day, then face-to-face verbal exchange becomes the communicative form which is generally dominant. This change occurs around one and a half years of age for most healthy children.[27]

Some kind of face-to-face positioning accompanied by physical contact seems to be the necessary condition for mutual exchange of vocal communication between caretakers and young infants. Lewis and Freedle, after studying vocal interaction between forty United States middle-class and lower-class infants (aged twelve weeks) and their mothers,[28] reported that in both social classes, when infants are distanced by being placed in an infant seat, the probability of vocal exchange is almost zero. Rather, vocalisation is unidirectional, mother-to-infant.[29] When contact was combined with face-to-face positioning, i.e. when infants were placed on mothers' laps, the vocal switching (participation by both mother and infant in a listener–speaker format) greatly increased in both the lower- and middle-class samples (Lewis and Freedle, 1977).

The relationship of body position to probability of vocal exchange may be quite strong. The communication form which allows for a combination of physical contact with face-to-face positioning is found in cultures in which children are carried on the caretaker's hip or arm. The !Kung San of Botswana, a gathering–hunting people, carry their infants in a side sling on the caretaker's hip. The sling allows infants a great deal of freedom of movement, and the face-to-face positioning is conducive to eye-contact and vocal exchange. Caretakers use conversation to distract a complaining infant, and in addition, side-carrying allows other children social access to the baby. Among the !Kung, Konner reports that older children frequently play with and talk to babies while they are being carried on their mother's hips (Konner, 1972; 1976; 1977). Additionally, the side-carrying form and all other communicative forms in which the infant is in both physical contact and a face-to-face position *vis-à-vis* the caretaker (e.g. on the lap) affords the highest input of stimulation, because stimuli are received simultaneously by virtually all sensory receptors.

Decidedly different sets of stimuli are presented to the infant's attention if the majority of messages are received through proximal sensory receptors (i.e. those communications mediated by physical contact), as opposed to reception through distal receptors (those communications mediated through the auditory and visual modes) or through a combined form of these. In each case, the cognitive structures of the infant, i.e. the anticipatory-schemata, which control the perceptions necessary to obtain information from a communication, will select and accommodate qualitatively different 'news' about the proximity and state of the caretaker.[30]

To help clarify this point, we have constructed a model accompanied by an explication (Table 10.1). The conditions for each interaction structure are stated in the headings, and the arrows indicate the directional flow of information. If a change were to occur in the structural relationship between mother and infant, it would necessitate a change in form; for example, if a mother is carrying an infant on her back, and then moves the baby to her lap in order to nurse it, the form changes from 'on the back' to 'face-to-face with contact'.

TABLE 10.1 THREE MODELS OF PROXIMITY SIGNALLING DURING CARETAKER–CHILD INTERACTIONS

	Communications		
Exchange mode	Contact: on the back	Contact: face-to-face	No contact: distanced
Tactile	MO ←→ CH	MO ←→ CH	MO CH
Visual	MO ←— CH	MO ←→ CH	MO ←→ CH
Auditory	MO ←→ CH	MO ←→ CH	MO ←→ CH
Vocal	MO CH	MO ←→ CH	MO ⇄ CH

As the model demonstrates, when infant and caretaker are in close physical contact, tactile stimulation is received by the proximal receptors of both interactors, whereas in the 'distanced' structure there is no tactile stimulation. Children carried on the back have visual contact with their caretakers although they can see very little of their faces; but caretakers do not have visual contact with infants' faces (unless, of course, the structure is changed to one of the other two forms). Auditory stimulation is present in all three forms, but as we have already noted, caretakers generally do not vocalise to infants on the back (LeVine, 1977; McKee, 1979). Distanced infants may initiate vocal signals to promote their caretaker's proximity, and caretakers talk to their distanced infants, which informs the baby about the caretaker's proximity, but this signalling across space is usually unidirectional. The optimal form for a vocal exchange is found in the contact: face-to-face model.

Can Infants Remember?

The suggestion that redundant perceptual experience influences the development of cognitive structures necessarily includes some notion of perdurable effects, that is, of infantile capacity to remember. Infants, to some degree, would have to be able to anticipate certain sets of stimuli pertaining to salient objects and to recurring events. Until recently, internal representation (i.e. both mental images and symbolic thought) was considered to appear in children at around 18–24 months of age (Piaget, 1973; Piaget and Inhelder, 1969). Thus, if infants could not retain a mental image of the objects in their environment, the effects of the environment could be considered as relatively negligible beyond the opportunities it offered for the development and rehearsal of action schemas.

It is of considerable interest, therefore, that evidence from recent research indicates that very young infants are able not only to make distinctions between persons and inanimate objects, but in addition they seem to be able to distinguish between familiar, salient persons, such as their own mothers, and other persons.[31]

Trevarthen reports the finding that infants respond to people and objects in a qualitatively different manner. When interacting with people, infants attempt to communicate with them, whereas they attempt to do things with objects: they visually explore them, and try to grasp, pick up, or step on them (Trevarthen, 1974).[32] Video-taped sequences of infants interacting with their mothers, or alternatively, with a stranger, show infants displaying a selective and affective array of responses to mothers, in contrast to a 'turning away' response to the strange woman (Brazleton, 1978).[33]

The selective attention awarded by infants to the voice, scent and face of their own mothers is evidenced in the results reported by several experiments using tasks of recognition.[34] For instance, infants of three days of age will turn more frequently towards their mothers who are standing out of the range of vision and calling the child's name, than they will to an unfamiliar woman who calls them (MacFarlane, 1978),[35] and Mills demonstrated that infants will exert considerable effort to hear their mothers' voices. She found that babies between 20 and 30 days' old would suck significantly more on a nipple in order to hear a recording of their own mother's voice than they would suck to hear the voice of a female stranger matched for volume (Mills and Melhuish, 1974). Infants of two weeks of age prefer looking at human faces rather than at other head-like stimuli (Fantz, 1961) and they prefer looking at their mother's face to looking at the face of a woman who is a stranger to them (Carpenter, 1974), an interesting finding given the general preference for viewing human faces.[36]

Spoken language is a unique feature of our species, and it is significant that infants perceive speech sounds as a special kind of acoustic stimulus (Friedlander, 1970; Morse, 1972; Trehub and Robinovitch, 1972). Paying selective attention to speech sounds, as Richards points out, 'will lead (infants) into the channel of communication which will eventually allow the acquisition of language' (Richards, 1974, p. 91).[37] New-borns (12–48 hours old) react to the speech of humans by displaying synchrony of movement to the speech rhythms of the adult interacting with them—an effect that has been observed also in conversing adults wherein speaker and listener move in synchrony (Condon and Ogston, 1967; Condon and Sander, 1974; Bullowa, Fidelholtz and Kessler, 1975; Brazleton, 1978; Trevarthen, 1974).[38] These tendencies on the part of infants are significant for they indicate that infants have some memory for salient stimuli (Bond, 1972; Friedlander, 1970; Salapatek, 1969) evidenced in their capacity to respond to stimulus discrepancy between 'mother' and 'stranger'.

Meltzoff and Moore (1977) have demonstrated that very young infants (16–21 days old) can imitate human gestures (protruding of the tongue, protruding the lips, opening the mouth, or clenching of the fists). Meltzoff's findings provide a further challenge to Piaget, who maintains that deferred imitation (the ability to imitate the action of a model when the model is not present), is not possible until Stage 6 (18–24 months) of the preoperational period: 'For Piaget, a mental image is not an image unless the child distinguishes it from a perception, he must differentiate the image from what it pictures' (Baldwin, 1967, p. 230).

Although the question of the age at which infants mentally are able to represent salient persons is far from settled, the research discussed above indicates that infants have the capability to act on the basis of a perceptually absent stimulus in the early weeks and months of life. We are increasing our understanding of the ways in which tactile, visual, olfactory and auditory perceptions offer us information about the physiological and psychological states of the persons with whom we interact. Furthermore, they afford us cues concerning the general orientations and intentions of persons in our environment toward ourselves (Hall, 1966; Montague, 1971). The susceptibility of infants to these cues as demonstrated by the research discussed above is leading to a radical reappraisal of infants: we begin to view them as receptive to the information the environment offers, and very early in life, as Richards puts it, actively negotiating with their parents to have their demands met.[39]

Trevarthen maintains that intelligence is the resultant of interpersonal interaction and that the 'maturation of consciousness and the ability to act with voluntary control in the physical world is a product rather than an ingredient of this process' (Trevarthen, 1974, p. 230). We have suggested that the roots of interpersonal interactions, as observed in the relationship between caretaker and infant, are distinctly cultural. With this in mind, perhaps we can begin, with a renewed respect for the flexibility of our species, to explore the richness and diversity displayed in the reflections of human intelligence in different cultural and ecological contexts.

Cognition and the Transmission of Cultural Knowledge

Many investigators have pointed to the effect of cultural environments on the socialisation of modal personality (Whiting, Child and Lambert, 1966; Whiting and Whiting, 1975; LeVine, 1969; Bacon, Barry and Child, 1959), and on the cognitive style of a cultural group (Berry, 1976, 1977; Dasen, 1974;

Wober, 1974; Deregowski, 1977; Witkin *et al.*, 1962; Witkin and Berry, 1975; Price-Williams, 1975). Based on the findings of these studies, it is clear that research into cross-cultural differences in cognitive orientations and abilities should begin with careful specification of macro-environmental factors and the delineation of cognitive skills requisite to the demands of subsistence in a given ecological setting. We have argued that the next step is to study the dynamics of the socialisation of cognition during infancy. Although this is a difficult assignment, we think it could be realised, at least partially, by examining the relationship between the phenomenal world of infants (the set of objects they have available to their perception) and the particular structure used by caretakers to transmit security-promoting messages about proximity to their infants. Now, relying on the model of infant-care customs outlined above, we proceed in the realm of speculation·and offer some tentative thoughts about how the study of the early socialisation of cognition in infancy could afford us some interesting problems for future research.

The preferred methods of educating children in traditional societies are often the informal or non-formal styles of instruction (cf. Wilbert, 1976, p. 8). Informal instruction is accomplished by means of a non-verbal performance by the teacher which the student carefully observes; non-formal instruction may utilise both verbal and non-verbal instruction, although verbal instruction may be indirect, making use of myths, songs or stories to teach the pupil. Both these traditional styles are characterised by a personal relationship between teacher and pupil which often is affectively charged. As Cohen (1971, p. 44) points out, in traditional forms of education pupils are encouraged to identify with their teachers. Additionally, in an informal or non-formal learning context, shared key symbols and cultural values often are communicated together with the pragmatics of the specific task at hand.[40] Although the use of language is certainly not excluded from the context of informal education, success in observational learning depends on practised perception of the performance of the instructor, and the altering states of the objects being manipulated whether, let us say, one is carving a canoe, gelding an animal or making a clay pot. Similarly, skill in observing minute irregularities or alterations in the environment is necessary if one is learning to gather vegetable foods, hunt, herd or cultivate plants.

Given the requirements for becoming a successful observer (in order to become a successful performer) in a society in which informal instruction is institutionalised, we should determine if there are specific forms of infant caretaking which are associated with this method of instruction. It might be possible to arrive at some of the early factors responsible for differences in cognitive skills and abilities if we could establish some kind of continuity between (let us say), a caretaking form which requires that infants be carried on the back and reinforced for silence, and an educational method that requires skill in observation. The suppression of vocality (which as we noted earlier is customary when infants are on the back) and the low degree of motor interference due to being wrapped in a shawl or swaddled (cf. Brazleton, 1977) allow infants more opportunity to observe, anticipate and attend to the activities and the perceived responses of their caretakers, and of other people within their perceptual field. To what extent, then, is the way information is picked up in infancy continuous and compatible with the way information is transmitted to older children in order to instruct them in the social, economic and ritual skills essential to members of their society? In other words, we are asking if it is possible that early-developed schemata (the anticipations developed during infancy) are functionally linked to the kinds of cognitive capabilities demanded by the cultural style of educating children.

We should also investigate the compatibility which may exist between the distanced caretaking form which prevails in Western cultures, and the kinds of cognitive abilities required for formal education in technological cultures. As we noted earlier, infants distanced in space from a caretaker are often required to take the initiative and vocally signal to caretakers to bring them into proximity. It would be interesting to investigate the extent to which continuities exist between our culturally preferred caretaking customs and our educational practices which require individual initiative, linear processing of information (through the medium of the written word) and verbal proficiency (cf. Cohen, 1969). We think it is important to examine the trajectory of cognitive skills which are developed during the course of interaction with environmental stimuli during infancy and early childhood. If anthropologists and psychologists are able to devise methods to accomplish this aim, perhaps we can discover, in our own and in other cultures, how the communication skills children acquire over time become linked to the cultural pathways of attaining knowledge and to the understandings which pre-exist as meaningful, valued and essential aspects of the adult world into which the infant is born.

Conclusion

We join other investigators in the plea for the cross-cultural study of the causal factors which produce differences in cognitive orientations and abilities (Nerlove and Snipper, in press; Ember, 1977). As yet, we know too little of the adaptive functions of our non-linguistic cognitive abilities, most likely because these adaptations appear useless or trivial in a technological society bent on 'modernisation', and thus, on standardisation.

The outstanding performance of Genie on gestalt tests is convincing evidence for the existence of non-linguistic abilities, and for the sensitivity of cognitive development to environmental contexts. We have suggested that the skills required by differing environments, and cultural differences in experience in early life, may be reflected in the development and elaboration of cognitive schemata. Moreover, we have offered the suggestion that if there is a continuity in the modes by which significant information is transmitted to children, from infancy through childhood, the anticipations thus developed may form a stable base for the learning style institutionalised by a culture. Finally, perception of the environment includes affective interaction with caretakers who are themselves socialised members of a culture. Socialised caretakers attribute meaning to their infants' behaviours on the bases of cultural premises and values. Thus meaning and perception may be inextricably entwined from the very start of life, and the structure of communication between child and caretaker affords the matrix from which perceptual schemata and meaningful understanding can be generated.

In order to understand and appreciate the range of cognitive *capacities* that are intrinsic to human beings, we must examine the cognitive *skills* that are brought to bear for the solution of similar problems in differing cultural and physical environments. Such a comparative, cross-cultural approach would provide the data to test an interactive theory of cognition, which proposes that perceptual schemata result from the selective attention of the child to the available and salient information in her/his environment. Cognition, then, is best studied within a relevant ecological context. We have suggested that ethnographies of the socialisation of cognition should begin with the study of the structured communication between infant and caretaker, and subsequently turn to the cognitive and perceptual opportunities children encounter as they move about in their social/ecological milieux. We should document how differential cognitive skills are enhanced as a developing child interacts with specific social and physical environments in order to become successful at specific tasks. We are suggesting that the place to begin such cross-disciplinary, longitudinal research is at society's cradle—the locus of the beginnings of interactive communication.

Acknowledgements

We are grateful to Margery Ciaschi, Denise Everhart and David Beyda for their aid in the preparation of this manuscript, and to William Lambert, Ulric Neisser, Bernd Lambert and Dennis Tedlock for their valued comments, although all responsibility for any errors rests solely with the authors.

B. J. Isbell is the author of the section on linguistics and the case study of Genie. The section on caretaking customs and cognition was written by L. McKee.

Notes

1. What we are thinking of here are the experimental designs that require subjects to verbalise the reasons for their actions. For example, standard Piagetian experi-

ments usually call for explanations of the reasons why a child made the choices executed during contrived situations (see Greenfield, 1976 for a critical discussion of this method). The usual method for the study of modes of classifications is to have subjects engage in the activity and then ask for their rationales. The ability to verbalise one's problem-solving strategies, as we have mentioned in the introduction, appears to be a skill associated with the impact of Western education. Recently, researchers have devised non-verbal Piagetian tests (Greenfield, 1966; Bovet, 1974; Cole *et al.*, 1971). Economically important skills such as weaving, pottery making and tailoring (Price-Williams *et al.*, 1969; Greenfield and Child, 1973; and Lave, 1977) are being studied as part of the new direction of research on cultural contexts of learning and thinking. (Cole *et al.*, 1971; Scribner, 1976; Cole and Bruner, 1974).

2. See Conklin (1972) for bibliography of more than 5000 references on folk classifications. It is interesting to note the sparcity of references on classification of non-verbal sensations such as olfactory, tactile and visual forms. The implicit assumption that language, to some degree, determines non-linguistic behaviour (for example, sorting out concrete phenomena into categories) follows from either the weak or strong version of the Whorf-Sapir hypothesis (cf. Rosch, 1974 for discussion). Formalism, another hallmark of cognitive anthropology, grew out of structural linguistics (Jameson, 1972). One of the debates that developed in the 1960s in cognitive anthropology is whether or not the orderliness of classificatory systems reflects the orderliness of cognition (cf. Burling, 1970). In other words, can we assume that classificatory systems are psychologically real? Other issues that have developed include the role of cognitive diversity within a population, and the acquisition of folk categories. In addition, a good deal of recent research (cf. *The American Ethnologist*, **3**, No. 3, 1976) is being directed towards 'discovering the constraints in nature and in the human mind which may account for the pan-cultural regularities [observed]' (Hunn, 1976, p. 508).

   Rosch and her associates (Rosch *et al.*, 1976; Rosch, in press) have set forth a theory of categorisation that addresses the basic question of the relationship between perceived phenomena and the construction of categories. Rosch (in press) explores two fundamental issues: the nature of categories and the role of stimulus attributes in the formation of categories. Her argument is that the prevailing 'digital' model of categories in terms of logical conjunctions of discrete criterial attributes (i.e. either/or, plus/minus contrasts) is inadequate for natural categories. An alternative 'analog' model is presented which represents natural categories as composed of a 'core meaning'—the prototype, or clearest cases or examples—'surrounded' by other members of decreasing similarity (the spatial metaphor is intentional). Rosch makes the strong claim that many categories (e.g. colour, form and facial expressions) become organised around perceptually salient prototypes, that is to say, those stimuli that attract attention and are more easily remembered. These categories are formed in such a way so as to maximise the correlation of attributes, or redundancy, within categories. Redundancy provides predictability and increasingly more information for the perceiver. Rosch argues that for such domains, both the content of categories as well as the process of formation can be expected to be universal. Cross-cultural research is needed to test these hypotheses.

3. Of course there are qualifications to be made. For example, even though Piaget's theory of intellectual development begins with motor development, the endpoint of the growth process is formal operations, or abstract thought. The means to decide whether a child has arrived at the level of formal operations is usually determined through verbal interaction between experimenter and child.

Greenfield (1976, p. 325) has noted that Piaget's notion of progressive development really depicts the development of a Western scientist. An idea which causes
considerable problems in the cross-cultural context.

Another major area of cognitive research which might be said *not* to be
logocentric is the study of vision (see Held and Richards, 1976, for recent research).
Nevertheless, some studies do require verbal responses, or the visual stimuli used
are letters, or words. We grant that it is difficult to design experiments without
verbal exchanges, but as will be seen later in our argument, naturalistic
observations of modes of perception and interaction are called for.

4. For a fascinating collection of papers on informal and non-formal education,
   which is preponderantly non-verbal, see *Enculturation in Latin America* (1976),
   edited by Johannes Wilbert. In the introduction, Wilbert proposes a heuristic
   model which consists of three dimensions: (1) the goals of enculturation consisting
   of: (a) the training of manual and mental skills, (b) socialisation (or the mode of
   transmission of skills) and (c) moral education; (2) the life cycle stages; and finally
   (3) the ambience or environment, culture and society within which enculturative
   processes occur.
5. Stevenson *et al.* (in press) found that 5- and 6-year-olds from remote tropical
   forest villages in Peru performed better than urban poor 5- and 6-year-olds from
   Lima on perceptual learning tasks. Familiar visual stimuli, and 12 transformations of line-to-curve, size, reversal, rotation and perspective were presented.
   The task demands systematic analysis of similarities and differences. The rural
   children perform the tasks better, regardless of whether they attended school or
   not. They also performed better on single and double seriation, showing greater
   flexibility (i.e. better scores on reverse seriation). The researchers conclude that
   their superior performance can be interpreted in part by the demands of everyday
   experiences to attend to systematic similarities and differences in their environment. It appears unlikely that school experiences would improve upon these skills,
   due to the fact that school is so often divorced from the demands and
   opportunities offered by the environment. A major question is whether the
   cognitive skills acquired through interaction with one's environment are transfer-
   rable to the tasks required in school, and vice versa. To answer this complex issue
   we must compare the demands and opportunities presented to the developing
   child in and out of school (cf. Cole, Gay, Glick and Sharp, 1971; Cole and
   Scribner, 1974; Cole, 1978; Wagner, 1974 and 1977; Goodnow, 1976). The
   knowledge that a 6-year-old child acquires in a non-literate society may appear
   complex and bewildering to an outsider. Bohannan (Smith-Bowen, 1964, pp. 15–
   16) describes her frustration in discovering that she was considered by the Tiv of
   Nigeria as someone with less than the intellectual capacities of a backward child
   because she could not readily differentiate and remember the names of leaves
   from different plants—a task any 6-year-old could perform without difficulty.
   Similarities and differences in the natural environment are vital for children, who
   are expected to be productive members of their society at an early age. We would
   advocate the investigation of the development of this type of knowledge in
   different cultures.
6. Note that the much discussed distinction between competence and performance
   loses its force if we focus rather upon a perceptual cycle in which the type of
   information or the stimuli and the act of 'becoming acquainted with', or cognition
   of the stimuli, are inextricably interconnected.
7. An excellent overview of the recent psycholinguist literature that addresses
   cognitive universals and the biological bases for languages can be found in Taylor
   (1976). Slobin (1971) edited a symposium held in 1965 that illustrates the

controversies concerning the adequacy of transformational grammar for psycho-linguistic research, the innate hypotheses, and finally the growing concern for semantic aspects of languages as possible universals (cf. Rosch, in press).

Another tack was taken by a branch of anthropology that has gained increasing prominence during the last decade: structuralism (Lévi-Strauss, 1963 and 1966) proposes another sort of universal—the universal operation of the human mind to order phenomena in bipolar transformational systems. In 1974, Laughlin and D'Aquili (1974) set forth an argument concerning the biological (neurological) bases for universal structural operations of the mind.

While these developments were taking place, many investigators turned to *The Ethnography of Communication* (Gumperz and Hymes, 1972), which focuses upon a wide variety of speech events as interaction taking place in specific cultural contexts. Meanwhile, within the mainstream of anthropology, the study of symbolic behaviour was beginning to be viewed as interactive communication as well (Turner, 1974 and 1975; Geertz, 1973; Umiker-Sebeok, 1977; MacCannel, in press). Abstract systems, such as symbols and signs, became described in terms of action, relationships or social dynamics. The impact of this trend has been felt within cross-cultural cognitive studies (Ember, 1977), as well as within psychologi-cal anthropology (Kiefer, 1977). Perhaps the convergence of this trend away from formalism and toward context-sensitive analyses within linguistics, anthropology, as well as within cognitive psychology (Cole *et al.*, 1971; see Nerlove's and Snipper's review, in press) has strengthened the same trend in studies of *Speech Play* (Kirshenblatt-Gimblett, 1976), and *The Social Use of Metaphor* (Sapir and Crocker, 1977), as special categories of verbal interaction that build relations between perceptual reality and cognition (cf. Isbell and Roncalla, 1977).

8. We have abstracted the following brief description of Genie's early environment from Curtiss (1977, part I).

9. Later we learn that Genie has a fetish for plastic objects (Curtiss, 1977, pp. 22–24). At one point she had 23 plastic buckets stacked by her hospital bed. One wonders if she was given plastic containers among the other 'toys' that she was occasionally allowed to handle. Also, it would be helpful to know whether or not she had been fed out of plastic containers.

10. We find this statement puzzling. Specifically we wonder what is meant by an 'incomplete' or 'gestalt' type of linguistic processing ability which makes use of context. Too often *logos* and syntax are taken to be so omnipotent that researchers forget that language (everyday English, for example) can be divorced from context by linguists, but not by speakers. Spoken communication would lose most of its meaning without such features as tone, rhythm and pitch along with gestural communication made with the face, hands and body. It appears to us that the grammar alluded to is the incomplete entity, whereas the gestalt type of communication is more complete in terms of information processing, and therefore more difficult to study.

11. For an introduction into the controversies concerning the hemispheric specialis-ations of the human brain consult the following: Gazzaniga (1973); Bogen (1973); Ornstein (1973, 1977 and 1978); Kimura (1976); Luria (1976); Geschwind (1976); and Semmes (1968).

12. We suggest that information about proximity may be highly cathected by infants due to the power of the messages to reassure them that they are 'in touch' with a protective other.

13. These interpretations are derived from cultural norms of behaviour. The cultural meaning of their own behaviour, thus, is first learned by infants through the

responses of others. This is a highly restricted view of meaning, but useful to the study of early, pre-verbal communication.

14. For a discussion of various forms of perceptual reception of non-verbal messages, see Hall (1966) and Montague (1971).

15. Wober has proposed that 'different styles of communication (oral tradition, print or electric recording) are related to different modes of sensory elaboration (apparatus internal to the individual) adapted to these media' (Wober, 1974, p. 127). He labels these different modes sensotypes.

16. In Neisser's theory of perception, the information the perceiver picks up from the environment is not altered (assimilated): rather the anticipations of the perceiver are altered by the perception. With each perception more information becomes available to the schema, which accommodates it and uses it to direct the succeeding perception. In this manner, perception becomes increasingly skilled, and the anticipatory schemata become richer in plan and format (Neisser, 1976).

17. Tactile perceptions include cutaneous contact (direct skin-to-skin) or contact mediated by clothing (and can include the 'touch' of radiated heat when registered by thermal detectors in the skin). Gustatory and olfactory perceptions are most often intermixed, as when infants suck on the skin, finger or nipple of their caretaker.

18. Visual communication is initially limited in young babies due to their restricted distance of focus: approximately 9 inches (MacFarlane, 1978). By three years of age children have attained adult acuity levels (Atkinson and Braddick, 1978).

19. Brackbill has demonstrated that continuous proprioceptive stimulation due to swaddling decreases arousal level in infants. The same effect is achieved if the infant is simultaneously and continuously stimulated in the auditory, visual and proprioceptive–tactile modalities. Chisholm, who studied the effects of cradleboard use on mother–infant interaction, notes that it is generally recognised that swaddling calms babies and induces sleep. One reason cited is that swaddling reduces spontaneous startle reflexes (Moros) which tend to waken infants. The diminishing of motoric responses combined with continuous presentation of stimulation tends to afford infants a more extended sleep period (Chisholm, 1977).

20. See Bowlby (1958, 1969 and 1973) for a discussion of his ethological theory which posits the existence of a phylogenetically adaptive bond between mothers and infants. In primordial times the bond functioned to promote the proximity of children to their mothers, and thus it served to preserve the child from predators. Also see Ainsworth (1963, 1967 and 1977a), Maccoby and Masters (1970); and Bernal (1974).

21. The work of investigators such as Richards (1974), Trevarthen (1974) and Brazleton, Koslowski and Tronick (1976) extends the adaptive functions of an attachment bond (Bowlby, 1969) between infant and mother into the here and now. They direct our attention to the multiple and relevant functions of caretaker–child association among which are the development of sociability and mutuality.

22. Cf. Robert LeVine (1977). However, the adaptation can and does alter rapidly in response to change in either the physical or social environment. Newson and Newson (1974) report the extensive changes in child-rearing customs and attitudes toward children that have occurred in the USA and Britain during the course of the past century.

23. We agree that most child-rearing customs exist because they promote the survival of the individual infant, but we would argue that some child-rearing customs can become institutionalised which may work against the well-being of individual children, while promoting the adaptation of the social group as a whole, over an

extended time period. For example, McKee (1977) reports a folk belief in a rural village in the northern Andes which effectively limited the period of time female infants were permitted to nurse. The cultural rationale of the practice was that the qualities of aggressiveness and heightened sexuality were derived from prolonged nursing; as these were culturally desirable traits for adult males, extended nursing was encouraged for male infants. Conversely, these were inappropriate qualities for adult females to display, and early weaning of female infants was necessary to limit the 'intake' of these male traits. In a tropical–alpine area in which infestations and infections of the intestinal tract are the major cause of death in young children, early weaning of females may be an evolved mechanism of balancing the sex ratio by allowing environmental selection pressures to act on female infants. To speculate that the custom exists because prolonged nursing enhances the survival chances of biologically more vulnerable male infants would be closer to LeVine's argument, but avoids the problem of the relative deprivation suffered by female infants in the society. For a discussion of Andean sex ratios see Bolton (1977). For a different model of demographic control, see Divale and Harris (1976).

24. Cf. LeVine (1977). Also see Brazleton's (1977) discussion of Maya Indians.

25. Whiting (1971 and 1977) correlated a high degree of physical contact between mothers and infants with mean annual temperature: cultures located in world areas with tropical climates were more likely to have child-care customs emphasising physical proximity. LeVine also associates a high degree of physical contact with tropical areas, and offers the explanation that it affords a means for constantly monitoring the state of the child's health in ecological areas characterised by a high infant mortality rate and little access to medical help. He outlines a hierarchy of conscious goals parents desire their children to achieve (e.g. physical survival and health, eventual economic autonomy and the ability to maximise behaviours compatible with cultural values), but he states it is evident that these subsequent goals can only be attained if the antecedent goal of defending the health and well-being of the child is realised (LeVine, 1977).

26. McKee (1979) considers physical contact as a medium of communication through which 'kinesic messages' are emitted by the child. Meaning is attributed to the infant's movements by caretakers, and the attributed meaning determines the kind of response caretakers make to the movement.

27. Klein et al. report a change in frequency of positive verbalisations directed by Guatemalan mothers to their infants as rising from 3 per cent of a half-hour period of observation at 8 months of age to almost 10 per cent at 16 months of age (Klein, Lasky, Yarbrough, Habicht and Sellers, 1977, p. 496). The group of 8-month-old children represented the youngest children in Klein's sample. The investigators reported that these mothers spent a large part of their time at some distance from their (8-, 12- or 16-month-old) infants, but that the total amount of physical contact was quite high, ranging between 18 and 35 per cent of the half-hour observations, whereas the level of caretaker vocalisation to infants was low (3 per cent at 8 months; up to 10 per cent of the half-hour at 16 months of age) (p. 392).

28. Twenty of the mother–infant pairs were middle class and twenty were lower class (Class V on the Hollingshead scale).

29. In the experimental format used by Trevarthen (1974), infants were placed in infant-seats and mothers were requested to 'chat' with their babies. However, mothers were in close proximity to their infants and frequently touched them. This positioning, which occurs frequently in natural mother–infant interactions, is characterised by intermittent physical contact accompanying vocal turn-taking. Such a structure best fits the contact face-to-face form, but the ambiguity of the

structure is a good illustration of the kinds of complexity we will encounter when we begin to apply our communication models to real-life situations!

30. This 'news' may not only be qualitatively different in structure but may also be different in meaning. Greenfield and Bruner note that 'Members of different cultures differ in the *inferences* they draw from perceptual cues, not in the cues they are *able* to distinguish . . . given complex input, the principles of selectivity will vary from culture to culture' (Greenfield and Bruner, 1969, p. 635) (italics ours).

31. Although he affirms that 'the first objects gifted with (cognitive) permanence were other persons and not inanimate objects', Piaget maintains that an initial adualism (the inability to distinguish self from other) characterises cognition in early infancy (Piaget, 1973, p. 46). For Piaget, decentring of effect only occurs during stages five and six of the sensorimotor period of development when the child is one and a half to two years' old.

32. In an earlier study Richards and Trevarthen had documented the reciprocal turn-taking which characterises vocal interaction between mothers and infants in Western cultures (Richards, 1971).

33. Brazleton (1978) maintains that trained observers analysing sequenced frames of film could look at the fingers, toes, eyes and mouth of a baby and determine whether a 3-week-old infant was looking at an object, a parent or a stranger.

34. Excellent reviews of this literature are offered by Pick, Frankel and Hess (1975) and MacFarlane (1977 and 1978).

35. Scent is also a salient proximity cue: MacFarlane (1978) reports from his research on perceptual abilities of infants that babies 6 days' old, presented with the breast pads of their mothers and those of strangers oriented selectively and more frequently to pads which bore the scent of their mothers' *bodies*, than they did to the scent of pads impregnated with their mothers' *milk*, but which had not been in contact with their bodies.

36. The experiments cited above have focused upon the infant's perceptual ability to attend selectively to its *mother's* voice, smell and face; what needs to be tested is infantile response to *any* person (e.g. siblings, grandmothers, etc.) who answers their needs and attends to their comfort in the days and weeks immediately following birth.

37. Kim Atkins (personal communication) suggests that we should find out what people say to infants depending on whether they are distanced or in close contact. It would be interesting to determine if differences in the frequency, content and goals of caretakers' utterances in relation to their preverbal infants could be correlated with the forms of caretaking we have discussed. For a study of cultural variations in mothers' speech to children see Harkness (1975). See also Rogoff (1978).

38. Research films made by Helen Blauvelt (1957) clearly show that there is also a synchrony of movement between parents when they are caretaking and interacting with their new-born infant.

39. Stimulating research investigating the ability of infants to modify the behaviour of the persons in their environment is found in the work of Rheingold (1969), Stern (1971, 1974); and Lewis and Rosenblum's edited volume (1974). Dunn (1976) reviews studies of the behaviour of infants and children in a variety of social contexts, and among other interesting queries, she raises questions about the extent to which the child is a self-directing actor.

40. In contrast to Western formal education, learning contexts in traditional cultures combine multimodal transmission of messages through dance, rhythm, music, myths, tales, ritual dramas and altered states of consciousness. The messages are

highly charged affective cultural statements which define the participants vis-à-vis society and ascribe specific skills to them on the basis of age, sex and status. The redundancy of the messages transmitted heightens the likelihood of successful communication, and thus, of successful socialisation. For an elegant description of the socialisation of children towards the achievement of trance-states, see Bateson (1975).

References

Ainsworth, M. D. S. (1963). The development of infant–mother interaction among the Ganda. In *Determinants of Infant Behavior II* (Ed. B. M. Foss), New York, Wiley

Ainsworth, M. D. S. (1967). *Infancy in Uganda: Infant Care and the Growth of Love.* Baltimore, Md., Johns Hopkins University Press

Ainsworth, M. D. S. (1977a). Attachment theory and its utility in cross-cultural research. In *Culture and Infancy: Variations in the Human Experience.* (Ed. P. H. Leiderman, S. R. Tulkin and A. Rosenfeld), New York, Academic Press

Ainsworth, M. D. S. (1977b). Infant development and mother–infant interaction among Ganda and American families. In *Culture and Infancy: Variations in the Human Experience* (Ed. P. H. Leiderman, S. R. Tulkin and A. Rosenfeld), New York, Academic Press

Atkinson, J. and Braddick, O. (1978). Development of spacial vision in the infant. Colloquium presented to the Department of Psychology, Cornell University, June 7, 1978

Bacon, M., Barry, H. and Child, I. (1959). Relation of child training to subsistence economy, *American Anthropologist*, **61**, 51–63

Baldwin, A. L. (1967). *Theories of Child Development*, New York, John Wiley and Sons, Inc

Bateson, G. (1975). Some components of socialization for trance, *Ethos*, **3** No. 2, 143–155

Bernal, J. (1974). Attachment: some problems and possibilities. In *The Integration of a Child into a Social World* (Ed. Martin P. M. Richards), London, Cambridge University Press

Berry, J. W. (1974). Ecological and cultural factors in spatial perceptual development. In *Culture and Cognition: Readings in Cross-Cultural Psychology* (Eds. J. W. Berry and P. R. Dasen), London, Methuen, 129–140

Berry, J. W. (1976). *Human Ecology and Cognitive Style: Comparative Studies in Cultural and Psychological Adaptation*, New York, John Wiley

Berry, J. W. (1977). Nomadic style and cognitive style. In *Ecological Factors in Human Development* (Ed. Harry McGurk), Amsterdam, North Holland Publishing Co, 229–245

Bever, T. G. (1970). The cognitive basis for linguistic structures. In *Cognition and the Development of Language.* (Ed. John R. Hayes), New York, John Wiley, 279–361

Bogen, J. E. (1973). The other side of the brain: an appositional mind. In *The Nature of Human Consciousness* (Ed. R. E. Ornstein), San Francisco, W. H. Freeman, 101–125

Bolton, R. (1977). High-altitude sex ratios: how high? Paper presented at the 76th annual meeting of the American Anthropological Association

Bond, E. (1972). Perception of form by the human infant. *Psychological Bulletin*, **77**, 225–245

Bovet, M. C. (1974). Cognitive processes among illiterate children and adults. In *Culture and Cognition: Readings in Cross-Cultural Psychology* (Ed. J. W. Berry and P. R. Dasen), London, Methuen, 311–334

Bowlby, J. (1958). The nature of the child's tie to his mother. *International Journal of Psychoanalysis*, **39**, 350–373

Bowlby, J. (1969). *Attachment and Loss*. Vol. 1: *Attachment*, New York, Basic Books

Bowlby, J. (1973). *Separation: Anxiety and Anger*, New York, Basic Books

Brackbill, Y. (1971). Cumulative effects of continuous stimulation on arousal levels in infants, *Child Development*, **42**, 17–26

Brackbill, Y. (1973). Continuous stimulation reduces arousal level: stability of the effects over time, *Child Development*, **44**, 43–46

Brazleton, T. B. (1977). Implications of infant development among the Maya Indians of Mexico. In *Culture and Infancy: Variations in the Human Experience* (Eds. P. H. Leiderman, S. R. Tulkin and A. Rosenfeld), NY, Academic Press, 151–187

Brazleton, T. B. (1978). *Mother–Father–Infant Reciprocity*. Colloquium presented to the Dept. of Human Development and Family Studies, Cornell University, Ithaca, NY, March 28th

Brazleton, T. B., Koslowski, B. and Main, M. (1974). The origins of reciprocity: The early mother–infant interactions. In *The Effect of the Infant on its Care-giver* (Eds. R. Lewis and L. Rosenblum), NY, John Wiley

Brazleton, T. B., Koslowski, B. and Tronick, E. (1976). Neonatal behavior among urban Zambians. *Journal of Child Psychiatry*, **15** No. 1, 97–107

Bullowa, M., Fidelholtz, J. and Kessler, A. (1975). Infant vocalization: communication before speech. In *Socialization and Communication in Primary Groups* (Ed. Thomas R. Williams), The Hague, Mouton

Burling, R. (1970). *Man's Many Voices: Language in its Cultural Context*, NY, Holt, Rinehart and Winston

Carpenter, G. (1974). Mother's face and the new born. *New Scientist*, **21**, 742–744

Carroll, J. B. and Casagrande, J. B. (1958). The function of language classifications in behavior. In *Readings in Social Psychology* (Eds. E. E. Maccoby, T. M. Newcomb and E. L. Hartley), NY, Holt, Rinehart and Winston

Chisholm, J. S. (1977). Developmental ethology of the Navajo: nature and culture on the cradleboard. A paper presented at the 76th Annual Meeting of the American Anthropological Association, Houston, Texas

Chomsky, N. (1957). *Syntactic Structures*, The Hague, Mouton

Chomsky, N. (1961). *On the Notion 'Rule of Grammar'*. Proceedings of Symposia in. Applied Mathematics, Vol. 12, Providence, RI, American Mathematical Soc., 6–24

Chomsky, N. (1975). *Reflections on Language*, NY, Pantheon Books

Clay, V. S. (1966). *The Effect of Culture on Mother–Child Tactile Communication*, PhD Dissertation, Teachers College, Columbia University, NY

Cohen, R. (1969). Conceptual style, culture conflict and non-verbal tests of intelligence. *Am. Anthropologist*, **71**, 828–856

Cohen, Y. A. (1971). The shaping of men's minds: adaptations to imperatives of culture. In *Anthropological Perspectives on Education* (Eds. Murray Wax, Stanley Diamond and Fred Gearing), NY, Basic Books, 19–50

Cole, M. (1978). How education affects the mind. *Human Nature*, **1** No. 4, 50–58

Cole, M. and Bruner, J. S. (1974). Cultural differences and inferences about psychological process. In *Culture and Cogniton: Readings in Cross-Cultural Psychology* (Eds. J. W. Berry and P. R. Dasen), London, Methuen, 231–246

Cole, M., Gay, J., Glick, J. A. and Sharp, D. (1971). *The Cultural Context of Learning and Thinking: An Exploration in Experimental Anthropology*, NY, Basic Books

Cole, M. and Scribner, S. (1974). *Culture and Thought: A Psychological Introduction*, NY, John Wiley

Cole, M. and Scribner, S. (1975). Theorizing about socialization of cognition. *Ethos*, 3 No. 2, 249–268

Condon, W. and Ogston, W. D. (1967). A segmentation of behavior, *Journal of Psychiatric Research*, 5, 221–235

Condon, W. and Sander, L. (1974). Neonate movement is synchronized with adult speech: interactional participation and language acquisition, *Science*, 183, 99–101

Conklin, H. C. (1972). *Folk Classification: A Topically Arranged Bibliography of Contemporary and Background References Through 1971*, New Haven, Dept. of Anthropology, Yale University

Curtiss, S. (1977). *Genie: A Psycholinguistic Study of a Modern-Day 'Wild Child'*, NY, Academic Press

Curtiss, S., Fromkin, V., Krashen, S., Rigler, D. and Rigler, M. (1974). The linguistic development of Genie, *Language*, 50 No. 3, 528–554

Dasen, P. R. (1974). The influence of ecology, culture and European contact on cognitive development in Australian Aborigines. In *Culture and Cognition* (Eds. J. W. Berry and P. R. Dasen), London, Methuen, 381–408

Deregowski, J. B. (1977). An aspect of perceptual organization: some cross-cultural studies. In *Ecological Factors in Human Development* (Ed. Harry McGurk), Amsterdam, North Holland Publishing Co, 261–271

DiVale, W. T. and Harris, M. (1976). Population, warfare, and the male supremacist complex, *American Anthropologist*, 78, 521–538

Dube, E. F. (1977). *A Cross-cultural Study of the Relationship Between Intelligence and Story Recall*, PhD Thesis, Cornell University

Dunne, J. (1976). How far do early differences in mother–child relations affect later development? In *Growing Points in Ethology* (Eds. P. P. G. Bateson and R. A. Hinde), London, Cambridge University Press

Ember, C. R. (1977). Cross-cultural cognitive studies. In *Annual Review of Anthropology* (Ed. Bernard S. Siegal), Vol. 6, Palo Alto, California, Annual Reviews, Inc, 33–56

Fantz, R. L. (1961). The origins of form perception, *Scientific American*, 204, 66–72

Fodor, J. and Garrett, M. (1966). Some reflections on competence and performance. In *Psycholinguistics Papers* (Eds. J. Lyons and J. R. Wales), Edinburgh, University Press

Friedlander, B. Z. (1970). Receptive language development in infancy: issues and problems, *Merrill-Palmer Quarterly*, 16, 7–15

Gazzaniga, M. S. (1973). The split brain in man. In *The Nature of Human Consciousness* (Ed. Robert E. Ornstein), San Francisco, W. H. Freeman, 87–100

Geertz, C. (1973). *The Interpretation of Cultures*, NY, Basic Books

Geschwind, N. (1976). Language and the brain. In *Recent Progress in Perception: Readings from Scientific American* (Eds. Richard Held and Whitman Richards), San Francisco, W. H. Freeman, 238–245

Goldberg, S. (1977). Infant development and mother–infant interaction in urban Zambia. In *Culture and Infancy: Variations in the Human Experience* (Eds. P. H. Leiderman, S. R. Tulkin and A. Rosenfeld), NY, Academic Press, 211–243

Goodnow, J. (1976). The nature of intelligent behavior: questions raised by cross-cultural studies. In *The Nature of Intelligence* (Ed. Lauren B. Resnick), NY, John Wiley, 169–188

Greenfield, P. M. (1966). On culture and conservation. In *Studies in Cognitive Growth* (Eds. J. R. Bruner, R. Oliver and P. Greenfield), NY, Wiley, 225–256

Greenfield, P. M. (1976). Cross-cultural research and Piagetian theory: paradox and progress. In *The Developing Individual in a Changing World.* Vol. I: *Historical and Cultural Issues* (Eds. K. F. Riegel and J. A. Meacham), Chicago, Aldine, 322–333

Greenfield, P. M. and Bruner, J. (1969). Culture and cognitive growth. In *Handbook of Socialization Theory and Research* (Ed. David A. Goslin), Chicago, Rand McNally College Publishing Co, 633–657

Greenfield, P. M. and Childs, C. P. (1973). Weaving, color terms, and pattern recognition: cultural influences and cognitive development among the Zinacantecos of southern Mexico. Paper presented at the First International Conference of the International Association for Cross-Cultural Psychology, Hong Kong

Gumperz, J. J. and Hymes, D. (eds.) (1972). *Directions in Sociolinguistics: The Ethnography of Communication*, NY, Holt, Rinehart and Winston

Hall, T. C. (1966). *The Hidden Dimension*, Garden City, Doubleday

Harkness, S. (1975). Cultural variation in mothers' language, *Child Language*, **27**, 495–498

Held, R. and Richards, W. (eds.) (1976). *Recent Progress in Perception: Readings from Scientific American*, San Francisco, W. H. Freeman

Hunn, E. (1976). Toward a perceptual model of folk biological classification. In *American Ethnologist*, Special issue: Folk Biology, **3**, 508–524

Isbell, B. J. and Roncalla, F. (1977). The ontogenesis of metaphor: riddle games among Quechua speakers seen as cognitive discovery procedures, *Journal of Latin American Lore*, **3** No. 1, 19–49

Jameson, F. (1972). *The Prison-House of Language: A Critical Account of Structuralism and Russian Formalism*, Princeton, NJ, Princeton University Press

Kiefer, C. W. (1977). Psychological anthropology. In *Annual Review of Anthropology.* (Ed. Bernard J. Siegal). Vol. 6, Palo Alto, Ca, Annual Reviews Inc, 103–119

Kimura, D. (1976). The asymmetry of the human brain. In *Recent Progress in Perception. Readings from Scientific American* (Eds. Richard Held and Whitman Richards), San Francisco, W. H. Freeman, 246–254

Kirshenblatt-Gimblett, Barbara (ed.) (1976). *Speech Play: Research and Resources for the Study of Linguistic Creativity*, University of Pennsylvania Press

Klein, R., Lasky, R., Yarbrough, C., Habicht, J.-P. and Sellers, M. J. (1977). Relationship of infant caretaker interaction, social class and nutritional status to developmental test performance among Guatemalan infants. In *Culture and Infancy* (Eds. P. H. Leiderman, S. R. Tulkin and A. Rosenfeld), NY, Academic Press, 385–403

Konner, M. J. (1972). Aspects of the developmental ethology of a foraging people. In *Ethological Studies of Child Behavior* (Ed. N. Blurton-Jones), NY, Cambridge University Press, 285–304

Konner, M. J. (1976). Maternal care, infant behavior and development among the !Kung. In *Kalahari Hunter-Gatherers: Studies of the !Kung San and their Neighbors* (Eds. R. Lee and I. De Vore), Cambridge, Harvard University Press, 218–245

Konner, M. J. (1977). Infancy among the Kalahari Desert San. In *Culture and Infancy: Variations in the Human Experience* (Eds. P. H. Leiderman, S. R. Tulkin and Anne Rosenfeld), NY, Academic Press, 287–328

Korner, A. F. and Grobstein, R. (1966). Visual alertness as related to soothing in neonates: implications for maternal stimulation and early deprivation, *Child Development*, **37**, 867–876

Korner, A. F. and Thoman, L. (1972). The relative efficacy of contact and vestibular-proprioceptive stimulation in soothing neonates, *Child Development*, **43**, 443–453

Laughlin, C. D. and D'Aquili, E. G. (1974). *Biogenetic Structuralism*, NY, Columbia University Press

Lave, J. (1977). Tailor-made experiments and evaluating the intellectual consequences of apprenticeship training, *The Quarterly Newsletter of the Institute for Comparative Human Development*, vol 1, no. 2, The Rockefeller University, 1–3

Lenneberg, E. H. (1967). *Biological Foundations of Language*, NY, Wiley

LeVine, R. A. (1969). Culture, personality and socialization: An evolutionary view. In *Handbook of Socialization Theory and Research* (Ed. David A. Goslin), Chicago, Rand McNally College Publishing Co, 503–541

LeVine, R. A. (1977). Child rearing as cultural adaptation. In *Culture and Infancy*. (Eds. P. Herbert Leidermann, S. R. Tulkin and A. Rosenfeld), NY, Academic Press, 15–27

Lévi-Strauss, C. (1963). *Structural Anthropology*, Translated by Claire Jacobson and Brooke Grundfest Schorpf, NY, Basic Books

Lévi-Strauss, C. (1966). *The Savage Mind*, Chicago, University of Chicago Press

Lewis, M. and Freedle, R. (1977). The mother and infant communication system: the effects of poverty. In *Ecological Factors in Human Development* (Ed. Harry McGurk), NY, North Holland Publishing Company, 205–215

Lewis, M. and Rosenblum, L. A. (eds.) (1974). *The Effect of the Infant on its Caregiver*, NY, Wiley

Luria, A. R. (1976). The functional organization of the brain. In *Recent Progress in Perception. Readings from Scientific American* (Eds. Richard Held and Whitman Richards), San Francisco, W. H. Freeman, 230–237

MacCannel, D. Ethnosemiotics, *Semiotica*, to be published

Maccoby, E. and Masters, J. C. (1970). Attachment and dependency. In *Carmichael's Manual of Child Psychology* (Ed. P. H. Mussen), Vol. 2, 3rd edn, NY, Wiley

McFarlane, A. (1977). *The Psychology of Childbirth*, Cambridge, Harvard University Press

MacFarlane, A. (1978). What a baby knows, *Human Nature*, 1 No. 2

Maclay, H. (1973). Linguistics and psycholinguistics. In *Issues in Linguistics* (Eds. B. B. Kachru, R. B. Lees, Y. Malkiel, A. Pietrangeli and S. Saporta), Urbana, University of Illinois Press, 569–587

Maclay, H. (1974). An experimental study of language and nonlinguistic behaviour. In *Culture and Cognition: Readings in Cross-Cultural Psychology* (Eds. J. W. Berry and P. R. Dasen), London, Methuen, 87–97

McKee, L. (1977). Socialization and the sexual source. Paper read at the 76th Annual Meeting of the American Anthropological Association, Houston, Texas

McKee, L. (1979). *Touch Me Not: An Investigation of the Relationship Between Sex-Role Characteristics and the Socialization of Attention-Getting Behavior*, PhD dissertation, Cornell University, Ithaca, NY

McLuhan, M. (1964). *Understanding Media: The Extensions of Man*, NY, McGraw-Hill

McNeill, D. (1966). Developmental psycholinguistics. In *The Genesis of Language* (Eds. Frank Smith and George A. Miller), Cambridge, Mass, MIT Press, 15–84

Marvin, R. S., Van DeVender, T. L., Iwanaga, M., LeVine, S. and LeVine, R. (1977). Infant-caregiver attachment among the Hausa of Nigeria. In *Ecological Factors in Human Development* (Ed. Harry McGurk), Amsterdam, North Holland Publishing Co, 247–260

Meltzoff, A. N. and Moore, M. K. (1977). Imitation of facial and manual gestures by human neonates, *Science*, **198**, 75–78

Miller, G. A. (1962). Some psychological studies of grammar, *American Psychologist*, **17**, 748–762

Miller, G. A. and Isard, S. (1963). Some perceptual consequences of linguistic rules, *Journal of Verbal Learning and Verbal Behavior*, **2**, 217–228

Mills, M. and Melhuish, E. (1974). Recognition of mother's voice in early infancy, *Nature*, **252**, 123–124

Montague, A. (1971). *Touching: The Human Significance of the Skin*, NY, Harper and Row

Morse, P. A. (1972). The discrimination of speech and nonspeech stimuli in early infancy, *Journal of Experimental Child Psychology*, **14**, 477–492

Nebes, R. (1971). Superiority of the minor hemisphere in commissurotomized man for the perception of part-whole relations, *Cortex*, **7**, 333–349

Neisser, U. (1976). *Cognition and Reality: Principles and Implications of Cognitive Psychology*, San Francisco, W. H. Freeman

Nerlove, S. and Snipper, A. Cognitive consequences of cultural opportunity. In *Handbook of Cross-Cultural Human Development*. (Eds. R. L. Munroe, R. M. Munroe and B. B. Whiting), Garland Publishing Co

Newson, J. and Newson, E. (1974). Cultural aspects of childrearing in the English-speaking world. In *The Integration of a Child into a Social World*. (Ed. Martin P. M. Richards), London and NY, Cambridge University Press, 53–82

Ornstein, R. (1973). *The Nature of Human Consciousness*, San Francisco, W. H. Freeman

Ornstein, R. (1977). *The Psychology of Consciousness*, NY, Harcourt Brace Jovanovich, Inc

Ornstein, R. (1978). The split and whole brain, *Human Nature*, **1**, 76–83

Piaget, J. (1973). *The Child and Reality: Problems of Genetic Psychology*, Middlesex, England, Penguin Books

Piaget, J. and Inhelder, B. (1969). *The Psychology of the Child*, NY, Basic Books

Pick, A. D., Frankel, D. G. and Hess, V. L. (1975). Children's attention: The development of selectivity. In *Rev. of Child Development*, Vol. 5. (Ed. Mavis Heatherington), Chicago, University of Chicago Press, 325–383

Price-Williams, D. (1975). The cultural relativism of intelligence. In *Explorations in Cross-Cultural Psychology* (Ed. D. Price-Williams), San Francisco, Chandler and Sharp, 51–64

Price-Williams, D., Gordon, W. and Ramirez, M. (1969). Skill and conservation: a study of pottery-making children, *Devel. Psych.*, **1**, 769

Rheingold, H. L. (1969). The social and socializing infant. In *Handbook of Socialization Theory and Research* (Ed. David A. Goslin), Chicago, Rand McNally, 779–790

Richards, M. P. M. (1971). Social interaction in the first weeks of human life, *Psychiat. Neurology Neurochir.*, **14**, 35–42

Richards, M. P. M. (1974). First steps in becoming social. In *The Integration of a Child into a Social World* (ed. M. P. M. Richards), London, Cambridge University Press, 83–97

Richards, M. P. M. (1974). Introduction. In *The Integration of a Child into a Social World* (ed. M. P. M. Richards), London, Cambridge University Press

Rogoff, B. (1978). Spot observation: an introduction and examination, *The Quarterly Newsletter of the Institute for Comparative Human Development*, **2** No. 2, The Rockefeller University, April, 21–25

Rosch, E. (1974). Linguistic relativity. In *Human Communication: Theoretical Explorations* (Ed. A. Silverstein), NY, Halsted Press, 95–121

Rosch, E. Universals and cultural specifics in human categorization. In *Cross-Cultural Perspectives on Learning* (Eds. R. Breslin, S. Bochner and W. Lonner), Sage Press, to be published

Rosch, E. *et al.* (1976). Basic objects in natural categories, *Cognitive Psychology*, **8**, 382–439

Salapatek, P. (1969). The visual investigation of geometric pattern by the one and two month old infant. Paper presented as part of the symposium on pattern perception at the meeting of the American Association for the Advancement of Science, Boston, December, 1969

Sapir, J. D. and Crocker, J. C. (eds.) (1977). *The Social Use of Metaphor: Essays on the Anthropology of Rhetoric*, University of Pennsylvania Press

Saporta, S. (1961). *Psycholinguistics*, NY, Holt, Rinehart and Winston

Scribner, S. (1976). Situating the experiment in cross-cultural research. In *The Developing Individual in a Changing World* (Eds. Klaus Riegel and John Meacham), The Hague, Mouton, 310–326

Semmes, J. (1968). Hemispheric specialization: A possible clue to mechanism, *Neuropsychologia* **6**, 11–16

Slobin, D. I. (ed.) (1971). *The Ontogenesis of Grammar: A Theoretical Symposium*, NY, Academic Press

Smith-Bowen, E. (1964). *Return to Laughter*, Garden City, The Natural History Library, Anchor Books

Stern, D. N. (1971). A microanalysis of mother–infant interaction: behavior regulating social contact between a mother and her $3\frac{1}{2}$ month old twins. *Journal of the American Academy of Child Psychiatry*, **10**, 501–517

Stern, D. N. (1974). Mother and infant at play: the dyadic interaction involving facial, vocal, and gaze behaviors. In *The Effects of the Infant on its Caregiver* (Eds. M. Lewis and L. A. Rosenblum), NY, Wiley

Stevenson, H. W., Parker, T., Wilkinson, A., Bonnevaux, B. and Gonzales, M. *School, Environment, and Cognitive Development: A Study in Peru*, Monographs of the Society for Research in Child Development, to be published

Sturtevant, W. C. (1964). Studies in ethnoscience. In *Transcultural Studies in Cognition*. (Eds. A. K. Romney and R. D'Andrade), *American Anthropologist*, **66**, 99–124

Taylor, I. (1976). *Introduction to Psycholinguistics*, NY, Holt, Rinehart and Winston

Ter Vrugt, D. and Pederson, D. R. (1973). The effects of vertical rocking frequencies on the arousal level in two-month-old infants, *Child Development*, **44**, 205–209

Trehub, S. E. and Rabinovitch, M. S. (1972). Auditory-linguistic sensitivity in early infancy, *Developmental Psychology*, **6**, 74–77

Trevarthen, C. (1974). Conversations with a two-month old, *New Scientist*, **62**, 230–235

Tulkin, S. R. and Kagan, J. (1972). Mother–child interaction in the first year of life, *Child Development*, **43**, 31–42

Turner, V. (1974). *Dramas, Fields, and Metaphors: Symbolic Action in Human Society*, Ithaca, Cornell University Press

Turner, V. (1975). Symbolic Studies. In *Annual Review of Anthropology* (Ed. Bernard J. Siegal), Vol. 4, Palo Alto, Cal, Annual Reviews Inc, 145–161

Umiker-Sebeok, D. J. (1977). Semiotics of culture: Great Britain and North America. In *Annual Review of Anthropology* (Ed. Bernard J. Siegal), Vol. 6, Palo Alto, Cal, Annual Reviews Inc, 121–135

Whiting, J. W. M. (1971). Causes and consequences of the amount of body contact between mother and infant. Paper presented at the Annual Meeting of the American Anthropological Association, NY, 1971

Whiting, J. W. M. (1977). A model for psycho-cultural research. In *Culture and Infancy* (Eds. P. H. Leiderman, S. R. Tulkin and A. Rosenfeld), NY, Academic Press, 29–48

Whiting, J. W. M., Child, I. and Lambert, W. W. (1966). *Six Cultures Series: Vol. I. Field Guide for a Study of Socialization*, NY, John Wiley

Wilbert, J. (ed.) (1976). *Enculturation in Latin America: An Anthology*, Los Angeles, UCLA Latin American Center Publications

Witkin, H. A. and Berry, J. W. (1975). Psychological differentiation in cross-cultural perspective, *Journal of Cross-Cultural Psychology*, **6**, 4–87

Wober, M. (1966). Sensotypes. *J. Soc. Psychol.*, **70**, 181–189

Wober, M. (1974). Towards an understanding of the Kiganda concept of intelligence. In *Culture and Cognition* (Eds. J. W. Berry and P. R. Dasen), London, Methuen, 261–280

11 Developmental Psychology and Society

JOHN SANTS

(*School of Cultural and Community Studies, University of Sussex, Falmer, Brighton, Sussex, England*)

Visions of a Better World

It would be reasonable to assume that psychologists in their everyday lives nourish within them, like everyone else, some concept of a better world. Few of them, however, have said very much about the consequences of their work for social policy. Indeed, when the President of the British Psychological Society in 1976 chose as the title of his Presidential Address *Psychology and Social Policy* (Tizard, 1976) he was breaking new ground and running some risk of offending 'scientific psychologists' who traditionally have not concerned themselves very much with the consequences of their discoveries. Tizard made an explicit plea for the recognition of the interdependence of scientific and professional psychology; he urged psychologists to seek their problems in social issues and devote less time looking in the laboratory for general laws governing behaviour. The view has had growing support from a number of psychologists in recent years.

For example, Nigel Armistead's (1974) *Reconstructing Social Psychology* brings together essays from social psychologists who 'while agreeing that social psychology can never be, and should never be, a total solution to the problems of living . . . have not given up hope that it can say a lot more to us than it says at present'. These psychologists look away from experimental psychology towards the three 'alternative' strands of humanistic psychology, phenomenology and Marxism. Their search for an alternative general psychology is perhaps a more radical solution than Tizard's in that he is more concerned with the systematic study of social problems than with reconstructing the concepts and methods of the discipline. What the approaches have in common is a concern for the social relevance of their work. The concern shows itself in many recent writings. David Elkind (1976) the Piagetian expositor explains in the Preface to his *Child Development and Education* that he finds in Piaget's writings 'a psychology that was sufficiently broad to satisfy my philosophical preoccupations, my clinical interests, and my scientific conscience'. He goes on to say that he believes that 'much of the research in educational psychology is too far removed from classroom realities to be of much help to teachers. I believe we need much more natural history in the science of education before we are entitled to become an experimental discipline'. The advice is sound; but educational psychologists claiming to be 'scientific' have not believed that they should start with the natural history of the classroom. They have instead started with the general laws of learning. Bruner, however, reveals a similar sense of the need for psychologists to start in the real world of social issues. The latest of his books on psychology and education does not even have a psychological concept in the title (Bruner, 1971) and was written with a constant awareness of 'social turbulence and human helplessness' and a worry about the 'relationship between knowledge as detached . . . and knowledge as a guide to purposeful action . . .'. In the last essay in the book, written in 1970, he explicitly addresses himself to the question of how the knowledge of psychologists might be more compassionately deployed.

Perhaps the most important example of a recent text in developmental psychology (written by a number of distinguished psychologists) which strives to get to grips with the social contexts of the real world is Martin Richards' *The Integration of a Child into a Social World.* Published in 1974, the title itself sounded an unexpected didactic note among psychological texts. The essayists are all researchers in child development, but what gives their writings a 'new look' is a common awareness that any meaningful description of the growth of the child must be interdisciplinary and look not only to psychology but also 'towards biology, and sociology and other disciplines' in order to get an analysis of the interactive system of child and environment rather than descriptions of simple rules of causes and effects. The comprehensive description, the editor argues, must go from the single cell of conception to the social human with some sense of continuity. The crucial message is that adaptation takes place in a social world. The message may not appear particularly novel to the layman but psychologists, hitherto, have not tried to be natural historians of the social world. Their selection of the stimuli to which they consider the child responds has owed much more to the variables of general psychology than to observations of the everyday lives of children.

We can see then that social psychologists and child psychologists have become impatient with concepts and findings constrained by the demands of scientific precision. They are impatient because what they have discovered does not enable them to say anything likely to be of much help to the parent, teacher or politician. It is all very well to know what would happen if the child were in a closed system controlled by an experimenter; but children are out and about in the open systems of their natural environments. I rather like what Marshall Sahlins has to say about the follies of reductionism: it is, he says, 'a kind of bargain made with reality in which an understanding of the phenomenon is gained at the cost of everything we know about it' (Sahlins, 1977, p. 15). The bargain is made, of course, because psychologists striving for scientific respectability are fearful that if they do venture out into the real social world they will sacrifice the very criteria which distinguish them from quacks, or indeed any wise, insightful observer of the human scene. I think we can conclude that many psychologists are now arguing for a study of the 'uniquely human nature of our own development' not only because they sense that their science is stagnant but because they want to do something about making a better world.

Visions of a better world loom repeatedly in the authors I have just mentioned. To take them in turn, Nigel Armistead ends his Introduction to his contributors on the reconstruction of social psychology with the explicit claim that a new psychology may be able to 'create a more human world'. David Elkind, in reviewing changes in psychology in recent years, believes that 'the social upheavals of the late 1950s and early 1960s made society look to psychology for help in providing better education for blacks, a better understanding of the psychology of persons who could assassinate a President, and a better understanding of youth who were alienated and alienating'. He concludes that the demands have changed psychology because it was 'suddenly confronted with a concept it had not had to face before, namely relevance' and it found that 'traditional learning theory had precious little to offer' (Elkind, 1976, p. 22). A similar utopian response to the anguishes of our age can be detected, as we have seen, in Bruner's writings. And the utopian vision comes to the surface in some of Martin Richards' contributors: the chapter by David Ingleby—significantly the concluding chapter of the book—argues that 'our most urgent task is to find a framework within which psychologists could work who do not share the conviction that the existing political order is the only possible or desirable one' (Richards, 1974, p. 306). This last quotation draws our attention to the question of whether the existing human sciences contain the necessary optimism for us to be able to shake off the ills of our age and move to a better world.

We have seen then that a number of psychologists are dissatisfied with the traditions of their science. The criticisms are of two kinds: (1) experimental psychology has come to a dead end and (2) psychology fails to tell us what we should do to improve life. A problem for psychologists concerned with the second criticism is that when they turn to the human sciences for guidance they are frustrated by what appears to be an inherent pessimistic acceptance of the *status quo*.

Pessimism and Optimism in the Human Sciences

Darwin and Freud, the founders of the human sciences, sought to enhance our understanding of the nature of man. Neither of them wished to pose as preachers or as social reformers; but both were moralists. Explaining man's altruism has been a continuing preoccupation in psychoanalysis and sociobiology. Analyses of altruism inevitably lead to pessimistic or optimistic thoughts about the future of mankind and, it must be conceded, we may have been profoundly influenced by the pessimism in these two nineteenth century scientists.

Freud's pessimism is illustrated in the frequently quoted last paragraph of *Civilization and its Discontents*: 'The fateful question for the human species seems to me to be whether and to what extent their cultural development will succeed in mastering the disturbance of their communal life by the human instinct of aggression and self destruction' (Freud, 1930, p. 82). Freud had some hope that 'eternal Eros' might eventually triumph, but a year later, in 1931, conscious of the looming menace of Hitler, he added a final pessimistic sentence to his book. The pessimism of Freud's writings on society were, perhaps, a product of his old age, accompanied by continual pain from the appalling series of jaw operations from 1923 onwards, when Freud was sixty-seven; but, it must be conceded that Freud's pessimism is an inevitable consequence of his initial instinct theory. Guntrip, in a series of publications, has spelt out the essential arguments of the psychobiology of Freud's early training. The Freudian infant arrives in the world with innate libidinal and aggressive instincts and his development is an outcome of the incompatibility of these instincts and the standards of civilised society. Personal development as an outcome of relationships was, it is true, emphasised in Freud's later theories but, Guntrip claims, Freud was never able to free himself from a preoccupation with a concept of man driven by destructive anti-social impulses firmly rooted in biology. He never quite let go of the scientifically respectable physiological principles of his youth acquired as a medical student, despite his preference for speculating about mental processes (Guntrip, 1961, pp. 58–65).

The classic Freudian psychobiology can offer little comfort for the future of society. In the editorial introduction to *Civilization and Its Discontents*, James Stratchey identifies the main theme of the book as 'the irremediable antagonism between the demands of instinct and the restrictions of civilization'. Nevertheless, there have been many attempts to construct an optimistic Freudian view of society by those who want to hold on to Freud's insights while rejecting his despair. Two of the most influential have been Marcuse and Norman Brown. Marcuse has been sustained in his writing by a belief that the institutions of civilised society can be made less repressive. Their present form is not inevitable. The family—the cauldron in which the Freudian conflicts express themselves—is, he argues, an archaic institution, a product of the capitalist society. We should, Marcuse continues, be able to harness technological achievements so that they can serve man's instinctual impulses and not forever be in conflict with them. Freud, however, had already offered his comments on the solutions of Marxists: he believed that the intractable nature of man would create difficulties in every kind of social community (Freud, 1933, p. 232). Norman Brown's basis for optimism derives from a belief that the psychoanalytical process can make Eros more conscious in all forms of intellectual activity, scientific as well as poetic, giving rise to more self-knowledge, humility and humanity. For him, Eros can triumph and then 'perhaps our children will live to live a full life' (Brown, 1959, p. 322).

Darwinism, in its return to psychology via ethology, has generated a new wave of pessimistic doom-watchers. But what of Darwin himself? The recent publication of extracts from Darwin's early Notebook, in the fascinating account of Darwin's thinking given in Gruber's *Darwin on Man* (1974), makes it possible to tease out some answers. Like Freud, Darwin pondered on the conflict between man's social and anti-social tendencies. At times he was optimistic. In the *Descent* he concluded that through natural evolutionary processes ' . . . the struggle between our higher and lower impulses will be less severe, and virtue will be triumphant'. On the other hand, Darwin saw nothing in the evolutionary process itself to make progress inevitable: 'In my theory there is no absolute tendency to progression, excepting from favourable circumstances' (Notebook quoted in Gruber, 1974, p. 371). Darwin's optimism does indeed appear to originate more in his general happiness from his scientific work than from a logical application of the consequences of his evolutionary theory. He had, as early as his voyage on the *Beagle*, abandoned Christianity for agnosticism; but some notions of Divine purpose remained with him, or at least were in his thoughts when writing publicly. A curious scrap from Darwin's B. notebook of 1837 appears on the fly-leaf of Gruber's book: 'If all men were dead, then monkeys make men— Men make angels'. Gruber's interpretation is that Darwin believed that if chance had not brought forth *Homo sapiens*, evolutionary conditions would have produced some other intelligent hominid. Chance does play a large part in evolution. Ecological niches do determine outcomes. Yet perhaps man will evolve into something higher: 'angels'. Darwin, nevertheless, returns to the logic of evolutionary thinking in his *Autobiography* when he concludes that in the end the sun and all the planets will grow too cold to support life and man, therefore, more perfect than he is now, is doomed to complete annihilation. The 'angel' that man is becoming will be annihilated (Gruber, 1974, p. 213). It is as if Darwin's subjective optimism allows him to tolerate the pessimism of his theory. The same can be said for many of today's evolutionists.

Darwinism has now as firm a stake in developmental psychology as it had in the genetic psychology of eighty years ago. What then are the characteristics of an evolutionary child psychology and what would be the consequences if— as Margaret Mead suggests—we put this evolutionary psychology to work in the upbringing of our children? E. O. Wilson in the controversial last chapter of *Sociobiology* (1975) allows himself to be apprehensive about the possibility that a complete understanding of man from evolutionary sociobiology 'would rob man of his humanity . . . total knowledge, right down to the levels of the neuron and gene . . . might be hard to accept' because we would then have lost the hope of a promised land. In the last sentance of his book, however,

Wilson takes some comfort in his prediction that we still have another hundred years before sociobiology wraps it all up. I think, however, we have more than that! In the meanwhile it is perhaps profitable to consider the effects of an evolutionary attitude on current studies of human development. They can be seen in the writings of ethologists who have applied themselves to the study of children.

Developmental Theories and their Implications

Theories and research in psychology are themselves cultural products. Consequently any attempt to describe what has been discovered by man about himself has to be seen as descriptions of his answers to questions which change as society itself changes in response to the answers given. What psychologists have 'discovered' about children has been the outcome of what they have studied, the kinds of questions they have asked and the ways in which their answers have been determined by the Zeitgeist. In this section I begin with some account of the questions taken over by psychologists from ethologists and then trace the changes in theorising about the smiles of infants. It may at first sight seem strange that smiling should have attracted such a weight of theories. Yet if one looks at infants what else is there to study? The smile is at once striking and identifiable. We think it is something we recognise. It is only when we try to explain it that we realise that the smile of infants can serve many functions except perhaps the function it serves in adults, which caused us to notice it in the first place. My survey of theories and studies of smiling moves from Darwin to Freud and then to Piaget. I dwell on the implications of the Piagetian developmental theory but do not, I hope, convey the impression that I believe that this fashion will remain unmodified by later fashions. But first, what are the questions?

There can be no doubt that ethology has had a liberating influence on the questions asked in developmental psychology. In particular, psychologists have benefited from the four questions distinguished by Tinbergen (1951, 1963) which have done so much for ethology, i.e. the questions of immediate causation, ontogeny, function and evolutionary history. Experimental psychologists have hitherto tended to restrict themselves to the first question of causation: (1) What made the child do that now? What are the neurophysiological mechanisms? But there are other questions. We can ask (2) How did the child grow up to do it that way? What is the developmental story? Then, (3) How does the behaviour aid survival? What good does it do the child? And finally (4) there is the question of evolutionary history: How did the behaviour evolve? Bowlby has demonstrated the value of keeping all four questions in mind in his work on mother–infant attachment. For him, a 'main reason for valuing ethology is that it provides a wide range of new concepts to try out in our theorising' (Bowlby, 1969, p. 7). But he adds that we cannot know how useful they may be until we have tried them.

The study of smiling in infants is a fascinating example of shifting emphases in developmental psychology. The influence of ethology can be seen in the post-war years but studies of this endearing feature of infants occur throughout the history of scientific child psychology (Freedman, 1974, pp. 177–183). Darwin as early as 1840 observed and recounted in his diary the smiles of his infant son. His observations about when and why the infant smiles and his general conclusions about the innate, universal and survival value of the baby's smile (Freedman, 1974) appeared again a century later. The changing fashions in theories and studies of smiling reveal the interplay of culture and science.

Throughout the 1930s the norm-gatherers were at work in the USA where smiling and laughter in infants and school children were charted in the fashionable descriptions of emotional development. At the same time, Kaila's ingenious studies in Charlotte Buhler's nursery in Vienna were rather different. Like Darwin, he noted that infants smile after staring at the adult face and he systematically explored just what the infant was looking at. He used cardboard models and decided that the infant was attending to a configuration or Gestalt of the eyes (Kaila, 1932). Another important contributor was Rene Spitz. His concern for infants in institutions is well-known: as with Bowlby, he drew attention to 'the restriction of psychic capacity', which he attributed to a lack of an adequate mother–child relationship (Spitz, 1945). His interest in the relationship prompted him to make an extensive study of smiling to a facial configuration. Spitz and Wolf (1946) picked up Kaila's hypothesis of smiling as an innate response to a pattern but concluded from 251 infants that by three months the initial inborn motor pattern of a smile has been integrated into a social response. Nevertheless, they suggested that the smile is an evolutionary product. Szekely (1954) turned directly to the ethologists for his interpretation of the smiling response to the eyes–nose–forehead configuration described by Spitz and Wolf. Subsequent research on smiling by Ahrens (1954) and Ambrose (1961) built up an explanation essentially aimed at explaining the functions and phases of smiling: a smile increases interaction between mother and baby, promotes proximity of one to the other and, thus at first ensuring survival, is one of a number of attachment behaviours which lay the foundations of a relationship from which the young can learn the characteristics of his species. It was noted that blind babies smile and this fact added to the evidence for believing that the first reflexive smile is innate. The whole story owes its impetus to the questions and methods of ethology applied to the mother–infant relationship.

Recently, however, another way of looking at the infant's smile has become fashionable. The origins of this approach, curiously enough, come from experiments in conditioning and from cognitive psychology. The basic idea is that babies smile when they solve a problem. If a baby discovers that a mobile suspended above him turns when he kicks his feet he is delighted, and smiles with apparent intellectual pleasure. He is playing the Contingency Detection Game. Watson (1970) to whom we owe the idea began by studying early instrumental learning and also the development of the perception of faces. He refers to his 'ethologiosociocognitive' hypothesis! The infant is pictured as a budding thinker and manipulator of the world around him. We have progressively shifted from a Freudian view of describing sociability as an outcome of social relationships, to a Darwinian view of programmed adaptation for survival, and finally to a Piagetian description of a cognitive being on the path towards intellectual mastery. Smiling, of course, may well be involved in all of these aspects of infant development. Any mother would probably agree with Bower's conclusion that it 'may well be that the smiles are different in each situation, that the baby has a social smile, a smile of appeasement, a smile of triumph, and so on' (Bower, 1977, p. 48).

The recent work on smiling as an accompaniment of problem solving in the earliest stages of development is very much in keeping with the current shift in developmental psychology to an emphasis on cognition as the core of development. We have seen how Freudian theories can so easily generate pessimism: Freudian instinct theory suggests that the child is imprisoned in his innate anti-social impulses and later Freudian relationship theory would have him imprisoned in his family relationships. Darwinism would have him imprisoned in the constraints of adaptation by natural selecion. Is the cognitive concept of the child as autonomous problem solver, internally propelled to ever increasing sophistications of intellectual mastery, a plausible description of development? And, if so, does this concept of the child generate optimism? The nature of the plausibility of the cognitive description of child development must now be looked at a little more closely. Is this the road to utopia?

Piaget, it can be said at once, has no doubts about the answer. In one of his rare pronouncements on education he tells us that if

'. . . childhood is thought of as endowed with its own genuine form of activity, and the development of mind as being included within that activity's dynamic, the relation between the subjects to be educated and society becomes reciprocal: the child no longer tends to approach the state of adulthood by receiving reason and the rules of right action ready-made, but by achieving them with his own effort and personal experience; in return, society expects more of its new generations than mere imitation: it expects enrichment' (Piaget, 1971, p. 138).

Utopians, however, have traditionally tried to find ways to arrange the utopia of which they already have a clear vision. They have not been content to let the next generation enrich society in its own way. This is the dilemma. Should we use our knowledge of child development merely to promote the optimal growth of 'learning and well-being' in our children so that they will transform society in their own way? Or should we use our experience to ensure that the next generation does not repeat our mistakes? We do not, of course, have such clearly separated alternatives. The child is not a free agent. In socialisation, the new generation has limited choices about what to internalise. Children grow up in a social world with all its values and beliefs. Berger and Luckmann (1971) go so far as to describe socialisation as society's 'confidence trick': cultural values are presented as if they were absolutes. Others are not so cynical and hold that it is our duty to transmit the benefits of culture: Bruner, for example, repeatedly asserts, in discussing our uniqueness, that man 'is not a naked ape but a culture-clothed human being, hopelessly ineffective without the prosthesis provided by culture', particularly in language and other forms of symbolism (Bruner, 1971, p. 131). But what the cynics and the custodians of culture have in common is the perhaps inescapable fact that growth cannot be generated as a potential free from its social context. Nevertheless, the concept of a child-centred education can be distinguished from an education where the child is explicitly managed to meet adult objectives. It is the Piagetian concept of child-centredness which we must now examine.

Piaget, as described in my first chapter in this book (chapter 1), distinguishes four categories in the determinants of development: (1) neurological maturation, (2) experience with things, (3) social interaction and (4) self-regulation. The trouble is that his emphases within these categories has varied as his researches and speculations have shifted over the years. Central, however, to our present discussion is the fourth factor of self-regulation: Piaget, more than any other, has made us aware of how much the child organises his own development. 'Development,' he tells us, 'is essentially dependent upon the activities of the subject . . . and not explicable solely by the external contributions of experiment or social transmission: it is the product of successive constructions, and the principal factor in this constructivism is an equilibration achieved by autoregulations . . . by a constant elaboration of fresh structures' (Piaget, 1971, p. 40). Piaget's first determinant acknowledges Darwinism: development is both promoted and constrained by neurological inheritance. It is Piaget's third factor which is bothersome. How does the child organise his social interactions? Piaget may recognise this determinant in his classification, but in comparison with his detailed investigations of experience with things (beads, beakers and balls) he rather evades descriptions of the influence of people on development. It would be foolish to conclude that anyone as perceptive as Piaget really believes that all children are merely busy little physicists in the making. Stages of development he says quite explicitly are 'always related as much to the particular surroundings and atmosphere as to the organic maturation of the Mind'

(Piaget, 1971, p. 173). In urging us to recognise that the child is an active organiser and not just a passive recipient of social rules and values, Piaget, nevertheless, acknowledges that 'memory, passive obedience, imitation of the adult, and the receptive factors in general are all as natural to the child as spontaneous activity' (Piaget, 1971, p. 138). Yet so long as Piaget concentrates his researches on 'the maturation of mind' as an outcome of spontaneous activity with physical objects he is not immediately helpful when we try to assess social influences. The clue to the essential feature of a Piagetian view, however, may lie in his concept of reciprocity: social development is a product of child–adult interaction and it is useless to specify particular causal effects as we are apt to do when we impose the concepts and methods of laboratory psychology on the developing child. All this is all very well, of course, but until we get more Piagetian research on social development we can never be sure about the part that adults might play in creating a new, enriched generation. Perhaps the best we can do is retain our optimism that a better world will come from autonomy rather than from obedience. Hitherto our nerve has failed: educational reformers from Rousseau to Plowden have preached child-centredness as the road to improvement but in practice we have always chosen the alternative of specified curricula and improved techniques of management.

Child psychologists are expected to know how to bring up children. But how can they respond when asked for guidance? The experimental psychologist will have nothing to say if there are no relevant experimental results. The behavourist will ask the parent or teacher just what they want the child to do and will then describe how to arrange it. The psychologist familiar with surveys and correlational studies will be helpful if the child belongs to a socio-economic group which has already been surveyed; but even then the advice may be hopelessly inappropriate for a particular child. Parents and teachers think they know what the Freudian will say and often make a joke of it. What kind of advice can be expected from the contemporary developmental psychologist?

Competence, as we have seen in studies of smiling, is a fashionable concept in developmental psychology and the fostering of competence is a fashionable aim. Contemporary child psychology has to do with arranging for the optimal development of resourcefulness and the avoidance of unfulfilled promise. The highly resourceful child is of course not necessarily a nice child, or even a happy one. But do we, nevertheless, know how best to arrange things so that our children could become resourceful? At the risk of reverting to what might look like a guide to child management, but inspired by Bruner (1971), I offer five principles which seem to reflect the spirit of the contemporary developmental psychology which draws rather more from biology and cognitive psychology than from psychoanalysis.

(1) Development is the child's construction.

(2) The child is naturally active and exploratory and seeks understanding and control of his environment.

(3) Adult interventions promote development when they are synchronised, supportive and encouraging rather than directive or corrective.

(4) The child moves through stages in his understanding of the world and thinking cannot be imposed by coercion.

(5) A child learns the culture of his society from the example of others and not from attempts at instruction.

These principles may look alarmingly progressive. Taken together they do imply that so long as the child is happily involved in any activity he must necessarily be developing at an optimal pace. Few parents have the nerve to avoid direction if the activity does not appear to be educationally relevant. They do not find it easy to tolerate a child's absorption in a task which strikes them as trivial, silly or liable to lead to interests they dislike. But the principles may not be so alarming if a distinction is made between the fostering of intellectual growth and the management of cultural development. Intelligence is crucially dependent upon early experiences. If the spontaneous activity of the young child is hampered by clumsy interventions then competence may be permanently impaired. Parents cannot teach a child to be intelligent but they cannot avoid shaping his cultural development by their own activities and the interests of the household. Parental influence on the dependent child is inevitably powerful by example. Most parents do in fact greatly underestimate the inevitable aspects of their influence. The 'confidence trick' of presenting values as absolutes works only too well. Parents bring a whole set of cultural assumptions to bear on the child whether they are aware of them or not. They cannot fail to be the chief architects of his interests and attitudes, but they will fail if they consciously try to be the moulders of his intelligence.

What would happen if parents stuck to the principles listed above? From what I have argued we could expect children to be more intelligent and more resourceful but also, as before, inevitably mere sustainers of the social system they learn from the adults around them. It is not obvious why the principles should lead us to expect—as Piaget does—enrichment rather than mere imitation. Margaret Mead (1970) provides a clue. She distinguishes three different kinds of culture. In postfigurative cultures 'grandparents, holding new-born grandchildren in their arms, cannot conceive of any other future for the children than their own past lives'. In cofigurative cultures the 'prevailing model for members of the society is the behaviour of their contemporaries'. In the final chapter of *Culture and Commitment* she sees the future as a prefigurative culture in which the child—and not the parent and grandparent—represents what is to come. The current generation are ready to present an unknown future to the child because 'none of the young, neither the most idealistic nor the most cynical, is untouched by the sense that there are no adults anywhere in the world from whom they can learn what the next steps should be'. Perhaps Mead is right and we are ready for a 'continuing dialogue in which the young, free to act on their own initiative, can lead their elders in the direction of the unknown'. Mead's utopia has all the dreamlike characteristics of its predecessors but current uncertainties make it just possible that we are readier now than we have ever been to invest optimistically in the resources of our children. But note her insistence on the need for the 'continuing dialogue' between the experienced elder and the resourceful young. As with Piaget, the road to utopia depends upon a truly reciprocal relationship.

It is of course an over-simplification to present contemporary developmental psychology as if it were only concerned with the growth of intellect. It is true that concern about educational failure in poor children has made Freudian psychology appear irrelevant and has favoured the cognitive psychology of Piaget. The Centre for Cognitive Studies at Harvard, for example, (Bruner, 1971) have drawn up a list of principles for use in day-care centres which are almost entirely cognitive. Yet the last is the Principle of Attachment. In this the Centre acknowledges that 'it is in interaction with a caretaker that much of earliest learning occurs' and that dependent human young need a caretaker 'who is there with warmth, certainty and effectiveness'. The Harvard psychologists thus introduce the main conclusion from Freudian psychology and make competence a product of the social interaction between the child and his parents. Commonsense as well as Freudian psychology suggests hat they are right but, as I have discussed earlier, Piaget is relatively silent about social influence. Nevertheless, his argument that society's enrichment requires a reciprocal relationship between 'the subjects to be educated and society' echoes Mead's concern for a 'continuing dialogue' between the young and their elders, even though she is prepared to give the unknown future to the child.

Reformers from Rousseau onwards have urged us to encourage autonomy in our children. In practice we have always drawn back at the last ditch and given the future to experienced elders. Why the reluctance to set up a joint enterprise in which innovation can come from a genuine partnership between youth and experience? The answer may be that the young always appear to want to go too far. In a child-focused society parents get a raw deal. This is the message from Rapoport *et al.* (1977) in *Fathers, Mothers and Others*: 'parents are people too'. It is carrying utopian thinking too far to believe that our task in society is no more than devotion to the next generation in the interests of cultural progress. The results of our understanding of child development should do more than create a happier future, even if we accept Mead's optimism and believe it to be possible. Adults and children alike have some claim on happiness here and now.

Psychologists and Social Policy

Psychologists have not paid much attention to culture. For them it is an unmanageable concept. The variables cannot be specified and have therefore been left out of developmental theories. We have seen, however, that developmental psychologists have grown uneasy about this neglect. A biological description cannot hold good regardless of the structure of the society in which the child develops.

> 'Who "winds up" the child, how and with what in mind, are questions that are likely to tell us far more about the end-product than a description of the knob' (Ingleby, 1974, p. 301).

Note also that physiological psychologists, when confronted with the human infant, are now beginning to argue that the 'human brain is . . . innately an organ of culture' (see Trevarthen, chapter 2). How then do we put 'society' into psychology?

We can begin with a rough description of what we have in mind when we talk about culture. Let us just say that we are dealing with all those determinants of development referred to as social rather than biological and which are characteristic of the society in which the child is growing up. We are talking about a way of life of a group of people passed on by language and imitation. It has to do with beliefs, morals and customs, with some continuity from one generation to another. Customs is a useful term because it simply means 'usual practices' or 'established procedures' in a society. Psychologists must now find some way of getting to grips with the interplay of the biologically given and the established social beliefs and customs.

Erik Erikson (1965) gives some indication of how this developmental story might be handled. His book, *Childhood and Society*, is regularly cited in child psychology texts but—possibly as a result of Erikson's amalgam of insight and idealism—has never quite registered a place as an important theoretical addition to academic psychology. Erikson is a Freudian and his formative professional experiences come from family psychotherapy. To understand what he is getting at you have to read his illustrative case histories with some care in order to grasp what is happening and not try to judge whether he has or has not demonstrated the efficacy of psychotherapy. Erikson himself says that he advances no claim of a cure but that he 'claims less—and aspires to more' (Erikson, 1965, p. 28). The 'more' is that a therapeutic investigation leads to an understanding of a crisis in family history. The technique is well illustrated at the beginning of the book in the history of the Jewish boy Sam who had been referred for convulsions diagnosed as epilepsy. Sam's crisis, Erikson concluded, could only be properly understood if it were related to a constitutional epileptic tendency and also to parental attempts to cope with his assertiveness, and also to the plight of a solitary Jewish family in an American

Gentile community. The case history has to be read in full to see a plausible account of the interplay of all three. In general terms, Erikson describes three developmental processes: (1) those inherent in the organism, (2) those concerned with the organisation of experience within the individual, and (3) those concerned with social organisation. He argues that these three processes—somatic, ego and societal—have been dealt with separately in the history of science as biology, psychology and sociology. He contends, however, that the meaning of an item in one process, e.g. a convulsion, is codetermined by its meaning in the other two. We will fail to understand, or formulate a satisfactory basis for a developmental theory, if we keep the processes separated in their scientific disciplines.

Erikson is, of course, not the only human scientist conscious of the consequences of dividing people up into processes to fit the needs of scientific practitioners. His merit lies in his making some progress towards an integration. He does, to be sure, begin by identifying some biological aspects of human growth, assumed to be universal. Here he borrows from Freud and settles for the oral, anal and genital biological processes which, for Freudians, dominate the transactions of early life. Having identified a universal set of biological stages, Erikson then offers analyses of how these biological processes are responded to in a particular culture and how the child himself constructs a satisfying identity from the clash of these pressures on him. His method can be seen at its most plausible in his analysis of the Sioux Indians. His biology may be inadequate but the method appears feasible.

The problem in this kind of approach undoubtedly lies in the identification of definitive biological universals. If we are to describe the 'vicissitudes of the instincts'—to borrow once again from Freud—we must first identify the instincts. The sociobiologists have been offering us their descriptions of our 'biogrammars'. By looking at non-human primates and living hunter-gatherer societies, and thus observing behaviour in the environment for which man evolved by natural selection, E. O. Wilson gives this brief description:

'What we can conclude with some degree of confidence is that primitive man lived in small territorial groups (100 or less) within which males were dominant over females . . . Maternal care was prolonged' (Wilson, 1975).

It is doubtful whether we can find enough in these characteristics to furnish a description of the universal biology of development. We are more likely to find the biogrammar in a neurology which follows Trevarthen's lead and studies the brain as an organ of culture. Nevertheless, mother–child attachment, stable-pair bonding and the co-operation necessary for group living have—as the 'instinct' theories of ethology—been more productive in developmental psychology than the cruder Freudian instincts.

Erikson remains a rare example in child-psychology texts of attempts to put culture into psychology although cross-cultural psychology has flourished for some years. From what I have argued so far in this section one would except development to differ from one culture to another. If we accept Erikson's analyses, it follows that how parents arrange things for their children is very much a product of the customs, perils and objectives of their culture as they see it. Parents seek to promote survival and success for their children within a particular social context. They do not as a rule seek to promote absolute development. And since success in one culture calls for skills which may not be appropriate in others, we should expect the skills of children to differ across the world. Western psychologists have tried to measure differences and then explain them.

Older anthropology texts are of course filled with descriptions of the exotic customs of tribal societies with a general acceptance of cultural relativism, i.e. each culture should be judged in its own terms and not evaluated as superior or inferior to the culture of the investigator. This assumption gives rise to the notion that anything is possible in human development and that human nature is of unlimited malleability. If we look around with open eyes, say the cultural relativists, we will find that there are many 'equally valid patterns of life which mankind has created for itself' (Benedict, 1934). There was even a trend towards attributing superior values to the cultures as yet untouched by technology and some romanticising of the noble savage.

Anthropologists adept at describing strange patterns did so because they were trained to submerge themselves in the native's point of view. Margaret Mead, trained by Franz Boas, the pioneer of the technique, describes how she was required to learn to 'think in another's terms and to view the world through another's eyes' (quoted in Harris, 1968, p. 316). The clinical methods of Piaget and Erikson have similar objectives. This is the emic approach in contrast to the etic. These useful terms were coined by the linguist Kenneth Pike (1954) and are derived from 'phonemic' and 'phonetic'. In language studies, phonemics involves the examination of sounds used in a particular language whereas phonetics attempts to generalise from phonemic studies in individual languages to a universal science covering all languages. Berry (1974) has set out the distinction in tabular form.

Emic approach	*Etic approach*
studies behaviour from within the system	studies behaviour from a position outside the system
examines only one culture	examines many cultures comparing them
structure discovered by the analyst	structure created by the analyst
criteria are relative to internal characteristics	criteria are considered absolute or universal

Psychologists have favoured the etic rather than the emic. Unlike anthropologists they have not seen a future for their science in piling up unlimited descriptions from within rather than from outside the system. Clinical psychologists have explored the individual's viewpoint, but academic psychologists have viewed this kind of exercise as more art than science. How, they ask, can we possibly derive general laws from emic studies? They have, in consequence, consistently failed to get the richness of human experience into their analyses. Instead they have been concerned with a few, very specific questions in their cross-cultural psychology.

Cross-cultural psychology is mainly about culture and cognition. Cognition, and in particular, perception, is the bedrock of experimental psychology. In contrast, the psychology of personality lacks a firm experimental basis and abounds with competing theories. It was not surprising, therefore, that when psychologists turned to other cultures they should take with them the concepts, techniques and questions from many years of laboratory experiments in cognition and also from intelligence testing, the two firmest foundations of their science. The first task was to discover whether there are cognitive differences among different cultures and, if so, whether the differences are differences in basic cognitive processes or merely differences in the ways in which culture influences basic processes. If there are differences in basic processes then there may be genetic determinants to be identified. However, the problem which has bedevilled cross-cultural psychology is the difficulty of discovering by experiment whether the differences really do exist: there are dangers in judging competence from performance. A subject from a different culture may fail the cognitive test not because he lacks the relevant capacity but because he is ill at ease or fails to understand the experimenter's question. Faced with this problem, some cross-cultural psychologists (e.g. Cole and Bruner, 1971) have advised that we should follow the example of the cultural relativists in anthropology and study differences and not deficits. But does this mean we should revert to the endless collection of strange cultural differences? Berry has an interesting alternative to get us from emics to an etic, i.e. from discriminations the participants themselves regard as meaningful to statements judged appropriate among scientific observers.

In his Introduction to *Culture and Cognition: Readings in Cross-Cultural Psychology* (Berry and Dasen, 1974), Berry proposes three aims in comparative psychology: (1) testing the applicability of our hypotheses in other cultures (2) exploring other cultures for new variations and (3) generating modifications of our hypotheses so that they become more general and can deal with our cultures as well as others and thus become universal. To do this, we should start with an imposed etic in another culture bearing in mind that it is likely to be only an approximation. Modifications are made until the imposed etic becomes a truly emic description for the new culture. We then see how much of the imposed etic is left (i.e. what is common to both cultures) and we have a derived etic from which we can get new hypotheses. The essence of the exercise is to be as flexible as possible in our formulation of hypotheses, learn from 'grasping the native's point of view' and thus arrive at true universals. We are by this method seeking neither unlimited differences nor 'deficits' but new universals which are not simply products of the conventions of Western psychology. Blurton Jones (Bateson and Hinde, 1976), in an interesting discussion of this issue, regrets that psychologists have not clearly recognised the distinction between emic and etic research and calls for more good emic studies so that we can 'test and if necessary reject our everyday culture's categorizations of behaviour'. It must be surprising to the layman to discover that psychologists have not been observing and describing the naunces of human experiences and thinking; but for reasons sound enough at the time psychologists opted for the study of observable behaviour. Today, many of them are pressing for more 'attention to the experience of the perceiver or actor, both the nature of the experience and how the experience is built up over time' (Armistead, 1974, p. 22). I think we will see a sharply increasing number of psychological studies in the next few years which will begin by trying to grasp the native's point of view. Only then will we know what it is we have to explain. Clinicians like Erikson and child psychologists following Piaget have already shown the way.

There may be signs that the tide is turning in psychology so that behaviourism in a strictly experimental science is giving way to a study of the development of human social experience; but it will be many years before we have anything like a comprehensive human science at our disposal. What then of the present? There are two aspects to consider: firstly, the value of what we know already—despite the shortcomings of text-book psychology—and, secondly, whether any short-term measures can be taken to bring psychology closer to social policy. The present achievements of psychologists are not, however, entirely trivial or irrelevant. A great deal has already been discovered, although in the absence of generally acceptable unifying theories, no single psychologist is able to identify or present what is here to stay. What psychologists do agree about may be more easily seen in what they do as practitioners than in what they publish in their learned journals. These agreed principles do filter through into social policy from time to time as evidence to committees. Occasionally, Governments are sufficiently concerned to finance large-scale research by consultative bodies which bring together large numbers of social scientists with enough time to distil the best of what they know. A good example can be found in *Learning about Learning* (Bruner, 1966) sponsored by the US Office of Education, which brought the psychology of cognitive development to bear on the political problem of school failure in poor children. The consequences were good for psychology as well as for education. Working parties and reports from professional associations are still the main links between psychologists and politicians. The process has its limitations because the relevant research is sparse, and psychologists as scientists are reluctant to advise without firm evidence. The new social and developmental psychology should, one day, generate more helpful links but in the meanwhile we have to think of what we might do while we await a richer psychology of human development.

Professor Tizard, as I mentioned earlier, would settle for research in 'significant problems that are within the field of competence' of present psychologists. The catch lies in deciding what is significant. Research on 'the rules governing the behaviours of individuals in differing environments' in order to 'foster learning and promote well-being' may look like the road to everyone's utopia but it is not always easy to know beforehand where learning and well-being are being threatened. Yet so long as we are prepared to discover failure and unhappiness in any social group the advice is sound. Psychologists now have a unique opportunity to liberate themselves from the constraints of their preoccupations with scientific status. They are already specialists in the techniques of a systematic study of human problems. A psychology responding to the human problems of society, and not to the problems of its own past, can only enhance its status.

In 1977, May Davidson succeeded Professor Tizard as President of the British Psychological Society. Her Presidential Address has the title 'The scientific/applied debate in psychology: a contribution' (Davidson, 1977). Successive addresses on the question of the social relevance of psychology can be taken as clear evidence of the dominance of the topic. Davidson spoke from a background in educational and clinical psychology and I can end the chapter by drawing on her analysis.

Davidson approaches the debate by shifting the analysis from psychology to psychologists. She suggests a tripartite classification: (1) scientist, (2) applied scientist and (3) practitioner. The scientist is the psychologist working in a university. He is a seeker after knowledge and his first obligations are towards knowledge itself. The applied scientist works in a unit or project supported by research funds. The practitioner is employed by the National Health Service or other government or local authority department. These distinctions, Davidson argues, suggest how we might remove 'an increasing burden from the backs of all psychologists'. All psychologists are educated as scientists: they internalise a demand for certainty and acquire 'the expectation that in the fullness of time both animal and human behaviour will be explained in all or at least many of its aspects'. Consequently they are uneasy when asked to respond as psychologists to messy, human problems and begin to share the layman's view that man is neither understandable nor predictable. Thus practitioners have the burden of guilt about forsaking their scientific standards and scientists are guilty about their inability to respond to public demands. The applied scientist in the research unit grows uneasy about the secondary nature of his small-scale work which lacks status as science and is often dismissed as an avoidance of what really matters in practice. If Davidson's analysis is right then few psychologists will be happy in their work. Scientists and practitioners will do little for each other.

The analysis does help us to understand why some psychologists criticise psychology. Any psychologist who tries to do more than one of the three jobs at the same time is bound to be frustrated. It may also be true that an explicit recognition of these distinct roles would make psychologists happier. But the question which has concerned us in this chapter is not the happiness of psychologists but the happiness of society. How might society benefit if psychologists were to put their house in order? Would psychology have a greater social relevance? Davidson's proposals give some hope.

Let us suppose that each one of three has settled for the job that suits him best. The scientist pursues his research with all rigour; the applied scientist picks up problems from the field and refines them for more elaborate and stringent evaluation by the scientist; the practitioner uses the best knowledge available but in the last resort is allowed to back his hunches for therapeutic purposes. Each carries out his task with a sense of appropriateness. By this means there is a two-way traffic from research to practical issues. The whole thing depends upon a recognition that there is no advantage in 'imposing one strategy of systematic exploration upon phenomena which, by their nature, require other strategies'. The upshot could well be the liberation of psychology from the laboratory with an increase of relevance and no loss of rigour. Something of the kind is happening already. Two Presidential Addresses must surely have some effect.

References

Ahrens, R. (1954). *Zeitschrift fuer Experimentelle und Angewandte Psychologie*, **2**

Ambrose, J. A. (1961). The development of the smiling response in early infancy. In *Determinants of Infant Behaviour* (ed. B. M. Foss), Methuen, London

Armistead, N. (ed.) (1974). *Reconstructing Social Psychology*, Penguin Books, London

Bateson, P. P. G. and Hinde, R. A. (ed.) (1976). *Growing Points in Ethology*, Cambridge University Press, Cambridge

Benedict, R. (1934). *Patterns of Culture*, Houghton Mifflin, New York

Berger, P. and Luckman, T. (1971). *The Social Construction of Reality*, Doubleday, New York

Berry, J. W. and Dasen, P. R. (eds) (1974). *Culture and Cognition: Readings in Cross-Cultural Psychology*, Methuen, London

Bowlby, J. (1969). *Attachment and Loss: Vol. 1, Attachment*, Hogarth Press, London

Bower, T. G. R. (1977). *A Primer of Infant Development*, W. H. Freeman and Company, San Francisco

Brown, N. O. (1959). *Life Against Death: The Psychoanalytical Meaning of History*, Weslyean University Press, Connecticut

Bruner, J. S. (1966). *Learning about Learning: a Conference Report*, US Dept. of Health, Education and Welfare

Bruner, J. S. (1971). *The Relevance of Education*, George Allen & Unwin, London

Cole, M. and Bruner, J. S. (1971). Cultural differences and inferences about psychological processes, *Amer. Psychol.*, **26**, 867–76

Davidson, M. A. (1977). The scientific/applied debate in psychology: a contribution, *Bull. Br. Psychol. Soc.*, **30**, 273–278

Elkind, D. (1976). *Child Development and Education: A Piagetian Perspective*, Oxford University Press, New York

Erikson, E. H. (1965). *Childhood and Society*, Penguin Books, London

Freedman, D. G. (1974). *Human Infancy: An Evolutionary Perspective*, John Wiley, New York

Freud, S. (1930). *Civilization and its Discontents*, Hogarth Press, London

Freud, S. (1933). *New Introductory Lectures on Psycho-Analysis*, Hogarth Press, London

Gruber, H. E. (1974). *Darwin on Man: A Psychological Study of Scientific Creativity*, Wildwood House, London

Guntrip, H. (1961). *Personality Structure and Human Interaction*, Hogarth Press, London

Harris, M. (1968). *The Rise of Anthropological Theory*, Thomas Y. Cromwell, New York

Ingleby, D. (1974). In *The Integration of a Child into a Social World* (ed. M. P. M. Richards), Cambridge University Press, Cambridge

Kaila, E. (1932). Die Reaktiomen des Sänglings auf das menschliche Gegicht, *Annales Universitatis Fennicae Aboensis, Series B*

Mead, M. (1970). *Culture and Commitment: A Study of the Generation Gap*. Panther, St. Albans

Piaget, J. (1971). *Science of Education and the Psychology of the Child*, Longman, London

Pike, K. (1954). *Language in Relation to a Unified Theory of the Structure of Human Behavior*, Vol. 1, Glendale: Summer Institute of Linguistics

Rapoport, R., Rapoport, R. N. and Strelitz, Z. (1977). *Fathers, Mothers and Others*, Routledge & Kegan Paul, London

Richards, M. P. M. (ed.) (1974). *The Integration of a Child into a Social World*, Cambridge University Press, Cambridge

Sahlins, M. (1977). *The Use and Abuse of Biology: An Anthropological Critique of Sociobiology*, Tavistock Publications, London

Spitz, R. A. (1945). Hospitalism. *Psychoanalytic Study of the Child*, International University Press, New York

Spitz, R. A. and Wolf, K. M. (1946). The smiling response: a contribution to the ontogenesis of social relations, *Genetic Psychology Monographs*, **34**, 57–125

Szekely, L. (1954). Biological remarks on fears originating in early childhood, *International Journal of Psychoanalysis*, **35**, 57–67

Tinbergen, N. (1951). *Study of Instinct*, Clarendon Press, Oxford

Tinbergen, N. (1963). On aims and methods of ethology, *Zeitschrift fur Tierpsychologie*, **20**, 410–433

Tizard, J. (1976). Psychology and social policy, *Bull. Br. Psychol. Soc.*, **29**, 225–234

Watson, J. S. (1970). Smiling, cooing and "the game". Abridged version in Stone, L. J. *et al.* (eds.) (1974). *The Competent Infant*, Tavistock Publications, London

Wilson, E. O. (1975). *Sociobiology: The New Synthesis*, Harvard University Press, Massachusetts

Index

Accommodation *see* Piagetian
   theory
Age as a *carrier* variable   120
Aggression
   aggressive drive   105
   measures of   263
   sex differences   263
Altruism
   evolution   109–12
   gene expression   48
   parental investment   110–12
Animal studies
   bird song   102–3
   generalisation to man   98–9, 108
   genetic component of
      behaviour   100
      see also Ethology, Imprinting
      and Learning
Aptitude   257, 258–9
Assimilation   *see* Piagetian
   theory
Attachment   86–7
   survival value   35

Behaviourism
   central tenet   169
   view of the human infant   77
Brain development   65–70
   after birth   73–4
   starvation, effects of   69

Central nervous system (CNS)
   function   52

   growth and development   53–7
Cerebellum   65, 69
Cerebral hemispheres   65, 70
   anatomical asymmetries   75
   sex differences and
      lateralisation   67–9
   speech centres   76
Child development
   commonalities   292–7
   cross-cultural studies   292–7
   evolutionary perspective   26–28,
      35, 38, 98, 292–7
   see also Cognition, Language
      acquisition *and* Piagetian theory
Child guidance, psychoanalytic
   theory and   33
Child rearing practices
   cognitive development   340–6
   hunter–gatherer societies   34–5
   implications for sex
      equality   34–5, 39
   learning   348
Children
   barriers in the study of   17–21
   generalisations about   15–16
Chomsky   170–3, 294, 332
   see also Language acquisition
Cognition
   adaptive function   349
   child rearing practices   340–6
   cognitive universals   333
   definitions (language based)
      328–9
   schooling, effect of   219,
      307–10, 327

Cognition (cont)
    see also Cross-cultural studies,
      Culture, Intelligence,
      Language acquisition *and*
      Piagetian theory
Communication in infancy 82–3,
    87, 197, 346
  cognitive development 340–6
  manual gestures 194–5
Competence 302–4, 332, 336, 380
  educational 218–49
Cross-cultural studies
  cognitive anthropology
    perspective 329
  cognitive differences 219–22
  cognitive and psychology
    perspective 329, 330–1,
    348–9
  conservation concept 300–4
  deficit hypothesis 219–22
  dreams 314–5
  language acquisition 187–88
  literacy and cognitive
    development 307–10
  methodology 132–9
  socialisation and sex
    differences 271
Culture, cognitive
    development 311–18
  definitions 329, 377
  types 375
Cultural relativism 379
  sex differences and 271–2,
    276–8

Darwin 17, 31–2, 253, 367, 369
Developmental psychology,
    definition 120
  dimensional model of
    research 121
  history 22–39, 166–7, 253–5
  methodology 120–39
  role of theory 122–3

Differentiation of cells 48–50
Drive theory 97, 105

Egocentrism *see* Piagetian theory
Electroencephalogram (EEG) 70,
    72
Epigenesis 50
Ethology, definition 34, 96
  evolutionary perspective
    106–12
  methodology 99
  relevance to developmental
    psychology 32, 96–116
  sex differences and 282
Evolution, adaptedness of man 35
  relevance to developmental
    psychology 26
  sex differences and 281–3

Fixed action patterns 100
Feminist movement *see* Women's
    movement
Freud 254, 268–9, 367–8

Genes 47–9, 264–6, 281–2
  see also Evolution
Genetic psychology 24, 26
Genie 209
  case study 234–9
Gesture 193
Gestural schemata 193

Hall, Stanley 22–6
  recapitulation theory 24, 25, 27
Heritability, definition 106
  misinterpretations 106
Hormones, definition 49
  sex differences 266, 274
Human behaviour
  foetus 70–2

genetic basis 112–16
newborn infant 76, 77
sleep 115
stable elements 114

Imitation
in infancy 83
sex differences and 270
Imp inting 34, 99, 103
Innate
critique of the term 100–2
various meanings 100
see also Instinctive behaviour
Instinctive behaviour 32, 99, 100,
105
Institutionalised operativity
310–14
Intelligence (IQ)
cross-cultural studies 296–7,
304
sex differences 262–6, 316–18
testing 26–7, 225–8
see also Cognition *and* Spatial
ability

Language acquisition
conversation, prerequisites for
204–7
critical period 336
cross-cultural studies 294, 295
deafness 187
disadvantaged children 260,
334–9
grammar
case 180–2
generative 171
pivotal 173–6
transformational 332
linguistic competence 175–6
linguistic universals 171, 294,
332

Piagetian theory 136, 183–6
prespeech 87, 206
production, syntactic limitations
188, 189
research into history of
169–208
research methods
conversational approach
201–9
functional approach
189–200
semantic approach
176–89
syntactic approach
174–6
sex differences 259–61
speech, holophrastic 123, 195
speech, telegraphic 174
Language and cognition 200–1,
328, 331–3
Learning
child rearing practices and 348
hierarchies of 232–3
nature of 218–49
in newborn infants 79–80
social policy and 381

Maternal deprivation 32, 33, 34,
69, 86
see also Genie
Mathematical ability
development of 261–2
disadvantaged children 261–2
sex differences 261–2
Memory
in early infancy 347
long term (LTM) 224, 232,
236–43
neuroembryological
analogue 63
short term (STM) 236–8
Memes 112

Mother-infant interaction
  cognitive development
    and   343–5, 347
  suckling   127–8
  see also Child rearing practices
Myelin   71

Natural selection   97, 105
  group selection   109–12, 116
  selective advantage   97, 107, 109
Nature-nurture controversy
    28–31, 61, 101, 168, 223–5,
    273
Neotony   64
Nerve fibres, organisation during
    development   57–63, 67
Naturalistic observation   124
  see also Ethology
Normative data   121–2
  see also Intelligence

Perception
  cognition and   329, 330,
    340–7
  colour perception and culture
    291
  in early infancy   78–81, 239,
    346
Piaget   17, 36–8, 77–8, 126,
    142–68, 183, 210–11,
    229–31, 254, 295–6, 300,
    314, 316–17, 372
Piagetian theory   142–68
  accommodation,
    144–6
  assimilation, definition
    144–6
  concrete operations   148–68
  consciousness   152, 153
  conservation tasks   261
  cross-cultural studies
    292–3, 295–6

determinants of development
    37, 150, 373
  dream concept   314
  egocentrism   77–8, 128–9,
    202–4, 346
  epistemology   142–3
  equilibration   150, 159–62,
    231
  formal operations   148–68
  formal schooling   305
  language acquisition   155–7,
    164, 165, 182–5
  object concept   147
  research implications   165–6
  schemes   144–68
  semiotic function   200
  sensori-motor intelligence   147,
    183–4, 199
  social interaction   154–5
  stages of development   37–8,
    157–9
  status of   162–6
  symbolic function   149–68,
    199–200
Predeterminist view of human
    development   16
Preformationist view of human
    development   16
Prespeech   83, 206
'Primitive mentality'   297–300,
    305–10
Prostaglandin   72
Psychoanalytic theory
  oedipal conflict   269
  sex differences and   268–9
  status of   317
Psychological reductionism
    278–81
Psychological universals   290
Psycholinguistics, history of   331–4
  see also Language acquisition

Rational task analysis   233–4

Research into developmental
    psychology
    cross-sectional approach   132–7
    emic approach   379
    etic approach   379
    laboratory research, criticisms of
        127–30
    learning theory strategy   129–30
    longitudinal approach   132–7
    nature of   41–2
    objectives   231–6, 327–8
    optimum strategies   138–9
    sequential strategies   136–7

Sex differences   253–84
    explanations of
        brain lateralisation
            266–7
        genetic   264–6
        hormonal   266
        maturation rate   267–8
        psychoanalytic   268–9
        situational   271–6
        social learning theory
            269–71
    research strategies   275–6
    role of culture   283–4
    social implications of   277–84
    variations with age   275–6
Smiling in infancy   370–2

Social policy   365–7, 370–83
Sociobiology   367, 369–70
Socialisation
    cross-cultural studies   271
    sex differences   269
Spatial ability   262–3, 264, 265,
        267, 270
Suckling
    experimental exploitation
        127–8
    inhibition   78
Synapses   67, 68, 69

Tabula rasa, child as   16

Verbal ability   259–61
Visual system, development of
    cortex   75
    in goldfish   60
    influence of external stimuli
        59–63
    plasticity of, in hamsters   64
    in Xenopus   58, 62

Whorfian hypothesis   33
Women's movement   271–2
Wundtian experimental psychology
        15, 22–3, 43

Lightning Source UK Ltd.
Milton Keynes UK
UKOW06f0745170416

272383UK00003B/137/P

9 781349 163335